Versions of English

Dorothy and Douglas Barnes
with Stephen Clarke

Based on a project financed by the
Social Science Research Council,
at the University of Leeds
School of Education

Heinemann Educational Books
London

Heinemann Educational Books Ltd
22 Bedford Square, London WC1B 3HH
LONDON EDINBURGH MELBOURNE
HONG KONG SINGAPORE KUALA LUMPUR NEW DELHI
IBADAN NAIROBI JOHANNESBURG
EXETER (NH) KINGSTON PORT OF SPAIN

First published 1984

British Library Cataloguing in Publication Data

Barnes, Dorothy
Versions of English.
1. English language - Study and teaching
I. Title II. Barnes, Douglas
III. Clarke, Stephen
428'.007'242 LB1631

ISBN 0-435-10170-6

Phototypesetting by Georgia Origination, Liverpool
Printed and bound by
Biddles Ltd, King's Lynn and Guildford

Contents

Preface

In this book we have tried to do something not attempted before, so far as we know: to describe the teaching of a subject as it appears to close observers, with its strengths and faults, its aspirations and frustrations, its successes and its daily trivia. It happens to be English that we have chosen, but it could have been another subject just as it could have been younger instead of older pupils. We cannot demonstrate the typicality of the teaching observed but the researchers, four experienced English teachers and teacher-trainers, recognised much of it as familiar from their own and others' class-rooms. Our account of English teaching will be of particular interest to teachers and lecturers concerned with that subject in its various forms, but the account is also relevant to others, particularly those who are concerned with curriculum development and the sociology of the curriculum, for we have been interested not only in what happened but why it happened.

The research was financed by the Social Science Research Council and based at the University of Leeds School of Education. The original research team comprised one full-time research officer, Dorothy Barnes, with Douglas Barnes and Stephen Clarke able to contribute only part of their time. (Stephen Clarke's participation in the fieldwork ensured that he contributed more widely to the ethnography than would seem to be implied by the one chapter that he wrote.) The School of Education also assigned to the project the part-time help first of John Seed and then of Pamela Jenkins, and during the third and final year released Douglas Barnes to give the whole of his time to the study. This additional support enabled us to work in greater depth than would otherwise have been possible.

We have benefited greatly from the help of co-workers and colleagues, and particularly from the initial help of John Seed. We have been fortunate in the fellow researchers who have been willing to read part of this book in draft and to advise us either in writing or in discussion: Stephen Ball, John Brown, Chris Day, Patrick Diamond, Margaret Gill, Martyn Hammersley, Geoff Higgs, Peter Medway, Michael Rayner, Andrew Stibbs, Frankie Todd and Mike Torbe. It is far from a formality, too, when we thank the project secretary, Elaine Nutter, for the care and hard work that she gave first to transcription of the data, and then to the preparation of this book.

Our greatest debt is to those many teachers, lecturers and students whom we cannot name because we offered them anonymity: all the names we use are pseudonyms. It is no light matter to admit observers into the lessons one teaches: the presence of another adult sometimes throws into uncomfortable prominence aspects of lessons that one has been glad to be unaware of. We enjoyed sharing their work – as this account will show – and thank them warmly for their generous collaboration, hoping that the experience has proved useful rather than discouraging. We thank, too, the principals, headteachers and other administrators who gave permission and smoothed our way.

Some of this material has appeared in another form elsewhere: as 'Between All the Stools: some methodological considerations in curriculum research' in *Journal of Curriculum Studies*, vol. 13:4, 1981; as 'Cherishing Private Souls' in Roslyn Arnold's *Timely Voices: English Teaching in the Eighties*, Oxford University Press, 1983; as 'Preparing to Write in Further Education' in Martyn Hammersley's and Andy Hargreaves' *The Sociology of Curriculum Practice*, Falmer Press, 1983; and as 'Finding a Context for Talk; aspiration and performance in some F.E. courses' in *Spoken English*, vol. 15:2, 1982. We thank the editors and publishers for agreeing to the reworking of the material.

Douglas Barnes
Dorothy Barnes
Stephen Clarke

Postscript

Readers primarily interested in our description of teaching are advised to read only the first two sections of Chapter 2 and then to skip to Chapter 3.

Glossary

Overseas readers may not be familiar with the examinations to which we refer. The General Certificate of Education (GCE) is examined at two levels: Advanced (A-level) and Ordinary (O-level). A-level is taken at 18 years of age, and is primarily a qualification for higher education. O-level, originally intended for only the top 20 per cent of the ability range, is a required qualification for many careers. The Certificate of Secondary Education (CSE) is the standard leaving certificate. Though its highest grade is equivalent to GCE O-level, CSE tends not to have so high a standing in the eyes of the public. Alternative examinations called 'Sixteen Plus' ('16+'), which seek to interrelate GCE and CSE grades, have been on trial since 1974.

Some other abbreviations may be unfamiliar to home as well as to overseas readers, so we supply a short glossary.

FE	Further education
HMI	Her Majesty's Inspector(s)/Her Majesty's Inspectorate
NFER	National Foundation for Educational Research
ONC	Ordinary National Certificate
OND	Ordinary National Diploma
HNC	Higher National Certificate
HND	Higher National Diploma
AEB	Associated Examining Board
JMB	Joint Matriculation Board
YREB	Yorkshire Regional Examination Board
TWYLREB	The West Yorkshire and Lindsey Regional Examination Board
RSA	Royal Society of Arts
BEC	Business Education Council
TEC	Technician Education Council
C & G	City and Guilds of London Institute
CITB	Construction Industry Training Board

CHAPTER 1

The Project: Purposes and Methods

'Curriculum is a selection from culture (Williams, 1961[1]; Lawton, 1973[2]) and a different selection is offered to different groups of students. The purpose of this study is to investigate differences in the versions of English curricula which are offered to various groups of students who are about to complete or have completed compulsory education.' These are the opening sentences outlining our research in the proposal which was accepted by the Social Science Research Council in 1979.

From the first, the study has been called *Versions of English*, with the sub-title 'Curriculum variation in relation to students and institutional contexts'. At the most superficial level what we are offering is a description, based on empirical evidence, of a range of curricula labelled variously English, English Language, English Literature and Communication Studies. Such a description is unique: the only vaguely comparable work is Weston, 1979[3], or the little known report of Squire and Applebee, 1968[4]. We can read historical accounts (Shayer, 1972[5]; Mathieson, 1975[6]; Ball, 1981[7]); ideological statements (Inglis, 1969[8], 1981[9]; Abbs, 1976[10]); pedagogical expositions (Pufford, 1978[11]; Sharp, 1980[12]) and persuasive polemics (Dixon, 1979[13]; Adams and Hopkin, 1981[14]). This, however, is the first attempt to demonstrate how the English curriculum is realised in classroom action through the interplay of ideology with practical exigencies deriving from the demands and expectations of schools, colleges and society as a whole.

We designed the study hoping that it would also throw light on theoretical issues. In 1971 M.F.D. Young challenged educational researchers to embark on studies that would make curriculum problematic and would relate the 'principles of selection and organisation [of knowledge] that underlie curricula to their instructional and interactional setting in schools and classrooms and to the wider social structure'[15]. The project was designed to take up that challenge, in so far as a limited short-term programme could do: Karabel and Halsey (1977)[16], adding their support to the 'interpretive sociology' proposed by Young and others, note that it 'focusses precisely upon those classroom processes that must be understood if there is to be any chance of reducing the class and racial differential in academic achievement that concern administrators'. Such processes as these constituted the deepest level of our concern, though we could hope to do little more than formulate some hypotheses.

From a practical point-of-view we wanted to know what curricula there are, not on paper but enacted in classrooms — what varieties of English are being taught, what knowledge, skills and values they emphasise, to whom they are taught, how teachers justify them, what pupils make of them, and so on. English curricula diversify sharply towards the end of compulsory schooling and even more afterwards; we wanted to know whether phrases such as 'literary heritage', 'personal growth', 'basic skills', 'communication studies' represent identifiable versions of English, and whether they are systematically distributed to groups of students.

Although we can express our interest in this detached academic way, as former teachers of English we retain a commitment to views about the value of various versions of English curricula. It seems to us perfectly proper — and indeed unavoidable — for researchers to hold such values, so long as they do not persuade them to select, emphasise and interpret in ways calculated to mislead. We embarked on our present research partly because of Dorothy Barnes' previous experience as curriculum officer with a Schools Council project. Because of the limited time available, that project began to develop programmes of curriculum change without either research into what English was being taught in schools and colleges, or into the purposes and concerns that were currently shaping teachers' attitudes to English teaching. The latter are of particular importance since it is precisely these purposes and concerns that guide their responses to any innovations proposed. If curriculum developers rely on their own intuitions they are very likely to find themselves addressing their persuasions to audiences whose concerns they have misjudged. A part of our motives as researchers is related to the concerns that guide teachers' actions. Curriculum proposals in English are unlikely to make explicit a model, for example, of what constitutes 'reading a work of literature', yet teachers differ sharply in the skills and processes they involve their pupils in, the aspects of the work they choose for emphasis, and the analytical concepts they use. Such differences are unlikely to become visible except in the minutiae of classroom communication, and may not be available by reflection to the teacher in question, having arisen less from deliberate choice than from a history of compromises between aspirations and resources.

In some earlier work Douglas Barnes discussed teachers' classroom language almost entirely in terms of pedagogical effectiveness. More recent work, such as that of Woods (1977)[17], A. Hargreaves (1978)[18], and Parsons (1981)[19], has stressed that the exigencies of keeping children under control may lead to strategies which are either ambiguous or directed primarily to ends which do not aid learning. Classroom control, however, is not the only concern of teachers. In *Versions of English* we should like to be able to relate classroom strategies to institutional factors, such as whether the course is situated in a school or further education college, the status of pupils in a setting/streaming system, or the examination being prepared for, as well as to the 'espoused values' of the teachers. All these play an important part in shaping the learners' experience of English curriculum, as does the students' perception of the salient costs and rewards (Willis, 1977)[20].

We have been able to identify four main strands in the motives that led us to research: (a) theoretical concerns; (b) atheoretical curiosity; (c) the desire to persuade; (d) information-gathering on behalf of policy-makers. The use to which our study is put is another matter: descriptive research is clearly valued by policy-makers, so we have to ask ourselves whether as researchers we want to supply data to enable — or is it to influence? — decisions over which we certainly have no direct control. The curriculum is very much a political matter: any information about what goes on in schools and colleges is of potential use in putting pressure for change — or opposing change. Nevertheless, we take the view that in the long run, making available more information about the curriculum will lead to better-informed debate.

The overall design

The study extending over three years was carried out at two levels: (i) in school fifth-year English classes; and (ii) in first-year courses in school sixth forms and in colleges of further education.

The first stage, concerned with school courses for all except remedial groups, was carried out in six schools. A particular interest was the identifying and describing of differences between courses offered to groups designated as more or less able and discovering how pupils assessed the value and relevance of school English courses. Since a considerable proportion of students end their schooling at this point[21] we presumed we would have defined the culminating experience of English for a substantial part of our student sample.

The second stage of the research followed some of the routes open to students who continue their education in English and Communication Studies. We worked in four further education colleges which received students from the six schools and continued on a limited scale in three of the schools. In further education colleges and school sixth forms we set out to describe the versions of English (and Communication Studies) offered to groups differentiated by the school/college distinction, by examination status, and by whether the course was intended as general education, such as O-level, or was part of a vocational package such as BEC or TEC. We hoped to discover how far post-compulsory courses, whether named English or Communications, reinforced students' previous experience of English and how far they offered something different.

We were interested in the possibility that there would be significant differences in English courses according to school status and the nature of the catchment area. We observed in the national statistics that there were some variations in staying-on rate and continuing education according to region so we hoped to set part of our study in a non-metropolitan area where the rate was higher, whilst the major part was based in a metropolitan area. Consequently four schools and three colleges were chosen in a large northern industrial city and two of our schools and one FE college in a smaller country town nearby. All the schools were mixed comprehensive schools; the ideal design was that they would be paired, with a low and high status school drawn from the city centre, a similar pair from the residential suburbs and the third pair from the small town.

The situational variants originally conceived in the design can be displayed in tabular form.

Table 1.1

Situational variables

Institution:	school/college
Nature:	compulsory/post-compulsory
Subject:	English/communications
Setting:	metropolitan/non-metropolitan
(schools):	city centre/surburban/small town
Academic status:	high/middle/low
Course:	general/business/technical

In the fifth form most pupils would be on GCE O-level or CSE courses: in the second stage we hoped to cover not only GCE O-level and A-level English in schools and colleges, but also to sample what was offered to the largest groups of FE students on vocational courses. In each institution we wished to have access to classes at three academic levels in accordance with our interest in identifying and describing the characteristics of courses offered to pupils (students) described as more or less able and to discover how those pupils/students assessed the value and relevance of their courses. This meant that we should have 18 fifth-year classes and probably three or four sixth-year classes in schools and 12 classes in the colleges.

Curriculum can be represented in various ways — through official statements of policy, school syllabuses, teachers' accounts of their intentions, events in classrooms, pupils' work, or pupils' perceptions of courses. That is, there are alternative sources of descriptive data beginning with intentions and moving progressively closer to pupils' experience. The research was designed to sample as wide a range of these sources as possible. We would collect public documents relating to the courses, examination syllabuses and papers, departmental syllabuses, course outlines and submissions. We would keep records and notes of all our meetings and visits to the schools and colleges. We planned to build up a profile of each teacher or lecturer in relation to the courses they were teaching. We would first interview the teachers and lecturers according to a schedule we had devised (see Appendix 1). We would ask them to allow us to observe what they considered a typical sample of their work with the class we were following. Ideally we hoped to tape-record lessons, but as we were not willing to press teachers who might be reluctant we devised a protocol for lesson observation. Although the tape-recordings and field-notes would be likely to pick up more of the teachers than the pupils, we were concerned to record the pupils whenever we could. When pupils were inaudible to us we were usually able to indicate the nature and length of their participation. We asked to have the opportunity to interview a third of each class towards the end of the course and we suggested that we should have a final meeting with the teachers and lecturers. In the event we were able to increase our demands, but we will deal with the additional material we collected as we describe the realisation of the design. Originally we also planned that we would devise a questionnaire for wider circulation, but as we were convinced by other researchers that such a mismatch of methods would not be productive, we soon abandoned that idea.

Realising the design

We had drawn up an ideal scheme, but its implementation was dependent on the willingness of colleges and schools to be involved in the study. Although we would not be working in the FE colleges until the second year, we had to approach them first because we wanted the schools to be ones which fed into the colleges. We hoped that we would pick up some of the pupils whom we met in the fifth year in the FE colleges in the following year. This preliminary stage of our work highlighted some differences between the two sectors. In colleges the decisions were made at a senior level, often with little or no consultation with the junior lecturers who would be involved in the research. Our approaches were made initially to the principal who made the decision in conjunction with the departmental head, who would often be an administrator rather than a teacher. We approached six colleges before we were accepted by four, and in only one case were invited to meet the lecturers before a decision was made. (It was not until later that we became aware of the implications of non-negotiated entry into college classes, non-negotiated, that is, with the lecturers themselves.)

Decision-making in secondary schools was quite unlike this. Headteachers consulted the teachers as a matter of course before accepting or rejecting our request. We approached schools within two local authority areas according to the criteria we have outlined. We were accepted immediately by the first two city-centre schools that we approached but there was more difficulty in finding small-town and suburban schools that would accept the research. We applied to 13 more schools, and in six cases met the English teachers to explain our intentions, before we found the four more schools that we needed. The contrast between school teachers' and college lecturers' control over access to their classes could not have been more patent.

It is fairly unusual for classroom observers other than officials such as HMIs to see examination classes. When visitors are shown the work of an English department it is often a lower or middle school class which is offered and we conjectured that teachers might be more sensitive about our penetration into examination classrooms because they felt there was a stronger disjuncture between their espoused theory and their practice. Whatever the reason, teachers in a number of suburban schools were not anxious for us to see them at work.

We have given the background of our entry into the six schools because it is important for readers to realise from the beginning that to some degree the schools and teachers were self-selected. The departments we were allowed to investigate were at least confident enough of their practice to feel that it could support and even benefit from our scrutiny.

Readers familiar with British schools in the 1980s will not find our descriptions of their physical characteristics contain many surprises. Two of our schools had been planned and purpose-built as local comprehensives, two were the results of the amalgamations of schools and two had been developed by the extension of an originally smaller school. Conditions such as pupil/teacher ratio were very close to the national norm. According to the national statistics, the average size of fifth-form English classes in 1979–80 was 24·5 pupils[22]: the average for our 18 classes was 24·3, so we were not seeing classes with a specially favourable or unfavourable pupil/teacher ratio. All the schools divided their pupils according to ability so in each school we planned to have three teachers: one with a top, one with a middle and one with a bottom group. Ideal designs, however, rarely work out in practice: we were dependent on the willingness of teachers. At Urban School the class which they designated as 'top' for the research was the one they described as the third in their ten fifth-form groups. In previous years this had been an O-level group, but in this particular year it had been decided that everyone should be entered for CSE. For most purposes of comparison, therefore, it was closer in its expectations to the middle band in the other schools. In the plan overall this was no disadvantage because we found that teachers were more anxious that we should see their teaching with their abler pupils, but we had to keep this inconsistency in mind when we were making comparisons between schools. At Greentown School where pupils were divided into two ability bands we secured the co-operation of only two teachers, but this was in part compensated for by the insistence of the teachers at Smalltown School that we saw five classes. We restricted our collection of data to four so that we retained our original plan of six classes from two schools in a small town in the total of 18 fifth-form classes. It is not surprising that fifth-form classes in the six schools had not been organised to provide us with neatly systematised research data: we had to deal as best we could with the real not the idealised version of reality.

We were torn between our desire to gain an ethnographic perspective and the logistics of being in 18 classes in six different schools at the appropriate times. Douglas Barnes and Stephen Clarke were having to fit in their visits in the interstices of a full university timetable, but we thought it important that everyone should be involved in all aspects of the research at this stage. The bulk of the fieldwork fell to Dorothy Barnes, but there was only one school, Greentown, where she was the only classroom researcher. Team meetings with these teachers, however, ensured that no school was being observed through only one pair of eyes. Early in the term we arranged the initial teacher interviews. Although they were structured we had decided to encourage people to be expansive in their replies, tape-recording the interviews so that we were not distracted by note-taking. We had suggested that they would probably take about three-quarters of an hour, but in practice many of them were longer. At this stage we were deliberately keeping our demands as low as we could because we were very conscious of the difficulties we had had in gaining access to examination year classes. As soon as we could produce a transcription of the interview we gave each teacher a copy asking them to alter or add anything if they wished.

The extent and time of our classroom observation was negotiated with each teacher individually and most of it took place in the first term and a half. In some cases we sat in on a sequence of lessons, perhaps a week's work, but in other cases we went in at spaced intervals. We tape-recorded a varying proportion of what we observed; when we were unable to use audio-recorders we all followed the same protocol for recording lessons. We entered the time, regularly noting particularly when there was any shift in the direction or activity in the lesson, and we scribbled down as many of the exact words that were spoken as we could. We expanded these abbreviated verbatim notes with a commentary as soon as possible after the lesson before the memory was overlaid with another observation period. Because our observation periods necessarily took place at different times in the year we decided it would be useful to have a diary return providing additional data from the same two-week period for each class and every teacher agreed to provide this.

Our sampling of written work was the least systematic aspect of our data collection. Our earliest request to headteachers had referred to 'appropriate documents, e.g. syllabus and textbooks', but from the beginning some teachers had offered us pupils' work. We were hesitant about renegotiating our terms of entry, but as time went on we felt that we were receiving an incomplete picture if we did not see a sample of the comments which all the teachers wrote. We slipped in a reference to written work when we were asking if people would fill in diaries for us and so in every class but one we succeeded in seeing work from a third of the class, but for all sorts of practical reasons our samples varied considerably in size. The interviews with pupils took place in a concentrated spell. We had originally asked to interview at least a third of the pupils in each class, and this was achieved. We had expected that this would be spread over a period of weeks and extend into the summer term, but we found in practice that as some pupils left or only attended for examinations after Easter we had to concentrate the interviewing period so the bulk of it fell to the full-time researcher. For the final meetings with the teachers we decided that it would be valuable to have the teachers we had worked with from each school together; surprisingly this proved very difficult to arrange.

As our study continued we found that we wanted to pursue this or that aspect in greater depth so we were making more and more demands which had not been in our original request. All the teachers filled in the diary of their lessons in a particular fortnight in March; later we asked them to check the lists we had made of all the written work they had set. At the beginning of the next school year we asked for the examination results of the classes we had been following and months later we asked them to fill in an open-ended questionnaire about their background and the influences on their teaching. That we were able to make these requests is a testimony to the patience and forbearance of the teachers and their conscientious professionalism.

In the second stage of the research we extended our institutional basis to four colleges, but as we wanted to make comparisons we continued to work, within limited boundaries, in three of the schools we had visited the previous year, choosing one from each of our subgroups (one city-centre school, one suburban school and one in a small town). The provisional arrangements for entry into the colleges had been made before we approached the schools, but the hierarchical organisation meant that the lecturers' willingness to participate had been taken for granted. The teachers may have been interested volunteers but the lecturers, with one exception, were conscripts. From the start we were clearer about what materials and access we wanted and these two factors probably shifted our position as researchers. We still had more than one researcher in all but one institution but, because of split sites and lack of central staffrooms, we found we were not so able to reinforce each other's impressions.

In the schools, we followed one O-level and three A-level courses: we wished to see similar English courses in a college setting, but as the balance was different there we placed more emphasis on O-level with only one A-level course.

The three levels of course, 'top', 'middle' and 'bottom', of the schools had no neat parallels in the college since academic levels were not comparable from one vocational area to another. RSA English courses as part of a vocational package proved to be heavily subscribed so we sampled those at two levels. The diversity of Communication Studies courses on offer made selection difficult: we wanted to sample the most significant groups in Business Studies (BEC), in Engineering and Technical courses (TEC), and in other craft courses (City and Guilds) but clearly, with our limited resources, we could not sample a number of courses at each level. We were able to follow BEC at National and General level, TEC I in two very different submissions, City and Guilds Communication Skills I, the communications elements in a City and Guilds Foundation Course and in a CITB (Construction Industry Training Board) course and one course which was described to us as equivalent to Communication Skills I, but was an internally assessed college course. The courses we have studied therefore are:

In six schools	Fifth-year sets	18 classes	O-level and CSE
	Sixth-year groups	4 classes	GCE O- and A-level
In four FE colleges	General courses	3 classes	GCE O- and A-level
	Vocational courses	10 classes	RSA, TEC, BEC etc.

In total this amounted to 35 classes and 34 teachers and lecturers. (The college classes are listed in Table 2.5 on p. 33.)

We followed at this second stage the same pattern of research, individual interviews with lecturers, classroom observation, interviews with a third of the students and group meetings at the end of the year. We discovered it was even more difficult to gain an ethnographic perspective in the colleges than in the schools because of the isolation of the individual lecturer and the very different working conditions. Most teachers worked the same hours as their colleagues and, although we encountered staggered lunch hours, most people's teaching days began and ended at the same times. The lecturer's timetable contained a specified number of contact hours, but these might be arranged so that one day started at 9 a.m. and the next at noon. We could not hope by arriving early to chat with people before their session, there was often no particular place where we knew we could find them: some would arrive, collect their papers and go straight to their class. If we sat in staffrooms they would often be empty, so although we spent more hours in the FE colleges both in and out of classes we had less sense of them as communities.

We had chosen colleges and schools in the same areas hoping that there would be some students who figured in both years of the enquiry. In the school sixth forms, of course, we achieved this, but we soon realised we would be very fortunate if any of our random sample of fifth formers chanced to reappear in the particular college groups. Only two individual students did, but in seven out of the 13 courses we were able to interview students who had either been in the classes we had observed in the fifth form or in parallel groups in the school. On a number of occasions we were recognised by students and cross-questioned about our activities: 'When is the book about us coming out?'

Towards the end of this second stage we asked all the teachers and lecturers to fill in an open-ended questionnaire about their backgrounds and the influences on their teaching. Answers in many cases merely substantiated what we already knew, but in some cases, especially when people replied at length, they provided us with valuable additional information.

The details of the schools and colleges, of the courses we followed, of the individual teachers and lecturers and of the sample of students will be the basis of Chapter 2, but it may be useful as a summary to this section to list the sources of our material.

a. Documents at national and local level, including examination syllabuses and papers.
b. Documents at institutional level, such as schemes of work.
c. Teachers' and lecturers' statements about their teaching and antecedents, gathered both informally and by structured interview and questionnaire.
d. Classroom observation.
e. Classroom materials, students' written work, teachers' comments.
f. Interviews with a third of the students in each class.

Methods and their rationale

No established tradition of curriculum research exists: it has borrowed its methodologies from various social science disciplines. We can identify seven possible modes:

i Assessment of learning outcomes (as frequently in the evaluation of curriculum materials: or in achievement monitoring by the Assessment of Performance Unit [APU] or National Assessment of Educational Progress [NAEP]).
ii Surveys (such as the studies of teachers' attitudes).
iii Historical accounts.
iv Studies of innovation. (These typically have a managerial bias, and can best be represented by the many studies discussed by

Rogers and Shoemaker, (1978)[23] and by House, (1974)[24].

v Classroom studies. (These are frequently descriptive but may be combined with assessment of learning outcomes, as in the ORACLE studies in primary-school classrooms [1980][25].)

vi Content analysis. (It is necessary to include this for completeness though it may occur more frequently as a part of larger studies. We have in mind the 'intrinsic' analyses of textbooks or other learning material, or perhaps of examination papers or syllabuses[26], in order to elucidate underlying emphases and values.)

vii Sociological studies. (These attempt to show curriculum as it exists in teachers' and pupils' practice, often using a mixture of ethnographic and other methods. Classroom studies may in some cases be a subdivision of this category.)

There is no doubt that *Versions of English* falls into the last of these categories. It also incorporates elements of the previous two: only a wide-ranging approach using eclectic methods is likely to feed back information and understanding relevant to our diversity of purpose. In part, our research design derives from the ethnographic perspective developed from the classical micro-sociological studies of Becker (1968)[27]. Yet Becker and British ethnographers such as Hamilton (1973)[28] and Delamont (1973)[29] have limited their attention to one or two schools. We wanted to gain the positive values which studies such as *Hightown Grammar*[30] or *Beachside Comprehensive*[31] possess, an awareness of the teacher in the cultural setting of the school, yet our purposes in *Versions of English* were different in that we wished to map a range of curricula on offer to different groups of pupils. In order to find this range we needed to go to a number of schools and colleges, which seemed to imply survey methods. The large-scale studies such as the Schools Council Survey (1970)[32], *Post Compulsory Education* (1974,5)[33], King (1976)[34], or the NFER projects (1977–81)[35,36,37] however, have not concentrated on the curriculum, but on different patterns of provision: 'where they should learn' rather than 'what they should learn'. Our concerns were different, so several considerations weighed against survey methods: first, teachers' reports on their own teaching are notoriously unreliable, so that some classroom observation would be essential if we were to find what the curriculum in action is in each classroom studied. Besides, we were uncertain what forms the matters we were interested in would take, so we would not know what questions to ask until we had looked. Furthermore, we were interested in how teachers justify what they are doing, what constraints they are aware of, and how their students interpret the curricula they are experiencing. With our limited resources it was clearly impossible to carry out ethnography in enough institutions to provide the range. Inevitably we compromised, trying to work in depth in six schools and four colleges of further education. We may, therefore, be vulnerable to criticism on one side for lack of generality and on the other for superficiality in that we were unable to spend as much time in each school as standard ethnographic practice recommends. Any researcher who follows Hirst's injunction to carry out small-scale studies of curricula 'to see both what happened in practice and why it happened . . . an explanation in terms of why people did what they did'[38] in the context of educational institutions and the education system will inevitably be led to mixed modes of research which seem indeterminate when compared with models drawn from the physical sciences.

In any ethnographic or quasi ethnographic research the definition of the role of the researchers is crucial. We were 'known observers' with the marginality which that position implies, hopeful that it would be 'out of the circumstances of being marginal man — the simultaneous insider-outsider — that creative insight is best generated' (Lofland, 1971)[39]. Our own personal histories as experienced schoolteachers of English meant that we were moving in familiar settings: to that extent we shared the assumptions and culture of the teachers, but we were conscious that our status in their eyes varied. 'Part of fieldwork is understanding what people understand you to be — spy, ally, journalist, etc.' (Bott, 1971)[40]. Most people knew we were former English teachers, but they also knew we were from the university: some had met us in different contexts, heard or read of our work. The majority, however (27 out of the 35 people), were strangers to us at the beginning of the project and in interpreting what they told us or showed us we must understand as far as we can the relationships which individually developed. Our role in the schools differed from that in the colleges for various reasons: our knowledge of the world of further education was much more limited. We had not been socialised into its expectations; only one of us had taught in a technical college and that was some years previously: our recent first-hand experience of classrooms in further education had been gained by observation and interviewing in four courses for the pilot study leading up to the project. We can realise with hindsight that two factors affected the basis of our relationships with the lecturers. The first was that, apart from Mr Davidson at High Street College whom we knew and had worked with in the pilot stage, we had not negotiated our terms of entry with the individual lecturers. The second was that, having established a research pattern in the schools, we tended to be less tentative in our requests. These factors were not major influences, but generally distanced us more from the lecturers. Our status as outsiders sanctioned by authority, was, perhaps, balanced by the fact that most of the lecturers seemed unaware of our previous academic work and the positions we had taken up in it. They were also more accustomed to presenting a public face than were the schoolteachers.

We did not set out with the Elliott and Adelman[41] premise of the teacher as equal research partners, although we were anxious to understand as fully as we could the perspectives expressed and enacted by them. We were conscious of the distinction which Keddie[42] draws between the perspective the teacher offers *in medias res* (the teacher perspective) and the position proffered in the relative calm of an interview or written reply (the educationalist perspective). When we talked to some educationalists of what we were doing they were concerned that we were not gaining the teacher's perspective on the lesson data. We were told we ought to give the teachers an opportunity to talk to us at the end of the lesson about what they had intended to happen. Comments such as this often come from those who have forgotten the hurly-burly of school and college life. At the end of a lesson there will be a couple of pupils with a query, someone perhaps wanting a new exercise book, two more wanting to check on the details of the work set and the next class will be arriving as the teacher is trying to get the right books out or move to another room. Whenever possible we were available to the teachers and lecturers and encouraged them to talk informally to us, but unless it was break or the end of the session this was far from easy. We offered ourselves as sympathetic listeners, we tried to arrive early, to sit around in staffrooms and not to rush away.

In order further to validate our accounts by presenting them to participants — respondent validation — we wrote a lengthy profile of each teacher and offered it for comment. Our accounts in these profiles were descriptive rather than evaluative, derived from the interview and classroom data and couched in positive terms. There was some surprise at how much we had noticed in lessons, various vaguely affirmative remarks, two people wrote offering correction or justification of very minor points and one person expressed hurt and indignation. We were very aware of the potential damage we could do and had deliberately presented what we saw as reinforcing accounts, but we were disappointed to have so little in the way of feedback. We intended to repeat the exercise at the end of the second stage in the research, but in the event produced profiles only for our own private use.

The teachers' and lecturers' perspectives are central to our understanding of what is going on, but caught up in the routinised tasks which necessarily inhibit reflection they will frequently not be asking the same questions of the data as we are. 'It may be the case that any account of institutions which isolates features in such terms as to make comparison with other institutions possible and useful will inevitably appear to distort reality to members of the institution'. (Strivens, 1980[43].) Some demands of the teacher's role are perhaps inevitably in conflict with a research stance: the need for a committed belief in what one is teaching makes a detached critical stance unlikely. A teacher 'does not begin with a set of goals and then develop means to achieve them: he is socialised into a culture which simultaneously provides a collection of routine concerns and practices which themselves define teaching (until further notice) and a set of accounts spelling out its purposes'. (Hammersley, 1980[44].) Our analysis is likely to be relevant to wider issues than those which the participants are immediately concerned to address. We are not setting out primarily to engage with teacher-defined problems (that is to 'take' problems), but to adopt a perspective which is outside and which to some extent transcends that of the participants. This implies that we hope to make explicit various patterns and consistencies that the teachers and lecturers may never have had cause to reflect upon or even be aware of. This is how we interpret Young's injunction to 'make curriculum problematic'.

Some writers recommend that the internal consistency of ethnographic accounts should be ensured by methods such as triangulation: 'In social research if one relies on a single piece of data there is the danger that undetected error in the data production may render the analysis incorrect'. (Hammersley, 1978[45].) Various methods are suggested, such as the comparison of data derived from different phases of the fieldwork or from different settings, the collection of data by different researchers and the comparison of data produced by different methods. Our research design had this diversity built into it: we must, however, remain aware of the inherent differences in status within data. Next it is necessary to explain why we chose to collect what we did.

The documentary evidence is of a public nature. Departmental syllabuses, for example, are public documents, intended as much for outsiders as for members of the department. They tend to be eclectic, seeking to accommodate competing ideologies within a tenuous consensus. They are sometimes defensive, all things to all people, and tend towards the blandness of the committee document. Nevertheless, each has its distinctive flavour and emphases, which can be related — rightly or wrongly — to what we know of the department from other evidence. Course outlines and submissions fall into the same category; the submissions and syllabus intend to convince, to be persuasive to outsiders. They tend to be problematic because they are at a remove from classroom action; there is no-one to enforce them, and at times there are sharp contrasts between values espoused in writing and the teaching we have observed, but this is not the normal state of affairs. Examination syllabuses and external guidelines (such as BEC) may explain some of the contradictions between espoused theory and action.

The data from interviews falls into the semi-public category. We are aware that since participants are face-to-face with their interviewer what they say may be influenced by views about what is currently acceptable, though on a number of occasions it was clear that teachers and lecturers were consciously taking up positions that they thought we would not share. There is likely to be a strong self-justifying element, particularly in the more informal departmental discussions we held after the classroom observation was completed. It is possible, but not certain, that teachers and lecturers were influenced by a wish to 'repair' aspects of the persona or role they had presented during lessons. Interview data is problematic in another sense in that in our semi-structured schemes we were pre-empting the topics to be dealt with. We had decided we wanted to elicit some statements about practice and belief before we saw people in action in the classroom, but believing that direct questioning about beliefs was likely to be unproductive we framed most of our questions in terms of the practical possibilities, realities and constraints of their situations rather than of ideal schemes. In retrospect we judge that the formal interviews might have been more productive if we had placed them later when we knew more about each individual and could adapt our questioning in the light of the issues that were emerging. Clearly we gained much material, of a more private category, from informal interviews, but this varied in amount according to the accident of place, time and our developing relationships with the participants. All researchers must discover in the course of the research refinements they wish they could make in retrospect, but if one made them the research would never end.

The open-ended questionnaire which we produced at the end of the second stage was yet another different invitation for participants to present themselves. (See Appendix 2.)

Our sampling of lessons may be open to criticism on the grounds of its representativeness since it may be said that teachers and lecturers showed us only what they wanted us to see. This is true to the extent that we were in no lessons without the prior knowledge and agreement of those concerned, but arrangements were frequently made weeks before the event and the amazement with which we were greeted on more than one occasion showed that there had been no careful planning of what we were to see. And even if we were only shown what teachers and lecturers wanted us to see, the process by which those lessons were selected tells us a great deal about the characteristics they preferred to display.

Data such as comments on written work, dictated notes, questions and topics set cannot be criticised in the same way. Our collections were, in the main, drawn from the students whom we randomly selected for interview. The problem of evaluating the student replies in the interviews, however, was one which exercised us. We were even more conscious of the effect of our role than we had been with the teachers. We had read in Woods (1979[46]) of the advantages of group interviews, but generally we interviewed pupils singly or in friendship pairs. We tried out both group and individual interviews but decided that on the limited access that we had asked for there was insufficient time for a group to establish its identity and provide us with the data we wanted. Our status as interviewers clearly varied: to some of the pupils we may have appeared to be part of the repressive apparatus of school, for although they had become used to our presence in their classes with notebook and tape-recorder, they generally knew little of our intent. We always asked their permission to tape-record what they said and reassured them, if they were worried, that we would respect their confidence. For some acutely aware of assessment we were clearly cast in the role of examiners to whom they must give little away. In the pilot study we had been amused to find that 'our cover had been blown': we were officials from BEC checking up on the new courses. In the fifth form generally it seemed the most able were the most suspicious of our motives; the least able, although not so articulate, were pleased to have a listener who was anxious for their opinions. (See Appendix 3, Interview Schedules.)

All researchers are faced with the problem of evaluating the version of reality which is presented to them, especially when people talk of their principles and beliefs. We tell people what we want ourselves and them to believe and our accounts will differ according to our state of mind and body as well as our attitude to our listeners. The materials we gathered and our classroom observation enabled us to see the values and perspectives espoused in interview and syllabus in the light of their practical enactment in teaching. It is possible that our sample of lessons is angled towards what it was people supposed we wanted, but we do not think that a great deal of such angling took place, because teachers are considerably constrained by course and examination limitations, by their sense of lack of time and by their normal strategies for teaching which often represent a kind of negotiated equilibrium between the teacher's intentions and the students'. As researchers we convinced ourselves of the validity and internal consistency of our study. The devices of triangulation, participant validation, cross-checking by using different sources of data, collected, described and analysed by different researchers were used to exclude obvious bias in selection and interpretation.

We can satisfy ourselves that we employed a scrupulous methodology, we can explain the research design and its rationale, but the greater problem will always be rendering explicit for others its validity, demonstrating publicly its credibility. It is impossible to make fully available to readers the processes by which the account was achieved. No outsider can fully understand the relation of each piece of evidence to the whole, because, unless they re-enact the whole research they can never experience the processes which caused hypotheses to be generated. The presentation of 'outcomes' inevitably misrepresents the processes. Ultimately as Anderson (1981) asserts 'there is no such thing as research only accounts of research'[47]. However objective researchers may claim to be, however firmly grounded the theories they pretend to operate, whatever means they employ to test hypotheses, there are *a priori* assumptions without which the research has no existence. There are no devices which can eliminate the part played by the observer's subjectivity in the making of an account. The researcher selects the area to be studied, the data gathered, the methodology, the mode of reporting, the basis of analytical categories, the emphasis on issues and the presentation of findings.

In the foregoing paragraphs we have made a deliberate distinction between two aspects of research reports in the social sciences — internal consistency and the observer-reporter's subjectivity. From the point-of-view of internal consistency, there are many devices — triangulation, multiple observation, respondent validation and so on — to minimise the effects of observer-bias. There is no escape, however, from the cultural perspective which makes the data meaningful yet is inevitably located in the socio-cultural life-history of the observer. As Anderson has shown, every research report will have something of the character of a persuasive account. We have made it our care in this report not to shelter behind an anonymous style that claims an objective authority, but to maintain the reader's awareness that he or she is seeing the world through our eyes. In our report we try to realise the ideal, to display data, methods and preconceptions in such a way as to provide purchase for others, so that they can weigh the evidence and have a ground for qualifications, judgement and disagreement. We present figures so that the extent and limits of our sampling can be seen and compared with accounts which may be made of similar curricula. We endeavour to keep clear the distinction between description and commentary and interpret the different kinds of data in the light of the conditions that generated them. Finally, however, it has to be: 'This is how it seemed to us; does it seem like that to you?'

CHAPTER 2

Institutions, People and the Use of Time

As the prime purpose of our enquiry was concerned with English teaching we did not set out to collect a mass of detail about each of the schools and colleges: we were focusing our attention upon the teachers and pupils in the particular classes involved. Nevertheless, it will probably be helpful if we attempt to provide our readers with some facts and impressions. No novelist or dramatist would expect his audience to memorise ten separate settings and 35 characters so we shall provide a table of information for reference (see Appendix IV), but some local colour may lessen the need to keep checking where which teacher belonged.

1. The schools and the teachers

Downtown School and Urban School could have been chosen to represent different stages in the history of educational expansion. Urban School belongs to the growth in grammar-school education at the beginning of this century: its now blackened buildings stand as a monument to solid northern municipal pride. The honours boards are proof of its past successes and its reputation is still high in the wide band of inner-city districts from which it draws the majority of its students. Since it became comprehensive and since the balance of ethnic minorities in those inner-city areas have changed, more and more black faces can be seen in the tiled corridors and the lofty classrooms. Indeed, in all the classes we observed we were conscious that a significant proportion, sometimes as high as a third of the pupils, was of West Indian or Asian origin.

Downtown School in contrast almost encapsulates the essence of the beginning of the comprehensive school movement of the late fifties and early sixties. It is a light, spacious concrete building, one of the first proofs of the post-war development of a run-down inner-city area. It is set in the hinterland where old respectable working-class terraces are surrounded by newer blocks of flats and prefabricated industrial units. We had the school described to us as 'rough' by a former pupil, but we saw no outward evidence such as vandalism or graffiti. In our 32 visits the only messiness we saw was the litter of crisp bags blowing about in a concrete play area and our over-riding impression was the spaciousness of the lay-out.

From our interview data the pupils at Downtown and Urban Schools stood out as predominantly lower working class: they had the highest proportion of parents with manual occupations, and more fathers who were unemployed. But even though there was this similarity, in appearance they seemed very different. All pupils at Urban School were in school uniform whereas one of our earliest field notes after a visit to Downtown School commented on the fact that the fifth-form girls seemed indistinguishable in their appearance and dress from the girls coming out of the local factory. It was unlike all the other schools in that we retain no impression of even the dominant colour of the school uniform. Certainly in the bottom group anoraks and outdoor coats were worn in class by almost all the girls and the boys sported magnificently striped sweaters. We have been interested in quoting these observations because such details were regarded as negative factors in Rutter's study *Fifteen Thousand Hours*[1]. The emphasis on uniform at Urban School might be thought to fit in with its grammar-school origins, but all the schools except Downtown seemed to expect conformity.

Significance of its origins was, however, demonstrated at Urban School in the harking-back to glories that were past in some of the comments we had from staff. Although all the teachers we worked with there had come to the school either when it was comprehensive or at the transitional stage there was a goodly number on the staff whose appointments dated from the old grammar-school days. The bridge-playing group of solid seniors in the corner of the staffroom at lunch time had no counterparts at Downtown School. Mrs Sutton, who was the recently appointed head of the English department at Urban School, looked too young to join their ranks, for her slight, youthful appearance belied her experience and qualifications. Hers was the velvet-glove approach, the quiet efficiency which influences her colleagues and manages her classes with a firm discipline. She had little time for 'bandwagons', describing herself as 'probably about middle of the range tending to formal', but she was nevertheless manoeuvring her colleagues into accepting less traditional syllabuses. Mr Callaghan and Mrs Sackville had both joined the staff in its transition period, she as a mature entrant, he as a young teacher with a couple of years' experience. Now struggling against ill-health, Mrs Sackville was acutely conscious of the growing gap she perceived between her pupils' worlds and hers. 'When we try to train them to speak correctly and make the best of themselves and write correctly and we correct their work then they think it's a fetish with us almost. We are superior beings or trying to make them into superior beings.' Mr Callaghan was energetic and enthusiastic and thought himself less formal than most of his colleagues. 'I don't overemphasise the mechanics . . . I think (others) might do far more grammar-based lessons and a lot more examples on the board.' The value he placed on oral work was what, according to his pupils, made his English lessons different. As one said, 'We usually have a right long talk . . . we discuss things all together'.

At Downtown School more of the department were involved because the school participated in both years of the research. The three fifth-form teachers — Mrs Brennan, Mr Richardson and Mrs Williams — seemed very representative of the staff as a whole, a young married group with similar interests, inside and outside school. As we sat in the staffroom listening to the usual conversations about pupils and school affairs, eavesdropping on talk of holiday arrangements or the planning of a wine and cheese party, we gained a strong impression of a community of shared interests.

Mrs Brennan was an outgoing young woman with a warm personal relationship with her pupils, in class and in her pastoral role. She recognised their strengths — 'some of them have a lovely way with words' — and wanted them to share her enthusiasms, to experience 'a certain joy' in reading. Mrs Williams, who did not regard herself as an English specialist, was, at this stage, finding her feet in the department. She was much influenced by Mrs Brennan's success, but she hankered after the security of more formal work. At the end of the year she was busily compiling worksheets and delighted to have found a book with 'some great exercises in'. Downtown was Mr Richardson's second school. He had had the good fortune to serve his apprenticeship in a lively department whose ideas were encapsulated in a course book he was still using. He had moved to Downtown School when a colleague became the head of department: he appreciated the support given by a good departmental team.

The three teachers we met in the sixth form were not as a group so typical. Mr Baxter had only recently joined the staff so was clearly not yet integrated into the staffroom community and the departmental ethos. It was only a matter of time for he was lively and energetic, very receptive to new ideas, but as a newcomer he worried about the sixth-form group, 'the kids here just don't seem to be trained to think'. Mr Underwood and Mr Holmes, as senior members of staff with wide and varied experience, were much more sure of their world. Mr Underwood, the head of department, maintained and supported the department in its liberal stance, but as an A-level examiner he was well aware of how the system operated. Mr Holmes was primarily an administrator but one whose humane outlook owed a great deal to his work as an English teacher in a pioneering department in another school during the sixties. From Appendix IV it will be clear that this was a strong department with a high proportion of its members in senior posts.

Our two suburban schools were less sharply contrasted in appearance than the inner-city ones: the most striking difference was in size for Catchwide School was by far the largest of our city schools whereas New Suburbia School was the smallest. Like Urban School, Catchwide School was the result of an amalgamation and we noticed that there was some of the same tendency to look back on old traditions. Both suburban school buildings were modern, set in pleasant surroundings on the edge of the town with New Suburbia School drawing most of its pupils from the attractive newly built estates nearby. Catchwide School, as its name implies, served a wider area; the rows of buses drawn up in the large forecourt were proof of that. Although New Suburbia School could boast some fine modern equipment and facilities, our impression of the school was coloured by the fact that we observed lessons there in the most inappropriate surroundings. It is, perhaps, worth commenting that the comforts of the conventional classroom can be forgotten in the architect's dream of social areas and linked workshops. The fine squash courts, excellent cafeteria, and generously equipped drama studios, however, make the school very attractive to parents and pupils and its reputation appeared high in the suburbs it served. Although the English department democratically shared the teaching at all levels, we had the sense that this was the school with the strongest chain of command. When the head gave his blessing to the school's involvement in the research the decision was accepted rather than discussed. This is not meant to imply any unwillingness of the teachers to participate but rather to give the feel of the school. At fifth-form level we worked there with Mrs Harrison, Mr Porson and Mrs Waterhouse, and Mrs King, the head of department, joined in during the second year. Mrs Harrison was talking of her lessons when she said 'I am quite a structured person', but it is a neat phrase to encapsulate her approach and her skills in classroom management. Mrs Waterhouse similarly liked a set pattern which, with her less-able group meant 'basic language skills and spellings', but even with the more able GCE classes it was 'on the whole a straightforward grind'. Mr Porson, the youngest of the teachers there, thought 'the teaching revolution of the sixties a mistake. When I was at school our attitude to work was much more serious' – a rather contradictory statement as the more serious school days he looked back to must have been in the early 1970s. Mrs King, although an able and experienced teacher, wanted us to adopt an authoritative role: she hoped we 'would tell (them) the kinds of practice that seemed admirable, the things that work — give (them) hints'.

The grey concrete of the Catchwide school buildings belonged to much the same period as Downtown's, but we were conscious of much more overcrowding in corridors and classrooms. The shift of population from inner-city areas has not always been anticipated in school provision as the planners are finding out. Male teachers considerably outnumbered the women in our sample and all the teachers from Catchwide School were men. It may have been by chance, but their experience was matched to the group they were teaching, a hierarchical practice which used to be a common one. Mr O'Donnell, the most experienced and the head of department, was teaching the top group, but the cramming he forecast we were going to see was 'not the sort of thing I would want to do if I were my own boss'. The hurdles of the examination equally preoccupied Mr Keegan, in his early forties, who taught the middle group. Mr Gilham, the relative newcomer, had the bottom group. Although he was still at the stage of struggling to collect materials, 'at the moment I'm literally working all the hours God sends and I'm still only half doing the job', he was nevertheless able to distance himself enough to worry about the danger of stereotyping his pupils. 'I've noticed this creeping into my own teaching. If I come across something that's difficult then I will do it with the top people; I'll keep them on their toes. But if it's with the bottom set we'll do Stan Barstow talking about having fish and chips on Friday night.'

The two schools in Smalltown were not perhaps so great a contrast to the city schools as might have been anticipated, because the small town we finally selected has to some extent become a dormitory town. But although according to our data the schools were similar in social mix to the suburban pair, there was nevertheless a different feel or atmosphere. Both of these schools, unlike our city schools, catered for 11–18 year-olds: this authority has not adopted a middle school system, so we were aware that the pupils had perhaps been more firmly socialised into the school's values. In many ways these were our most attractive schools although they lacked some of the facilities of New Suburbia School and were more cramped than Downtown School. Both were set in pleasant tree-lined roads in residential areas: as we walked past the flower-beds to the highly polished entrance halls, peace and quiet prevailed. It was a different scene when we left at the end of the day amid the convoys of buses and staff cars, but it was all an orderly and controlled affair.

Greentown School's secondary modern origins seemed unimportant superficially, but from comments we heard in the local FE college it seemed they still affect its reputation, especially if one contrasted it with Smalltown School. It was significant, we thought, that our collaborators at Greentown School were the two most recent members of the English department, young men who had wider experience than most. Mr Tremaine was head of the department and Mr Saxon his second. The more established members of the department included some who were part-time or had other loyalties as well as English. Mr Tremaine caricatured his teaching beautifully, 'There's the formal Tremaine who stands up and says William Blake was born in 1757 . . . take it down please. There's the, "Should we hang IRA men? — What do you think, Janet?" sort of lesson', but he went on, 'I like also to have small groups working and reporting back and there's a certain amount of drama work . . . ' He devoted much of his time in and out of school hours to working with individuals, but 'this is a very formal school and children, if they don't get their shot of formality, will feel uneasy and unco-operative about what might go on'.

Perhaps this tension accounted for some of the doubts Mr Saxon expressed. He was trying to put the emphasis on his pupils 'as developing individuals', trying 'to follow leads'. He was not abrogating responsibility, 'I'll do typing through the early hours of the morning for them, but I don't want to lapse into teaching from the front because it's an easier life . . . it's fine as long as I am bursting with energy, but . . . once you're down things fall apart'.

It is difficult to account for the sense of confidence of Smalltown School solely in terms of its origins. It is true it was the oldest grammar school foundation, but in its progress towards comprehensivisation it had absorbed various less prestigious schools. It could not be said of any of the English departments that we worked with that their morale was low, indeed, the opposite was true: we would not have been allowed into a department which had many self-doubts. The difference, perhaps, at Smalltown School was that morale throughout the school was high. It was the staffroom in which we felt we had become accepted as familiars and where we were expected to form part of conversational groups and not be just eavesdroppers. There was plenty of the usual talk of the misdemeanours of the fourth form, but there was also discussion of the staging of *Oh, what a lovely war*, the novels people were reading and the films they had seen. We worked there in both years of the research and, particularly at fifth-form level, saw a large sample of the teaching because people were so insistent that we should. Mr Squires, the head of department, was teaching a middle-ability group, but we also saw some of his work with a more able group. His fairness and sympathetic understanding as a head of department was valued. He said of himself as a teacher, 'I tend to talk too much', but his aim was for 'as much variety of approach as possible' and to 'make appeals as personal as possible'. Of all teachers he placed the greatest stress on widening the cultural horizons of his pupils. Mr Austin was initially to be the teacher of the bottom group, but he also taught the most able class and he was anxious to have our reactions to his work with both groups. He was an unusual person, strongly committed to his academic interests yet also able to establish a strong bond with those expected to be anti-school. For one able pupil English was pleasant because 'it expands your mind', for John in the bottom class it was good because 'the group gets on well, we all mix together and work as a team . . . as a team you find you can get through more'. His was the most interesting and exciting teaching we saw: there are plentiful references to it in the sections which follow. Mrs Wood was nearing the end of her career and she savoured the opportunity to talk and think about her teaching. 'Perhaps I enjoyed the opportunity of showing that us old chalk and talk old-timers still have a trick or two up our sleeves', she wrote in a letter giving us a delightful picture of the 'dreadfully marvellous send-off' the school had given her on retirement. Our involvement in the sixth form was more limited, much more in line with the other departments in that we observed Mr Austin sharing the teaching of one A-level group with Mr Anderson who described his sixth-form teaching as 'compromise all the time. Compromise and wait . . . you sit and lurk then you pounce on something . . . But you have to get them through the exam'. We saw least of his work, but he was respected by the others and apparently shared many of their interests.

2. The colleges and the lecturers

The account of our entry into the colleges probably tells as much about them as any description of their buildings or situation, for it was an instance of their compartmentalisation and bureaucracy. The last two decades have witnessed a massive expansion of the further education sector and our college buildings were evidence of this. Even in the city where the greater part of the colleges were housed in impressive modern buildings, annexes and outposts were needed to cope with the increasing numbers; for example, only in one college, City Road, were all the Communications classes in the main block. Since all the colleges drew their students from a wide area, their actual location was not so important a variant as in the case of the schools. The social background of the students at Smalltown College which distinguished it from the city colleges was concomitant with its setting, but in general the course rather than the college determined its public status.

High Street College was the largest of the colleges and most of the students and staff there were housed in a fine purpose-built building. When the students we interviewed said how different college was from school we remembered our first impressions of High Street College. The expansive reception area with its potted palms and comfortable couches, the notice boards announcing student elections and urging people to vote for John Smith or Rafiq Mirza as entertainments secretary all seemed a far cry from the lists of house detentions and the shrill school bells, but behind the facade even in this impressive building it was not always so different. The A-level students were sitting behind the old desks in the prefabs, the RSA classes were even referred to as form 1B or form 5, and those silent ranks of would-be shorthand typists poised waiting for the next instruction were becoming part of a hierarchical system more rigid than many a school.

The English or Communications Department as such did not really exist in any college, but at High Street College we did meet most of the lecturers, for we attended the only English 'syndicate' meeting that the 30 or so of them had had during the last two years. The three experienced lecturers we eventually worked with were all in different departments and despite this meeting seemed to know little of each other's work. When we visited one of them we never encountered any of the others and we realised when we entertained them at the end of the year in our rooms that we probably knew them better than they knew each other. Mr Davidson, the only English graduate of the three, was enthusiastically developing Communications courses in the Business Studies Department: BEC Communications seemed the embodiment of all he had been trying to do in the department for the last ten years. Mr Peel in the Secretarial Department was fighting a rearguard battle convinced that the real values of O-level and RSA English would ultimately prevail against the innovations of BEC. And Mrs Lincoln was building a bastion of culture in the A-level literature courses in the General Education Department, housed in the old school down the road. All were experienced lecturers and the two latter also had years of experience in commerce and government service. Although the three we worked with did not know each other well, in each department there were enough lecturers engaged in similar work for there to be some sense of a department identity, but it was only the lecturers involved in the BEC Communications who worked as a team, jointly preparing materials and following the same plan.

At City Road College, although we rarely encountered anyone but the lecturer we were visiting, all the lecturers were administratively in the same General Studies Department. In contrast with those at High Street College they were either relative newcomers or outsiders because of their part-time status. Two of the four, Mrs Brown and Mrs Fraser, although teaching almost the equivalent of full timetables were unestablished; a third, Mr Turner, had only just been appointed: only Mr Blackburn had been on the full-time staff any length of time. At City Road College we really felt that we had been passed down the line; anyone of relative seniority suggested that we saw someone else's work. But we were glad to have the opportunity of seeing what in theory was part-time teaching as this constitutes so much of English and Communications work in colleges. Mrs Fraser and Mrs Brown had both originally trained for teaching in school and had found themselves almost by chance in their present jobs. Mrs Fraser had left school-teaching whilst her children were very young and had heard from an acquaintance of the need for some part-time help at City Road. Mrs Brown had been drawn in through her work with unemployed school-leavers. From the sessions we saw we assumed that they had easy access to the banks of teaching materials which the departmental head had encouraged and helped lecturers to develop, but we learned that it could take three or four years for a part-timer to find what was available. Whatever the difficulties had been, the degree of commitment and enthusiasm with which the part-timers prepared and presented those materials was remarkable. It may have been due to their personalities rather than their part-time working, but the organisation of their sessions contrasted sharply with those of the full-timers. Mr Blackburn, perhaps more than any of the others, fitted the stereotype of the General Studies lecturer which he had himself volunteered, 'slightly unreliable, a bit scruffy, somewhat lefty'. Like Mr Turner he had come to FE after experimenting with a range of jobs: they could both present a persuasive and well-thought out rationale, but in class they aimed at an easy-going and relaxed approach. Facilities at City Road College seemed to be in every respect ideal for Communications: light attractive furniture could be arranged at will in the carpeted rooms, overhead projectors waited to be plugged in, sophisticated audio-visual equipment was readily provided.

Square Hill College provided a stark contrast: it was the college where Communications teaching struggled against the most obvious difficulties. Ironically, the reputation at local and national level of the band of lecturers who worked here in the seventies has almost become a legend, but through administrative changes the department had been split and the lecturers we saw were working under the most difficult conditions. Only the quiet and gentle Mr Benson, who had been there 13 years, was in the main block with the TEC students. Mrs Brindley, a comparative newcomer, was mothering her boisterous clumsy lads in the old huts scheduled for demolition, but she was at least in five minutes' walking distance of facilities of the main block, whereas Mr Wilkinson in the converted factory was a couple of miles away. Although he was the most highly qualified lecturer in academic terms, he remarked rather ruefully that it was his manual working experience, his years learning a craft, which gave him status and credibility. Their professionalism was impressive under these isolated and difficult conditions.

Unlike its city counterparts, the main buildings at Smalltown College belonged to the early years of the century and there was no fine foyer to impress visitors or bustling cafeteria as a student meeting place. The College had spilled over into any available adjoining premises and had sites scattered throughout the town. Each of the three Communications lessons Mr Hemmings was timetabled to teach during a week to the BEC class we observed took place in a different building and as we sat there we could speculate what their former histories had been. It was easy to imagine that the low narrow room must have been two rooms perhaps servants' bedrooms, but what could have been the functions of the heavy rails on the ceiling in what seemed to have been built as a small office block? It could not have been that all our visits to Smalltown College chanced to be on rainy days, but when we recall Mr Hemmings we see a youthfully enthusiastic figure in a bright blue waterproof clutching his papers in a plastic bag to protect them. He had some responsibility for student sport and leisure so was much in demand as he hurried across the town. Young Mrs Sands had no established base beyond her share of a shelf and table in the pokey staffroom: she, too, flitted from site to site with her RSA students. Only Mr Pattison, the most senior of the three, could be regularly found with his O-level class in the former drawing room of an Edwardian house — a setting somehow appropriate both to his manner and to his references to the superior social background of his pupils.

3. Resources in schools and colleges

It is significant that when we were describing schools their settings seemed important both from the point of view of status and our sense of the dominant atmosphere in the school and department. The community of the school staffroom with most people working the same hours and talking of the same concert or outing or fund-raising activities had no parallel in FE. Individual departments were almost schools in themselves for they were catering for hundreds of part time students as well as the nucleus of full-timers, and it was usually the status of the departmental course which mattered. Whereas English in school is a highly esteemed academic subject, its status in colleges is much more ambiguous. If the college stresses A-level courses English may be accorded parity with other specialist subjects, but this is not automatic even when its student numbers are high. Technical colleges were set up to teach vocationally-linked courses and in most colleges the strong and powerful departments are those with trade and business links. Our account will have shown that English and Communications teaching was generally organised within the vocational departments even if it was technically in General Studies: it was only at City Road College that we had any sense of the subject having general status, and that may have been because it was the head of department's specialism.

Readers familiar with national statistics will know that teaching groups in English at fifth-form level are larger than for any other subject (24.5 pupils). The class sizes in our sample averaged 24.3 pupils, but there was quite a considerable variation between schools. We produced a notional figure of the teaching time allocated to each pupil by dividing the teaching time for English each week by the number of pupils in the class and this enabled us to see which classes had the most favourable provision. For example, all groups at New Suburbia School tended to have the shortest teaching times, but to some extent this was balanced by the favourable pupil-teacher ratio of their smaller classes.

Table 2.1

Teacher time allocation per pupil per week (minutes)

Sets:	Top			Middle		Bottom	
	Downtown		10.4	Catchwide	11.2	New Suburbia	10.3
	Smalltown	(a)	7.8	Downtown	8.3	Catchwide	9.5
	Urban		7.6	New Suburbia	8.3	Smalltown	9.2
	Greentown		7.5	Smalltown	7.3	Downtown	9
	Catchwide		7.3	Urban	6.9	Greentown	8.1
	Smalltown	(b)	7.2			Urban	7.6
	New Surburbia		6.5				

Even though some teachers placed great stress on the importance of individual teaching these figures are not to be taken as an actual measure of the time they could spend with each pupil, but rather as an indication of the generosity of teaching provision which, coupled with other resource allocation, may be significant. Overall, Downtown School had the most generous allowance and Urban School the least, but the more striking comparison was in the provision for classes within each set. A pupil in the top set at Downtown School had much more teacher time than a pupil in the top set at any other school (60 per cent more than at New Suburbia School). There is an even wider variation between the most and least generous provision for the middle set.

In the sixth and FE the figures look very different and, because of the status of the course, are not so comparable. The national average for teacher–pupil ratio is 11.1 in sixth-form English groups. The largest group we observed was 17 strong at New Suburbia School, the smallest at Downtown School was only seven. The classes in FE varied from 11 to 20. The largest classes were at Smalltown College where they ranged from Mrs Sands' RSA Secretarial course with 20 students to the O-level course with 15 students. Secretarial and Business courses seemed likely to have higher numbers than the Craft and Technician courses where the average was 13, but these smaller figures were probably determined by workshop accommodation. The notional figures we produced in Table 2.1 have validity for comparative purposes since at fifth-form level all the pupils were taking either GCE O-level or CSE and so could expect a roughly similar provision. In the post-compulsory year the courses varied so greatly in the emphasis and importance which English or Communications receive, that the notional figures range from 40 minutes for A-level English at Downtown School to six minutes for RSA English at Smalltown College. It is perhaps worth pointing out how much more favourable the provision for O-level English Language is at this stage with notional figures of 20 minutes per student at Smalltown College and 16.6 at Downtown School.

Although there were differences in the allocation of material resources to English in schools they were not such wide variations as in the colleges' provision; but even those limited variations in schools such as accommodation had implications of the valuing of English as a subject. More than half of the fifth-form English lessons took place in 'English' rooms, although in some cases these were no more than the form room of the English specialist who had some kind of linked subject display on the walls. At Downtown and Greentown Schools the English rooms formed a real subject base with cupboards and storage facilities to hand. When Mr Saxon urged his class at Greentown School to borrow books for home reading they could do it there and then as the store cupboard opened off the room. On the walls of the classrooms there were displays of posters, some professionally produced, others made by staff. Alongside the photographs of productions and pictures of characters from plays there was pupils' writing on a variety of topics. In one classroom at Downtown School there was an effective presentation of the uses of punctuation marks. Although general facilities were not so good at Catchwide School, the walls of Mr Gilham's room were covered by his collection of theatre posters and in Mr O'Donnell's room there were advertisements for the Book Club and displays of its offerings. Such presentations owed as much to personal enthusiasm as to resource allocation, but they were more likely if rooms were set aside for English. The worst conditions probably were those at Urban School where we saw lessons taught in impossibly cramped partitioned rooms, but it was not that English was singled out; conditions were not worse than those generally prevailing for academic subjects in an old building. But it was in one of the newest buildings, New Suburbia School, where the subject apparently fared the worst. Home economics demonstration complexes, open plan social areas, technical drawing rooms were all pressed into use for English teaching. Boxes of books had to be carried from room to room and although there were excellent audio-visual resources, as we know from carrying out interviews in a store room piled with electronic equipment, there was no technician to provide the help which was so readily available at City Road College.

Generally, teachers had few complaints about their limited resources: Mr Gilham at Catchwide School was the only person who said that he would probably teach differently if, for example, he had access to television. He would have liked to encourage a more critical appreciation of programmes and considered that this should be an element of a fifth-form English course. The brevity of many lessons made it difficult for teachers to set up equipment, although at Smalltown School facilities were such that Mr Squires regularly used video recordings with his middle ability group, and Mrs Wood was able to use the record player for her lessons on *Romeo and Juliet*. Although most teachers said that they did not think that more resources would have changed their approach, they were not happy about the limitations imposed on their buying of books. We ought to remind readers that these remarks were made before severe cuts had been made. Mr Tremaine, at Greentown School, remarked that the copies of *Woman in White* he had to buy as an examination set text had taken half of the English allowance for the whole school. Mrs Sutton, at Urban School, felt that she would like to have spent more on books and equipment for the less able. Examination set texts clearly had to have priority. One contrast we picked up incidentally was in the amount of money available for the library in two of the schools. We were told that in the previous year the librarian at Urban School, for the whole school for all subjects, had £100 to spend, whereas we heard that at Smalltown School the Parent–Teacher Association had allocated £1000 from its funds to supplement the authority allowance. There is perhaps no need to comment on this except to add that the proportion of pupils in our sample who came from social classes I–III (non-manual) differed in a similar ratio for these two schools: thus the least affluent pupils had the least money spent on books.

4. Social backgrounds of pupils and students

We have made passing reference to the social class background of the pupils and students in our sample and here may be an appropriate place to elaborate on that.

Our allocation of pupils and students to social class was based on the information which they gave us incidentally in the interviews as we asked them about the relevance of English in schools to their parents' work. We used the Registrar-General's categories for father's occupation, but in a small number of one-parent families with widowed or divorced mothers we used the mother's occupation. We suspected that sometimes jobs were up-graded to sound more important than they were: we had rather more people in charge of this or that than seemed probable, but on the occasions when we cross-checked because a job sounded particularly unlikely our doubts were proved wrong. We therefore accepted what we were told and on that basis the differences between the populations of the three groups of schools was clearly marked. Only 13 per cent of the parents of our sample in the city-centre schools fell into classes I and II, compared with 30 per cent in the pair of suburban schools and 52 per cent in the schools in Smalltown.

Table 2.2

Pupils' social background by location of school

Schools	Registrar-General's Classification of Occupations I & II	III	IV & V	Not classifiable	
City Centre	13	55	16	16	100
Suburban	30	54	8	8	100
Smalltown	52	23	13	2	100

The figures for I and II from the Smalltown schools are higher than they should be for purposes of comparison because there were in the six classes three 'top' groups which are more likely to be drawn from I and II. Our figures for the so-called top, middle and bottom groups from all the schools reflected a marked differentiation according to social class patterns.

Table 2.3

Pupils' social background by groups/sets

Groupings	I & II	III	IV & V	Not classifiable	
Top	52	33	3	12	100
Middle	18	48	14	20	100
Bottom	17	54	19	10	100

It is clear that with two suburban schools and the two schools in prosperous Smalltown we have an unrepresentative picture for the whole comprehensive school population. Classes I and II, however, according to the Registrar-General's classification, are not narrow groups: the entries in Class II were often nurses, teachers or owners of small businesses.

It is worth commenting that in the data from the sixth form and FE which was collected in the second year of the research a few parents were allocated according to employment who were in fact unemployed. For example, only one of the three A-level students we interviewed at Downtown School had a parent who was working, but in cases where unemployment was recent students usually told us the jobs that their fathers had had. Unemployment was rising sharply in all sections during the later stages of the research and more parents would now probably figure in the last column (not classifiable).

School-leavers were already finding great difficulty in getting jobs: most of the City and Guilds I group at Square Hill College had tried for manual work, some for as long as a year. They were taking the craft course using 'it as a last resort, if I don't get a job I can come here' and hoping that in the future it might tip the balance in their favour.

The very clear relationships we could see between social class and schools had no close parallel in the post-compulsory year as Table 2.4 demonstrates.

Table 2.4

Students' social background by colleges

	I & II	III	IV & V	Not classifiable	
High Street	21	31	26	21	99
Smalltown	35	54	0	12	101
Square Hill	26	52	22	0	100
City Road	39	26	26	9	100

Smalltown College stands out with no students drawn from IV and V and High Street College is the only college where the proportion from IV and V is higher than that from I and II. If we examine the social class background of the most highly qualified students, the 32 (50 per cent) who had more than two O-levels or their equivalent, 14 came from I and II, 12 from III and only 6 from IV and V. Social classes I and II were, in fact, providing more of the highly qualified students. In the survey which Dean and Steads undertook in 1978[2] of students on one-year courses in colleges and sixth forms the highest proportion (30 per cent) came from IIIM and 24 per cent came from I and II. If we extract from our sample the students on one-year courses the figures are 31 per cent from IIIM and 26 per cent from I and II so it appears that our sample, although small, was not atypical. It is the two-year courses which recruit substantially (41 per cent) from social groups I and II.

We were interested in the general levels of educational achievement of the students who chose to continue their education in FE and particularly in their success in English. Venables' research in the sixties had found that highly able first year ONC (Ordinary National Certificate) students performed comparatively badly on verbal tests[3]. We expected that as Hordley and Lee (1970)[4] found a disproportionate number of FE students from selective schools we would find that the majority of our students would have come from groups equivalent to our 'top' groups, but would not necessarily be those who had been successful in English. Our findings did not bear this out

Table 2.5

Previous achievement of students

	COURSE	No. in Sample	GENERAL EDUCATIONAL ACHIEVEMENT 5 or more O level	 2–4 O-level	 At least 4 CSE 2–5	 Fewer than 4 CSE 2–5	ACHIEVEMENT IN ENGLISH CSE I (O-A/B/C)	 CSE 2/3 (O-D/E)	 CSE 4/5	 U
COLLEGE										
High Street	A-level	[illegible]	4	–	–	–	4	–	–	–
	BEC Nat.	[illegible]	2	2 (BEC Gen.*)	–	–	2 + 2*	–	–	–
	RSA III	[illegible]	–	2	3	–	5	–	–	–
	RSA I	5	–	–	5	1	–	2	4	–
Smalltown	RSA I/II	[illegible]	2	2	2	–	5	–	1	–
	BEC Gen.	[illegible]	–	3	2	1	2	2	–	2
	O-level	[illegible]	–	3	2	–	3	2	–	–
Square Hill	TEC I	[illegible]	–	3	2	–	1	3	–	1
	CITB	[illegible]	1	–	3	–	2	1	–	1
	C & G I	[illegible]	–	–	5	1	–	1	4	1
City Road	TEC I	[illegible]	5	–	–	–	5	–	–	–
	Coll	4	2	1	1	–	2	2	–	–
	C & G Foundation	[illegible]	–	–	4	1	–	2	1	2
	TOTAL	6[illegible]	16	16	29	4	33	15	10	7
	%	10[illegible]	25	25	45	6	51	23	15	11
SCHOOL										
Downtown	A-level	3	3	–	–	–	3	–	–	–
	O-level	4	–	1	3	–	–	4	–	–
New Suburbia	A-level	6	5	1	–	–	6	–	–	–
Smalltown	A-level	4	3	1	–	–	4	–	–	–
	TOTAL	17	11	3	3	–	13	4	–	–

Table 2.6

Social class distribution of sample interviewed (raw scores)

INSTITUTIONS		Registrar-General's Classification of Occupations							
FIFTH YEAR	Group	I	II	IIIN	IIIM	IV	V	N.C.	TOTAL
SCHOOLS	T	–	1	2	3	1	–	1	8
Downtown	M	–	1	–	3	1	1	4	10
	B	–	–	1	4	1	1	–	7
	T	–	–	4	4	–	1	–	9
Urban	M	–	2	1	3	1	1	1	9
	B	–	3	–	5	–	1	3	12
	T	1	4	–	1	–	–	2	8
Catchwide	M	–	2	1	6	–	–	–	9
	B	1	–	–	4	–	2	–	7
	T	1	5	3	–	–	–	–	9
New Suburbia	M	–	1	3	2	–	–	1	7
	B	–	–	2	5	2	–	1	10
Greentown	T	2	5	1	–	–	–	1	9
	B	–	4	2	1	1	–	–	8
	Tl	3	5	1	–	–	–	1	10
Smalltown	T2	3	2	–	1	–	–	2	8
	M	–	2	1	1	2	–	3	9
	B	–	1	1	3	2	–	1	8

SIXTH YEAR SCHOOLS	Course								
Downtown	A-level	–	–	2	–	–	–	1	3
	O-level	–	1	–	3	–	–	–	4
New Suburbia	A-level	1	3	–	–	1	–	1	6
Smalltown	A-level	1	1	1	1	–	–	–	4
FE COLLEGES									
High Street	A-level	–	2	–	–	1	–	1	4
	BEC Nat.	1	–	1	–	–	–	2	4
	RSA III	1	–	3	–	1	–	–	5
	RSA I	–	–	–	2	2	1	1	6
Smalltown	RSA	–	2	1	1	–	–	2	6
	BEC Gen.	–	1	2	3	–	–	–	6
	O-level	1	2	1	1	–	–	–	5
Square Hill	TEC	–	3	1	–	1	–	–	5
	CITB	–	–	–	3	1	–	–	4
	C. & G. I	–	1	1	2	1	–	–	6
City Road	TEC	1	2	–	2	–	–	–	5
	COLL.	1	–	–	1	3	–	–	4
	C. & G. Found.	–	2	–	1	1	–	1	5

as Table 2.5 shows. The fact that 50 per cent of the sample had two or more O-levels showed that they had been in the most able classes during their schooling, but the figures for English achievement showed that an even higher proportion, perhaps two-thirds, were from the groups which had formed our 'top' ones in the fifth year. They were not those likely to do less well in verbal tests, but conversely the more successful. We had assumed that few of the 'bottom' group would continue in the educational system and this was borne out. Even the students who had few qualifications seemed generally to have come from the 'middle' group.

5. Teachers and lecturers: personal histories

We have indicated in a summary fashion the relative status of the teachers and lecturers within their institutions, but we have given very little impression of them as individuals with their own private histories. The reduction of the schools and colleges to tables and lists has taken away the living atmosphere: a similar exercise for our teachers would be even more inaccurate although we have produced some information in tabular form for ease of reference.

In all we observed 35 teachers and lecturers, 17 in the first year, 18 in the second. Because our school observation was spread over both years the school sample is considerably larger than that from FE colleges: we have 22 teachers in schools as against 13 lecturers in colleges. It can hardly claim to be a representative sample, but it is not an inconsiderable one: in two respects, however, it is unrepresentative and that is in the proportion of men to women and the qualifications of the teachers. We will discuss qualifications later, merely remarking that it seems reasonable to assume that the less highly qualified a teacher the more unwilling he or she would be to be involved in classroom research. The fact that we had 22 men compared with 13 women when there are more women English teachers than men is not so easy to explain.

The profiles which we presented to all the teachers for their comment at the end of the first year were based on all the data we had collected about them and their courses, but as lessons will be analysed in the other sections we shall try to exclude that material here and use the interviews, conversations, group discussions and questionnaire which most people filled in at the end of the second year. The questionnaire was not returned by seven people, three from the second year and four from the first year. One of those we had lost touch with when he moved during the first year, another was seriously ill and had left teaching and three were heads of departments who, burdened with paper work, were perhaps tiring of our demands which had fallen most heavily upon them.

The striking difference between the people in schools and those in colleges was not so much age or experience, as in their positions in their institutions. As well as the six heads of departments in schools we had two heads of year and one deputy headmaster — all very senior posts in the school hierarchy — and five others had graded posts. In further education, in contrast, most of the lecturers (nine out of thirteen) were at the lowest grade, (two were unestablished) and only one had reached the position of senior lecturer. As would be expected the majority of the teachers in senior positions had taught in other schools (68 per cent), but most of the lecturers even some of the most experienced were in their first permanent and full-time teaching posts. Mr Davidson had been 13 years at High Street College, Mr Benson 14 at Square Hill College and Mr Pattison even longer at Smalltown College.

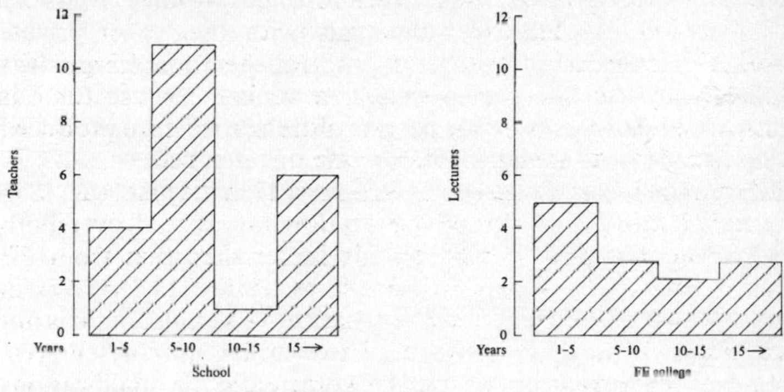

Figure 2.7(a)

Years of teaching experience

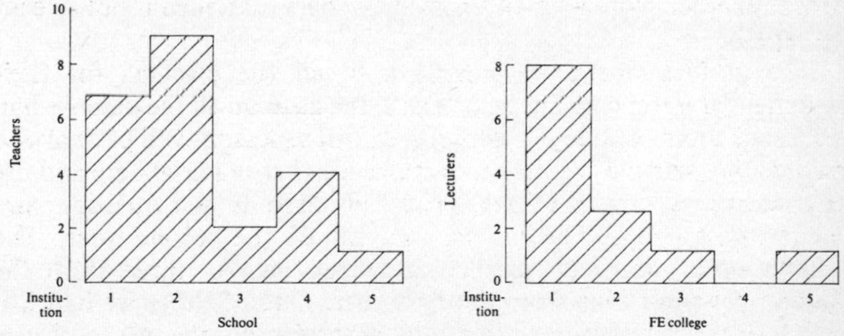

Figure 2.7(b)

Range of experience of teaching
(i.e. number of teaching jobs)

We expected the lecturers to have spent longer in other occupations and this was in fact the case; whereas 12 teachers had spent all their adult working lives in teaching this was true of only one lecturer. Mr Peel had more than 20 years' experience in banking, the army and the colonial service, Mrs Lincoln, Mrs Brindley and Mr Wilkinson each had more than a dozen years in other jobs. Many lecturers, therefore, had experience of the kind of offices for which the students on business and secretarial courses were destined, but few had substantial experience of manual work. Mr Wilkinson, who had spent his first 12 working years as a skilled craftsman, was the exception. But whatever work experience they had had, even if it was comparatively limited, was an important element in the establishing of their credibility with their students and indeed with their colleagues. In contrast, we never heard Mr Keegan refer in classroom or staffroom to his years in the Forces or his other varied working experience. When Mr Saxon was teaching writing he did not prove his point by reference to his work as a journalist; it was the pupils' teenage world about which anecdotes were told. The 'real' world at school is home, the domestic world, where relationships with parents and friends and private feelings matter: the 'real' world of FE is work, the demands of industry, the striving for success.

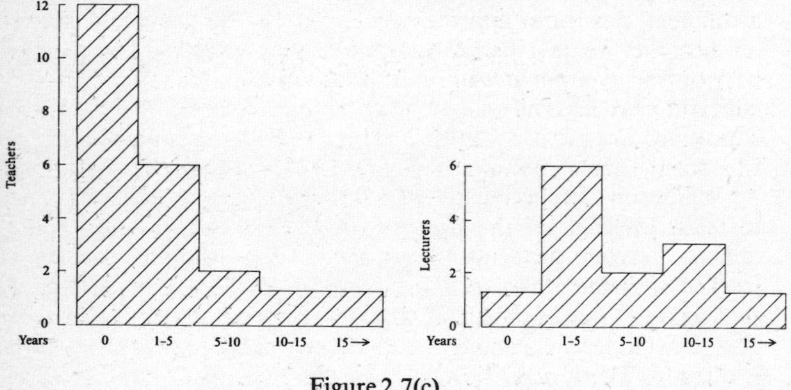

Figure 2.7(c)

Time in occupations other than teaching

Our sample of teachers and lecturers was, by any standards, highly qualified and, in that respect, unlikely to be typical. Most of them had first degrees (31 out of 35), seven had master's degrees (four in English, three in Education) and all had trained for teaching. Only four of the FE lecturers had trained specifically for work in further education, but all seemed happy in that sector and no-one wanted to teach in a school, even if they had initially intended to do so and had only moved into further education because of the difficulty of obtaining a job in school. Only one of our schoolteachers, Mr Anderson at Smalltown, had planned to teach in further education, but he no longer cherished that idea. Although they considered their chances of promotion to be low and largely dependent on chance, the FE lecturers generally thought their working conditions more favourable than those in schools.

Table 2.8

Status and qualifications of teachers and lecturers

	Holding Senior Post*	Graduate	Main qualification in English
Teachers N=22	9	19	21
Lecturers N=13	1	11	6

*Senior post = head of department, head of year, deputy head, senior lecturer

We have been asked by a number of people whether we could detect a different classroom approach from college- or university-trained teachers and we have had to disappoint them. Most of our teachers were university graduates in English with post graduate certificates in education: we had only six who had entered teaching via colleges of education. The picture was different in further education where there was not the same common background, for only Mr Davidson and Mr Wilkinson had specialised in English at university and then trained to teach English. Of the schools, Smalltown had the most highly qualified teachers academically for three out of the four teachers we worked with there had second degrees in English. But perhaps we shall answer some of the queries about the effects of training when we analyse what teachers and lecturers wrote when we asked them about it directly. There may, however, be other consequences of college training in that three of the teachers who were initially college trained were less closely linked to English and had respectively responsibilities for general studies, outdoor pursuits, and careers, although these did not take up the major part of their timetables. All of our schoolteachers except Mrs Williams at Downtown School had qualifications in English and spent most of their time teaching it.

The lecturers teaching English and Communications had, in contrast, degrees which included Zoology and Psychology, History, Sociology, Theology, Archaeology, and Business Administration, and although Communications or English represented a considerable proportion of their timetables they were sometimes teaching general studies on vocational courses. Their positions as English or Communications specialists were consequently more isolated with less support from the team or department. Subject qualifications and the courses taught were much less likely to be matched in colleges than in schools: for example, a lecturer in one college with no special qualification in English, appointed originally to teach accounts, taught nothing but English, whereas a lecturer at Square Hill College with a master's degree in English Literature taught mainly Industrial Studies. College lecturers in General Education were expected to be much more adaptable either than their colleagues in practical subjects or their counterparts in schools, and qualifications mattered for less.

These differences in subject affiliation and attitudes to work experience may point to a different set of values. One of our early purposes when we were planning the research was to study the explicit and implicit justification for their subject which practitioners offer to their students. Those will be found in our lesson data or in the comments on the students' work we collected, but it will be interesting to examine what the people said and wrote about their general purposes and aims when they talked to us and also what they considered had had most influence on their views on English and Communications teaching.

6. The teachers' espoused values

Believing that direct questions are frequently an inappropriate tool for eliciting our deep-seated beliefs and the principles which govern our actions, we avoided asking people about their ideological positions. However, through their comments and their answers to other questions we gained insights about the circumstances and principles which determined their teaching. All the teachers in our sample were aware that their effectiveness would be measured by their pupils and the community at large by examination success, so examinations were always a determining factor. Our analysis of lessons will establish the extent to which this was so in practice; examination assumptions varied in their influences upon teachers' conception of English courses and their own teaching. We must not think of examinations as an external force beyond the teachers' control: even though schools are often limited to a particular GCE board because of expense and to a particular CSE board by geographical area, through Mode 3 and similar schemes the examination demands may, in part, be the choice of the department or even the individual teacher. Assessment via coursework enabled Smalltown and Downtown to have almost complete control over the content of all their English (language) courses and it is perhaps because of the administrative co-operation which internal moderation forces upon the participators that we had the impression of the most unified departmental position from the teachers at these schools.

However, as we worked through the material from our first interviews with the teachers we became increasingly aware of how frequently there was similarity in the underlying assumptions within a department in all the schools even when teachers were speaking specifically of the particular 'top' or 'bottom' set we were going to see. Much of what was said about literature or language teaching will be dealt with in those sections, what will follow here is an attempt to pick out some of the salient recurrent ideas and themes rather than coherent philosophies.

When Mrs Harrison at New Suburbia School referred to the 'common starting point' shared by all members of the department, she was in fact referring to a textbook which everyone was expected to use. But that agreement that a textbook should determine the course showed a desire for order and conformity which was important in this department. One of the women teachers whom we worked with there pointed out that they had all been appointed at the same time and so had 'started doing similar things in similar ways'. Mrs Harrison described herself as 'a structured person . . . I like to have things self-contained'. Mrs Waterhouse liked a set pattern, particularly enjoying working with her bottom group through the exercises in the coursebook: 'I love doing basic language skills and spelling'. This was the department where we found most frequent references to the constraints of parental and pupil pressure. Mrs Harrison felt that pupils 'seem to want their thinking — well, their written work — to be narrow', and Mrs King confirmed this viewpoint when she commented that open-ended exercises were very unpopular. 'I think they see as more fair questions which can be answered just by looking at a passage . . . put into my own words to show that I understand it'. Mr Porson thought as the most recent comer he was likely to differ in his approach, but he found the complaints of his O-level group about homework difficult to understand: 'when I was at school we just did it'. These nostalgic references and his criticism of the sixties which we quoted earlier seemed rather strange since Mr Porson was one of the youngest of our teachers, but his remarks seemed to typify the department's stress on order and 'diligence': 'it's not so much to do with teaching English, it's more to do with the socialising of the kids really', socialising them into an acceptance of the coursebook and assumed requirements of the examinations.

We have remarked on the high status of English as a school subject, but not all schools felt that this was the case. Mr Keegan at Catchwide School deprecated the idea that English was 'just another subject'. He accepted as a fact of life that in the eyes of officialdom examination success was all that mattered and he presumed that everyone would feel similarly 'circumscribed by the demands of the syllabus'. All his comments on fifth-form teaching were couched in terms of the examination; for example, he would begin to explain his aim but turn immediately to the examination: 'my emphasis is on individual understanding of things and I tend perhaps to have in mind the fact that in the examination they will have to grapple and sort things out for themselves'. It was interesting that whenever he used the term literature it was always synonymous with the literature examination and not the general meaning of the word. He did not express the bitterness of his colleague Mr O'Donnell at the manacles which examinations placed upon him: 'the hurdles which have to be jumped at the end of the year', the 'three texts to be got through', 'the language course to be covered'. 'It's not the sort of thing I would want to do if I were my own boss.' Mr Gilham, the most recently appointed, shared Mr O'Donnell's concern with literature: he thought his bottom stream was motivated by the possibility of examination success but as he was choosing his own texts he was not so constrained by set texts. The expression 'related to their experience' was one which he used more than once, as did Mr Keegan when he spoke of teaching the less able, but Mr Gilham was worried lest his view of that experience was stereotyped in the working-class stories he used. He would particularly have liked to extend his English work into criticism and evaluative appreciation of the media whereas Mr Keegan felt that there was a need for work more related to the functional use of language.

The regret that English should be 'just another subject' was in itself staking a claim for the subject which was made most explicit by the Smalltown teachers. Mr Squires' belief in the importance of extra-syllabus knowledge for success in English was an example of this — 'it's the quality of interest that they've shown not only in the immediate syllabus, but . . . their awareness of the world around them and of other people. I don't think they can do well at English in the fifth unless they've got a reasonable knowledge of ideas'. English to all the teachers at Smalltown School was an over-arching subject and their conviction that their content was the whole person came out in a variety of statements. Mr Anderson's desire in the sixth form 'to break down some of these dreadfully crippling categories, the disciplines . . . you seem to get lower down the school, "Ah, but Sir, that's Geography isn't it".' Mrs Wood's reply to the parents who get 'upstage about the things we do'; in this particular case, reading a poem which touched on abortion. Social responsibility, the integrity of the individual and the importance of relationships were all essential parts of the ideal English for these teachers. They wanted pupils to think for themselves about society and their social obligations, an approach which seemed to imply 'challenging' teaching stretching the 'bright kids' and exploration of personal ideas for the less able (Mr Squires). They described their teaching styles with such phrases as:

'most of it by instinct' (Mrs Wood), 'the pattern . . . very uneven' (Mr Austin) or simply informal, which contrasted strongly with the terms, for example, New Suburbia used.

At Downtown School we were perhaps conscious of the solidarity of a departmental approach because of their use of some jointly prepared materials. Mr Richardson thought that they would all be likely to follow a similar method of working in units or themes rather than individual lessons. It was rather more difficult to establish a common theoretical position. Mrs Brennan's attitude seemed to be very much concerned with giving her pupils confidence so that they would succeed in examination terms, but she also wanted them to become readers, 'to start thinking about quite serious topics on their own' and to be able 'to write to a friend . . . and enjoy composing that letter'. Her colleague, Mrs Williams, stressed that the purpose of the general discussions which took place in English was to help pupils cope more effectively with talking to adults, but she felt that her concern to produce the required number of coursework assignments determined her English teaching. Mr Holmes, the most experienced of the Downtown teachers, saw the school as providing a secure base for some children from very impoverished backgrounds and he felt he was doing his best work when he was preparing his classes for writing an assignment that they would enjoy or reading when 'they're absolutely hooked'. He believed in writing and reading that was closely linked to his pupils' backgrounds and experience.

The teachers we worked with at Urban School seemed less unified in that they represented different positions. Mrs Sackville, for example, seemed to want to combine two models of English; the stylised English essay, the formal values she associated with old school certificate, with the more limited functional usage which the everyday and business world demands. She felt her pupils were weak in ideas and powers of expression so that her teaching had to be geared to remedying those weaknesses. Ideally she thought the examination should be based upon the needs of employers and higher education. Mr Callaghan emphasised the value he placed on oral work and the discussion of social issues through literature. Although, on looking back, he said how constrained he considered he had been by the need to prepare for the examination, in our earliest interview with him he seemed to feel relatively free from the examination pressure which pervaded many comments made by the head of department, Mrs Sutton. She too would have liked an oral element in that examination, but until the examination system changed she saw her work as all directly or indirectly governed by it. (Interestingly, the year after we worked in the school she, as head of department, steered a change-over to a system of coursework assessment. It would have been valuable to compare her ideas and practice in the changed situation.)

A similar change took place in Greentown. When we observed and talked to Mr Tremaine he was preparing his class for O-level language and literature by final examination, but the following year all the department moved into the 16+ language scheme which involved coursework assessment. Although he and Mr Saxon worked closely together, different emphases came out in their initial interviews (not our first meeting as they had invited us to spend an evening with them socially before term began). Mr Tremaine saw his fifth-form teaching to be perforce tailored to examination requirements because he appreciated that success was so important for parents and pupils, but he was concerned also that language work should provide 'the kids with some kind of equipment to cope with written arguments'. The salience of his pupils' appreciation of his own valuing of books was very like Mr Austin's, as was his emphasis on the importance of the pupil–teacher relationship. 'I'm sure the commitment of the teacher is the biggest single factor . . . they've got to have a real experience when they come to the classroom, shared with someone who likes books and is committed to them as people . . . I know this sounds like the back page of a Penguin book . . . the more you throw in the more fun it is . . . they've got to know that you like it first and foremost, that you read books . . .' Mr Saxon was much more conscious of the tension in his lower ability class between two principles: 'this young liberal approach of I am making you better citizens and I am making you more effective operators in the outside world'. Although he had 'certain types of work, or certain English skills that . . . they should master . . . I put most emphasis on *them* as developing individuals'. He returned to this later: 'I'd certainly want the English skills like imparting information or instruction. Something practical with an end in view . . . some life skills, as far as they relate to English'.

The quotations from interviews do not purport to offer coherent statements of theoretical positions, but rather to suggest some of the underlying assumptions which informed teachers' thinking. The influence of colleagues was one which people judged important and the similarity of views expressed in departments suggest that this was much more likely to be true in the schools than in the colleges which we shall consider next. Some teachers from schools which had no strong departmental ethos would have other affinities. Mr Callaghan of Urban School would have been happy at Downtown School. Mrs Sutton seemed to belong partly with New Suburbia School in her statements, but her practice at times accorded more with the Smalltown School philosophy. Considering practice and theory we may be able to distinguish clearly marked strands, but not from statements alone.

7. The lecturers' espoused values

In our initial interview with Mr Davidson at High Street College he interestingly distinguished between three definitions of the subject which he had experienced:

i. Old-fashioned English which he described as 'based upon a continuation of the O-level idea . . . which wasn't particularly useful or relevant'. Although earlier he had conceded that girls doing secretarial courses needed 'a bit more emphasis on English in the old-fashioned sense'.
ii. 'Literature, liberal studies that sort of area.'
iii. Communications which 'certainly contains English and to some extent is about English, but it's English plus a lot more'. His enthusiastic advocacy of Communications saw it as equipping students 'with certain written and oral skills so that when they get into the big world they can cope with demands that are made on them . . . give them confidence'.

His definitions were his own but they were borne out by others. Mrs Sands of Smalltown College contrasted creative and traditional English, saying that her teaching was 'very traditional' and this linked well with Mr Davidson's old-fashioned English for the typists. 'It's important that people should spell correctly and punctuate correctly if they want to do well in their shorthand and typing exams' (Mrs Sands). Mr Hemmings, also at Smalltown College, was 'one for formal English' and Mr Peel at High Street College believed in English teaching which would get his students examination qualifications and equip them for a job. It is difficult to write on the philosophy behind this point of view, because most of the lecturers' beliefs were revealed by individual examples, their return to the topics of punctuation and spelling, in practical rather than general terms. But two justifications were consistently offered, examination qualifications and usefulness for a job; there was sometimes an implication that schools had failed, but also an appreciation of the problem: 'I just didn't realise that people found English so difficult' (Mrs Sands). Indeed, although Mrs Sands saw her individual contribution as narrow and limited, this should not imply that this was her view of the purpose of education. She would probably have echoed Mrs Brindley's 'Exams open doors'.

The other lecturer who placed the examination high in his priorities was Mr Pattison at Smalltown College who was teaching O-level English Language. The students on his course were, in fact, repeating or upgrading their fifth-form work hoping to achieve the O-level success they had failed to gain at school and, in appearance, many of the boys were particularly immature. So far as they were concerned examination success was the only criterion.

Although several of the lecturers valued the general or 'liberal' studies which provided Mr Davidson's second category, it was only Mrs Lincoln who saw this primarily as the study of literature. She was preparing for the English Literature examination at A-level a self-selected group of relatively able students at High Street College, and probably had the most academic approach of the four A-level teachers, despite her lack of formal qualifications. ('Academic' here implies that she presented to her students some of the concepts of academic literary criticism, carefully using technical terminology.) Mrs Lincoln asserted energetically the value of literature as a moral and cultural force and, like many of the schoolteachers, justified its study in terms of personal growth and understanding: '... it has a relevance to the individual ... Poetry is not something that is outside them but is indeed a way of helping them to understand themselves.' The final meeting we had with the lecturers from High Street College became a battle between the advocates of vocationally-linked courses and Mrs Lincoln. Her assertion of the value of literature is illustrated here:

> It seems to me that language is communication and it seems to me that the skills of being able to order your experience are absolutely basic to all human beings and that whatever technological equipment we may end up with we are human beings first and last and the important elements in all our lives are in fact private, personal. And the ability to be able to say exactly what you mean is something that we will try to do all our lives, desperately try to find the right words, not just the right words or the right context, and the right mood. I think it's a great mistake to see oral language as an alternative, or as a balance, to written language, it seems to me that they are two quite different skills.

Mrs Lincoln's position was certainly not shared by Mr Wilkinson at Square Hill College who was perhaps talking of the kind of course Mr Davidson had in mind, although not probably the same kind of students:

> I think it's a real assumption on my part that they will be at all interested in literature and in fact I've never ever tried to teach anything of literature — because I would have felt when I was their age, when I went to the ... college, if anybody had come in and said we'll read a short story or do some creative writing, I would have turned off immediately ...

Mr Wilkinson has a master's degree and was contemplating embarking on a doctorate in literature yet he commented:

> Literature for me answers certain needs I have but they don't necessarily have those needs and I think the whole deal with General Studies has been so much of a middle-class assumption about working-class kids, what they need. From Matthew Arnold right down the line, you know that you somehow cultivate working-class kids. Well, OK, you can argue that working-class kids have no culture. I get really angry at that kind of assumption.

> I'm, perhaps, far more screwed up having become interested in literature and looked for answers in literature, or I did, than most of these kids who seem far more able to cope with things than I did at their age — I mean with relationships and things like that — they may be coping in very traditional patterns . . . but I would hate to take away that kind of security from them, in any way. . . . I've become very cynical about it actually, about what I can actually pass on to them. I can teach them to write a letter, teach them how to set out a report, but very little else I think. Anything else that comes over might be attitudes towards things, I might, just by the way, spark off something.

Mrs Lincoln spoke for a large body of committed teachers of English literature, perhaps larger in schools than in colleges; Mr Wilkinson was unusual in that, though he shared with many college lecturers a scepticism about the value of literature to students, he had no doubt of the great value he himself had derived from it. The likenesses as well as the contrasts of perspective are instructive. Both lecturers implied that the source of values lay in everyday life: Mrs Lincoln made this clear in her reference to the private and personal elements in our lives, Mr Wilkinson by his rejection of the idea that working-class students lack culture. Mrs Lincoln insisted — rightly in our view — on the importance 'of being able to order your experience' but this (it seemed) was carried out not through discussion but through the study of literature. (Her teaching as well as her other contributions to the discussion warrant this interpretation of her rejection of 'oral language' in favour of 'written language'.) Thus she relates ordering everyday experience to giving primacy to literary studies. Mr Wilkinson, since he teaches in another college, was not present to respond to her statement but he would clearly have accepted the potentially high value Mrs Lincoln placed upon literature. Where he differed was in placing the source of the value in the receptiveness of the learner rather than in the works of literature themselves. People like him gained from literature partly because they were 'screwed up'; and in contrast to this he admired young people who coped with relationships without the benefit of literature. Though he said that his students would dismiss literature if it were presented to them, he was not falling into the weak stance of basing the curriculum on 'interest'; he was challenging the widespread assumption amongst English teachers that reading literature is beneficial irrespective of the concerns and state of mind of the student. He felt that this assumption arose from middle-class values and beliefs about the richness and validity of working-class life, and these he wished to reject. This led to a general doubt whether educators have any right to impose their views of the world upon their students, and particularly to attempt to change their perspectives on first-hand experience. (If Mrs Lincoln, or some of the sixth-form teachers had been present, they might have retorted that he was depriving working-class students of the right to have access to literary culture.) Such an emphasis upon the rights of the learner to determine what he should learn appeared to us more common in some parts of further education than in schools, where a paternalistic attitude to pupils' values is usual.

Mr Benson, in answer to our invitation, fantasised about his ideal course which would use literature to look 'at different belief systems . . . to find out as much as we can about human nature', but he meanwhile contented himself with the 'closely constructed courses we're doing nowadays', the detailed learning objectives spelt out in the TEC submission from Square Hill College. Probably he would have agreed with his colleague Mrs Brindley who remarked, 'I was all for the book culture and I still think it's important, but these students are frightened by books'. Mr Peel with his girls at High Street was the only person who saw literature as part of a vocational course. 'We feel that if they are going into an office, literature is very important, not only does it broaden their outlooks but in giving them literature it gives us the opportunity of talking about another age . . .' This may match with Mr Wilkinson's 'middle-class' assumptions, literature as one of the social graces which equip a girl for the office, but if it had in fact provided the opportunities for talk about another age it would not necessarily have been an assault on their values. Mr Wilkinson was clearly not denying the students' right to knowledge of a different set of values from their own: he was reacting against the rejection of their culture.

The third option in Mr Davidson's list was equipping students with the communication skills they needed to function successfully in the world of work and enabling them to understand the communicative processes which operate. The BEC philosophy had spurred him to develop some imaginative and skilful assignments, but when challenged he found it hard to defend them. Their outcomes were mainly written, which worried him for he himself felt there should be a much greater emphasis on oral work than external bodies allowed.

> I wouldn't say there'll be no written work, of course there'll be written work. But if you try and analyse the sort of written English skills which most of these people need at work or even in their daily lives, it boils down to what, the ability perhaps to put a decent letter together and that's it really . . . certainly if we look at it from a purely functional (view) of what they're going to need as opposed to perhaps what we'd like to give them over and above that, the ability to put a letter together, make a few notes, sending a memo, there's not a lot more really.

He believed in their value to his students, but in the heat of battle could not justify it. It is an irony that the most telling justification for vocationally tied communication studies came from the most ineffectual of lecturers who had none of Mr Davidson's qualities as a teacher. 'If you give people skills which might make them good employees, you also give them the skills to be more independent.'

Mrs Brindley at Square Hill College and Mrs Brown at City Road College, whilst stressing their belief in enabling their students to cope with the communicative demands of work, saw their roles as closely tied with their students' personal welfare. A collection of Mrs Brindley's remarks demonstrates the complexity of her position which was very similar to Mrs Brown's:

> In the end you have to teach them to conform because that's what life's about really isn't it?
> I would aim to give them some skills to get by . . . the basic life skills.
> They are dependent on the trade they've got and I think it can harm a student to give them too many liberal ideas.
> That is the real value (of communications) when they begin to understand themselves and why they behave in certain ways.

The group of girls whom Mrs Brown was teaching had not been successes at school; she hoped that as a result of the course, 'They'll know how to cope in a work situation, they'll know where to go in their lives, to different social agencies . . . I hope they'll be able to write letters, to fill in forms and things like that. I take that for granted. I hope they'll acquire the skills that we want them to, but I don't just want it to be for the exam . . . I hope they'll make the best of themselves'.

Two of the lecturers have not been mentioned in this section, Mrs Fraser and Mr Turner, who were part of the team teaching TEC communications at City Road College. Mrs Fraser was particularly enthusiastic about the area of study skills and problem-solving which she saw as a valuable part of Communications. She welcomed us into her classes, but as she was not one of the lecturers we had arranged to work with we never recorded an interview with her. Mrs Fraser saw the understanding of communication processes as a neglected area of practical value to students which could be filled in Communication Studies. Mr Turner's concern was rather with 'affective education which seems to be just virtually ignored in our educational system . . . ' He 'tried to avoid . . . teaching students how to write letters or use the telephone. They are not the things I want to do, basically. I'm not trying to say they have no value: they're essential. It's just an area I don't want to be involved in. I'd like to be involved in something which has a little more mystery to it than something which is essentially practical'. A statement such as 'the kind of things I try to emphasise pull people out of the prisons they erect for themselves' placed him in the second of Mr Davidson's areas although his consciousness-raising was based on very different premises from Mrs Lincoln's.

We have spent time on these three positions because they seem to provide a key to the way in which lecturers viewed themselves, and most of the lecturers can be placed somewhere on the scale. (See Table 2.9.) The positions they stated did not necessarily match the principles of the course they were teaching. The lecturers whose names we have marked with an asterisk expressed ideas which were directly in contrast with the principles of the course they were teaching, the lecturers' names which straddle two columns showed some ambivalence of attitude. These positions are drawn mainly from the initial individual interviews; in the later more public group interviews lecturers sometimes presented viewpoints more in harmony with the course philosophies. In Smalltown College we discovered that the lecturer appointed to organise the BEC courses had 'refused categorically to have anything whatsoever to do with BEC at all'. Mrs Sands preferred the Communication Studies approach to the English course we had observed her teaching, ('beautiful English essays . . . not a skill they will be able to market') but both she and Mr Hemmings agreed that 'providing you can justify yourself in BEC jargon you can do anything really'. Communication Studies was preferable to English, but Mr Hemmings felt so strongly about the fact that it had also displaced general studies that he had produced an outline of a general course with communications elements for consideration by the vice-principal. 'I've been very unhappy these last few years about the way in which BEC, for all its other qualities has taken over. Liberal studies has really gone out of the window in terms of current affairs and elements of a wider general knowledge.'

Table 2.9

Lecturer's espoused positions

<table>
<tr><th>Traditional 'old-fashioned' emphasising form and examination requirements</th><th>Liberal/literature/consciousness-raising personal growth</th><th>Communication studies — functional competence understanding of process</th></tr>
<tr><td>Mr Hemmings*
Mr Peel
Mrs Sands</td><td>Mrs Lincoln
Mr Turner*</td><td>Mr Davidson
(Mrs Fraser)
Mr Blackburn
Mr Wilkinson</td></tr>
<tr><td colspan="2">Mr Pattison</td><td></td></tr>
<tr><td></td><td colspan="2">Mr Benson</td></tr>
<tr><td></td><td colspan="2">←—— Mrs Brindley ——→</td></tr>
<tr><td></td><td colspan="2">←—— Mrs Brown ——→</td></tr>
</table>

8. **Affiliations and networks**

In our initial interviews we had been concerned with the account the individual teacher or lecturer gave of their teaching and ideas about the subject. As the research progressed and we talked informally with them we became interested as to whether we could generalise about the teachers and lecturers as a group. One headmaster who invited us into his study to chat, interestingly described the teachers who were working with us as the outward-looking members of the department; was this a generally applicable statement? When we came eventually to formulate the questionnaire about backgrounds and influences we asked, 'Who or what do you think has had most influence on your views (and practice) in English and communications teaching?' and included 'people you have known' as one of the possibilities. However, before we analysed the replies we had already charted some of the networks which we had noticed in operation. Three schools (Downtown, Smalltown and Greentown) were all involved in internally assessed 16+ or O-level; one of the teachers at another (Urban) had been. JMB O-level (Syllabus D) and JMB/TWYLREB 16+ both demand that teachers meet regularly to discuss the grading of candidates' work, so that anyone who has participated in the schemes has a reference group outside the school. The discussions in such groups are not at a theoretical level: decisions about appropriateness and assessment have practical implications and become part of a teacher's practice and way of looking at the subject. Smalltown College staff were involved in 16+ coursework assessment for the first time during our year with them so they were also becoming used to justifying their ideas more publicly. If lecturers teaching TEC courses had been involved in the preparation of their college submissions they too had had to couch their ideas in a public terminology to secure validation. The adoption of BEC and City and Guilds Communication Skills or Foundation Course syllabuses was recent enough for lecturers to be accustomed to a common language of learning objectives. It is not surprising that we found the FE lecturers involved in new courses generally readier to offer theoretical justifications. Only a minority of teachers and lecturers are involved in professional subject associations; both NATE (National Association for the Teaching of English) and ALE (Association for Liberal Education) groups in the area have always been small, but we knew four of the group (two teachers and two lecturers) through NATE whilst some of the lecturers at City Road and Square Hill knew each other through their activities in ALE. The involvement in professional organisations outside the school or college seemed to predispose people to be willing to be part of a research project. In the main, the connections our sample of teachers and lecturers shared were professional ones but we were surprised that we crossed some quite separate friendship links. Our attempts at confidentiality were somewhat defeated when we were greeted with, 'You were in my friend's lesson yesterday', or 'So-and-so saw you in Downtown staffroom last week'.

Our sample, we decided, tended to be drawn from the

'cosmopolitans' rather than the 'locals': that is people who saw their roles in a larger educational context. Interestingly, they were not predominantly 'local' in the usual sense of the word. Only four or five of our teachers and lecturers had been born and bred within 20 miles or so of where they were teaching, but a third or more had remained in the area after they had initially trained and, in that, they were probably typical of secondary and college teachers. Heads of departments in school had generally travelled furthest, but individual histories would have to be described in detail to prove these points.

Gerald Grace quoted one senior teacher in London as saying, 'There is more liaison between English departments and they have a very active professional group. I think it is true to say that there is an alternative form of education being espoused by English departments in London.'[5] Grace's evidence did not support the second part of the assertion; our evidence supported neither part. There was exchange of views amongst those involved in the same form of examining, but it was at the very practical level of materials and classroom strategies, where the networks were most important for our teachers and lecturers.

The replies we received in answers to the question about important influences varied in length from five words to a thousand or more. Some replies were in personal terms referring to particular formative events in their own lives, to accidents tragic or happy which still seemed to have powerful reverberations; others, however, listed in barer and more general terms the institutions and experiences which they thought had had most influence on them. Many of the replies, of course, concerned themselves with educational experiences and these were framed in negative as well as in positive terms. Six people stated emphatically that they were determined not to teach in the way they had been taught. Their criticisms were mainly of narrow, examination-dominated, 'boring' teaching, but in one case the teaching had been unsatisfactory because it was too informal.

We were surprised that schooldays were less rather than more likely to have produced enthusiasm for English. It is worth noting that it was generally particular teachers who had had the power to inspire enthusiasm: 'I was heavily influenced by the humane and pleasant men who taught me at my secondary school. Peter H___ and John A___ infected me with an enthusiasm for reading and the stage, which I took to with all the passion of adolescence and have kept ever since. They did it, I think, by simply communicating to me their own interest in literature and drama, rather than by direct teaching' (Mr Tremaine). 'A man called John F___ (to whom Ted Hughes dedicated his *Poetry in the Making*), an immensely civilised man of considerable personal warmth, a man who had suffered great personal tragedy in his life, yet remained optimistic about life and its possibilities, . . . a man who valued the human spirit above all things' (Mr Austin).

Schooldays and teacher-training were among the most important influences acknowledged, much more important than academic or university experiences. The majority of people made no reference to their specialist study: four of the five who did emphasised its importance in increasing their appreciation of literature; language study either had not happened or was ignored. Our own position in a School of Education quite likely provoked comments on the value of initial training. It gained qualified approval from three ('interesting but irrelevant', or 'necessary but unexciting'), dismissal by another three ('remarkably little influence'), and an 'almost useless' or rather stronger condemnation from five others. Only Mr Tremaine wrote at any length picking out two of his tutors at Bristol as providing 'an interesting perspective on my job and its environment'.

Half-a-dozen respondents named formative books: Mr Porson produced a list of six which he claimed were far more useful than the lectures and seminars provided by his education tutors. Only three writers, however, were mentioned more than once. J. H. Walsh wrote *Teaching English 11–16*[6], from a grammar-school background in the mid-sixties, but it seemed it was still having an impact on beginners 15 years later. Michael Marland was another shared influence and for Mr Saxon his books and courses provided 'that timeless moment of recognition — this is how it should be'. Flower's *Language in Education*[7] had been a powerful influence on two FE lecturers soon after it was published, 'the seminal work as far as development of my ideas went' (Mr Davidson). Books on teaching a subject are likely to diminish in importance as practitioners develop their own skills and ideas, so it is perhaps not surprising that the longest list of influential books came from one of the least experienced teachers.

In the interviews or in conversation, people often referred incidentally to a textbook or materials they liked using and we noticed in lessons how closely some teachers and lecturers followed them. We were interested that no-one referred in their written replies to their teaching being influenced by a textbook but Mrs King, who had returned to full-time teaching after seven years' domesticity, wrote of how she had been influenced by the range of textbooks which 'seemed to bring together in convenient form just what I had tried, more haphazardly, to accumulate'. Her use of 'accumulate' suggested sources and resources and, as our own observation had led us to expect, the replies showed that the sharing of materials which such developments as JMB/TWYLREB 16+ English Language and JMB Syllabus D involved was a powerful influence on teaching. As Mr Holmes wrote, 'Perhaps the single most formative influence on my approach to teaching, that development completely changed my thinking...Also for the first time I really communicated with dozens of teachers and shared and swapped ideas'. Informal contact with other teachers and lecturers in ALE and NATE and this more formal contact which trial markings and panel meetings necessitated were referred to by nine out of the 14 who were involved in such activities and constituted by far the most important source of influence generally recognised. Only four teachers and no lecturers referred to departmental colleagues, which reminded us that teaching can be a very isolated activity. It made us realise that the opportunity we have had of seeing so many teachers and lecturers at work and talking with them about what they were doing is unique.

9. How time was spent: the categories

For each lesson we observed there exists a lesson protocol, either an annotated transcript of the recording or, for those lessons we were unable to record, as verbatim an account as it was possible for us to make accompanied with annotations from the field notes. From these protocols we have been able to produce an analysis of the amount of time spent on different activities, but for these tables we divide our data according to the purpose of the activity rather than its inherent nature. In any one classroom at a given time a variety of activities are likely to be happening. The teacher may be reading aloud, interspersing the reading with comments and questions; the pupils may be following the reading but also making notes in their books; so even when the whole class is seemingly engaged in the same activity, some pupils may be writing, some may be reading and listening and others may be speaking in a questioning exchange. When individual or group work is taking place the picture will be even more complicated. From the protocols we can demonstrate this complexity; from the detailed analysis of the lessons we can show the nature of the activity as well as its purpose: the reduction of the data to a simplified basis enables us to provide general impressions and to draw useful comparisons.

The categories which we have adopted arose from the data. The first group relating to the study of complete literary texts resulted from the sharp contrast between practice in schools and FE colleges, as did also the attempt to distinguish between material drawn from literary and non-literary sources. But before we generalise about practice we should explain the meaning of the headings we have used.

There is no significance beyond convenience in the ordering of the categories and no implicit evaluation of the different activities and purposes: the headings are intended to be descriptive. We must emphasise that allocations on a simplified basis such as this can only provide overall and general impressions: much more detailed analysis is necessary for fine discrimination.

(*1–4 Study of complete literary texts*)

1. *Localised, close textual study* indicates the reading of a text when

the teacher takes the class through the play, story or poem slowly, page by page and line by line. The commentary is mainly localised, usually containing a considerable proportion of paraphrase and gloss on individual words and phrases and on stylistic features. Occasional discussion of associations and emotional response is so embedded in the commentary that the time spent on it cannot be quantified. The category may include talking, reading and some writing.
2. *Reading* can be a teacher-directed or individual pupil activity when reading rather than commentary is the major activity. It can often be a first reading when detailed study is not the aim or it can be a re-reading of a text previously studied.
3. *Study of themes, topics and selective narration* indicates discussion which is not subordinated to textual analysis as in (1) above: much of this interpretive study is within the traditional examination framework of characters and themes but not all. It may include talking, reading and writing.
4. *Writing* on literary topics has been kept separate from writing on general topics. It may be closely related to work in (1) and (3) but in this case writing is the predominant activity.
5–6. *Understanding extracts* is a kind of close study: its purpose is to answer questions mainly designed to test comprehension. It may be based on textbooks, worksheets or examination papers. As an activity it may include talking, reading and writing. We have separated work on literary passages as this distinction seemed likely to be significant.
7. *Writing on general topics* includes the preparation which may be substantially talking and reading. When literature is used either as a model or as stimulus it is marked (L). Preparation may provide substantial opportunities for oral work which, without the ultimate writing outcome, would have been placed in (10) and (11).
8. *Practice of written conventions* indicates the emphasis has been on 'correct' written usage, e.g. spelling and punctuation exercises, letter or memo layout.
9. *Reflection on language/communication* includes such activities as considering appropriateness, discussing bias in language, instruction in the terminology of communication studies.

(*10–11 Oral/talk*)

10. *Practice and presentation* is talk as an end in itself, e.g. preparation for reading a passage, prepared talks and role-play. The preparation may involve writing and reading.
11. *Socio-moral-cultural attitudes* is a category, predominantly talk, where the purpose appeared to be the reinforcing and modifying of attitudes. Examples of the transmission of values are also found embedded in (1), (3), (5), (6) and especially in (7), but in colleges, particularly within the ideology of 'social and life skills', this category existed in its own right.

12. *Miscellaneous* contains those activities which would not usually be considered part of English (e.g. calculations and numeracy).
13. *Non-teaching and control* includes administrative tasks and time spent in persuading pupils to carry out the teacher's wishes. Although this often contained considerable socio-moral elements it cannot be considered as part of the English curriculum.

10. How time was spent: the fifth form

From the first year when we worked in the six schools we analysed the material from 77 separate fifth-form sessions (114 school lessons) amounting to 72½ timetabled hours. Table 2.10 represents in percentages the time allocated to specific activities during the actual teaching time (66 hours 51 minutes).

Within each school we have indicated whether a class was one offered to us as a representative top (T), middle (M) or bottom (B) group and the course it was following. As we describe elsewhere, the label O-level language or CSE English can mean that there are very different examination requirements.

Most of the interviews were completed in September and it was during the next five months that we observed and recorded a sample of lessons with the classes. The teachers themselves agreed which lessons we went into, but the aim was that they should show us what they considered a typical sample of their fifth year work. This is the material which forms the basis of Table 2.10, but we were aware when we started to generalise or think of what went on in a lesson with 5X in one school comparing it with one with 5X down the road, that we had seen the first in the last week of October and the other perhaps just after the Christmas holiday. One teacher, in particular, had stressed in his interview that he was very aware of the emphasis falling on different activities at different times of the year. Consequently, we decided that we would ask each of our teachers to fill in a diary of their lessons for the first two weeks in March, eight to ten teaching weeks before the examinations. We realised that the emphases may be different from those in the first two weeks of October but, at least, all our data would be drawn from the same period and when eventually we added it to our own observations we might have a more accurate picture.

In the diary returns we had 199 lessons from 18 classes; for some unexplained reason one class lost their Friday afternoon lesson preventing us from having the convenient total of 200. The figures do not correspond precisely to our Table 2.10 as one of our original 17 teachers left the school at Christmas so we had no return from his class. But two teachers from Smalltown School supplied details of their lessons with two classes, hence the 18 classes.

Our figures from these diaries are obviously based on much cruder

Table 2.10

Schools—Fifth-form English (based on classroom observation)

SCHOOL		COURSE	1 STUDY OF COMPLETE LITERARY TEXTS: Close, textual, localised	2 Reading	3 Themes, characters, narration	4 Writing	5 UNDERSTANDING EXTRACTS: Literary	6 Non-literary	7 PREPARATION AND WRITING ON GENERAL TOPICS	8 PRACTICE OF WRITTEN CONVENTIONS	9 REFLECTION ON LANGUAGE/ COMMUNICATION	10 ORAL/TALK: Practice and Presentation	11 Socio-moral-cultural attitudes	12 MISC.	13 NON-TEACHING AND CONTROL	% TOTAL
DOWNTOWN	T	'O' Lang. & Lit.	33	–	28	5	–	–	28 (L)*	–	–	2 (L)	–	–	5	101
	M	CSE Lang. & Lit.	36	–	19	13	–	–	23 (L)*	–	–	–	–	–	10	101
	B	CSE Lang.	–	25	6	–	–	–	65 (L)*	–	–	–	–	–	4	100
URBAN	T	CSE English with Lit.	–	–	–	26*	–	19	39 (L)*	11	–	–	–	–	5	100
	M	CSE English with Lit.	23	–	–	–	33	–	29*	–	–	–	–	–	15	100
	B	CSE English	–	17	7	–	27	–	20	11	–	10 (L)	–	–	8	100
NEW SUBURBIA	T	'O' Lang. & Lit.	40	–	18	–	–	–	11	27	–	–	–	–	4	100
	M	16+ English & CSE Lit.	43	–	16	–	–	–	19	–	–	16 (L)	–	–	6	100
	B	16+ English	–	31	7	–	–	–	–	49	–	6 (L)	–	–	7	100
CATCHWIDE	T	'O' Lang. & Lit.	50	3	–	–	–	–	6	33	–	–	1	–	7	100
	M	'O' Lang. & Lit. with CSE	51	–	–	35*	–	10	–	–	–	–	–	–	4	100
	B	CSE English with Lit.	10	7	37	24*	–	–	4	–	10	–	–	–	8	100
GREENTOWN	T	'O' Lang. & Lit.	24	–	19	–	–	12	3	–	5	–	27	–	10	100
	B	16+ Lang.	–	–	1	–	–	–	82*	–	–	–	–	6	11	100
SMALLTOWN	T	16+ Lang. 'O' Lit.	55	–	35	–	–	–	–	–	–	–	–	–	10	100
	T	16+ Lang. 'O' Lit.	25	11	–	–	–	–	49 (L)*	–	–	–	–	–	15	100
	M	16+ Lang.	6	10	–	–	–	–	58 (L)*	11	–	–	7	–	9	101
	B	16+ Lang.	–	–	–	–	–	–	79*	–	–	–	15	–	6	100

(L) indicates significant literary element * indicates writing for coursework folder

Table 2.11

Time allocation from diary returns

SCHOOL		COURSE	1 STUDY OF COMPLETE LITERARY TEXTS: Close, textual, localised	2 Reading	3 Themes, characters, narration	4 Writing	5–6 UNDERSTANDING EXTRACTS: Literary/non-literary	7 PREPARATION AND WRITING ON GENERAL TOPICS	8 PRACTICE OF WRITTEN CONVENTIONS	9 REFLECTION ON LANGUAGE/COMMUNICATION	10 ORAL/TALK: Practice and presentation	11 Socio-moral-cultural attitudes	12 MISC.	13 NON-TEACHING AND CONTROL	% TOTAL
DOWNTOWN	T	'O' Lang. & Lit.	8	–	67	8	–	17*	–	–	–	–	–	–	100
	M	CSE Lang. & Lit.	–	–	–	–	–	–	–	–	–	–	–	–	–
	B	CSE Lang.	–	30	–	–	–	60 (L)*	10	–	–	–	–	–	100
URBAN	T	CSE English with Lit.	25	–	10	10	–	45*	5	5	–	–	–	–	100
	M	CSE English with Lit.	–	10	–	–	40	40*	–	–	–	–	10	–	100
	B	CSE English	20	–	–	10	25	40	5	–	–	–	–	–	100
NEW SUBURBIA	T	'O' Lang. & Lit.	50	–	10	20	–	20	–	–	–	–	–	–	100
	M	16+ English & CSE Lit.	10	–	10	20	15	–	10	–	35 (L)	–	–	–	100
	B	16+ English	–	50	–	–	11	11	17	–	11	–	–	–	100
CATCHWIDE	T	'O' Lang. & Lit.	80	–	20	–	–	–	–	–	–	–	–	–	100
	M	'O' Lang. & Lit. with CSE	25	–	12	13	19	13	6	6	–	–	7 (L)	–	101
	B	CSE English with Lit.	–	33	8	–	–	42	17	–	–	–	–	–	100
GREENTOWN	T	'O' Lang. & Lit.	42	–	8	–	25	–	8	–	–	17	–	–	100
	B	16+ Lang.	–	–	–	–	33 (L)*	33*	–	–	33	–	–	–	99
SMALLTOWN	T	16+ Lang. 'O' Lit.	25	–	25	–	–	33 (L)*	–	–	–	–	17 (L) (Cinema)	–	100
	T	16+ Lang. 'O' Lit.	33	17	17	–	33 (L)*	–	–	–	–	–	–	–	100
	M	16+ Lang.	–	10	–	–	30 (L)*	60 (L)*	–	–	–	–	–	–	100
	B	16+ Lang.	–	10	–	–	–	60 (L)*	–	–	10	20	–	–	100
	T	16+ Lang. & 'O' Lit.	20	–	40	–	33 (L)	7*	–	–	–	–	–	–	100

(L) indicates significant literary element

* indicates writing for coursework folder

data than those from our carefully timed protocols. The teachers did not attempt to provide a detailed breakdown of everything that happened in each lesson, but they gave enough information for us to be able to make an analysis on broad lines. We were interested later to look back at the teachers' estimates in the interviews and compare them with the tables our analyses produced. The majority of replies were reasonably close to our figures with a tendency to spend somewhat more time on O-level literature than people estimated. In Mr Keegan's and Mrs Sackville's replies it seemed that if what they had shown to us was typical they had considerably underestimated the amount of time they spent on literature, but this seemed to be explained when we realised that they regarded writing on literature as essay writing if it were intended for a CSE English Studies coursework folder.

In the first broad survey the most interesting variation seems to be in the time given to work on literature; in the lesson data 49 per cent and in the diary returns 53 per cent of the whole. But these totals mask distinct variations in the kind and proportions of work done by different classes. In a cursory glance we can notice differences between individual classes, for example, 90 per cent for a class at Smalltown School and 1 per cent for one at Greentown School, but we wanted to find out if the differences followed any pattern. The crucial variant appeared to be the literature examination course, but that in its turn was decided by other factors which we will discuss later. First we will ascribe all the classes to groups according to their literature examinations.

All 18 classes were being entered for a language examination or one with a strong (more than 50 per cent) language element. Seven of those classes were also taking an O-level examination in English Literature; this is group A. Five were also taking CSE Literature (or English Studies); these constitute Group B. The six classes who were aiming for only one qualification in English or English Language form Group C.

Table 2.12

Time on literature according to examination (lesson protocols)

	% of time on literature	% of literary element in language	Literature % of whole
A O-level literature (7 classes)	57	8	65
B CSE literature (5 classes)	51	17	68
C No literature examination (6 classes)	18	16	34

In the diary returns we were not able to estimate so accurately the literary element; for example, if we were told that a lesson was spent on an extract used for O-level or CSE comprehension we were not always given details of the passage nor did we know the kind of questions. The picture that emerged, however, seemed not dissimilar.

Table 2.13

Time on literature according to examination (diaries)

	% of time on literature	% of literary element in language	Literature % of whole
A O-level literature (8 classes)	68	3	71
B CSE literature (4 classes)	49	8	57
C No literature examination (6 classes)	23	16	39

The groups A, B and C correspond approximately — that is, with the exception of one or two classes — to our top, middle and bottom groups.

Two comments can immediately be made on the figures displayed in Tables 2.12 and 2.13. First, English meant something very different for the more able than it did for those of lower ability — for the able it was predominantly work on literature and this emphasis decreased proportionally as one went down the ability range. The second comment is that teachers were not, as is often asserted, completely dominated by examination requirements. Even for those pupils who would not be examined on particular books, in most classes literature was important and accounted for about a third of the course. Most of the teachers in our sample, whatever the class they were working with, said that literature teaching was what they enjoyed most.

But it is not only in the total time spent on literature that the differences were important; it is in the way that time was spent. In our tables we identified four categories and we should examine the time accorded to them. Our divisions for the diary returns have perforce to be arbitrary because of the limitations of the information given, but we have been able to make distinctions; for example, if a teacher has said that the class read two chapters of a novel in a lesson it had clearly been a different kind of reading from that which took place when the class spent a whole lesson reading one or two short poems.

Close study was what was important in both tables for Group A: it averaged at 40 per cent per class in the lessons we saw and at 37 per cent from the diary returns. Reading without comment was not significant in either table, but the time given to general literary study increased considerably in the March returns when, as to be expected, there was much more stress on topics that might occur in the examination. We have included some lessons spent in writing out dictated notes in this section, reserving the 'Writing' column for pupils' own written work. The proportion of time spent on examination-type written work had increased slightly, but it was still very small.

Table 2.14

Proportions for different literary activities according to examination

	A		B		C	
	Lesson protocols	Diary	Lesson protocols	Diary	Lesson protocols	Diary
1. Close study	40	37	22	7	1	-
2. Reading	2	2	1	19	13	21
3. Themes, characters etc.	14	25	15	11	4	-
4. Written work	1	4	13	12	-	2
TOTALS	57%	68%	51%	49%	18%	23%

For our second group the pattern in the lessons was quite similar: close study, although not so important, took up the largest amount of time but the significant difference was in the amount of written work done in lessons. Classes preparing literature work for coursework folders often discussed and wrote their essays in class, whereas their counterparts in A who were working for a final examination would be expected to do them at home. The figures from the diaries did not produce the same pattern and this in part can be explained by the fact that at Catchwide School the coursework folders had been completed at that time.

For Group C we see that reading was, in fact, the main activity in literature study: close study was virtually non-existent and there was very little discussion of literature.

We noticed with interest that there seems to have been developed an accepted order for dealing with set books in Group A. Shakespeare or the longest text comes first, with poetry, because it is considered the most difficult, usually left until the end. When we were observing 'close study' lessons in the first term these were on texts such as *Twelfth Night*, *Romeo and Juliet* or *The Woman in White* with Goldsmith's *The Deserted Village* as an exception. In the March fortnight there were 21 lessons on poetry, none on drama and only seven lessons for fiction (*Great Expectations* and some modern short stories). It was interesting that in this same period Group C were reading only prose fiction (modern novels or short stories). As a general conclusion we can remark that for Groups A and B thinking, talking and writing about books is as important as reading or studying them: for Group C reading may take up to 21 per cent of their time, but reflection on the books read was almost minimal.

Although we have indicated in Tables 2.12 and 2.13 the literary element, particularly in the preparation of coursework essays, we have not included it in the totals that we have been using up to this point. Most of the lessons we recorded in the protocols that were intended to be preparation for writing general essays for coursework folders included some reading of short stories, poems or extracts, as is indicated by (L) on the table: it was, however, 'reading' rather than close study. This pattern was not so strong in the returns and this may be attributed to the timing of the sampling: the argumentative/discursive type of essay which was considered more difficult than narrative or personal writing was left by some teachers until the end of the course and it was not so likely to have a literary stimulus.

The overall figure for writing changed little from 29 per cent of the lesson protocols to 26 per cent from the diaries, but it will be interesting to observe the variations the totals conceal. The striking difference is in the amount of time spent on teaching essay or assignment writing: for those classes presenting a coursework folder it is 38 per cent of the whole, for those classes taking a final examination only it is 10 per cent. For example, New Suburbia School, where all the language work was examined by final examination paper, was the school which placed least emphasis on teaching writing in the fifth form: we recorded no writing lessons either in the lessons we saw or in diary returns from the bottom group; one lesson for the middle group; and the times recorded for the top group relate to unprepared writing on topics chosen from examination papers written under examination conditions in class. We can thus say that essay topics were prepared in class whenever they were to form part of a coursework folder, whatever the ability of the pupil. With middle and bottom groups they were frequently written in class under the teacher's supervision. No such preparation and instruction was given to classes whose writing abilities were to be assessed in a final examination.

In considering writing, which was the next most important area after literature, we have passed over the column 'Understanding extracts' which, although it is a kind of reading, is usually placed under the Language heading. Every English or English Language examination designed for 16-year-olds that we have encountered includes a test of comprehension, and in our initial interviews most teachers considered that they spent a great deal of time in the fifth form teaching and practising comprehension. Interestingly, there are many more entries in the diary returns than from the lessons we observed (from ten classes in the diaries, from five classes in the lessons) and the proportion of time spent on it is higher (an average of 28 per cent per entry compared with 20 per cent). We observed surprisingly little comprehension work, five sessions in all. In two of the lessons teachers were returning work which pupils had already done, explaining what kind of answers were required, and in three others they were discussing passages, preparing for the actual written work to be done later. This small amount may have been because teachers were reluctant to show us the lessons when they expected the class to work individually on a comprehension exercise in class. As Mrs Harrison said to us, 'With respect, if you know you're having somebody coming into a lesson you will have more of an oral lesson'. For pupils who were being assessed on coursework folders much of the comprehension work was done in class under supervised conditions; as these were tests rather than lessons we saw none of them. A further likely reason why more comprehension lessons were recorded in the diary returns was the imminence of the examinations or completion of the coursework. Smalltown School, which showed high figures, had estimated that it spent least time on comprehension work; as the head of department Mr Squires wrote on his diary returns 'two atypical' weeks. But although the weeks may have been atypical for some nevertheless the average figure of 16 per cent for comprehension work seems more likely than the 5 per cent from the lesson protocols. As we have said, we could not ascribe some of the material to the literary/non-literary categories, but it seemed significant that the passages used in the coursework assessment classes were predominantly literary, which moves us on to our next point — the division of English into language and literature.

The language/literature distinction tended to operate most strongly in classes using final examinations. In the top classes at Catchwide and New Suburbia Schools the emphasis was on the study of set literature texts and the preparation for writing on general topics seemed to consist of giving a list of titles. Boundaries were blurred at Downtown and Smalltown Schools where literary material was likely to be used for comprehension and reading was a basis for writing. The practice of having an extended piece of writing as the final question in comprehension work was an established feature in these schools. These variations may be institutional, but they seemed to be linked also to the mode of assessment. Schools which were involved in cross moderation had evolved similar practices and attitudes.

Decontextualised practice of written conventions was most frequent in schools and classes using coursebooks and a final examination: for example, whereas bottom classes presenting course-work folders spent a great deal of their time practising extended writing, the bottom class at New Suburbia School concentrated on punctuation and spelling exercises, rarely writing at length. It is worth pointing out that for 12 of the 18 classes (two-thirds) there was no entry in this column.

Most of the lessons we saw were predominantly oral in the sense that the teacher talked and that pupils answered questions, but their apparent aim was not to improve pupils' oral skills. Some literature lessons with the top classes at Downtown, Smalltown and Greentown Schools were spent by pupils preparing topics and then presenting them to the class. Our placing of these in the 'Close study' category does not reflect adequately the classroom experience there. Mrs Brennan, Mr Austin and Mr Tremaine were all teachers whose active encouragement of their students' oral abilities should be emphasised, but the oral presentations which followed group or private preparation of a topic were seen as spoken rehearsals of a written answer, a convenient way for everyone in the class to listen and follow. In some instances they were read verbatim. The oral emphasis shown at New Suburbia School in both the middle and bottom groups can be attributed to the fact that it was the only school where oral work formed part of the 16+ examination and the oral element of the 16+ examination was being assessed when the researcher was present and when the returns were made. The oral work of Mr Tremaine's class at Greentown School we have placed in the 'Socio-moral-cultural' column, but this attribution needs further explanation. Mr Tremaine was the only teacher who set aside time for discussion of general topics without expecting any written product or situating the discussion within the context of other work. The discussions may have been intended indirectly to relate to general essay writing in that they offered an opportunity to air views on topics similar to those which might be found on a final examination paper and they rehearsed pupils in the techniques of argument, such as the use of examples and illustration, but it was significant in the lesson we saw that no reference was made to the likelihood of writing about the topic. (It was lessons such as these which provoked us to include 'public rationality' amongst the versions of English discussed in Chapter 6). The anecdotal exchanges with which one or two teachers prefaced their lessons, we have placed in 'Non-teaching and control' because they did not seem specifically related to the teacher's view of the English curriculum.

11. How time was spent: sixth form and further education

In the second year our observation had as its main focus a variety of FE courses labelled English or Communication Studies, but we continued our observation in three of our original six schools. We observed 53 sessions in the four colleges (recording 49): that amounted to 81½ timetabled hours (73¼ hours' teaching). We observed 16 sessions in schools (recording 15): the whole school total was roughly equivalent in time to one college, so to make the school/FE comparison easier we have represented it as such in the following table (2.15). We have no diary returns from this year: in colleges

Table 2.15

Schools (sixth form) and FE colleges

INSTITUTION	COURSE	1 STUDY OF COMPLETE LITERARY TEXTS	2	3	4	5 UNDERSTANDING EXTRACTS	6	7 PREPARATION AND WRITING ON GENERAL TOPICS	8 PRACTICE OF WRITTEN CONVENTIONS	9 REFLECTION ON LANGUAGE/ COMMUNICATION	10 ORAL/TALK	11	12 MISC.	13 NON-TEACHING AND CONTROL	% TOTAL
		Close, textual, localised	Reading	Themes, characters, narration	Writing	Literary	Non-literary				Practice and Presentation	Socio-moral-cultural attitudes			
SCHOOLS															
DOWNTOWN	'O' Lang.	-	48	17	-	-	-	31 (L)*	-	-	-	-	-	5	101
	'A' Lit.	48	11	17	-	-	-	-	-	-	11 (L)	-	3	10	100
NEW SUBURBIA	'A' Lit.	50	12	36	-	-	-	-	-	-	-	-	-	2	100
SMALLTOWN	'A' Lit.	43	8	49	-	-	-	-	-	-	-	-	-	1	101
COLLEGES															
HIGH STREET	'A' Lit.	33	-	30	33	-	-	-	-	-	-	-	-	4	100
	'O' Lit. and RSA Lang.(1)	14	-	-	-	-	39	29	13	-	-	-	-	5	100
	BEC (Nat.)	-	-	-	-	-	-	56*	28	9	-	-	-	7	100
SMALLTOWN	'O' Lang.	-	-	-	-	11	10	74*	-	-	-	-	-	5	100
	RSA Lang.	-	-	-	-	-	36	48	4	8	-	-	-	4	100
	BEC (Gen.)	-	-	-	-	-	-	-	37	18	20*	-	18	7	100
SQUARE HILL	TEC I	-	-	-	-	-	-	-	-	16	67*	-	6	11	100
	C. & G. I Comm. Skills	-	-	-	-	-	-	44*	9	14	-	24	4	5	100
	C. & G. C.I.T.B.	-	-	-	-	-	12	46*	30	-	-	2	-	10	100
CITY ROAD	TEC I	-	-	-	-	-	-	22*	-	9	32	21	-	16	100
	Coll. Foundation†	-	-	-	-	-	-	57*	-	-	-	-	37	6	100
	C. & G. Foundation	-	-	-	-	-	-	-	12	11	-	46	21	10	100

(1) from two classes
† equivalent to C. & G. Communication Skills I
* for coursework assessment

Table 2.16

Allocation of time according to course (%)

COURSE	STUDY OF COMPLETE LITERARY TEXTS	UNDER-STANDING EXTRACTS	PREPARATION AND WRITING ON GENERAL TOPICS	PRACTICE OF WRITTEN CONVENTIONS	REFLECTION ON LANGUAGE/ COMMUNICATION	ORAL/TALK		MISC.	NON-TEACHING AND CONTROL	TOTAL
						PRACTICE AND PRESENTATION	SOCIO-MORAL/ CULTURAL ATTITUDES			
'A' Literature (schools & colleges)	94	-	-	-	-	2	-	-	4	100
English 'O' & RSA (schools & colleges)	10	28	50	5	1	-	-	-	5	99
BEC — People & Communication (colleges)	-	-	36	31	13	7	-	6	7	100
Communications TEC & City & Guilds (colleges)	-	1	28	6	9	21	14	11	10	100

sessions tend to be longer and less frequent than in schools and we arranged our visits generally so that we sampled the course at different times during the two terms.

The immediate contrast is the preponderance of literature study in schools: English study there is more or less synonymous with literature study. If we look at the individual colleges, different emphases stand out immediately: the literature entry for High Street College, the importance of talk in Square Hill College, the emphasis on overt shaping of attitudes in Square Hill and City Road Colleges. But a more useful way of approaching the analysis is by grouping together similar courses.

The overall picture presented in Table 2.16 is very different from that in Tables 2.10–2.14 from the fifth year. Literary texts had little importance in FE colleges, either in their own right or in the preparation of writing: indeed no books were important unless they were to be examined, for with one exception (Downtown School O-level Language) we saw no reading in this second year of a complete text unless it was an examination set text. Understanding work in contrast with the fifth year was based mainly on non-literary extracts.

Although writing was still important, it was not so frequently continuous or essay writing. The concentration on writing on general topics that we noticed in classes using coursework for assessment was apparent at Smalltown College, but was not generally paralleled in further education. The proportions of time spent in practice of written conventions were not significantly higher than those we had recorded in the fifth year except in the BEC courses, but we find entries in this column in the majority of college courses. Alongside this practice of conventions, however, there was more reflection on the principles of language and communication than we had observed in schools.

We noticed the greater emphasis placed on oral work in technical courses and the increasing likelihood of socio-moral-cultural activities existing as a discrete category. Simulated interviews for jobs were particularly chosen for oral practice, but at Square Hill College the presentation of a prepared talk or project was also an important part of the final assessment. In the schools, oral practice could be tied to literature but, as was to be expected, this was never the case in the FE colleges: oral practice emphasised interview skills and the social skills of self-presentation. The institutional variant was not so important as the course: A-level Literature and O-level Language in High Street and Smalltown Colleges matched schools more closely in their time allocation than they did the other courses in the same college.

The allocation of time on task is a comparatively crude instrument of analysis: for finer discrimination we need to look at individual lessons and sessions in detail and the rest of our study will endeavour to do this.

CHAPTER 3

Preparing to Write in the Fifth Form

1. Communicating criteria

Since literacy has so long been the central concern of education it is not easy to look afresh at the teaching of writing, and to shake ourselves free of taken-for-granted assumptions in order to describe present practices as no more than one set of possibilities amongst many. Of course, children have to learn to write, and as they get older they write stories and compositions or essays; we have all done it. But writing is not all of a kind; quite apart from fiction, writing can deal with different topics, and can be addressed to different readers from the writer him or herself through known audiences to the faceless public. It can expound and inform, but it can also question, analyse, persuade, contradict, mock or merely entertain. In some writing the writer is present throughout, voicing qualifications, admitting to a perspective and acknowledging responsibility, whereas other writing assumes the anonymous voice of authority. Learning to write involves learning to deal with different material, to assume different voices and styles, to address different audiences and to carry out different rhetorical functions. Nor is the teaching of composition unproblematic. At one time, for example, it was thought appropriate to teach words, then sentences, then paragraphs and finally essays. Though we no longer believe that writing can best be learned in that way, there remains nevertheless the question of what abilities are involved, how they relate to one another, and how they can best be taught. Teachers have to answer such questions practically rather than theoretically, and their practice has varied even during this century. In seeking to find out from what they do today how teachers are implicitly answering the questions, we are freezing momentarily the flow of cultural history.

Our task in this section is to question that part of our material that was gathered in school fifth-year English lessons in order to find out what activities constituted for those classes the teaching of writing, and how teachers and pupils perceived these activities. Writing retains its centrality; in GCE and CSE examinations it remains the dominant means of evaluating young people's achievements in English

Language. We are taking the arbitrary but convenient decision to deal here only with 'continuous' writing, treating in Chapter 4 the writing of exercises, including 'comprehension' tasks structured by a series of questions requiring the interpretation of a given passage. Writing concerned with literature is also being dealt with elsewhere. In separating the three categories 'composition', 'comprehension' and 'literature' we are following teachers' usage, which itself follows the structure of examinations.

The material on which this analysis is based includes lesson observation — recorded in fieldnotes or by tape-recording — interviews and informal discussions with teachers, writing topics set to pupils during the year, some of the pieces which they wrote, and interviews with a third of them. The lessons used are those in which time was devoted to preparing pupils to write, to setting topics for writing, to the writing itself and to the handing back of work previously done. They amount to 29 lessons of which 12 were double periods; in two cases only part of the lesson was concerned with writing. Nine of the lessons were taught to top sets, six to middle, thirteen to bottom, and one to a sixth-form 'O-level retake' group. (The proportion is uncharacteristic in that analysis of the 'diary' completed by teachers in the second term showed that top sets spend considerably less classroom time on writing than other sets do.) The total teaching-time was just over 20 hours, this constituting 31 per cent of our fifth-year classroom material. (This can be compared with the 'diary' analysis, which showed that 28.5 per cent of the total time for all pupils was devoted to writing.) It should be added that writing was not mentioned in some of the lessons; they have been included in this analysis because we know that the class was later required to write upon the topic discussed.

A complete answer to our questions would require a study that extended throughout schooling. In looking at what for many pupils will be the final year of schooling we are not unaware of what has gone before. Teachers expect their fifth-year pupils to have mastered many skills during the preceding years; what we can expect to see will combine the further extension of previous approaches with attempts to remedy whatever some pupils have failed to grasp. Our impression is that for the most part the further extension is done publicly by class teaching and the remediation of faults by written comments and private advice. For practical reasons, the former is more fully represented in our data; but at an appropriate moment we shall refer to teachers' written comments and to individual tuition.

Our interest in this material is not simply to find out how writing is being taught in the last year of compulsory education, important though that is. English is sometimes described as 'a subject without a content' but this is far from being the case, as observation of secondary-school English lessons soon shows. Most English teachers, when they ask pupils to write, spend a good deal of time preparing them by preliminary reading and discussion which displays possible topics and approaches and perhaps enacts the presence of a concerned and sympathetic audience, and this is true of fifth-year examination classes. Although there is an unspoken assumption that each pupil will choose his or her content and treatment uniquely within the framework of a given topic, English teachers do not usually leave the responsibility to their pupils' unguided choice. Since the boys' and girls' skill as writers is to be assessed partly on the basis of their choice and arrangement of material, and the attitudes and styles which characterise their presentation, it behoves their English teachers to take an interest in the repertoire of possibilities they are able to select from. In order to make appropriate choices of content and approach pupils need to learn the criteria by which their writing will be assessed.

The criteria of assessment can be thought of as falling into two groups. 'Surface' criteria, such as length, spelling, punctuation, and the more obvious conventions of lay-out and genre (such as fiction/non-fiction) are relatively easy to communicate to pupils, though they certainly do not always apply them correctly. However, there are 'deep' criteria which are much harder to communicate but have more influence on grading; the deep criteria refer to preferred topics and preferred ways of writing about them, including arrangement, emphasis, values, style and tone. The transmission of these criteria becomes more urgent as pupils move into the examination years, whether their work is to be assessed by a faceless examiner or by a moderator from another school. In the latter case it may be more urgent still, since the pupils are to be assessed on the basis of a folder of coursework for which the teacher feels directly responsible.

There are two reasons for finding the transmission of criteria for writing particularly interesting. The deep criteria for writing amount to a set of preferred pictures of the world which gain good examination grades; the teaching of these criteria is potentially the teaching of deep criteria for living. No doubt young people do not always believe — or even listen to — what they are told, yet the pictures of the world which are presented to them in the curriculum are clearly a matter of public importance. The other important aspect of the deep criteria is the possibility that they are more available to some pupils than to others: certainly some use them more effectively. One of the many explanations that have been given for differences in school success between children from different social milieux has been Bourdieu's argument[1] that some bring with them from their homes 'cultural capital' in the form of sensitivities and preferences for what amount to little more than differences of style and perspective. Since style in this sense is almost identical with deep criteria, further understanding of what these criteria are and how they are communicated should throw light on some aspects of school failure.

How do young people gain access to deep criteria? They certainly do not come to school in cultural nakedness: they will have talked with other members of their families, read newspapers, magazines and books, watched television programmes, shared the interests and activities of a peer group, and all of these will have supplied them with information, preferred topics and points of view. In some cases they will even have been provided with styles of writing. These deep criteria which they bring to school may or may not be of a kind to earn an examiner's approval. An example which most English teachers will recognise is the essay on popular music which grates upon their sensibilities by adopting the subject matter, perspective and specialised style of pop music magazines. It would not be unfair to say that a substantial part of English teaching is concerned with offering pupils a wider range of options and making partly available to them an examiner's likely judgements about their relative worth. In order to observe this happening we shall give our main attention to lessons in which pupils are prepared for writing. The next two sections are devoted to two main groups of influences upon what happens in English lessons: teachers' priorities, values and perspectives as they were expressed in syllabuses (and to a lesser extent in discussion), and the influence of examinations. The third major influence on lessons — the pupils' priorities, values and perspectives — is dealt with later in Chapter 8. Before that, however, there are four chapters which constitute an analysis of what teachers communicate by the content of writing lessons; they are based upon classroom observation, on written work done by pupils, and on the views of the teachers themselves, which are included whenever they throw light upon the classroom procedures.

2. Departmental perspectives

We had hoped to receive an English syllabus from each of the six schools, but in spite of more than one request we were not given one from Greentown School or from Urban School; it seems likely that in both cases a relatively new head of department was moving cautiously towards the time when it would be appropriate to produce a document which implied some consensus about English teaching. Thus we are dealing with documents from only four schools. None of these syllabuses dealt with fifth-form English in detail, so the quotations that follow tend to be drawn either from sections concerned with both fourth- and fifth-year classes, or — when it seems appropriate — from the general introduction, which in two cases constituted over half of the document. In most cases the explicit reference to the fifth-year course was no more than a sentence or two in length, and related to examination requirements.

Because syllabuses serve as 'shop window' documents, they tend to include various perspectives in an ad hoc consensus. Nevertheless, the author or authors usually show their own preferences by emphasis, selection and practical advice, so it is possible to characterise their differences by passing over what they have in common. We propose, therefore, to draw major themes from each of these four syllabuses before assembling parallel accounts of the other two schools.

Downtown School's syllabus came closest to the 'personal' approach which is to be characterised in a later section. We have described elsewhere the inner city area from which the school draws its pupils. In spite of the social problems of such an area, school morale seems high, and the English department has had for some years a reputation for energy and enlightenment. The syllabus speaks for what is often called the 'personal growth' model of English teaching. John Dixon's *Growth through English*[2] is quoted, a passage in which he presents the classroom as a place for 'talk about people and situations in the world as they (the pupils) know it'. The author of the syllabus writes of the involvement of the whole personality and 'the appreciation of self in relation to all around'. In the lessons we noticed an emphasis on the content of writing, and the syllabus makes this explicit: 'Language and experience grow from each other, hence the importance of the subject material within our thematic approach'. These were to include 'human relationships and questions of our time': themes suggested for the fourth-year course included Living in Cities, Work and Leisure, and Authority. In spite of the social background of the pupils, no mention is made of the transmission of values, but 'thought-maturation' is mentioned as equal in importance to 'the development and projection of personality'. The three teachers at Downtown whose lessons we observed were Mrs Brennan, Mr Richardson and Mrs Williams. Certainly there was relatively little deliberate attempt in the lessons we saw to transmit values, the exception to this being Mrs Brennan's lesson on war. The three teachers shared an emphasis on literature and a wish to relate it to their pupils' perspectives. There was also less sign of a concern to teach modes of reasoning than in some other schools. In most respects, however, there is a good match between teaching strategies and syllabus, which expresses the personal growth view of English in a relatively pure form.

In the Smalltown School syllabus the 'personal' emphasis is reinterpreted into something rather different. We have described elsewhere the school and the favoured social background of many of its pupils. The morale of the English department is high: Mr Squires is head of department, and amongst his colleagues are Mrs Woods and Mr Austin, three highly committed and skilful teachers. The syllabus asserts that 'accurate and sincere' writing arises from 'involvement'; pupils are to learn to write well by constant writing. For older pupils 'subjects dealt with should be biased towards their own adolescence and their relationships'; they should 'probe the consciousness' of each pupil. So far this sounds not unlike Downtown School's approach to public topics from a personal perspective. But another element appears which reflects a different emphasis. Some pupils are said to have a 'culturally impoverished background', so part of the purpose of English is to 'expose them to facts, information and ideas' and 'to widen their often narrow boundaries and reveal to them how rich life can be'. (The idea of Smalltown pupils being culturally impoverished would ring strangely in the ears of teachers in Downtown and Urban Schools, but this is how the Smalltown teachers perceived some of them, enough to give these concerns a substantial place in the syllabus.) Partly the remedying of this impoverishment would be done through literature, but it was also made plain — in the section on CSE courses — that 'the pupils must be made to consider some of the problems of their time, political, industrial, commercial, personal, to make them aware of the responsibilities of citizenship'. By talking to the culturally deprived the English teacher is to 'take them beyond television, football, pop and bingo'. We found in many lessons, not only those in Smalltown School, teachers who took the responsibility for presenting to their pupils certain attitudes, beliefs and values that they held to be important. Such purposes were clearly present in the lessons taught by Mr Squires, Mrs Wood and Mr Austin, though it seems unlikely that the last of these, who had remarkable rapport with his bottom-stream pupils, would entirely relish the implications of some of the phrases quoted above. Undoubtedly, the syllabus interprets thematic work for less-able pupils in terms of a kind of social rescue work, undertaken from a position of cultural advantage which only partly drew its credentials from high literary culture.

Some remarks made by Mr Squires and Mr Austin reinforce aspects of the syllabus and were entirely consistent with their lessons. Mr Squires spoke of the importance of 'the social element', especially with very low-ability children:

> I find I'm frequently talking to them — this sounds snobbish — in a way to try to civilise them in some ways, either to calm down frustration or gee them up, very often just to calm them down . . . 'Now let's have a look at this' . . .

Mr Austin added that he puts the child before the examination, whether it's CSE or GCE, but that nevertheless:

> They will pass and they will pass well, because I think I've put in a lot of work in talking about so many other aspects of life and seeing the literature is relevant to that.

Mr Austin, perhaps wishing to make repairs in the impression he had given, insisted that he was not pursuing social goals at the expense of his pupils' examination prospects. The Smalltown emphasis on social goals does not, however, include within it 'nourishing the poetic function'. Mr Squires made it clear that, though he valued 'the free, informal, imaginative, creative' aspect of his subject, these ideas are 'very alien' to less-able children:

> when their ethos is toughness and there's little room for compassion in the lives of some of them. They live very much in the world of soccer, leather jackets, jeans and motorbikes.

(It is interesting to notice that it is the boys' ethos that affects Mr Squires' priorities: the girls have disappeared from sight.)

Like other departments, Catchwide wanted a balance between 'personal and impersonal' writing, but it is possible to read between the lines a somewhat greater concern with the latter. The syllabus begins with aims; the first aim refers to 'personal development and social competence', and the second to 'basic, practical English'. (Something of the tone can be caught from the sentence that follows: 'Letter writing is the only form of creative writing that all pupils will need in adult life.)

One phrase in the Catchwide syllabus urges that, by the fourth year, 'personal writing should be set in a framework of general comment', thus implying a preference for writing that goes beyond the anecdotal and towards reflection and analysis. In the same paragraph comes a reference to 'writing verging on the official, the academic, the detached'. Taking these emphases from their context in the general part of the syllabus to some extent misrepresents what, in our view, is the most analytical and sophisticated of the four syllabuses. Our purpose in doing this is to indicate that not all English departments are devoted to an unqualified personal development view of English: the author of the Catchwide document had thought to some effect about alternative kinds of writing. There was not, however, a close match between what the syllabus said and what we saw in Mr O'Donnell's and Mr Keegan's lessons, though it is relevant to add that both of these teachers felt strongly constrained by examination requirements. (See page 85.)

The syllabus from New Suburbia School was quite different, but it too placed more emphasis upon impersonal writing than upon personal. The influence of examinations was patent; only one sentence of the syllabus referred to the fifth-year course: 'Work in the Fifth Forms is closely tailored to the examination requirements of individual groups'. This means that our impression of the principles informing the teaching of English in the school will have to be drawn from elsewhere in the syllabus, particularly the section that deals with fourth-year courses. The more able fourth-year pupils were to 'attempt the more difficult types of essay (descriptive, polemical, discursive)' while for the less able there should be 'emphasis on the personal'. However, the syllabus as a whole made few references to personal writing, and went into some detail about other kinds. For example, 'shorter pieces' are specified: 'summaries; reports; newspaper articles; letters provoked by various stimuli; dialogues', and this is quite unlike the other syllabuses. Indeed the flavour of the fourth-year syllabus can be gathered from the opening sentence: '*Language*: Language work will be done from the course books . . . ', and from other headings in the list, '*Spelling*', '*Vocabulary*', '*Comprehension*'. Here we find a quite different construction of 'English' from that in Downtown School or Smalltown School: the interest in written conventions and the more public functions of writing are in the foreground as the references to coursebooks imply. (A surprising aspect of New Suburbia's concern for examinations is that, in our judgement, the activities we saw in lessons were often a poor match with the skills likely to be tested in the examinations that the pupils were taking.)

It was Urban School and Greentown School that did not provide us with syllabuses. We now turn to the informal discussions with members of these departments — which took place after the completion of classroom observation — in order to characterise their approaches from what was said in the discussions. As it proved impossible to arrange a joint meeting with the Urban School department we talked separately with Mrs Sutton, the head of department, Mr Callaghan and Mrs Sackville. As in the other discussions, we introduced into all of these informal interviews a sheet of quotations about English teaching; one passage urged that 'nourishing the poetic function is the most important thing an English teacher can do with less able children', and another that 'only in English is the whole man catered for'. These views were generally rejected, especially by the teachers from Urban School. Mr Callaghan, speaking for the English teachers as a whole, said: 'We think we're catering for the whole man and we do no such thing'. Mrs Sutton made it clear that she did not give the poetic function a high priority with less-able pupils, saying, 'I think we've got a responsibility to make them literate when they leave, otherwise they are not going to get the jobs . . . they could aspire to'. On another occasion, Mr Callaghan, after reading the 'profile' of his teaching that we had written, commented that our data lacked the following: (1) the formal part of the course (e.g. letter writing, especially letters of application); (2) examination practice of comprehension exercises; (3) the transfer of diagrammatic material into written (e.g. a series of lessons on the siting of an atomic power station); (4) the writing of publishers' blurbs after hearing a radio programme on the work of advertising copy writers. It is clear that he wished to repair some aspects of our presentation of him — perhaps the place of the private/personal in it — but it was not clear whether we had a genuinely biased sample of lessons, or whether he merely wished in retrospect to detach himself from our account. The omissions he spoke of leaned towards public/impersonal, and the last two (3 and 4) seemed to point towards the contextualised writing tasks that we found in some further education courses. Mr Callaghan was one of the teachers who said that he did not 'go in for writing stories', that is, did not often set them to pupils. If we add to this that Mrs Sutton described her teaching as 'tending to formal' this would suggest a department unlikely to place strong emphasis on the personal. (See page 146 for Mrs Sutton's definition of 'formal'.) As Mr Callaghan indicated, this is not the impression we received from their lessons; some of Mrs Sutton's lessons were characterised by a combination of personal content, emphasis on useful skills, and a desire to transmit views about proper behaviour.

The discussion with Mr Tremaine and Mr Saxon of Greentown School threw rather less light upon their views about the teaching of writing, so this account will use material taken more from the individual interviews than from the discussion, though at the risk of conflating unlike data. Mr Tremaine, the head of department, placed considerable emphasis on the rational aspects of writing: 'various ideas that they might argue with or argue about, abstract concepts. We do some syllogisms as well, ways to attack arguments', he said. He thought that the department should be providing pupils with 'some kind of equipment to cope with written arguments that they read and construct their own written arguments themselves'. He did not 'find a lot of opportunity at this stage' for story writing and therefore his classes 'do quite a lot of work on substantial journalism and on major controversial themes'. Mr Tremaine mentioned a fourth-year project on the General Election in which groups of pupils each represented a political party, and a sequence of letters placed in the simulated context of an exchange between zoo-keeper and headmaster about the behaviour of pupils during a visit. Our observation of lessons and of pupils' writings confirmed this emphasis. Mr Tremaine rejected the view of English which links it to personal experience, to spontaneity and to a creativity denied to other subjects. Writing for him seemed to be not primarily an occasion to explore the self, but a cluster of abilities closely linked to logical thinking and relevant to writing on public themes and for public purposes — a perspective unique amongst our 17 teachers, which we have called the 'public rationality' version of English.

Mr Saxon was the only other member of the department who took part in the research. Although he accepted much of Mr Tremaine's perspective, it was possible to detect in what he said during the initial interview the traces of another and partially contradictory viewpoint. He claimed to work from a range of kinds of work to be covered in English, mentioning a tension between the claims of 'creative writing' and the ability to give clear and concise instructions. He represented this as a tension between making pupils 'better citizens' and making them 'more effective in the outside world'. Coursework assessment had enabled Mr Saxon, he told us, to go beyond the 'formal essay', and he instanced handing round contrasting fabrics — fur and so on — so that pupils could write in response to this 'tactile stimulation', a method unkindly characterised in the sixties as 'kipper sniffing'. We found that Mr Saxon's lessons answered to his account by including not only private topics but also a serious attempt to teach pupils how to structure an essay on a public issue. It was clear to us that Mr Saxon was a teacher who was in the process of shifting his perspective away from a personal growth approach towards one which acknowledged some of the public functions of writing.

It would have been no great surprise to find a wide gulf between syllabus aspirations and fifth-year realities, but in the event we found that the emphases detected in three of the syllabuses corresponded reasonably well with what we had seen in lessons. These main emphases can be summarised thus:

Downtown School:	Personal growth in a social context
Smalltown School:	Access to culture
New Suburbia School:	Examination requirements and useful skills
Catchwide School:	Personal growth balanced with useful skills

In the last of these, Catchwide, there was some division between syllabus and fifth-year practice in that we saw little interest in the personal growth aspect of English and much concern with examination requirements. Mr O'Donnell and Mr Keegan of Catchwide seemed to feel more constrained by examinations than many other teachers did, even those at New Suburbia who were undoubtedly much concerned with examination results. On the basis of other kinds of evidence we can characterise the other two departments:

Urban School:	Literacy and literature for the deprived
Greentown School:	Public topics and rationality

It must be admitted, however, that to reduce the work of skilled teachers to homogeneous slogans is a convenience that is potentially highly misleading. The teachers themselves would undoubtedly reject such crudely simplified accounts. Their function here is merely to record our impression of a tendency, though the labels disguise the great deal all the teachers have in common as well as the not inconsiderable differences of emphasis within each department.

There is one issue unrelated to our analysis of teaching that can usefully be discussed by way of a coda to this section. English teachers lack a well thought-out and consistent framework for talking — and thinking — about writing, and this shows most obviously in the lack of an agreed taxonomy of kinds of writing. At times a simple two-category model appears both in the syllabuses and in what teachers say. The introduction of the New Suburbia syllabus mentions 'a wide variety . . . from factual answers to factual questions, to the kind of writing in which the pupil may feel the most intense pleasure in expressing and creating', though later it does suggest other categories. The syllabus from Smalltown School calls for a balance between 'imaginative' and 'factual' writing. Catchwide School syllabus mentions 'from the very formal to the very informal, and from the objective to the highly subjective', and later 'personal and impersonal' topics, but without explaining whether this is one dimension or three. Our own distinctions between public and private, and personal and impersonal belong to this tradition. Other categories are mentioned elsewhere in the syllabuses, though it is often hard to relate them to the paired categories or bipolar dimensions cited above. Some of the distinctions relate to format: 'letter', 'dialogue', 'diaries'. Others are based on content: 'science fact and fiction', '(descriptions of) places and people', 'fantasy'; or on the fiction/non-fiction dichotomy. Some categories are drawn from contexts in life outside school: 'the business letter', 'summaries, reports, newspaper articles' and presumably imply an audience and an appropriate style. Other distinctions are essentially rhetorical ones, concerned with purpose: Catchwide School refers to 'essays putting forward a point of view', while New Suburbia distinguishes 'descriptive, polemical, discursive' writings, describing them as 'the more difficult types of essay', perhaps in contrast with 'narrative', a commonly used category throughout. 'Discursive', too, is a commonly used term, probably because it is used by some examination boards: it seems to mean little more than 'non-narrative'. Downtown School mentions the Writing Research Unit's three categories — Expressive, Transactional, Poetic[3] — but does not relate them to the more commonly used terms which appear elsewhere in the same syllabus. Catchwide School uses a stylistic criterion in the phrase 'writing verging on the official, the academic, the detached' — or are they three different styles? The distinction between reflective and non-reflective writing occurs infrequently: Catchwide asserts that as pupils mature their 'intense personal writing, whether narrative or descriptive, needs to be set in a framework of general comment'. What is worth noting is not merely the diversity of dimensions, which have clearly not been sorted out by the authors of the syllabuses, but the lack of any serious attempts to make the categories explicit; one is led to suspect that when teachers talk to one another about writing, many ambiguities and disagreements are papered over by the vagueness of the terms used. The teachers probably believe that natural language provides all the terms they need; it might be proposed, however, that both thinking and communicating about writing would be aided by a common terminology and some clarification of meanings.

3. The influence of examinations

Secondary schoolteachers of English all feel in some degree constrained by examinations, though some perceive the conflict between their priorities and the demands of an examination to be greater and more oppressive than others do. Indeed, it is not unlikely that those teachers who found the conflict most oppressive eliminated themselves from this research by refusing to take part. The purpose of this section is (i) to describe the demands for writing made by examinations, (ii) to relate the writing done by pupils to the mode of examination they have been entered for, and (iii) to display the teachers' perceptions of examination constraints.

We began with topics set in examination papers for the General Certificate of Education (GCE) Ordinary Level and the Certificate of Secondary Education (CSE) in England and Wales during 1979. Analysing these papers[4] led us to make a general distinction between 'public' and 'private' models of English; here we are applying the distinction only to essays in English Language papers. The public approach tends to detach English from the concerns of everyday life. Essay topics require the writer to stand back from social issues and coolly put arguments from various viewpoints. Some topics recall the *belles lettres* tradition; for others the expected style of composition seems more usually to correspond to middlebrow journalism. Questions tend to be 'open', apparently leaving to the writer the choice of subject matter, form and style, though one senses in the impersonal style of the rubric a whole world of assumptions and values by which those choices will be judged. That is, in the public model what is being tested includes whether the candidate has internalised these assumptions and values enough to judge what topics and perspectives will be preferred, and what kinds of writing will count as well-balanced, rational and inventive. This is a typical public writing task:

> Write, in any way you wish, about ONE of the following titles:
> Peace, Exhaustion, Hatred, Laughter, Hero-worship, Desolation, Memories, Meditation.

The private approach differs from this in two respects: the topics tend to be personal and domestic, chosen to be close to the writers' supposed private concerns; and the tasks often spell out a context and purpose for the writing. It is as if the examiners, wishing to avoid the possibility that the assumptions and values implicit in the public approach do have a social class bias, have made the criteria they will use so explicit that no candidate is disadvantaged by not having access to them. An unfortunate outcome is that in searching for a context and purpose supposed to be relevant to young people, the examiners embed the task in a stereotype of domestic life — the family, the peer group, the club — at worst a parody of urban working-class life. If public issues appear in the private approach, the writer is frequently encouraged to deal with them through their impact on individuals. An example that illustrates the private content is:

> Teenagers are often criticised for not behaving as parents expect. On some occasions, however, teenagers are anxious that their parents' behaviour will not let them down. Describe exactly how you hope your parents would behave if you were to bring your boy or girl friend home specially to meet them, and mention some mistakes that you might fear that they would make.

Some 'private' examination topics go to much greater lengths in indicating what content, style and tone is expected.

The public and private approaches to English are idealisations which seldom appear in a pure form. There was some tendency for the (higher status) GCE papers to lean towards the public and for CSE papers to lean towards the private, but many were mixed or even showed the opposite tendency to that expected.

By analysing examinations we had arrived at what were more likely to be loose clusters of emphases and preferences than two coherent viewpoints. These would have to be clarified. Moreover it could not be assumed that teachers' perspectives and practices would be a close match with examination questions, particularly since many pupils in the study were to be examined in English by a selection of the work done during the course, instead of — or as well as — an examination paper. It would be necessary to find out empirically how far teaching strategies and the writing actually done by pupils fell into similar categories.

In our first attempt to get an impression of what pupils wrote about we categorised 263 titles which teachers had set, giving these results:

Table 3.1

Analysis of topics set for writing

Public topics for discussion etc.	38%
Public topics requiring personal/narrative treatment	14%
Private topics (self, family, friends, school, work)	30%
Subject matter not specific enough to be categorised	18%

This seemed to contradict our impressions by placing too much weight on public topics, so we decided to look instead at our fieldnotes on the 770 pieces of writing by pupils which we had inspected. This allowed us to take into account not merely the titles set but which of them the pupils had chosen to write about and how they had interpreted them. In order to describe the results of this second analysis we must first explain the categories we used.

1. *Private/Personal* This included autobiographical writing which varied from the anecdotal — purporting to be true but not necessarily so — to the introspective and reflective. The topics were usually private and the treatment always personal. Examples were:

My earliest memories
My grandmother
The pains and pleasures of teenage life.

(We can illustrate how misleading a title alone can be by taking as example 'The European Cup Final', which we placed in this category because the writer made of it an opportunity to write about the excitement of a trip to London.)

2. *Fictional narrative* It was often very difficult to determine whether a particular first-person narrative — the most common kind — belonged here or in the 'personal' category. The following titles clearly invite a narrative:

The day the lift stuck
Maybe next time.

However, titles such as 'Old Age' or 'Prejudice' frequently appeared at the head of fictional narratives, which partly accounts for the over-emphasis on public topics in our analysis of titles. (The former might be a Pinteresque sketch of two old ladies talking in a pub; the latter a sentimental tale of love triumphing over all.)

3. *Belles lettres* We placed in this category those pieces of writing in which the writer had treated a topic as an invitation to display literary skills, without much personal involvement or serious engagement with public issues. Such writing frequently occurred in the 'examination paper' classes when a teacher set topics from a previous paper and in classes working from textbooks. The mode of writing was often mixed, including passages of anecdote, generalisation and description; older teachers would recognise the traditional O-level essay.

4. *Public issues* These we subdivided:

a. *Personal treatment of public issues* Here the writer either through choice or following the terms of the set task, dealt with a public topic mainly in terms of its effects on individuals, often himself/herself.
b. *Impersonal treatment of public issues* This included tasks which

specified a persuasive or instructional mode, such as:

A speech presenting the facts against smoking

For the most part however, public topics were open to treatment in either an impersonal or personal manner:

Pop music
'All young people should learn a language other than their own.' Do you agree?

5. *Letters* Letters in general might fall into any category, but all those in our sample were either applications for jobs or complaints about faulty goods or services, so we categorised them separately.

This analysis of pupils' written work (see Table 3.2) enables us to compare classes entered for different modes of examination: (i) by examination paper, (ii) by folder of coursework, (iii) by a mixed mode combining the two. In interpreting Table 3.2 it is useful to keep in mind that the overall amount of writing done by classes preparing for examination papers was considerably less than that done by classes in the other categories. One first notices the high proportion of fictional writing: 50 per cent in the coursework mode. It is less easy to come to conclusions about the relative emphasis on personal and impersonal writing. If we omit column 4a (public topics but personal treatment) since it is ambiguous, and treat the first two columns as personal and the remaining three as impersonal, we can then say that 'examination paper' classes' written work divided into 30 per cent personal and 64 per cent impersonal, 'coursework' classes write 73 per cent personal and 24 per cent impersonal pieces — a striking contrast — and 'mixed mode' classes fall between them at 55 per cent personal and 34 per cent impersonal. This is an interesting and unexpected finding in that it predicts a strong relationship between mode of examining and a leaning towards either personal or impersonal writing. However, this is not the only relationship between the examination and the version of English presented to the pupils, and it is to these other relationships that we now turn, leaving to later sections the further development of the personal/impersonal dichotomy.

For the minority of more able pupils who are to sit an examination paper in literature, this fact is the best predictor of the main emphasis in the version of English that they will experience. This can be shown from the 'diary' analysis: classes sitting papers in O-level literature spent 68 per cent of lesson time on literature and 10.5 per cent on general composition, whereas those not entered for any examination in literature spent 23 per cent of lesson time on literature (mainly reading) and 46 per cent on general composition. (See Table 3.7 on p. 149.) This is somewhat counterbalanced by the writing which some of the former groups did for homework; pupils in the latter groups —

Table 3.2

Pupils' treatment of writing topics in relation to mode of examination (in percentages)

	1. Private/ personal	2. Fictional narrative	3. Belles lettres	4a. Public/ personal	4b. Public/ impersonal	5. Letters
Examination paper (5 classes)	16	1[illegible]	30	5	16	18
Coursework folder (8 classes)	23	5[illegible]	11	3	10	3
Mixed mode (4 classes)	34	2[illegible]	22	11	12	0

mainly bottom sets — are unlikely to have done much writing at home. The overall effect of literature on their English course was particularly marked for three of the top sets who were to sit examination papers — as against coursework assessment — in language as well as in literature. These three sets did hardly any extended writing at home or at school apart from that relevant to the literature examination. Mr Tremaine of Greentown School accounted for the small number of pieces of general writing he had set the top set by telling the investigators that each of his pupils had seven exercise books, one for each of the books they were studying: the focus was on literature rather than on language. Mr Squires of Smalltown, teaching for a paper in literature though not in language, found that he was 'pressurised by exams' and dramatised it as: 'I must do twenty pages of *Great Expectations*, which isn't the ideal way of doing it'. Mrs Sutton of Urban School, speaking apparently of the one O-level group in the school — which we had not been able to observe — said, 'I think in the top set groups there has been very little specific language work; the language work has come out of studying the literary texts'. Since this corresponds with what was said in some initial interviews (by Mr O'Donnell, for example) with our observations and with the data drawn from the diaries, it can be taken to be a well-established description of the version of English likely to be experienced by most top sets.

The second basis on which the version of English experienced by pupils can be predicted is the chosen mode of examination in English Language: this was used in Table 3.2 to differentiate the kinds of writing done by different groups of pupils. It is not clear whether the mode of examining should be seen as an influence on the version of English or whether teachers' preferences for one version or the other guided their choice of examination. As the analysis showed, there are marked differences between the three groups of classes; at this point we shall consider what teachers said about examinations and in later sections return to the differences in what the pupils wrote, particularly in relation to the proportions of private/personal and public/impersonal writing.

When we talked to the 17 teachers who took part in the fifth-year section of the study, we found that those who were preparing pupils for an examination paper mentioned it frequently, as if it were salient in their minds. New Suburbia School English syllabus contained no section outlining fifth-year work, merely referring to 'examination requirements' as if this made both goals and means fully available. Mrs King, the head of department at New Suburbia, acknowledged in both interview and post-observation discussion that their fifth-year teaching was much influenced by the examination. She and her colleagues differentiated the effects of O-level, however, which they felt greatly constrained by, from those of the 16+ paper which the school's two lower sets were taking. Even past papers do not necessarily define a curriculum, and we thought we detected a mismatch between the activities practised in many New Suburbia lessons and the skills likely to be tested in examinations. (This will be discussed in Chapter 4, which deals with those aspects of language teaching not relevant here.) Catchwide School, too, was highly conscious of examination results; when the researchers suggested during the departmental discussion that Catchwide was more examination oriented than other schools Mr O'Donnell, as head of department, replied: 'We're here to do the best we can for our kids . . . in terms of the world these kids are going out into. The more examinations they have, the better it is going to be for them.' Mr Callaghan thought that his school, Urban School, was 'very, very examination biased' and clearly found this a marked constraint on his approach to English teaching. These are the three schools which we perceived as most leaning towards the public/impersonal side of English.

English teachers have campaigned for many years to achieve school-based assessment, but when we turn to what teachers in this study said about helping pupils to prepare assignments for the folders it appears that this too has proved to be a constraint. Mrs Williams of Downtown School felt that her work with the bottom set was 'dominated by the assignments', that is by the task of obtaining from each pupil 12 satisfactory pieces of writing. Similarly, Mr Callaghan felt 'shackled by the syllabus' which again referred to the 12 pieces required for CSE English Studies and Mr Saxon spoke of 'a shameless conveyor belt'. Mr Austin of Smalltown School made a characteristically reflective comment:

> I was very much in favour of 16+ English, and although I am still in favour of it I've been more under pressure from marking this year than I've ever been before, and the tendency has been that the assignment has to be over and done with and move on to the next one, so really there are fairly tight limits to 16+ even though it seems very open-ended, and possibly one would like to spend more time on certain issues but it's impossible . . .

Work with less-able classes became dominated by the need to persuade them to produce 12 assignments suitable in length and quality for inclusion in a folder. Mr Tremaine, who was teaching a top set at Greentown School, helped us to understand why some teachers had campaigned for this opportunity. He disliked the traditional examination because it allowed him no contact with what his pupils wrote in the examination room. The effect of changing to the other mode of assessment was that he was now teaching 'almost exclusively language' and 'fitting the literature in, rather than the other way round'. Assessment by coursework allows teachers to take direct responsibility for what their pupils write, but at the same time makes their work more visible to other teachers. This probably accounts for the elaborate preparation for writing which we noticed: communicating deep criteria becomes of urgent importance.

In the lessons themselves there were signs of a change of emphasis that echoed the changed mode of assessment. The fact that the teacher decides what topics are written about and assessed, and indeed controls the criteria of assessment, frees him or her to pursue intrinsic aims, instead of directing attention to the aims imposed extrinsically by a public examination paper. Even in the coursework sets all teachers and pupils must have been fully aware of the examination as an overall goal, yet there were considerable differences in the salience given to it when teachers made justificatory remarks during lessons. Teachers often account to their classes for what they are doing, since the pupils are likely to devote themselves more assiduously to work they perceive as justified; indeed, teachers who feel uncertain of their grasp on a class refer more frequently to examination requirements. (The teachers may also have been aware of the observer as a potential source of evaluation whose perceptions needed to be educated by means of justificatory accounts.) The following are typical of lessons in which pupils are preparing to write assignments.

Mr Richardson of Downtown School began his lesson, after a brief reference to the theme of family life in the play they had read in the previous lesson, by saying: 'What I want you to be thinking about in your next language assignment — so I'm trying to tie literature and language up — is your own family life or anyway a family life nearer the norm than we had in the play.'

Mr Callaghan of Urban School began likewise with the discussion of characters in a play, *Hobson's Choice*, but moved out on to other topics such as divorce. The purpose of this discussion, which moved rapidly from one topic to another, came out incidentally in the course of the lesson when he said: 'I want to give you a wide variety of things you can write about.' Mrs Williams and Mrs Brennan of Downtown School filled the blackboard with long lists of relevant vocabulary which either awaited the pupils when they came into the room at the beginning of the lesson or were shown to them later. The former who was teaching a bottom set made it explicit that the purpose of the activity was the production of an assignment; the latter clearly had other important purposes, but the listed words were a potent reminder of the implicit framework.

However, not many of the teachers displayed a single-minded commitment to the production of examinable assignments. Many teachers in this group could be seen to pursue intrinsic goals such as the communication of values and (less frequently) the encouragement of particular styles of thinking; these will be illustrated and discussed in sections 7 and 6, respectively, of this chapter.

4. The private and the personal

At this point it became important to make a distinction between *topics* set, either in examinations or as assignments, their *treatment* by the teacher in a lesson, and their *interpretation* by the pupil who writes. Each topic can be allocated to a point on the scale from the private to the public. For example:

Loneliness	Private
Bringing up children	Domestic
Attitudes to people who are different	Local (face-to-face)
War	Public

At one end we have topics directed towards the exploration of aloneness and uniqueness, then aspects of a domestic context, then a group of topics related to relationships amongst acquaintances, and finally some issues that come from the world of social awareness and responsibility. Even this range is highly selective: a topic from the physical sciences would be unlikely to occur, for example. The major concerns of English lessons point towards such areas as childhood, family life, the peer group concerns of adolescents, employment, and a restricted range of public issues.

This placing of the topic on the private-public scale can be distinguished from whether it is treated by the teacher who sets it as personal or impersonal, and similarly from how it is interpreted by pupils. 'Loneliness' could possibly be an introspective account of one's own experience, or an impersonal analysis of a social phenomenon. (It could also be a story; the discussion of fiction is being held over to the next section.) Some topics have a built-in indication of whether they are to be treated personally or not: '*The experience* of loneliness' and '*Feelings about* brothers and sisters'. In analysing the pupils' treatment of writing topics in Table 3.2 we utilised both scales, private-public and personal-impersonal: column 4a, for example, referred to public topics which the writer had dealt with in a personal manner.

The subject matter of the personal approach to experience is typically domestic; the book of poems used in one of these lessons was called *Generations* and contained a section headed 'Family Life'. Such source books, which contain poems and passages of prose mainly extracted from fictional and biographical works, are organised in 'themes' which communicate persuasive messages about the nature and organisation of the English syllabus. They have to a considerable extent supplanted the older English textbooks, which indeed contain some extracts for reading but are mainly concerned with providing exercises based upon that reading. Many of the source-books would appear equally open to use in an impersonal approach to experience, since they also contain themes such as 'War';

whenever the extracts are mainly devoted to accounts of first-hand experience rather than to reflections on general issues, however, the source-book would seem to encourage the personalising of these public topics.

The purpose of this section is to characterise and illustrate a group of lessons in which teachers were implicitly or explicitly conveying to their pupils that a personal approach to the piece of writing in question would be preferable. In identifying these lessons we sought to go beyond impressionistic judgements by selecting indicators of personalising that might be somewhat less inferential.

Table 3.3

Indicators of personalising

Teachers tell anecdotes or encourage pupils to do so	10 lessons
Teachers ask for the expression of feeling in writing	10 lessons
During the lesson the teacher seeks to transmit values	10 lessons
The discussion takes off from the reading of a literary passage	11 lessons
Narrative treatment of the topic is acceptable	12 lessons

Table 3.3 shows the indicators chosen and their frequency of appearance in the 29 lessons on which we are basing this account of preparing to write. Since they are not randomly distributed, their occurrence can be used to distinguish two groups of lessons.

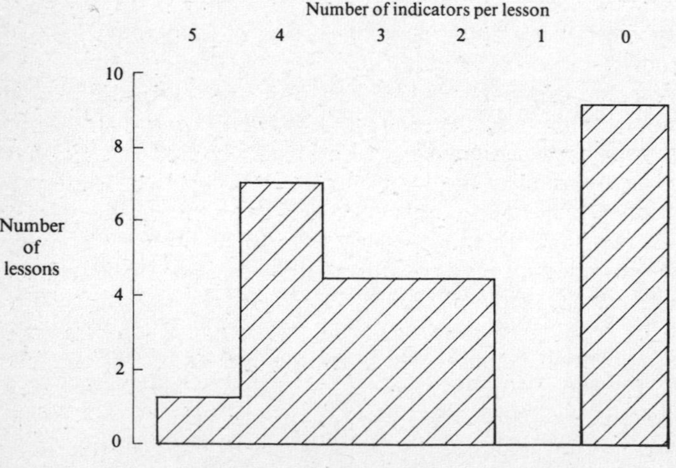

Figure 3.1

Distribution of indicators

The quantitative analysis shown in Figure 3.1 enables us to distinguish a group of 16 lessons which contain two or more indicators from another group of nine lessons which contain none. (Four lessons in which there was little or no comment by the teacher have been omitted from this analysis.)

Although we have called these 'Indicators of personalising', they amount less to a sharply defined single category than to a loose cluster of associated characteristics. The telling of anecdotes and the expression of feeling are central to a personal presentation of experience, and, as we have seen, the kind of literature usually read points in the same direction. The other two characteristics, the use of narrative including fiction and the transmission of values, are more loosely associated and will be dealt with in their own separate sections. (Two other potential indicators were considered: whether episodes of rational-reflective discussion occurred (13 lessons); and whether the teacher made any attempt to teach writing techniques (11 lessons). These turned out to be randomly distributed with respect to the two groups identified in Table 3.4. They too will be discussed elsewhere.)

This quantification of indicators, however, gives no more than an impression of the content of the lessons, the messages transmitted to pupils or the means used to do so; to do this it will be necessary to exemplify and discuss the details of particular lessons. It will have been noticed from Figure 3.1 that one lesson contained all five of the indicators, and it is this one that will be used to present the ideal type of a private/personal approach. Indeed the lesson might be held to represent what has been called 'the progressive consensus', since it encapsulates the essence of the personal perspective while at the same time showing occasional public elements. The teacher, Mrs Wood, was highly experienced and taught this lesson to a top set in Smalltown School.

Mrs Wood's original justification for the discussion was unambiguous: 'This morning we're going to do some preparatory work for your next assignment, which is "Myself" '. This was mentioned again briefly at the end of the lesson; apart from these two brief mentions teacher and pupils alike seemed to join in the discussion for its own sake. In this and in a number of other lessons the assignment provided an occasion for a discussion which the teacher saw as intrinsically valuable. Mrs Wood set the scene for the discussion by reading two extracts from biographical and fictional works, both of which exemplify the narration of events from a child's viewpoint. Then she invited members of the class to tell anecdotes — chosen in advance — from their own early childhood. They can be illustrated from our fieldnotes: 'Catherine tells of pulling up flowers thinking they were weeds, getting into trouble so hiding in an old pram for three hours, mother being very angry when she found her.'

Mrs Wood, very confident in her relationship with the class, was able to give greater status to anecdote-telling by adding some of her own, which had an intimate quality that made her potentially highly vulnerable to rejection by the class. We are reminded of Bernstein's suggestion that one implication of what he called 'invisible pedagogy' is to make more of *the pupils*' private lives open to evaluation and to influence.[5] Mrs Wood responded to Catherine's anecdote with one of her own: she told in some detail of losing one of her own children on Scarborough beach, expressing her recollected feelings of rising hysteria. Later in the lesson she contributed an even more private recollection: 'My mother died when I was very small and I used to snuggle up to my father's back on the sofa . . . , I used to sneak into his bed and snuggle up to his back; it stood between me and the world.'

The style ('snuggle') and the domestic references define quite sharply a particular mode of dealing with experience; Mrs Wood's relation with this particular class was such that they could talk about experience in this way in spite of the public associations of the classroom. Here we have a domestic topic dealt with in a style of introspective self-awareness: the two together illustrate an extreme of what we call the private/personal mode of representing experience.

A wide range of topics and experiences was touched on during the lesson:

first day at school
a child's relation with an adult
childhood fantasies and punishments
compelling children to eat food
research on children's diets
children being lost by their parents
interest in astronomy
children as judges of character
difficulty of remembering childhood
effect on children of parents' quarrels
physical appearance of people as misleading
tolerance for people who are different
bringing up children
sex roles.

Although most of these were dealt with in a personal manner there was at the same time the frequent presence in what Mrs Wood said of a certain kind of rationality which was parallel to that present in lessons taught by other teachers. Such a lesson cannot be fully accounted for in terms of preparation for a particular examination. Both the close attention to the texture of personal awareness and the particular world-view are clearly valued by Mrs Wood for their own sake and, though they match with certain characteristics valued in English examinations, they probably go beyond what is functionally necessary to prepare for it. Mrs Wood was engaged in educating her pupils and not merely in preparing them for examinations.

At several points in the lesson certain of Mrs Wood's concerns were made more explicit. In response to a girl's anecdote about refusing to eat 'scrambled eggs for tea', Mrs Wood first provided a parallel instance from her own childhood, and then turned to the more general discussion of whether parents should compel children to eat. She elicited from the class that adults assume that they know best what is good for their children, mentioned some research on the effect of different diets, and ended with the idea that children should be given choices as a preparation for eventual autonomy. The topic was still a domestic one, but the mode had swung away from the anecdotal-personal to a public analytical discussion. Moreover, Mrs Wood clearly wished to communicate to the class her views on the upbringing of children. Later in the lesson there was a similar discussion of the unreliability of physical appearance in guiding our attitudes to people. People who were unusual or ugly in appearance may generate 'a shock of revulsion that is very quickly covered up'. Very clear messages were being sent to the class about the necessity for sensitive treatment of outsiders, on the basis of a self-critical awareness of one's own impulses. It was clear that Mrs Wood valued sensitivity to other people's viewpoints. Indeed, the whole of the lesson was a celebration in the romantic-liberal tradition of self-awareness and sensitivity to others. Preparation for an assignment had given Mrs Wood the opportunity to engage in the teaching of values; this is discussed more generally in section 7 of this chapter.

Although Mrs Wood provided us with this 'ideal type' of lesson, her views and her teaching at other times were both more complex and more various. In our interview with her the stress fell upon her pupils' 'willingness to take in new ideas'. She regretted that the examination created in her able top-set pupils so much anxiety and reliance on note-taking, since it was 'lively minds' that made pupils 'interesting to teach'. The nature of Mrs Wood's concern, however, came out obliquely when she talked about an occasion when some mothers complained about their daughters having been given a poem about abortion. She had said to them:

> Isn't it better for them (the girls) to be prepared and read a poem about abortion and for me as a representative of authority to stand at the front and say, 'I cannot think of anything more appalling for a teenage girl to go through than to conceive a child and have it aborted', then for us to (say), 'O that's not nice', and wrap it up?

This characterises well Mrs Wood's policy of tackling public issues in a way that brings out their implications for individual people, her combination, that is, of public topics, moral concern, and 'personal' treatment.

Although, from the point of view of our observer, Mrs Wood's lesson was an impressive display of skill and confidence in which the boys and girls of the top set took a lively part, we found when we talked to them that not all were enthusiastic about the personal approach. Sandra said, 'It was very hard but I enjoyed it in the end; you had to be very, very honest', but Catherine said, 'I prefer to keep my feelings to myself'. Simon did not like the prescription of topics for assignments: 'We did have one entitled "Myself", but the sort of things we put in it, it wasn't what I wanted to do really'. Chris said that he would rather make things up. Pupils' attitudes to personal writing will, however, be taken up in more detail in a later section.

Mrs Wood presents us with a relatively extreme example of personalising, yet she helps to characterise a view of the world which we have found to be strongly represented in English teaching. Experience centres on personal relationships with family and friends; high value is placed upon self-knowledge and sensitivity to others' perspectives in these relationships. The typical mode of writing derives from late 19th- and early 20th-century novels and autobiographies with their introspective concern with protagonists' mental states — how they suffer the world's blows. Experience tends to be decontextualised, or at most located in the family or peer group; when public issues are addressed they are dealt with in terms of the texture of individual experience. It is as if our sole moral responsibility is to those whom we meet face-to-face. The liberal teacher's dilemma of how to cope with controversial and political issues in school is avoided by a concern for private areas of experience. The strategy was incisively characterised by Fred Inglis:

> Most English teachers, I suppose, teach from a mixture of personal writing, halting talk on tape, improvised drama, and Modern Short Stories, in the interests of a low-key individualism, a deep sense of personal helplessness in a pretty grim world, from which you rescue such meaning as you can from the intimate texture of your private life . . .[6]

He went on to urge that 'cherishing private souls is not enough'; English teaching 'cannot remain pottering in its own back garden and its private ethic'. English should return to 'the radical tradition', he concluded. Later we shall turn to Mrs Wood's colleague, Mr Austin, whose teaching had moved some way towards this ideal.

No other lesson in our 'preparing to write' sample was so extremely personal as Mrs Wood's. However, as Figure 3.1 shows, 16 other lessons displayed aspects of the personal. Not all of these were unambiguously personal, however. Mrs Brennan, for example, who had developed unusually warm relationships with many of her pupils in the top set at Downtown School, valued her pupils' experience highly, and spoke enthusiastically of the essays they had written about their earliest memories: 'I haven't enjoyed marking a piece of work so much for ages'. Her appreciation, however, seemed to be focused as much upon their skill with language as upon the intrinsic quality of the experience: 'Some of them have a lovely way, they do... they paint images...'

Two of the indicators of the private/personal approach were 'Teachers ask for the expression of feeling in writing' and 'The discussion takes off from the reading of a literary passage', and these will provide two convenient focal points for illustrating the characteristics of some of these 16 lessons. In ten lessons the teacher explicitly urged the expression of feelings as a valued aspect of writing. Mrs Sutton of Urban School spoke of what she had done as a girl upon returning from school:

> What do you do when you get home after school? Do you change out of your uniform? That always used to be what I looked forward to, perhaps because our uniform was a lot stricter than yours. That was the first thing I did when I got home, got out of that uniform into clothes that I felt were more me and not like all the other people at school, so that was a symbol if you like of being free of the discipline of school. I used to get into the kind of clothes that I liked to wear rather than those the school wanted me to wear.

Such precise identification of motives is not untypical of these lessons, though it is often the motives of characters in literature that are in question. Later in the same lesson, Mrs Sutton's concern with feelings was made explicit. After a lengthy commentary (mainly given by Mrs Sutton) on a group of topics that included 'My first experience of being away from home' she settled her (bottom) set to write, and moved about the room giving advice to individuals. To one pupil she said: 'No, what I want is not just the facts about... (omission) but your feelings, about your feelings when you left home'. Mrs Sutton was far from being a single-minded personaliser; in interviews and lessons alike she showed a marked concern that the bottom set should master orthographic conventions, partly through the use of exercises. In a lesson focused upon loneliness, Mrs Williams of Downtown School read an appropriate passage from a novel and then asked the pupils to 'describe the children's feelings'. Throughout the lesson feelings were emphasised: 'If you are writing about being alone what must you write about apart from your feelings?' and 'You yourself have been taken to jail... What would your feelings be?' This culminates in a direct challenge, 'How many of you think basically you're shy?' (We shall have occasion later to remark upon the pupils' response to this.)

In 11 lessons literature played a central part. When a teacher is introducing to a class a new topic for an assignment, the most frequent pattern is for the lesson to begin with the reading of several poems and prose passages that deal with the topic. Any discussion that follows is unlike that in literature lessons in that there is seldom any exploration of the meaning of the passages. It is tacitly assumed that the pupils have grasped the meaning and implications, so little or no time is allowed for them to penetrate deeper by rereading or discussion although the pieces chosen are often quite difficult; the implicit model of reading for these lessons seems quite different from that which shapes literature lessons. (This contrast between models of reading is explored in more detail in Chapter 5 on literature teaching.) Discussion frequently moves rapidly away from the poems or extracts to the topic itself, and it is at this point that anecdotes may be encouraged by some teachers. The reading of literature as part of preparation to write is not of itself a signal that personal responses are required; this must depend on the choice of literature and how it is dealt with. As we have seen, the reading of extracts in the context of writing is in fact a member of the cluster of characteristics round the private/personal approach though such lessons are not always highly personal, as some of the examples will show.

In our first example the pupils did begin with an admirable grasp of the text. Mr Callaghan of Urban School began his lesson with an exchange about the different attitudes to marriage of two characters in the play *Hobson's Choice* which they had been reading in a previous lesson, so they were able to join in with considerable interest and knowledge; for example:

T. What did Maggie compare courting to?
P. She said a buckle can make a shoe look nice but you can have a shoe without it.

After some minutes, however, Mr Callaghan shifted the focus of the discussion by asking:

T. If you get married does it mean wanting to spend all the rest of your life with that person?

Some of the pupils were not sure; their contributions included:

P.1 A lot of people just live together if they think they're not going to stay forever.
P.2 If you've no prospect of happiness you shouldn't get married to someone.
P.3 More people get divorced who marry young than those who marry at twenty-odd.

Although the discussion moved on later to other topics, most of it was similar to this. Typically it was concerned with people's motives, though with a strong tendency to generalisation, and a simplistic view of cause and effect. It was of considerable interest to many pupils, and might be said to display concerns and attitudes like those in the Problem Page of some magazines in answer to readers' letters, and indeed the teachers at Smalltown School did base a piece of work on the writing of such letters. This restricted but not irresponsible view of life provided a significant strand in several lessons with bottom sets; it would not be appropriate to quantify it since it merges imperceptibly into a number of rather different perspectives.

Another teacher, Mr Richardson, devoted almost all of his lesson to discussing poems and prose extracts. He led the discussion partly towards interpreting the texts ('. . . how fragile she is — "fragile" is the word I'd use, but "weak" will do. . . .') and partly towards relating the methods of presentation used in these literary examples to possible choices that the pupils (a middle set at Downtown School) might make in their writing. For example, the poem 'My Sister', written by a 14-year-old girl, was based on an extended metaphor that attributed cat-like characteristics to the sister; after pointing this out Mr Richardson asked: 'Have you any feelings about your own sisters or brothers that are like that?' This makes it unusually clear that the works of literature were intended to perform the function of model for the pupils' own writing. Similarly in discussing the passage from *Sons and Lovers* in which Paul Morel takes Clara home to meet his mother, Mr Richardson said:

> Thing I want you to notice in that passage, and you could try and capture it if you write something similar as part of your assignment, is the way in which the people in it think that they know what the other person is thinking but really they don't. Mrs Morel is sitting there weighing Clara up and thinking, 'I can sort her out; I'm stronger than her; she's no trouble'. And Clara's thinking, 'I expected something hard and cold, but she's quite a nice little woman really when she's chatting'. And Paul's thinking, 'They're going to get on very well together', and he doesn't see what's underneath it.

This perceptive commentary on the scene is worth quoting at length for several reasons. First, because it makes it entirely explicit that Mr Richardson is trying to communicate to the class skills which are essentially those of the novelist and poet, and to encourage them to practise these. In so doing he is undoubtedly making available to them some of the deep criteria appropriate to fictional and personal writing. Second, the passage illustrates once again the area of experience so often focused on in these lessons: what is being valued is sensitivity in face-to-face, particularly domestic, relationships, and insight into people's perspectives and motives. Those of us brought up on the particular sensibilities of the English novel tradition find it difficult to see this as a cultural choice, a choice, that is, from amongst alternatives. Here in Mr Richardson's lesson we can see this tradition being passed on to young people as part of their preparation for an examination.

Two lessons taught by Mr Squires of Smalltown School have to be accounted for differently. In one of them, a double period, the topic was 'War' and the time was devoted to reading poems and watching a film. In discussing these he seemed to be primarily concerned to help his pupils obtain access to the experience and attitudes which he believed to be available in the literature and film; the syllabus for English at the school included an emphasis on widening pupils' cultural boundaries. During the lessons his questions were confined to interpretation at a relatively literal level. ('Could there be an even grimmer meaning in "Time died smiling"?' and 'Can anyone give me a phrase or word perhaps that indicates just how unpleasant this death was?') Learning to read a poem is not just a matter of responding to something objectively present in it: literature can only become meaningful if interpreted in the light of a complex of cultural beliefs, concerns, attitudes, assumptions and values. Mr Squires' lessons may have presented to pupils appropriate cultural complexes, but unlike those in other lessons his were not focused upon personal versions of experience.

To avoid oversimplification in describing the functions played by literature, it should be made clear that when works of literature are read in these writing lessons the following strands can be identified. The reading and subsequent discussion seems on various occasions to function:

i. To communicate attitudes and values
ii. To display material that can be used in the writing
iii. To provide a model of style and content for imitation
iv. To encourage a reflective attitude towards experience
v. To provide a 'virtual experience' of value in its own right
vi. To be an occasion for literary critical analysis

It is the first three of these that predominated in the 18 lessons in question, and the effect of this is not only to define implicitly preferred genres of writing but also to place value upon a highly personalised view of experience. With the exception of Mr Squires' lessons, the function of literature in the teaching of writing seems to be the establishment of a pre-emptive framework which offers to young people models of suitable content — as well as practical possibilities for the topic in hand — and with them the particular voices, styles and perspectives that we have been attempting to characterise. Of course, the framework excludes other possibilities, at the same time strengthening and weakening the learners' control over what they write.

We had heard teachers elsewhere rejecting energetically what they called 'sociological English', and when in an interview Mrs Sutton of Urban School turned to this topic her remarks threw light on what seems an ideological struggle within English teaching. We had asked Mrs Sutton about 'general (social) issues' and she wished to make it plain that there are general issues that should not be called 'social'.

'You can discuss family matters, for example, that you wouldn't talk about in sociological terms.' Mrs Sutton went on to illustrate her point, but in a slightly ambiguous way:

> Last week I had a lesson with the fourth year about responsibilities at home, and who was doing what at home, how they felt about doing jobs at home, earning money and so on for doing their jobs, or having a right to live at home without giving anything to the family. Maybe that is sociological English. I hope not.

She justified her rejection by saying that pupils had already experienced 'this dreary kitchen sink stuff' in their middle schools, and needed more imaginative work. 'I think there should be a balance between this kind of issue and work based on literature for its own sake.' Mrs Sutton was not rejecting public topics so much as impersonal ('sociological') approaches to them; this would account for the uncertainty implied when she *hoped* the fourth year lesson was not sociological English. There seemed to be two elements in this rejection: first, a deliberate choice of a personal ('imaginative') approach to experience, and second, a belief that literature should be read 'for its own sake', not contextualised in a thematic discussion. Mrs Sutton was far from being an extreme personaliser; her rejection of 'sociological English' on the basis of these two values is probably characteristic of a majority of English teachers. The link between personalising and an insistence on literature as a value in its own right is highly significant, in that for teachers like Mrs Sutton it is literature which provides apposite models for interpreting public issues through their impact upon individuals.

It might be expected that an emphasis on private topics and on writing as an exploration of the writer's unique response to the world would be accompanied by an eagerness to accept responsibility for 'the whole child', for young people's social and moral attitudes as part of the context in which writing abilities are developed and refined. As we shall see, many English teachers do act as if the transmission of values were part of their responsibilities, though in informal discussions we found them very cautious about accepting a wide-ranging 'pastoral' responsibility for their pupils. Mr Callaghan of Urban School said firmly, 'We think we're catering for the whole man and we do no such thing'; Urban School department was, however, one of the three schools which tended to be less than wholehearted in participating in the 'progressive consensus'. Yet even Mr Squires, whose syllabus at Smalltown School at times came near to presenting English as cultural rescue-work, was sceptical about 'nourishing the poetic function' with boys in lower streams. It was he who directed our attention to a complex issue related to the part played by personalising in classroom control with those pupils for whom distant examinations are not a sufficient inducement. In establishing 'the correct working atmosphere and relationship' with his middle set pupils he thought it necessary to 'give as much variety as possible . . . to make appeals as personal as possible, to bring in individuals as much as you can . . .' He had earlier said, 'The lower down the ability scale I go . . . the more emphasis I put on narrative writing and on personal writing — (exploration) of personal issues, personal behaviour and experience'. However, Mr Squires did not make it plain whether he varied his approach in this way primarily because he saw personalised approaches as less intellectually demanding, as more acceptable to his pupils, or as appropriate to classes not being prepared for a literature examination. One or two (male) teachers occasionally engaged in vicarious participation in teenage culture by expressing a knowing acquaintance with under-age drinking, sexual activities, and such mild dishonesties as travelling on buses without a ticket. Nor was this only a mark of the less secure teacher. It appeared to be part of an attempt to lower the boundaries between teenage/out-of-school culture and English/in-school culture that would be an expected accompaniment to an ambition to penetrate more deeply into pupils' sense of themselves and their place in the world.

We have already noticed that there is a connection between the assessment of coursework and an emphasis on personal writing. For Mr Gilham, a young man in his second year of teaching at Catchwide School, it was the requirement to write assignments that had helped him to control the pupils in his bottom set: 'I'm eternally grateful for the CSE coursework which has to be done in stages over the year, because I do find that that keeps their interest and is one of the few things which enables you to insist (on writing) because they examine it all for the exam.' It is significant that all of the assignments he set were highly personal, whereas the tendency in the Catchwide department as a whole was away from the personal.

Beside Mr Gilham's and Mr Squires' remarks we must set several contrary indications. Not all teachers perceived personalised English to be only suited to the less able, as Mrs Wood's teaching of her high-ability group showed. Later in this chapter (section 8) we will produce evidence from interviews with pupils that more of them disliked writing on personal topics than liked it; moreover, it was less popular in the lower sets, not more. Evidence from lessons is ambiguous. Mrs Wood's top set joined in her lesson on 'Myself' but many — as we have seen — were privately unenthusiastic. Mr Callaghan's group talked about their own concerns when they were protected by the anonymity of the characters in a play. So did Mr Austin's bottom set at Smalltown School, but in the manner of chorus to a raconteur. Several teachers, Mr Richardson (teaching a middle set) and Mrs Sutton (a bottom set), received restricted contributions from pupils. Mrs Williams of Downtown School, a young teacher with limited experience of English teaching, met an extremely unco-operative response from her bottom set. She began one typical lesson by reading literary extracts, a passage from *Walkabout* and an autobiographical passage expressing an author's sense of exclusion when as a boy he watched from the bank other boys' horseplay in a canoe. The pupils had little to say about the two passages, perhaps because they needed longer to get inside them, and even less to say when pressed directly to express personal experience or to reflect on themselves. Mrs Williams said: 'He's envious of any group of people . . . There are people about him but he doesn't feel he can make friends . . . He is taken about by his family, or he's too shy to make friends. "Never 'as owt to say for 'imself." What would you think of somebody who was too shy to respond to overtures . . . ?' And went on to ask: 'How many of you think basically you're shy?' No pupil responded and one boy who was eventually addressed directly rejected the idea vehemently. When asked to describe the feelings of persons in the passages read, the class offered only single words in reply: 'lonely', 'eccentric'; and, similarly, when asked about the emotions of people in imaginary situations they suggested, 'sadness', 'resent', 'helpless', 'desperate' and so on. In this class there was resistance to the teacher's attempt to break down the boundary between school and private life, which became almost overt at one moment when Mrs Williams asked, 'What was he (the narrator in the second passage) like?' and one boy — the one who had refused to admit to shyness — replied sotto voce, 'Thick'. The pupils rejected this direct approach to their private experience, and this, according to Mrs Williams, was typical of her relationship with this class. In sum, the emphasis on personally relevant learning cannot be persuasively accounted for in terms of classroom control, even though it may at times perform that function; it is far more deeply embedded in the sub-culture of English teachers.

Older pupils are not always very ready to accept the goals of the curriculum as valuable, realistic and relevant. By the fifth year they have views about the world they will go out into, their own likely roles in it, and the likely relevance to it of various parts of the curriculum, including the version of English which they have experienced. Though some accept the goals of English as worthy of their efforts, others see writing — at least in the form they have experienced it — as irrelevant (see section 8). Whether or not their view is a just one, it affects what they do in school.

It would be quite inappropriate to complete this section without illustrating from written work done by the classes we were observing what is meant by 'private' and 'personal', and the problems that some — perhaps many — young people have in achieving work likely to satisfy their teachers. Of the several hundred pieces of writing which we read and took notes on, we have full copies of 98, and it is from these that the examples used below have been taken. The following, written by a girl in a bottom set, is perhaps typical of what teachers are hoping for when they set such a topic as 'Jobs I wanted as a Child', though not typical of what they receive. (What follows is an abbreviation of the first paragraph.)

> I think My Very First Job I wanted to do as a child, was to be a mother . . . , I used to feed the babies, wash them then put them to bed. At a night time I would put five dolls in my bed. I used to shout at them and spank them if they started to cry, or would not eat. I used to pretend I was taking them to my aunties house and I would make them up special. I copied everything my mother did to me, and I used to do it to the dolls. I felt really good because I had someone to look after. I wanted to be just like my mother, and I felt grown up.

What defines this as 'personal' is not merely a topic which directs attention to private experience, but the author's reflective reinterpretation of experience; the task is used as an opportunity to reconsider and reshape personal history; 'to come to terms with experience' is the phrase commonly used by writers on English teaching. In particular she tries to express the feeling tone: 'I felt really good . . . ' and 'I wanted to be just like my mother'; we have seen from the lessons that requests for this are typical of the personal approach.

Another characteristic commonly valued is the provision of realistic detail which serves to substantiate the author's implicit claim to a meticulous truthfulness to the texture of experience. Such detail has been a commonplace in an English novel tradition stemming probably from Dickens. Though a frequent accompaniment of autobiographical writing it does not necessarily lead to introspection, as the following passage illustrates. The writer, a boy in a top set, describes a visit to his mother in hospital; he found her asleep.

> I pulled up a chair and opened a plastic carrier bag which I had been carrying. I took out a brown paper bag out of which I rustled some grapes. The flowers which I found in the bottom had been squashed and crushed by a bottle of Lucozade . . . It was at that moment that my mother woke, stretching and rubbing sleep from her eyes.

We have the private topic, the autobiographical stance, the detailed recollections, and the personal relationship to be explored, but the author makes of all this a screen behind which to conceal the feeling tone of the occasion. In satisfying the teacher's requirements yet keeping his private world intact he showed impressive skill as an author.

When we read this sample of essays our attention was frequently caught by uncertainty in the writer's adoption of a tone or persona. In writing for an unknown or imaginary audience about private or relatively private topics, young people find themselves faced with this dilemma: if their own everyday spoken style and perspective are not appropriate, where must they look for a voice to assume? It is a dilemma faced by every writer, but it becomes acute for 16-year-olds writing about private topics apparently for a public audience but in fact for a teacher with whom they may or may not be on easy terms. Here are some hints of their attempts at a solution.

The first is naïvely vulnerable, pitching his tone uncertainly, near to everyday speech:

> When I leave school sometimes in the future I hope to become an engineer. It is a very good job and you will get paid a lot also. But if I don't become an engineer . . . (bottom stream)

The next, also a boy, attempts a more generalising stance and a style further from everyday speech:

> In some shops you will meet some very rude assistants, they will totaly ignore you and stand chatting to their friends, and will not even appologise to you for the delay. When you are eventually served the assistant will speak curtly to you and even a protest to a high authority will go unheeded, as such an act will cause the assistant to become even more bitter with you. (top set)

This boy has an impressive repertoire of linguistic resources; he has dealt with the problem of tone by withdrawing into a generalising 'high style' that does not match well with the anecdotal subject matter.

The next example comes from what purports to be a realistic account of being snowbound. It begins:

> The snow fell heavily upon the full car as it hurried quickly to take us to Scotland. Visibility was poor and Dad had to strain his eye to keep us on the road . . .

and later continues:

> The car began to swerve gentle from side to side and I became a bit paniky. 'Ice', I thought to myself, 'Only ice' . . . (top set)

The author is pulled in two directions between alternative strategies, one leaning towards the colloquial and the other towards quasi-poetic fine writing. The latter tends to win, perhaps because it distances her from the events and allows her to take up conventional attitudes; the whole account reads like a fictional construction, not a reflected-upon anecdote, whichever in fact it was.

Very occasionally a pupil will attempt to solve the dilemma by an equally artificial display of aggressive sophistication:

> Teenage life, is, as most people put it, 'Alright', as I am old enough to go to the occasional Disco and get away with buying fags. I also like to get slightly pissed at parties . . . (bottom set)

Far from self-exploration, this is self-concealment. The boy's failure to solve the dilemma of persona shows itself not only in the choice of content but also in the uncertain tone; he is addressing himself informally to his teacher but attacking his sensitivities at the same time, daring him to disapprove. Personal approaches are a potential threat to teachers as well as to pupils.

Much more common was a flat lack of expressiveness. It might arise from failing to discover that written language can express attitudes, or from too restricted a repertoire of forms and rhetorical devices, or from withdrawal into a policy of minimal satisfaction of school demands — covering the pages with writing, and little more. It is impossible to discover from the writing itself when, if ever, the inexpressiveness is a defence against the demands of personal writing. In speech we express attitudes and emphases, indicate certainty or doubt in the strength of what we say, present ourselves as people engaged in what we have to say, all through tone, rhythm and gesture. In writing these have to be expressed through the choice and ordering of words, and some pupils whose control of the surface conventions of writing is good may never grasp that this is lacking from what they write, even in letters to friends. Here a girl imagines herself in a year's time:

> Its Monday and I get up at eight o'clock. I dress and have breakfast. Then I go out to get the morning paper. Then my Dad got up at eight thirty and when he was dressed we both went into the shop through the door . . . (bottom set)

The whole account is similar to this: there is no sense of presenting a version of oneself — a persona — to an imagined audience. Such inexpressive writing was very common amongst the work of the pupils in bottom sets. If it is based on a model it must be the elementary textbook which selects, simplifies and washes clean of emphasis and dispute. The models that these young people meet in newspapers and teenage magazines are very different, but would not be acceptable in school.

We end with two pupils who have found confident solutions to the dilemma, both of them — interestingly enough — from Mr Austin's top set at Smalltown School. The topic of the first one is 'Censorship', a public topic indeed, but treated by one boy in an interestingly personal way. Here is the third paragraph:

> The aspect of censorship that really annoys me is film censorship. Here we have a bureaucratic type system of a panel of people sometimes old, representing the opinions and making the decisions of a town. I would say its fair to assume that older people are bound to be shocked by nude erotic scenes, but why cut it out of society? It occurrs!

It will be noted that this is 'personal' in a quite different sense from that in which we have been using the word. Here there is no introspection into the texture of private areas of experience. The topic is public, but the writer is making explicit his own relationship to what he asserts: the thinking and judging self is placed centrally in the account rendered, persuading and evaluating but taking full responsibility for doing so. This is a stance that occurs all too seldom in these writings, and it may not be unreasonable to relate it to the encouragement Mr Austin gave his pupils during lessons to formulate and develop their views orally.

Here is a girl in the same class setting out on the topic 'The English Abroad':

> Let me begin by stating the obvious — we English are streets ahead when it comes to holidaying abroad. We're the ones who really make the holiday go. Its not Germans you'll find dancing on the tables in the beer kellers, but we English — throwing ourselves into the holiday spirit with gusto . . .

And she maintains it for nearly five pages. Now, in spite of 'me' and 'we', this is not personal; it is a display of middlebrow journalism of the kind once called *belles lettres*. It is the achieved 'voice' that is so impressive, light, uncommitted, witty, apparently engaged in a flow of informal chat but entirely detached, acting a part for an audience that wants nothing more than lightly mocking entertainment. Such writing, which is very infrequent at this level of skill, sets a problem for the prevailing private-personal ideology of English teaching. From a 'personal' perspective it is insincere, manipulating and entertaining its audience, not exploring the psyche or the social world. Yet it is undoubtedly highly skilful writing, almost publishable — on the right page in the right newspaper. And for us it points to one of the limitations of that perspective, that it devalues writing that is skilful but detached. Our impression from this study is that only a small proportion of fifth-year boys and girls use the opportunities for writing to explore and reshape their own experience; most of them, as we have seen, either retreat into the inexpressive or devise elaborate masks which enable them to demonstrate verbal skill without endangering their privacy.

In bringing this long section to an end, we reiterate the distinction between private topics — related to self, home, peer group, school and future work — and a personal approach to them. We have shown teachers implicitly recommending personal treatment of topics, and many pupils either avoiding this or becoming trapped in uncertain or inappropriate styles of writing. In the personal approach, the quality of first-hand experience becomes the measure of all things. This emphasis on the uniqueness of experience implicitly devalues concern with those whom we do not meet and with those public issues that resist personalising. Protestant, individual, romantic, this is the liberal's dream of transcending his own time: it goes with social deracination. Its advocates claim that in personal writing the writer is able through introspection to reorder experience, to observe new relationships, to assign meaning to the raw material of everyday life.

For some young people, perhaps only a few, it appears to do just that, offering them an unusual opportunity to value their own concerns, perceptions and experience in the midst of a school curriculum that for the most part rejects and devalues that experience, and ignores their ability to order and interpret the world. Because they are required to open some of the most private and vulnerable parts of their lives, many others cannot accept the opportunity. There must be other means by which the English curriculum can confirm their ability to make sense of the world without assaulting their privacy.

5. Narrative writing, especially fiction

One of the indicators used in the previous section to narrate the private/personal approach was the teacher's acceptance or encouragement of fictional writing. This is a paradoxical relationship: fictional narrative, though often told in the first person, need not be in the least introspective or expressive of the feeling-tone of experience. The inexpressive narratives quoted in the previous section show how far from personal such writing can be even when concerned with events of the kind we are calling private. Indeed, for many pupils it seems probable that this is part of the appeal of fictional writing, that it allows them to deal with areas of life that directly concern them, in their own experience or in fantasy, without committing them to public self-examination. This is because fiction can distance private experience from the self of the narrator, if he or she wishes, and because popular fiction provides voices and personae that can easily be assumed.

Narrative of any kind also provides a simple basis for sequence, and for this reason too is likely to appeal to pupils who are aware of having difficulty in non-fictional writing first in generating appropriate content and then in finding an appropriate structure for it. Narrative goes far in solving both of these difficulties, and for this reason this section refers to narrative as a whole, and not just to fiction.

Teachers' attitudes to fictional writing proved to be somewhat ambiguous. In 12 of the 29 lessons which were concerned with writing it was either implied or said explicitly that fiction would be acceptable. Fictional writing is always possible in English Language examinations at this level, GCE O-level, CSE, and 16+. In the papers set in 1979, for example, in most cases from one to three of the topics set asked for fictional writing, and in all papers there were topics which did not specify the mode of writing required, and which could therefore be satisfied with fiction.[7] Both teachers and pupils saw stories as easier to write than any other prose genre;[8] many pupils choose the fictional mode whenever they are allowed to do so, so teachers from time to time nominate a topic for 'discursive' treatment, that is, not narrative. Discursive writing tends to be seen as real work, in that it requires knowledge and possibly rational argument. Lessons show that rational argument implicitly holds a high place in teachers' estimates of the value of writing.

Of the teachers we observed only Mr O'Donnell of Catchwide School and Mrs Williams of Downtown School said that they emphasised story writing, and this with less-able pupils whom they found unable to write at length in other modes. The other two mentions of fictional writing were by Mr Callaghan of Urban School and Mrs Brennan of Downtown School: Mr Callaghan said that he did not emphasise story writing. Mrs Brennan's remark was in response to an explicit question about story writing predominating in the assignments; she replied that this was true of her work with CSE groups, but that with her present top (GCE) set, although she set more 'imaginative' assignments, she had no difficulty in finding pieces of 'discursive' and 'descriptive' writing when she wanted to include them in a coursework folder. An inspection of the first 12 writing topics set by Mrs Brennan to her top set suggests that nine could be satisfied by a narrative, and most pupils whose work we read had taken this opportunity. The exceptions were: a descriptive piece on 'Wind and Weather', a persuasive argument 'Against Smoking', and a review of a theatre visit. Mrs Brennan mentioned 'Capital Punishment' and 'Teenagers' Rights' as non-narrative topics set later in the year. In one case, 'Commercialism at Christmas', she had given way to pressure from pupils to allow a fictional response. She commented to the researchers that 'they do tend to be better at them' (i.e. stories).

Mrs Brennan's treatment of the topic of 'War' throws light upon the status of fictional narrative in some English courses, in particular those examined by the assessment of coursework. In a lesson which will be illustrated in a later section (pp. 121–22) Mrs Brennan gave an impassioned account of the horrors of war, based on Wilfred Owen's poems and some other literary texts. When she discussed the assigned piece of writing she said, 'Write a realistic piece on the topic of war'. Although napalm had been mentioned in one of the poems read, it seemed implicit that World War I was intended to be the focus. Our fieldnotes read:

> Day in the life of a soldier in the trenches. Can put character in war situation. . . . Nurse or doctor . . . folks back home. Can do diary entries — soldier's, mother's . . . *Or* letters home . . . series to soldier and return. Not limited to simple story.

In answer to a pupil's question Mrs Brennan added: 'Diary — put down thoughts not what you did in the day.' The predominant expectation was of fiction, though not necessarily of consecutive narration. At the same time this lesson shows how fiction can become the means by which public topics are treated in a personal manner, for the more impersonal ways in which war might be considered, presented and discussed were hardly mentioned.

Although some of the writing which came out of this assignment achieved passages of imaginary exploration of the suffering of war, it also allowed for more superficial kinds of writing. One girl who told a story of a newly married couple separated by war fell into an undemanding novelettish mode:

> Sam and June had been married for almost a year. They hadn't had a great deal of money when they were first married, so they lived with Sam's parents . . . (top set)

The narrative continues its untroubled way through the husband's death and loss of their baby, and implicitly raises questions about the purpose of teaching writing. This pupil writes adequate prose, but fails to penetrate beneath the surface of experience; it seems trivial to focus English teaching on the production of acceptable discourse without involving far more of the boy's or girl's abilities, including cognitive, imaginative and ethical elements.

Not all fictional writing was either as naïve as this nor as flat and inexpressive as some already quoted. Quite a number of pupils in middle or bottom sets are impressively able to adopt the style and mannerisms of popular fiction:

> Jane sat on her bed the coffee was spilt all over the bed and floor. . . . The books were thrown on the floor . . .
>
> Jane sat there looking out of the window. All she could see was an old brick wall that was falling down.
>
> Everything was going wrong for her nowadays . . . (bottom set)

The story was rounded off with an ironical twist and a sentimental reunion with Jane's mother. Apart from intermittent fullstops and some misuse of paragraphing the literary skills shown are impressive, leaving the reader in some uncertainty whether or not the mechanical externality of the narrative was relevant to assessing its value as a piece of writing.

The obverse of such writing appears in pieces where the writer is imaginatively engaged but lacks the literary skills to make the quality of that engagement available to the reader.

> Every year the Fifth Form of our school has a race. It is a race using machines, which are handbuilt by the pupils of the Fifth Form. The machines in question are karts, not the type with a bit of string for a steering mechanism, but the type with a 'two hundred and fifty c.c.' engine . . . (top set)

The events of the tale show the author to be naïvely involved in his fantasy, but his account is no more than bare statement of a series of actions. Apart from his failure to use those devices which make for rhetorical cohesion, his control of written English cannot be faulted. Indeed his prose would be admirable for the technical purposes for which — judging from the interests shown in this piece — he is most often likely to use it. In terms of the expressive values implicit in the private/personal approach to English teaching, however, such work is a relative failure.

So far we have been illustrating skills qualified by inadequacies, but many children write very impressive stories. It is not always easy to show their virtues by brief quotation. One girl picked up precisely the attitudes and concerns of novels such as Stan Barstow's *Joby* and utilised them to create a tale of warring gangs of small boys. At the end one gang was dangling the youngest member of another over the parapet of a railway bridge. (His 'medals' were milk-bottle tops.)

> 'listen' shouted one kid 'listen, can ya hear it, it's a train, a bloody train; pull him up, quick'.
>
> They were all frightened now, even the Englands. 'Pull him up, I can see t'train.'
>
> They all rushed forward to help, the train was close. They pulled with all their might.
>
> Suddenly it was all over. The train had missed the younger by a foot and he was crying
>
> 'I've lost me medals' he whimpered.
>
> 'Never mind' said the General 'We'll give ya another'. (top set)

Although by this point in the story the author's punctuation has become uncertain, her control of this quasi-naturalistic literary mode and her timing of incident, dialogue and comment are faultless.

A few boys and girls of this age are, however, capable of writing short stories that are fully comparable with adult writing. One begins like this:

> Billy sat on his father's knee, his back bent, picking thoughtfully at his shirt-buttons; Aunt Pol was talking to his father while she did the washing. They seemed to like talking to each other, thought Billy; after all, they were sister and brother. He thought back two Saturdays to the first time his father had come — the first time Billy had met his father. It seemed terribly long ago, yet very vivid in his mind. Ever since his aunt had mentioned his father, two years since, he had very much looked forward to seeing him . . . He felt it would cause a change, and at seven years of age he felt the time was ripe for a change . . . (top set)

The control of tone, shaping of sentences, the interlinking within the paragraph and the hinting at themes for the story, all are masterly. This is the kind of reward for their efforts that most English teachers look for, since behind the control of language can be detected a particular kind of interest in people and their perceptions: these are the goals to which private/personal approaches are heading. That is, such approaches lead more to fictional writing than to autobiographical-reflective modes, though this last quotation was chosen partly to show how the two can merge.

When the sample of written work was analysed (Table 3.2) it turned out that in 'Examination paper' classes there was little difference in the amount of personal writing and fictional writing done, 16 per cent and 14 per cent respectively, though the two together amounted to nearly a third of the writing done. In contrast, the amount of fictional writing done in the 'coursework' classes was proportionately much greater (and absolutely very much greater). In the latter classes 50 per cent of the writing done was fiction, and 23 per cent was personal, giving a total of 73 per cent, more than two-thirds of the writing done. The dividing line between fiction and personal writing is indistinct. Much fiction, as we have seen, is essentially personal in its focus, even though externalised by the use of fictional characters. An unknown proportion of personal writing is in fact made up, as one or two of the pupils explained to us. It is less important to distingush the two than to grasp how large a proportion of the writing done in fifth-year English classes falls into the two categories, something over half of our sample.

We shall illustrate later a remarkable lesson taught by Mr Austin to his bottom set at Smalltown School. His themes appeared to the observer to be poverty and the rights of the impoverished, though talk in the lesson touched upon a wide range of topics. It was not until the following lesson that it became clear that Mr Austin was preparing his pupils to write a story of a boy from a poor family who was resisting authority. He did not expect his pupils to bare their souls in writing; their written work was allowed to remain within the safe limits of fictional stereotypes. The virtue of fiction for such young people is that it can offer them a literary mode — *Cider with Rosie*, *To Kill a Mockingbird*, *Joby* — that they can adapt to their own ends, and by accepting these adolescent voices enable their pupils to explore their real or imaginary worlds without the need to adopt a more distant persona. Mrs Brennan was one of the most successful teachers in terms of examination results. As we have seen a large proportion of the writing done in that class was fictional, and much of it showed admirable sensitivity to people and skill in using words. If Bourdieu's treatment of the knowledge of deep criteria (which he calls 'style'[9]) as cultural capital is correct, examination by coursework enables working-class pupils to do themselves justice in fictional and quasi-autobiographical modes of writing when other modes are more inaccessible to them.

6. Impersonal modes of writing

During the initial interviews with teachers we asked questions about their emphases in teaching, about their conception of the ideal pupil, and about individual pupils in their classes. In their replies all 17 teachers included phrases from which it is possible to infer the values with which they approach the teaching and assessment of writing, though the fact that the fullness of the replies varies greatly from teacher to teacher must be taken to limit the usefulness of this evidence. This data was not structured by the interviewer, and in many cases was not offered as a statement of values. Table 3.4 indicates how frequently each value was referred to.

Table 3.4

Teachers' espoused values for writing

	Teachers	*Relevance*
1. Orthographic conventions	10	All writing
2. Vocabulary	5	All writing
3. Confidence	2	All writing
4. Structure and planning	7	Impersonal writing
5. Logical argument	4	Impersonal writing
6. Clarity	3	Impersonal writing
7. Awareness of ideas	2	Impersonal writing
8. Abstract or reflective thought	6	Impersonal writing
9. Ability to make value judgements	4	Personal or Impersonal?
10. Originality and imagination	7	Personal or Impersonal?

Although it would not be useful to attribute very precise meanings to these categories, there does seem to be a heavy emphasis on the characteristics proper to impersonal writing. There was some tendency for references to value judgements to occur alongside those to originality and imagination, which seemed usually to refer to personal writing or fiction. The choice of the word 'reflective' in some cases in category 8, and the references to 'value judgements' (and also sometimes to 'self criticism') may imply that the writing which moves from narrative/personal towards reflective/analytical modes is valued highly. However, the seven references in the 'originality and imagination' category seem insignificant beside the 22 references in the 'impersonal' categories (27 if the value judgements category is included). Thus we can say that in the interviews the teachers showed a predominant concern with the rational aspects of writing.

Ten of the 17 teachers mentioned some aspects of written conventions, but inspection of the data could produce no evidence of any alternation between written conventions and the mention of other values. It is likely that all English teachers consider written conventions to be important, though some give them greater prominence than others. It is interesting to note that though punctuation and spelling were frequently mentioned in this category, only one teacher mentioned paragraphing as a convention to be taught.

The discussions with the teachers from Urban School were characterised by an emphasis on impersonal kinds of writing, and similar emphases were found in the syllabuses from Catchwide and New Suburbia Schools. Mr Squires, head of department at Smalltown School, believed that 'there are occasions when writing has got to be de-personalised' and that it did pupils a disservice if all writing was 'extremely subjective'. Mrs Brennan of Downtown School responded to a passage about 'the poetic function'[10] by reasserting the importance for less-able pupils of being able to 'apply for a job and write a letter'; this matched what the teachers from Urban School said about 'formal' writing. Mr Tremaine, head of department at Greentown School, rejected the passage more vehemently, saying that it was 'total rubbish' and 'typical of the mid-sixties English teachers' arrogance'.

It will be remembered that of the 29 lessons observed 16 had shown signs of a leaning towards personal writing; indeed this bias dominated our subjective impressions of the lesson observation as a whole, particularly in Smalltown and Downtown Schools, and to a lesser extent at Urban and Greentown Schools. It is not easy to interpret this evidence of personalising in lessons and the teachers' assertions of the importance of impersonal forms of writing. If the latter had appeared only in the post-observation discussions it could have been accounted for as a kind of retrospective repairing of personae by teachers made aware of a difference between aspiration and reality. However, as we saw, a similar emphasis appeared in the pre-observation interviews, so this explanation cannot hold. Nevertheless, for some of our teachers it is true that there is a discontinuity between our classroom observations and their assertions of purpose: it is particularly true of Mrs Sutton and Mr Callaghan of Urban School. Several explanations are possible: teachers may — as some syllabuses assert — set a range of tasks from personal to impersonal and we may have seen more of the former. Why might this be so? Could some of the teachers have biased their selection of lessons because academic educationists are expected to prefer 'progressive' teaching methods? It is possible. Do teachers find pupils more co-operative when topics relate more directly to their own lives, and so prefer such topics when a visitor is expected? This seems unlikely, since we have evidence that many pupils dislike the personalised approach. It remains possible that there is a genuine gap between some teachers' ideal image of themselves and the strategies they find themselves adopting in the face of the exigencies of classroom and examination: this may be true of a few teachers at most amongst the 17 in the fifth-year part of the study.

The analysis of pupils' writing (Table 3.2) gave us a more objective measure of emphasis: impersonal writing amounted to 64 per cent and 34 per cent respectively of that done in examination paper classes and mixed mode classes, though the proportion fell to 24 per cent in coursework classes. There is some difficulty, however, in illustrating how impersonal writing is dealt with in lessons because much of this writing was done with little or no preparation, and in many cases was written as homework, so we found that few of the lessons we observed were concerned with impersonal writing, in spite of teachers' assertion of its importance. They did not, however, always mean the same kind of writing: sometimes they were referring, not to writing that engaged with public issues, but to that with narrow functional purposes. In Table 3.2 we divided impersonal writing into three categories: (i) *belles lettres*; (ii) impersonal treatment of public topics; and (iii) letters, and these will now be discussed in turn.

The *belles lettres* category includes those pieces of non-fictional writing in which it is the writer's intention to present to the reader a pleasantly entertaining persona without touching upon issues of private urgency or public importance. (A few pieces written to practise particular styles or perspectives, such as three accounts of Lord Mountbatten's funeral written as if from three points of view, were also included here.) The model for such writing is middlebrow journalism of a kind more common a generation or more ago, especially in volumes of 'essays'. The genre survives in many English textbooks. Mr Keegan was using a textbook published in 1978, which dealt with writing under a series of headings that included: The Descriptive Paragraph; The Reflective Paragraph; The Imaginative Paragraph; The Introductory Paragraph; The Concluding Paragraph; The Light Humorous Essay; and which provided tasks of writing such paragraphs. The socio-literary values embodied in the approach can be judged from the following sentences which are taken from the paragraph given in the book to exemplify 'The Descriptive Paragraph':

> This puppy have I called the Lord of Life because I cannot conceive of a more complete embodiment of vitality, curiosity, success and tyranny. Vitality first and foremost. It is incredible that so much pulsating quicksilver . . .

What do pupils make of this verbal posturing? One wrote for another teacher on the topic of 'Fire' (a typical *belles lettres* topic):

> The flames looked like people running after you, shouting death, dressed in falmboyant clothing. The tips of flames looked like daggers, cutting in to everything. The trees which had been captured by the flames looked like mourners all in black. . . .

The girl who wrote this earned high marks; she had picked up some aspects of the manner, and had also learnt that it is possible to manipulate words so as to present oneself elegantly without risking commitment to anything of weight. We might surmise that from the pupil's point of view this offers her partial entry to the manners of an unfamiliar social milieu without threatening any penetration of her private life.

One of the pieces already quoted would have been categorised as *belles lettres*, the witty and inventive account of 'The English Abroad' (p. 103). In contrast with the passage on 'Fire' it is very skilful indeed: elegance and detachment are at a premium in such writing. While a few pupils are able to make use of the mode, many even of the more skilled writers achieve little more than a show of verbal dexterity.

> The market was a hive of activity, the people moving like worker bees from one stall to another . . . The clink of money and the shouts of traders' claims for their produce, as well as the ever present babble of the crowd, formed an unintelligible din that drowned out any lesser sound . . . (top set)

Many pupils told us that they liked 'descriptive' writing of this kind, which allows them to display their abilities without commitment and without endangering privacy. For an observer brought up on the personal approach there is something objectionable about writing of this kind; perhaps it is the combination of self-display with inauthenticity — the 'worker bees' and 'the clink of money'. Once again the dilemma about the boundaries of English is pressed on our notice; is it enough for teachers to encourage pupils to increase their control over language and turn aside from judgements of authenticity? Many, perhaps most, of the teachers who took part in the project would not think so.

Writing that we categorised as *belles lettres* accounted for 30 per cent, 22 per cent and 11 per cent respectively of that done in examination paper classes, mixed mode classes and coursework classes. At its best it reaches 'The English Abroad'; at its worst it leads to a mindless covering of paper. The latter was unfortunately a good deal more common in our data, many of the examples coming from New Suburbia School, where the teachers seemed to place less weight than most others on finding topics for writing that were acceptable to their pupils. For classes preparing for an examination paper rather than coursework it is reasonable to see *belles lettres* writing as a kind of depersonalised alternative which could deal in its detached way with any topic, public or private. Although unacceptable to those teachers who see writing as a means of self-exploration, for a substantial number of others it remains as an important alternative, perhaps because the triviality of many topics set in examinations does not encourage any more profound purposes.

The second mode of impersonal writing is that which deals with a public topic. Our analyses of examination papers and of the topics set by teachers (Table 3.1) show that public topics are undoubtedly set, though Table 3.2 shows that they are chosen by a minority of pupils (10–16 per cent of the writing done). This is confirmed by our interviews with pupils: nearly a sixth of them said, without being asked directly, that they enjoyed expressing their opinions. Almost all of these pupils were, however, in top sets; this kind of writing is not viewed with favour by pupils of average or below average ability.

Although there were — as we have shown — so many references in the interviews with teachers to the values and concerns underlying the teaching of impersonal writing, there was almost no direct reference to the teaching itself. (Once again no direct question on this was addressed to the teachers.) Because of this we shall turn first to the lessons.

The influence of impersonal writing on lessons proved to be strangely oblique. It was noticeable in many lessons — including those, like Mrs Wood's, which were notable for personalising the topics discussed — that now and again the teacher would adopt a strategy that seemed to be directed to teaching a form of reasoning. We were able to collect and categorise these; the most common forms consisted of (i) an insistence on pupils giving 'evidence' to support an assertion, and (ii) the analysis of a discussion in terms of 'points for and against'. The latter appeared to embody a conception of how to approach impersonal writing. This became very clear in a lesson taught by Mr Saxon to the bottom set at Greentown School. He said explicitly to his pupils '. . . I want to teach the principle of having two sides to an argument', and told them to:

> Put a sub-heading 'For and Against the Fifth Year': the columns needn't go more than five lines . . . When we make a point, pop it down either side of the middle line . . .

Later he explained the purpose of this:

> It's a sequence of paragraphs. Each point you make will become a paragraph, because you have a paragraph for each point.

Mr Saxon here seems to take the formal debate as his model of rational discussion. It assumes two opposing sides that can be supported or opposed by arguments which can be conceived of as a sequence of 'points'. It matches perfectly with what English teachers call 'discursive writing', essays in which a detached balancing of points is likely to be valued by an assessor. However, it would be unrealistic to dismiss it as merely the teaching of examination skills. Standing back from one's own thoughts in order to segment them as 'points' and to categorise them as 'for' and 'against' is a valuable preliminary to more subtle kinds of analytical thinking, and at the same time acts as a paradigm of liberal rationality, which is free to 'see both sides' of every issue and to engage in cool debate because unthreatened. This model of rationality turns even those topics that appear to be private into public ones. Mr Saxon's topics included, 'Marrying at Sixteen', 'Reintroducing Capital Punishment' and 'Fee-paying Schools'. The list looks like a typical set of O-level topics — though Mr Saxon seems to have chosen them himself — and Mr Saxon's way of teaching writing fits a similar pattern. (It is appropriate to note, however, that the previous assignment written by the class had been 'A Family Row' which had been treated in a fictional manner.) However, the class discussion of these topics was less rational than Mr Saxon would probably have liked, as his pupils were not always willing to join in his version of serious discussion.

As one would expect, Mr Saxon presented an impersonal view of experience in this lesson, which would be suited to the techniques of abstraction that he was trying to teach. In the previous lesson he had seemed to be primarily concerned to extend the range of their ideas, for intrinsic reasons rather than for examination purposes. He had played to the class a recording of a discussion from a local radio station about raising the school-leaving age, asking them to pick out 'points' as they listened. ('If you're writing an argumentative essay you want to pick out points' — that is, you *should* pick out points.) He asked a pupil: 'Karen, what do you think would be useful work experience?' and eventually received 'community work' and 'helping old people' as answers. He then challenged the value of this from the point-of-view of an imaginary parent coming to the school to complain, and received justifications from several pupils, such as 'He's learning to cope with outside life'. Episodes of this kind are not simply devoted to examination preparation nor to intrinsic goals alone since, though they are undoubtedly relevant to preparing a 'discursive' essay, they also embody reflexive thought of a kind highly valued in our culture. This other form of rationality appeared quite frequently in the lessons, and can be represented in this example from the same teacher: 'Don't just say "Rubbish!" Give us a reason.' Many English teachers make it part of their business to communicate to pupils the necessity of supporting statements of opinion; this will include conveying to them what counts as 'evidence' under these circumstances, another category that does not come from nature. This form of reasoning may be established more in literature lessons than in those we are considering.

Mr Saxon was unusual in the emphasis that he gave to the teaching of forms of reasoning, yet similar concerns showed themselves in other teachers' lessons (in 13 out of 29), usually in short episodes. One teacher spoke to her pupils about 'training your thoughts' though the subsequent lesson was more concerned with awareness of tone than with rationality. When attempts to improve the logic of pupils' thinking do occur, they are often subordinated to other goals of a more personal kind; rationality of one kind or another is an implicit goal for teachers who take a personal approach as much as for others, yet — with the exception of Mr Saxon — they showed little awareness of this. The fact that it is mentioned in only two of the four syllabuses and by one teacher in the discussions suggests that it does not have great salience in English teachers' models of what they do. For example, in the Fourth Form section of the New Suburbia School syllabus some mention of rationality appears in a heterogeneous list under the general heading of 'Language', a list that includes 'metaphor, simile, alliteration' and ends '. . . abbreviations; *definitions*; *logical thinking*; more difficult punctuation (brackets, hyphens)' (our emphases). The other mention of reasoning is a mere passing reference to 'thought maturation' in the Downtown School syllabus. Neither shows any sign of a considered and articulated policy. The only reference in the discussions occurred when Mr Keegan of Catchwide mentioned using de Bono's CORT materials[11] (intended for training in problem-solving strategies) in English lessons with third- and sixth year classes, and this was clearly a much more deliberate approach to rationality than the brief and extempore episodes we had observed. Rationality has a curiously half-submerged position in English teachers' self-awareness.

In several lessons, including Mr Saxon's, the teacher displayed a direct interest in the content suitable for an essay on a public topic, in contrast with the oblique concern with reasoning which has just been illustrated. We illustrate this with an example that differs sharply from Mr Saxon's in that the teacher was content solely to discuss relevant ideas and opinions and made no attempt to teach a technique for structuring an essay. In this respect it is more typical of the several other lessons which dealt with a public topic.

One of Mr Squires' lessons on violence and war was mainly devoted to the reading of literature; the other, which was quite different, provides us with another example of a lesson based on a public topic. He began by asking whether violence settled anything, and received an unexpected reply:

P.1 Er freedom to — On telly, when you get watched if they know who it is.
T. Yes, so um, what is almost certain to happen in the future, as a result of violence?
P.1 There's more action going to be taken against you.
T. More violence, is that what you mean?
P.1 Yeah, violence used with violence.
T. And it will go on and on . . .

This seems to be one of the occasions when a pupil's contribution recognisably introduced a new perspective, apparently through unawareness that in Mr Squires' lessons this kind of personal experience was *not* acceptable. Mr Squires wanted a generalising reply about violence solving nothing but received a response from the point-of-view of an individual caught up in violence. The teacher made a 'public' bid, but received a 'private' response, though he was soon able to reinterpret what his pupil had said by generalising it. Indeed, much of this lesson operated at a similarly public level. For example, the Tom and Jerry cartoon films were mentioned as possible to influence young children, and Mr Squires commented:

> That, I think, is a possible danger, that in a cartoon like that tremendous violence can be used. A cat may become a corkscrew and a second later of course perfectly all right. So it could — and this applies to you, Mark — it could mean people are becoming immune to violence, that they . . . they . . . forget the physical effect of it.

The discussion in Mr Squires' lessons was concerned with issues seen in general terms as detached from the subjective self-awareness of any individual. Subjective experience would be treated as relevant evidence: Mr Squires asked his pupils later in the lesson to write down answers to questions about violence in their own behaviour and attitudes, their replies were discussed in the general terms befitting violence as a public issue. Mr Squires offered to this middle set an education in the rational discussion of public issues. In spite of the fact that three of the private/personal indicators — one anecdote, signs of the intention to communicate values, and an explicit request for anecdotal writing — occurred in the lesson, the overall bias was undoubtedly public.

It will not be necessary to illustrate at length this mode of writing. Amongst the more successful pieces is the essay on Censorship quoted on p. 102 and a critical account of a play seen during a theatre visit. It is worth illustrating, however, the qualities that make for success. Compare these two attempts at writing about learning foreign languages:

> I think young people should learn a language other than there own because it can helpful if you wan't a job at a travel agency or a local representer. However, I think foreign languages should ('not' inserted later) be compulsory . . . (top set)

One can almost share the writer's agony in squeezing out sentences on this topic. Another boy in the same class wrote:

> Firstly, a foreign language would help one to increase one's understanding of foreign culture and could provide an insight into the structure of the native language as many words in the English Language are derived from foreign languages . . . (top set)

Why is it the second writer signals social confidence so strongly even in one sentence? What lies behind words such as 'style' and 'persona' which we have used previously? It is partly the technical vocabulary — 'culture', 'structure', 'derived' — and his control of complexity within the syntax of a sentence. But there are also social gestures such as the 'firstly', the use of 'one' as an impersonal pronoun, still acceptable in this kind of writing, and the mannerisms of academic prose such as 'provide an insight' — mannerisms that the authors of this report too are not unaware of using. The point being made is that the difference between the two pieces is social as much as it is linguistic, 'social' in the sense of the writer's ability to assume and maintain a role.

Although the third kind of impersonal writing was represented in the sample of pupils' work solely by letters, these are part of a much wider category. When we originally interviewed teachers several of them made us aware of an alternative perspective to the dominant personalising, though it was expressed in muted tones as might be expected from teachers aware of being in a minority. Three teachers — Mr Keegan of Catchwide, Mrs Waterhouse of New Suburbia and Mr Saxon of Greentown — all expressed an interest in what one of them called 'functional' writing. These teachers seemed to feel that the current emphases in English were not well matched with the needs of some of their less-able pupils, and their alternative emphases were intended to match these needs. (It should be noted that Mrs Waterhouse and Mr Saxon were teaching bottom sets in the fifth year, and Mr Keegan had for some years taught less-able pupils.)

Let us begin with functional writing as the teachers themselves presented it to us in interviews; in each case it was the teacher who raised the matter. Mr Keegan wanted an unexamined course for pupils who were not interested in a qualification:

> I'd like to make the course for those people more practical, (but) more related to the functional use of language like filling forms, reading telephone directories.

He continued: 'There are all sorts of things we don't do . . . newspaper language, Radio Times and television programmes . . . ' which seemed to refer to something rather different from 'functional uses'. Mr Keegan acknowledged that it was possible to deal with these in the existing CSE course 'but in practice they tend not to get done'.

Mrs Waterhouse seemed to have something similar in mind when she said that instead of an essay she would like to see in the examination 'a more factual piece of writing where they're asked to communicate a set of instructions, or writing a letter'. Elsewhere in the interview, when explaining her aims for the bottom set she included 'a simple sort of factual expression, a system of notes'. When she said, 'the actual essay, story writing, I honestly do not see the point of' she appears to have been implicitly rejecting the personalising tendency that many other English teachers were committed to, and this rejection was reflected in the lessons we observed her teach.

It is not clear from what Mr Saxon said how far he would have agreed with Mr Keegan and Mrs Waterhouse. The following quotations from his interview should be read in the context of an account of thematic teaching which has yet to be described (see p. 145) and which contrasts with the views expressed here. It seems possible that Mr Saxon, unlike Mrs Waterhouse, was willing to accord some value to both personal and impersonal modes of writing. In an unmistakably self-deprecating tone he referred to 'this young liberal approach of "I am making you better citizens, I'm making you more effective operators in the outside world" '. And when he was rejecting essay topics such as 'Childhood Memories' he said that he looked for 'material that was relevant to (the pupils) on their way out into the world', referring for an example to their part-time jobs. It is interesting to note that both Mr Saxon and Mr Keegan were late entrants to teaching; the former had worked as a journalist and the latter had been in the army. No doubt these other experiences had decreased the strength of their literary studies as a source of values.

Mr Saxon said that the ideal examination for his bottom set would include both 'some kind of self-presentation' and 'different English skills, like imparting information, or instruction', and he went on to provide a useful illustration of the latter:

> The comprehension exercise for me wouldn't be something from *My Family and Other Animals* but would be something like, 'Your father is a very busy man. He's asked you to go into the pro's and con's of fitting seat belts to his car', or something like that.

Mr Saxon appeared to be dichotomising writing tasks into two categories which correspond roughly with the extremes of the private/personal and public/impersonal dimensions, and to wish to give more emphasis to the latter than many other teachers did. It is worth noting that in his example the impersonal task had been contextualised in the manner of writing tasks in Communication Studies. (The value of this last evidence must be qualified by the admission that Mr Saxon may have believed that the person interviewing him was committed to this approach, and that none of the work we have seen, or heard being read aloud, by Mr Saxon's pupils fitted this pattern.)

It can be seen from the remarks made by Mr Keegan and Mrs Waterhouse that one aspect of this instrumental view of writing is an emphasis on literacy skills that can be practised in separation from continuous writing; those departments preparing pupils for examination papers tended to make considerable use of textbooks. This led — particularly in New Suburbia — to the expenditure of a great deal of pupils' time on exercises; our concern in this paper is with continuous writing, however. A surprising amount of letter-writing was done in the classes we observed, rising to 18 per cent in the case of the examination paper groups. Almost all of these letters were applications for jobs, the exception being an assignment on letters of complaint about faults in goods or services provided. This emphasis on letters could not be accounted for solely by examination paper demands: only one of the examination papers that pupils were to sit contained a compulsory task in impersonal writing, and this was not always a letter. We might surmise that teachers and pupils alike value social relevance, and the 'business letter' stands as a — very inadequate — symbol of this. Teachers seemed eager to display to us the lessons in which they taught letter-writing: perhaps they valued the security of transmitting surface rather than deep criteria, though in one interesting lesson a top set pushed an unwilling teacher into some discussion of tone and content. Both teachers and pupils saw this work as relevant to real life; from a different perspective one might relate it to learning how to carry out some aspects of a subordinate role in our economic structure. (In this respect, however, these lessons were a pale and ineffective equivalent of the socialising processes we found in colleges of further education.)

Mrs Sutton, the head of department who was teaching the bottom set at Urban School, spoke of a textbook whose exercises she valued because they were contextualised in apparently 'real life' situations and at the same time gave much needed practice in skills. She spoke of one section of the book which was based on an imaginary girl who had been caught shoplifting in a supermarket:

> There are various interviews with people involved, such as the store detective, her mother, and so on, and you have to write the evidence as to whether she was guilty or not. It showed you a map of her route to the supermarket, and you have to see how far that corresponds with what she said she did. And the social worker says a bit about her background, and the relationship with her mother is bad, and so on . . .

Mrs Sutton appeared to be justifying this contextualised task as a way of making work on skills 'more real' to pupils who in her view needed a good deal of it. However, she had earlier mentioned the same book, saying that it was 'the only one I know with the language work that we need' because the exercises involved the pupils in 'inducing opinions from facts given'. This suggests that she approved of the book more because it exercised cognitive skills she thought important for less-able pupils, while at the same time noting that it made English more acceptable to them by being contextualised in a situation they were willing to consider 'real'. (One wonders what impact television programmes have had upon adolescents' conceptions of 'real life'.)

Several other pieces of writing were set which did not quite match any of the three categories of impersonal writing, though they were included in the *belles lettres* group. Some — like the exercise outlined by Mrs Sutton — were an attempt to make writing tasks more real by setting them in an imaginary context; others were devoted to developing pupils' awareness and skills without any attempt to involve their personal feelings and commitments. Mr Tremaine, for example, after a discussion of bias with his top set at Greentown School, asked them to write short newspaper accounts of the same event from different perspectives. This was in line with what he said in his initial interview, though it relates more to 'substantial journalism' than to 'controversial themes'. (See p. 76.) The purpose of such writing is less to develop skills than to increase pupils' understanding of the effect of audience and the author's perspectives and motives on writing, which matches Mr Tremaine's stress on public and rational aspects of writing. Mrs Sackville of Urban School had her middle set write a Personnel Officer's Report about the character Billy Liar in the novel of that name. Such tasks occurred in the textbooks available in some schools; Mrs Sackville, who made considerable use of textbooks, set tasks such as analysing the programmes available on two radio channels and reporting the results in continuous prose. These tasks reach out towards the contextualising of written work in simulated 'real life' situations that has been taken much further in Communication Studies in FE colleges. They encourage the practice of writing detached from personal commitment, but their values and expectations are quite different from those implicit in the writing we are calling *belles lettres*.

The school sample of lessons included only one that appeared to be directed towards increasing pupils' awareness of the relationship of communication to context, though it became something different when the boys and girls began to write. Mrs Harrison of New Surburbia School was using a textbook which she justified to her middle set pupils as 'exercises like you'll get in 16+ to train your thoughts in certain situations'[12], thus combining an extrinsic and an intrinsic justification. The exercise involved the consideration of accounts of a road accident written from the perspectives of various participants. Discussion concerned both what information each would be likely to include, and the tone which each might appropriately adopt. For example:

T. Would the statement from B be in the same tone?
P. (Inaudible)
T. No, right, he's probably more on the defensive.
T. How would he act, in his statement . . . ?
P. He should have waited until the lorry passed . . .

(Although these fieldnotes make omissions they give the flavour of the discussion.) One of Mrs Harrison's comments precisely defined her concerns in teaching this lesson: '. . . Don't worry about the right or wrong answer; you've got to argue your case'. The focus was not on accurate content but on the mastery of skills; this is a long way from the private/personal perspective where what was most highly valued was subjective truthfulness to experience. Eventually Mrs Harrison set the class a letter-writing task which was precisely situated in an imaginary context: a girl, training abroad as a nurse, has asked a friend for the names of unattached boys as penfriends, and she then writes to one of them, or one of the boys writes to her. The emphasis in discussing the task fell upon appropriateness of content and tone, and here the relevance of the first part of the lesson became clear.

T. What tone...?
P.1 Friendly.
P.2 Impersonal.
T. What do you mean by impersonal?
P. You can't say 'I love so and so' at the end.

If Mrs Harrison in her attempt to teach the concept of appropriate tone was concerned with deep criteria, what one at least of her pupils drew from this was a surface criterion to do with conventions for closing a letter. (Surprisingly Mrs Harrison accepted this.) In the exchanges about the letters we once again have the antithesis of the personal: Mrs Harrison is endeavouring to teach writing skills and conventions in separation from particular content or cultural values, an approach much more common a generation ago. In the last section we shall discuss some implications of emphasising personal writing, skills and conventions, situated tasks, public topics or *belles lettres*.

7. Beyond deep criteria

This section is focused upon the transmission of values; first we shall display what happened in lessons and then briefly explore the teachers' perceptions of what they were doing. To give some idea of scale, it is worth saying that we detected episodes of value transmission in 11 of the 29 lessons, and other lessons not included in the 'preparing to write' sample had similar episodes. Some of these episodes were short, little more than an aside; others continued for much of a lesson. We were impressed by the diversity of the values being transmitted; in this section this diversity will be illustrated from lessons taught by six teachers.

Three lessons were concerned with war, the most frequent public topic. In one, although the explicit purpose was the preparation of an assignment, Mrs Brennan of Downtown School clearly wished to influence pupils' attitudes to war through the reading of Wilfred Owen's poems and letters, and of other texts in prose and verse. In particular she spoke with some passion about the passage in the poem 'Dulce et Decorum' in which a soldier dies in a gas attack. (The field-notes on this lesson are disjointed but give some impression of the style of her fluent presentation.) 'What's happened to the pride of man in death?' She used the word 'degrading' and explained it as 'degrading us for trying to kid ourselves'. Commenting on the ironical title of the poem, she said:

> Owen is saying: 'It's not like that... You must know what it's like... You couldn't possibly say to children it's sweet. It's not romantic; it's revolting and horrible'.

This part of the lesson seemed to be intended to shape pupils' attitudes irrespective of any relevance to an examination; and indeed the teacher's impassioned presentation had a visible effect on some of her pupils. One aspect of departmental policy at Downtown School was an emphasis on building pupils' vocabularies, thought to be particularly deficient, and Mrs Brennan incorporated the provision of appropriate words into her preparation of pupils for writing an assignment. Her commentary on the list of 41 words which she had written on the blackboard before the top set arrived for the lesson amounted, however, to something considerably more than the provision of vocabulary. (Some of these words appear in the following quotations from our fieldnotes, and have been underlined.) After reading the poems and letters and talking with some passion about World War I, Mrs Brennan turned suddenly to the lists on the blackboard and went through them systematically commenting on most of the words and linking them with the poems that had been read. (The following is a greatly abbreviated account taken from fieldnotes.)

> T. talks about Owen's state: 'numb': The poetry will be found in the pity, poetry that will last. (Quotes lines from 'The Send-Off'.) When they get back life's changed, they'd changed... were different people. So you get hypocrisy. The parliamentarians send people off to war... (etc.) Told lies to keep us fighting. Heroism, Indifference — you don't want to know. Survival, Beastliness; Owen likens the battlefield to an army dying of disease (Ref. to maggots): war is dirty and degrading. Grief — Owen feels for their grief, the people at home.

Although superficially Mrs Brennan is providing her pupils with appropriate vocabulary for their writing, this also amounts to a set of appropriate attitudes. It is as if Mrs Brennan — who is unlikely to have heard of Bourdieu — wished to provide her able working-class pupils in Downtown School with a repertoire of attitudes and evaluations which would be acceptable in a school assignment. It should be remembered (see p. 105) that much of the writing done as an outcome of this lesson was fictional, so that most of the pupils would not be using this terminology in an impersonal discussion of the nature, causes and results of war. This makes it hard to account for the presence in the lesson of this extended episode other than as a means of communicating attitudes and values to the class.

Mrs Brennan influenced her friend and colleague Mrs Williams, who used similar lists in lessons with a bottom set. Mrs Williams asked members of her class to suggest occasions when people might be lonely, and for each of these 'occasions' asked for words to describe it. For example, when a boy suggested 'In gaol' as an occasion for loneliness she asked for words to describe the cell, accepting 'dark', 'cold', 'isolated', 'square', 'small', 'just bed', 'little window', 'helpless', 'desperate'. Other situations suggested included running away from home, in hospital, old people without family; in each case the class was asked to provide suitable words, and did so, though with some resistance. Mrs Williams in an interview had mentioned her emphasis on vocabulary; in practice these episodes seemed to function at least equally as a means of communicating a range of stereotyped situations, with attitudes to match, that would be acceptable in an assignment. It is interesting to notice from these two examples that the stereotyping of subject-matter is equally applicable to public and private topics.

Another teacher who communicated moral values in the course of discussing writing topics was Mrs Sutton, head of department at Urban School. One lengthy episode concerned the importance of the family in our lives. I shall abbreviate Mrs Sutton's lengthy expansion of a pupil's contribution in order to illustrate her style:

> The people (you suggest) if you have a good relationship with your family they'll be closest to you, will know how you'll react to problems, they'll know when you need help. They've brought you up: they know you better than anyone else...

And later:

> ....if you have a good relationship with your family, it's quite likely that there will always be, somewhere, some people on whom you can depend. 'What is the most important thing that your parents have provided for you? What in turn do you think will be the most important thing to provide for your own children?'

(These two questions came from the textbook on which the lesson was based.) Pupils suggested first 'security' and then 'love', Mrs Sutton providing an extensive commentary on each of these, such as:

> It may not always look like that from where you stand, it may not always look as if they're behaving as if they love you, but what they do is usually in your best interests even though it may be difficult to see...

Mrs Sutton too was in effect transmitting values as an incidental part of preparing her pupils for the writing of an essay. This mingles in a characteristic way with her rejection of impersonal ('sociological') English and her emphasis on skills and conventions.

Mr Squires began one lesson with a sentence that was archetypal: 'I want to...um continue with the theme we were talking about on Tuesday and which you've done some writing about it and thinking about it since then on this question of violence...'

We saw two lessons taught by Mr Squires of Smalltown School which arose from the general theme of War and Violence. In one he read poems by Wilfred Owen to his middle set, but did not provide an interpretive commentary in the manner of Mrs Brennan. The other lesson dealt with football violence, and this did contain a number of episodes with an undeniable moral content. One of these episodes has already been quoted for another purpose on p. 115. Mr Squires, like Mrs Sutton and Mrs Brennan, held strong opinions on certain topics and was not unwilling to communicate these to pupils. After asking, 'What is in human nature that leads people to fight?' he accepts the answer 'aggression', and develops it:

> And when you are in a temper, when you're...em...in a highly emotional state you stop thinking sensibly and um... rationally, so there's no doubt that it's part of not only human nature but of animal nature as well that we've got these instincts of aggression within us.

Later he continued: 'Do you think we'd be as civilised as we are today without an instinct for aggression?' and linked this with primitive man's struggle to survive:

> ...some people have got a lot more aggression than others; to some extent it's nature, to some extent it's upbringing and circumstances of one's life.

My purpose in quoting this is not to approve or disapprove Mr Squires' model of human behaviour but to illustrate once again the wide range of purposes that an English teacher may pursue in the course of preparing pupils to write. Mr Squires was communicating these views to his pupils because he believed them to be true, not because he expected them to be reproduced in their essays.

Some of the English teachers' values were expressed in an almost unnoticeable fashion in the course of classroom discussion, particularly of private topics. We have already quoted at some length (pp. 89–91) Mrs Wood of Smalltown School, when we used her lesson on 'Myself' as our ideal type of the personal approach. Some of Mrs Wood's questions during that lesson asked for pupils' opinions; they were talking about bringing up children:

> T. What difference does it make if you're the eldest?
> P. In some ways it's harder, because when you start a family you have very strict ideas about how you should bring children up...

Other questions she asked, however, contained implicit in them answers that pointed to a particular opinion:

> T. Why is it bad for a child never to make a decision?
> P. Because it'll never be independent...

Most of the values implied in exchanges such as this second one are unexceptionable; it is only when we ask ourselves how strong the evidence is that decision-making is essential to children's moral development that we realise that the teacher is taking a moral stance.

This is true irrespective of whether we agree with Mrs Wood about this matter.

Episodes like these raise the question whether it is possible for a teacher to conduct discussion of value-laden issues without expounding or at least implying where he or she stands. The Humanities Curriculum Project recommended the stance of neutral chairman, but on the basis of a carefully prepared body of 'evidence', documents that would ensure that a variety of viewpoints were considered. In the absence of such evidence is it possible to ensure that alternatives are expressed if the teacher does not take on that responsibility? There were not many occasions in the lessons observed when anything of the sort took place. On one occasion, Mr Callaghan of Urban School, leading off from a play they had been reading, encouraged a rapid move from one topic to another — youthful marriages, the responsibility for pregnancy, marriage in church, parental arguments, and so on. The framework was unambiguously preparation for writing: 'I want to give you a wide variety of things you can write about', and much of the talk was in fact exchange of views:

T. What can cause that kind of argument?
P. Money.
T. Not giving her enough?
P. Not earning enough!

Unlike almost all of the other teachers, Mr Callaghan was not attempting to encourage his pupils to discuss logically, nor transmitting values, nor teaching techniques of writing; as he said, he was simply displaying a range of possible topics.

To find a more persuasive example of neutrality we have to go outside the lessons in which pupils were prepared for a piece of writing to a lesson in which Mr Tremaine led a discussion with his top set at Greentown, apparently for its intrinsic value. Throughout he was careful to remain neutral, even when the opinions expressed almost certainly contradicted his own. His style can be briefly illustrated from fieldnotes. At one point they were discussing the film *Holocaust* and pupils said that it was 'too gruesome' and that it 'went a bit too far'. Mr Tremaine probed for other views:

P.1 I think it's got to be shown.
P.2 You can't hide an event like that.
P.3 War's finished; we ought to forget about it.
T. (To rest of class) What do you think about that point of view?

Later he asked:

T. A lot of propaganda against war . . . Is there an argument for war?

(It must be remembered that these fieldnotes provide no more than an abbreviated version of what was said.) Mr Tremaine's teaching here seems in line with his declared interest in 'controversial themes' and in teaching pupils to express and criticise arguments (p. 76). He provided his pupils with an impressive model of a liberal interest in public themes combined with rational detachment, which seemed to go along with social poise and a certain aloofness from the more disturbing aspects of life.

Mr Tremaine's and Mr Callaghan's lessons were atypical, however. Most English teachers when they engaged in discussion are likely to be pursuing other goals as well. Giving pupils access to what to write about and how to write about it can easily be translated into attempts to influence their view of life and their values, and this may be inherent in the current literature-based version of English.

In the section on personal writing, we quoted (p. 92) from a passage in which Fred Inglis argued that 'cherishing private souls is not enough' and urged that English teachers should return to 'the radical tradition' of moral and social criticism. Mr Austin, who taught a top and a bottom stream at Smalltown School, was the teacher who came closest to acting upon this prescription. When he was teaching the top set he went further than any other teacher in trying to initiate his able pupils into the values and procedures of literary criticism: in those lessons he might be taken to represent both the kind of teaching we are describing as initiation and also the view that English is concerned with the continuation of a cultural tradition. Here we are to illustrate his teaching of the bottom set, the lowest of 11 streams, with pupils who had earlier been categorised as 'remedial'.

In the first lesson we saw he appeared merely to be talking informally about some things that interested him, loosely linking them together by reference to a conversation with a man met in a public house the previous evening. During the lesson, however, it became clear to the observer that his implicit themes were poverty and the right of the individual to fight back against the system, and that this was part of the preparation for writing a story. In the course of a lengthy narrative-cum-discussion, Mr Austin touched on a remarkable range of topics, including the rock group Steel Eye Span, learning Latin, black magic, Airfix models, the names of foreign tanks, the difficulty of getting a rebate on income tax, postal codes and a public swimming bath that was never built. Most of these topics belong at the public end of the topic continuum, but Mr Austin treated them in a highly personal manner. One underlying theme came through when Mr Austin asked, 'How many people tell me what to do?' and made a list on the blackboard. A generalising analysis was being formed out of the private particularities: being 'forced into a mould' was linked with income tax, postal codes, the numbers on driving licences, and the anonymity of being given a number in the army. It was in part a tour-de-force by a master of talk; yet the pupils joined in with some eagerness. Mr Austin's view of his pupils' world was far from the urban stereotype ('kitchen sink') that we observed some teachers of bottom streams to fall back upon. He actively opposes stereotypes and expects all his pupils to have wide interests; the pupils' enthusiasm shows him to be right. The peroration which concluded this lesson partly sums up his unusual values. (Here it has to be represented not in Mr Austin's own words but in the cold reduction of our fieldnotes.)

> I like the man in the pub because he was only twenty-one — teachers probably heaved a sigh of relief — but what was he doing? Thinking for himself, following a group no-one had heard, making models, mates probably mocked him but he kept on. Won £20. Looks like a punk rocker and yet sings traditional folk songs. Failure at seventeen, at twenty-one married, looking after wife, saving for baby, interested in all sorts of things. I want to bump into you in the *Prince of Wales* in six years' time and be as impressed by you.

This remarkable plea to the members of the class to resist the stereotyping that comes from institutional authorities and from the mass media, and to defend their autonomy and self-respect goes further than anything else we have ever met in English lessons. It was a kind of lay sermon, that through its celebration of the individual and its rejection of determinism became the apotheosis of liberal romanticism.

The second lesson was more explicitly concerned with preparing for writing, yet the story was still the occasion for reflection on life. By means of informal questioning and discussion Mr Austin gradually built up on the blackboard sets of notes relevant to the planning of the story. With the pupils' aid he first reconstituted the list of social authorities with power to constrain individuals. Next he elicited a notional income and expenditure account for the fictional family, this giving rise incidentally to some discussion of the problems of managing on a low income. Finally he led the class to make decisions about the members of the family who were to be the *dramatis personae* of the story. Mr Austin at one and the same time was modelling publicly for his pupils the processes of analysis, note-taking and planning, and also transmitting values. This became explicit at one point in the lesson when one girl who had not taken the message said, 'It's no good really us feeling sorry for 'em 'cos I mean it's them that get into that mess, int it?', and this drew from Mr Austin the reply, 'I've been talking for an hour . . . and Dawn has cut the ground right away from me 'cos she's saying it's their own fault. . . . ' It was clear that such attention had not been given by accident to the problems of families with low incomes.

The writing to follow would thus be couched in the domestic fiction of a boy in a poor family resisting authority. Mr Austin did not demand that his pupils bared their souls in writing; their written work was allowed to remain within the safe limits of fictional stereotypes. By encouraging his pupils to talk freely, however — for example, of what they perceived of injustice in their own experience — they developed some sense of the interaction of forces in society. The talk about the privations of the fictional family allowed personal anecdotes about the regulations in a local authority home or favouritism in families, but it could also encompass comment on policies about rents and public transport or on sex-stereotyping. This heightening of awareness placed the fictional family more firmly in a real world, and allowed for reflective discussion of the pupils' own everyday experience.

Mr Austin seemed always ready to turn from his planned lesson in order to recognise and respond to issues raised by his pupils: 'I tend to feed on what they offer me', he told us. The discussion of parents' power over adolescents included a reference to their insistence on an early return at night. Mr Austin introduced another aspect by saying, 'I've often known it happen where it's all right for the lads to stay out as long as they want (omission) and I've known sisters get furious about it'. A sequence followed in which he tried to enable boys and girls alike to reflect on male responsibilities in sexual relationships. As the sequence is a long one, in order to illustrate Mr Austin's style we can quote only a part and must abbreviate that by making omissions.

Girl 1 There's more chance of us being beaten up . . . (omission)
Girl 2 Or being followed, attacked, something like that . . . (omission)
Girl 3 You know, they don't trust you.
T. Trust you in what way?
Girl 3 They think you're going to do something that you shouldn't do . . . (omission)
T. Lot of embarrassment about. (omission) Fear of getting pregnant, that's what the worry is, if you're staying out with lads, isn't it? (omission) Your parents are protecting you against the wolves and sharks; keep the wolves and sharks locked up and you'd be all right. Unfair, isn't it?

Mr Austin did not touch frequently upon sexual issues and here he was directing attention more towards the effects of gender upon personal freedom. In such episodes, he tried to encourage his pupils to reflect on a wide range of moral and social issues in their own lives; in the course of this he inevitably projected some of his own values, as in the sequence quoted.

In a third lesson the class were to have continued writing the story but Mr Austin had just seen a BBC documentary film about Cambodia, and had been very moved by it. When he mentioned it and the class showed interest, he embarked on an account of some of the horrors, invoking the pupils' moral responsibility:

> All right, we live in Smalltown but they're human beings. If you saw this film and saw this suffering . . . It could be you, it could be your brother and your sister. It could be somebody you love dying, starving horribly, flies crawling all over them. They couldn't move, they hadn't the energy to swat the flies away.

His account was impressive enough for some boys later to begin discussing ways of collecting money for an Oxfam appeal. Here Mr Austin's intentions had been to transcend his pupils' everyday lives and extend their moral sympathies.

Mr Austin's rationale for his teaching of this bottom set deserves some attention before turning to what other teachers said about values. What he was doing was fully deliberate: in discussion he accepted Mr Squires' view that they were 'carrying the banner for civilising influences'. Later he wrote in response to our questionnaire, 'Teachers of English are defenders of the spirit and should always be a radical force helping to make for life'. He also wrote, 'The more wide-ranging social and cultural role of the teacher is . . . in constant need of positive defence' against the pressures to give primacy to examination results. There was no doubt of the high priority that Mr Austin gave to what he considered to be his socio-moral responsibilities. With the top set he made wide references to English literature, with the intention — as he told us — of showing that it 'has a relevancy for me as I live day to day'. With the bottom set his references were to television and to everyday life; as he said, 'With the bottom set, discussion of social issues will probably occupy . . . half of the time'. In both cases, however, 'It's got to come through you to them and they've got to pick up something genuine within you'. Even though Mr Austin's work with the bottom set did not depend heavily upon literature, many of the expressions he used — 'civilising influences', 'make for life', 'genuine' and 'integrity' — seem to refer back to that account of the literary tradition as defender of moral and cultural standards which was developed in Cambridge in the 1930s and 1940s. However, what was most noticeable to an observer of his teaching was not something he shared with other teachers, but his unusual sensitivity to his pupils' worlds. Most teachers offered to their classes a model of social experience and moral concern that was considerably more stereotyped and restrictive than Mr Austin's.

The syllabuses from Downtown School and Smalltown School laid claim to intrinsic goals in the teaching of English, and what we saw of lessons made it clear to us that, particularly for teachers in those two departments but also for some teachers from other schools, such claims were no façade to conceal a single-minded commitment to examination results even in the examination year. The desire to transmit values did not seem to be linked to a particular social background: it was strongest in Downtown School and Smalltown School, two schools which were in sharp contrast when the social class background of their pupils were compared. The reader will recollect the belief expressed in the Smalltown syllabus that their pupils were 'culturally impoverished', a state which English should help to remedy. In this section we have shown the teaching of Mr Squires, Mrs Wood and Mr Austin, all three members of this department, illustrating how they acted upon these beliefs. Certainly their priorities seemed different from more examination-oriented departments such as those in New Suburbia and Catchwide Schools. Those teachers who did give the transmission of values a place in their teaching nevertheless found it possible to achieve the extrinsic goal of good examination grades as well.

Our next task is to illustrate what other teachers said about values. One of the most surprising aspects of teachers' accounts of their teaching was that they seldom laid claim to moral intentions, in spite of what we had seen in their lessons. They talked of the importance of 'relevance to pupils' lives' and not of transmitting a value-laden account of some aspects of those lives. Mr Austin's colleague, Mrs Wood, acknowledged a moral aim obliquely in her anecdote of the poem about abortion (p. 91); and Mr Squires, the head of department, said that in teaching literature for the 16+ examination (that is in preparing assignments) he was concerned with enjoyment and with 'social matters that arise and behavioural matters'. Apart from these three references, all from Smalltown School, the moral goals that were pursued in lessons seemed not to be acknowledged in the interviews. (We did not ask directly for them.) They may constitute an implicit rather than an acknowledged strand in the personalising tendency.

It might also be asked whether the values leant in one direction or another. For the most part they were the typical views of liberal-minded, professional class, Sunday-newspaper-reading adults who believed their world-views not only to be true but to be important enough to share with their pupils. The focus was upon face-to-face personal and domestic morality; on the occasions when attention was given to public issues they tended to be matters such as war, and even this was usually held at arm's length by being dealt with in terms of World War I. That is, this privatised ethic presented public issues in terms of attitudes and interpretations rather than of actions. English teachers in schools are often thought to be subversive, but — as Gerald Grace has pointed out[13] — this is a myth. We attempted to collect together any topics that might lead even to mild criticism of the status quo and found only the following:

Greentown School	Mr Tremaine	i. discussion of censorship of films by borough council
		ii. discussions of school assemblies
	Mr Saxon	iii. pupils wrote letters of complaint about faulty goods

Smalltown School Mr Austin

iv. discussions of 'people who can tell me what to do'
v. discussion of poverty
vi. expressions of indignation about persecution in the third world.

None of these could be called subversive, though they did amount to attempts to persuade pupils to look more critically at the world about them. They took place in the two schools with the highest proportion of middle-class children; we found nothing comparable in Downtown School or Urban School.

It might well be asked why it is that English teachers do not confine their attention to the teaching of writing, and so avoid involvement in matters of value. The elementary school tradition which this century inherited from the previous one provided a model of such teaching: attention was concentrated upon handwriting and orthographic conventions — spelling, punctuation, and paragraphing — a model based on the requirements of a copying clerk. A secondary tradition co-existed which saw writing in terms of the 'essay'. Elegant, disengaged from context and from any purpose but amusement, the essay was the goal of the kind of writing we are calling *belles lettres*. At this point the part played by writing in the public testing of English becomes relevant; if the content of an essay is assessed, and with it the shaping of the content and the style adopted, then these have to be included in the teaching of writing. Up until the 1950s, English teachers — with an increasing minority of critical dissenters, however — tended to teach deep criteria for writing by communicating the implicit demands of *belles lettres*, a strand which we have shown to continue in some English teaching today. When writing was taught explicitly it was treated as a hierarchy of linguistic skills separated from the intentions of the writer: teachers taught 'the effective use of adverbs', 'sentence-combining', paragraphs with 'topic sentences', and pupils were expected to combine these in a whole. During the 1950s the objections of the critical minority began to be the opinions of the majority; English teachers discovered that most pupils wrote better if they wrote about something that mattered to them, and if their teachers accorded validity to what they wrote by responding to it as a serious message. Writing was seen as a purposive act, not merely the exercise of skills but the shaping of linguistic resources by the desire to communicate. In the years that followed, the teachers came to believe that preliminary discussion of the topics also improved the quality of the writing done, partly — as we have suggested — by making more available to pupils the deep criteria on which the writing would be assessed, but also by displaying possibilities and giving the teacher the opportunity to play the part of interested audience. Changes in the teaching of literature that were taking place concurrently also influenced the teaching of writing. Teachers were more hesitant to hand over authoritative readings, ready-made literary opinions; the idea of 'personal response' meant that each reader should shape his or her unique interpretation of a literary work — except on those occasions when an examination made this inadvisable. Not only was literature visibly the centre of English by the early 1960s, but it carried with it expectations about the development of an individual viewpoint and of 'relevance' to pupils' concerns. If literary study was to be relevant to life, this meant that it could not avoid involvement with the moral concerns that shape works of literature, nor avoid asking pupils to write about them as a part of their response to the novels, poems and plays they were reading. All of these characteristics were mirrored in the teaching of writing. To prepare boys and girls to write, a teacher must choose a topic relevant to their lives or to their fantasies, encourage them to use the writing to explore their individual experiences and at the same time make adult criteria available to them. It is this that has led to the large amount of personal writing we have observed; it has also led to a concern with the transmission of values. The engagement with ethical issues, felt to be inevitable in literature teaching, has carried over to writing.

To sum up the material discussed in this section, it would be true to say that some teachers were going beyond the demands of communicating deep criteria, but that the personalised ethic they were transmitting was for the most part congruent with the view of writing — and also the view of literature — that they were seeking to communicate. Nevertheless, it is a moot point whether values transmitted explicitly or implicitly as the *content* of lessons speak as persuasively to young people as those which through the very processes of teaching and learning ascribe to them a role and a stance in the face of experience.

8. What the pupils said

This section deals with four issues: (1) What topics do fifth-year pupils enjoy writing about? (2) What instrumental value do they believe writing skills to have in employment? (3) What are they able to formulate as the criteria on which their writing will be judged? (4) What do they think they (or their teachers) can do to improve their writing?

We asked the pupils what writing they liked or disliked, and in most cases followed this up with a probe about what they thought of writing about themselves, their families, and their own experiences. It was no surprise to find that most pupils preferred writing stories; this was particularly true in lower sets some of which, we found, had been given mainly fictional tasks. Able pupils too liked writing short stories: a boy in Mr O'Donnell's top set at Catchwide said of writing in English, 'It's more fun because you can write down your own ideas.

I like writing short stories; I often try to put a twist in the tail'. Our probe about personal writing drew surprising results, however. Of the 157 boys and girls whom we interviewed, 83 gave replies explicit enough to be used, and these were predominantly negative, 22 girls claimed to enjoy personal writing, while 25 were antagonistic to it. 10 boys liked it, while 26 disliked it. We did not ask an explicit question about impersonal writing but it was mentioned unprompted by 35 pupils mainly from top sets; 25 said they enjoyed expressing their opinions on a general topic, and 10 disliked it. Quite often the expression of preference for discursive writing was accompanied by a rejection of personal writing. It will be necessary to look in detail at what was said in order to understand the nature and basis of these attitudes.

The most frequent explanation of a dislike of personal writing was that the writer became 'stuck for ideas' or 'I can't think what to write'. One boy suggested that 'you need a poetic gift to write about family and feelings', a gift he clearly felt to lack. To understand why some pupils found it difficult to write about themselves, a topic most of us are interested in, we must look elsewhere. A girl in Mrs Williams' bottom set at Downtown, a set highly resistant to personal talk, said, 'I think it's personal', apparently meaning too private to put on paper, though two other pupils in the class liked personal writing. There were signs of feeling that English trespassed on private matters when 'you ought to keep them to yourself'. For some pupils this may have been combined with the sense that there were parts of their family life that they would not wish to be public property. Moreover, when a pupil says that there is 'nowt interesting about me' it suggests that some sense of personal inadequacy is making privacy something to be cherished. On the other hand, one boy said that 'writing about yourself sounds like boasting'. Another, who 'can't stand' writing about himself, explained:

> I'm scared of it. I don't know what to write, whether I'm being vain or whether I'm being dishonest or whether I'm being too honest... You always try to picture yourself something that you aren't, always try to grade yourself above everybody else. Everybody does; it's nature. But if you put it on paper, people who are reading it will think that's not you.

This diverse collection of attitudes does not cohere conveniently, but suggests three motives for uneasiness about personal writing: conflict with sub-cultural values, a desire for privacy, and conflict with some young people's self-images.

Some pupils however said that they liked writing about 'the things of everyday life', and there were references to particular pieces they had enjoyed. One mentioned a portrait of her grandmother she had written and another had been able to write about visiting her mother in hospital. Ruth, in Mr Austin's bottom set, liked writing about people: 'People are really different... There's always something you can write about', but was not so enthusiastic about writing about herself. 'I know about myself. Some people want to know, but you can normally just tell them instead of writing it down.' It seemed that many used fiction as a way of dealing with first-hand experience, since it freed them from the danger of giving too much away or of adopting an unacceptable persona. A girl in Mr Porson's top stream at New Suburbia, who had done little writing during the year apart from that concerned with literature, said that she liked writing stories, for example, an account of 'people's experiences at work'. When writing such stories she was able to put into them incidents that had happened to her, and how she felt. Catherine in Mrs Wood's top set at Smalltown School preferred to 'keep my feelings to myself' but was able to 'live with the part' when she wrote about characters in books. Perhaps these should be counterbalanced with the boy who said that he enjoyed writing about his family but always 'made it up'.

Quite a substantial minority of pupils said that they enjoyed 'descriptive' writing, though this might not always mean the same thing; classes preparing for assessment of coursework would be likely to write extended pieces on *belles lettres* topics such as 'A Forest Fire', whereas those classes preparing for examination papers had often used textbooks which included short descriptive paragraphs amongst the exercises. It might be surmised that the appeal of descriptions is that such writing is free from the problems of personal writing which have been discussed above, while it does not demand the organisation of thought required by discursive essays.

It was an able and articulate subgroup, about a sixth of all those we interviewed, who told us that they enjoyed writing what one of them called 'documentaries and opinions', this being slightly greater than the proportion of our sample of pieces of writing that fell into the 'public impersonal' category (p. 83). These pupils appreciated the freedom of choice given to them by what we have called elsewhere 'public, decontextualised' topics. Nearly all spoke of enjoying the opportunity to 'give an opinion', 'write what you want', 'give your own views', and a few added that in such writing there was no right answer, as in other subjects than English. For some of these pupils it was important that the topic was right: 'sex equality' and 'the views of young people' were mentioned with approval. Some of the smaller group who expressed dislike of such writing said of topics like Capital Punishment that they 'don't know enough about it', and two girls said that it was only boys who knew about topics such as War and Inflation. A girl from Mrs Brennan's top set at Downtown School found the requirement for a balanced argument inhibiting: 'If you feel strongly about one thing you can't put an argument against it... if you don't think that's right'. (It is perhaps relevant to remember that Mrs Brennan's success with this group seemed to us to depend on her engaging their enthusiasm for the books and topics they were dealing with.) It seems likely that there is at the very least a minority group of more able pupils who appreciate being given public topics which they can deal with in a relatively impersonal manner, though with considerable personal commitment.

So far we have been considering the intrinsic value of writing in English lessons as perceived by the pupils themselves. Almost all liked writing stories; subgroups expressed a liking for descriptive, discursive or personal writing. About a third of the pupils, however, expressed uneasiness, lack of confidence or dislike of personal writing, and this seems to be a matter that should be taken seriously by English teachers since it included many pupils taught by highly skilled teachers such as Mrs Wood and Mr Austin. Next we turn to pupils' views of the instrumental value of English, and particularly of writing.

It was somewhat disturbing to discover that the majority of pupils did not see the English they were doing at school as having any relevance whatsoever to their parents' work or to the jobs they themselves hoped to do. This was true of many pupils who enjoyed writing and were relatively successful in it. As might be expected, opinions appeared to be quite closely related to social class. On the one hand there was Elizabeth at Urban School who could see no relationship between the demands made in everyday life for talking, reading and writing and what went on in English lessons and said, 'I don't think you need "O" English except in higher jobs'; on the other hand there was Carol at New Suburbia School who said, 'You've got to be able to express yourself in any kind of job, so I think you have really to have quite a high qualification in English'. The former perspective was far more common, and this enables us to understand how a large proportion of pupils, particularly those in middle or lower sets, or in Urban and Downtown Schools, see the nature of English. Amongst those who said that their fathers do not 'use English' in their jobs were the children of at least two teachers and a university lecturer. This should warn English teachers that their view of what they are teaching is not only different from that held by many pupils and members of the public but may even differ from that held by some colleagues. For most of the young people it was oral skills that mattered in real life, including employment, and many would not consider taking a job that involved much writing, a question which we put to them directly. For example, Shirley at Catchwide School, whose father was a dustman, said that in a job 'where you're writing all the time, you'd be feeling as if you were back at school again', which may suggest that in her eyes writing tasks are associated with immaturity. Further light is thrown on this by some rather diverse remarks which indicate some of the social meaning of school English to certain pupils. One girl at Downtown School who did think English important associated it with 'a position of responsibility', and a boy at Urban School (who emphatically did not) said that 'if you're a good writer and can spell good they (the other boys) look down on you', adding that to be good at English you had to be 'snobbish'. Such remarks suggest that for some working-class pupils, not only the use of standard English speech but even success in essay writing can be taken to indicate that one has ambitions that will eventually bring about separation from the values of family and friends. It seemed, too, that in some working-class families all the writing of letters is done by the mother, so that this played a part in some boys' dismissal of writing as not relevant to their future lives. English was sometimes seen as relevant only to office jobs, themselves associated with feminine roles, and in these cases reference was usually made to the importance of spelling, punctuation and neatness. (We shall return later to the pupils' perception of criteria.) For some pupils in top sets it was the concentration on the study of literature that was not relevant to employment, but this can apply only to a few. Lynne in Mr Austin's bottom set at Smalltown School can be taken to represent many less-able pupils. She did not think that the English done in school would have been any use to her father who owned a small haulage firm: the only writing he did was to take down notes from telephone calls. A number of boys in lower streams spoke with approval of work they had done on the writing of job applications: this seemed to represent their sole conception of a mode of writing relevant to employment. To sum up so far, it seemed that those children, a majority, who saw school English as irrelevant to real life did so for several overlapping reasons: it was irrelevant because they perceived spoken language to be more important than written in the jobs they knew about and aspired to, because literature and personal writing seemed not to be of instrumental value, and because writing was for many of them associated with sedentary activities, particularly in offices, which did not match their self-image. The failure of fifth-year English to respond to the pupils' perceived needs for abilities in spoken language cannot be brushed away as an artefact of young people's shortsightedness.

It is now appropriate to turn to some pupils who did not share this view. Sean, who was in Mr Tremaine's top set at Greentown, made the penetrating remark that though he was not sure that essay writing had any practical application, he thought it made 'you more aware of the possibilities of English' rather than helping with a job. A committed apologist could not have put it better. Another boy in the same set said that in 'nearly every job you get you've got to express yourself sometime'. Several young people related English to effective communication in general; Martin in Mrs Brennan's top set at Downtown School said that you 'need to be able to communicate with people and express, write properly and well in good form'. One or two pupils, but very few, mentioned the academic importance of written

English: one of these who was unusually articulate said that English 'links all subjects together', but his father was a training adviser in a large firm. Although the English courses experienced by top streams concentrated on literature it was pupils from top streams who tended to express views like those quoted, and particularly pupils whose parents were in non-manual employment. In part this can be explained by the hypothesis that pupils from middle-class homes rightly believe written language to be relevant to the jobs they aspire to, just as working-class pupils aspire to jobs that do indeed require competence in oral more than written language. But this is probably not entirely true: it seems probable that the latter underestimate the part played by writing in the world they will find themselves in as adults. Those taking apprenticeships will find it important in the FE courses they attend; it will certainly be important in commerce in more ways than the writing of error-free letters; and it will be important in industry for anyone who takes on even minor managerial responsibility. This can perhaps be related to Paul Willis's demonstration of how working-class pupils' conscious cultural choices can operate to exclude them from better jobs, though his study[14] seems to have related to a much smaller subgroup than those I am here referring to, most of whom had certainly not rejected school values as a whole. It seems that there are social-class-oriented differences in how English is perceived, which may affect many young people's commitment to the subject and therefore their level of achievement in it.

The interviews also throw valuable light upon what the young people consider to be the characteristics of good writing, these inevitably providing the basis for any efforts to improve. Our first interest here is to consider the relative emphasis on surface and deep criteria. All of the references to criteria were incidental to other questions, since we made no attempt to discover them by direct means. There were more references to surface than to deep criteria. Although in some cases particular boys or girls mentioned both, there was a considerable tendency for those in lower streams to show more awareness of surface criteria, possibly because they are easier to talk and think about. The 157 interviewees mentioned these surface criteria with the frequencies shown in Table 3.5.

Table 3.5

Pupils' references to surface criteria

Spelling	15 times
Handwriting and neatness	13 times
Vocabulary	11 times
Punctuation	9 times
Paragraphing	2 times
Sentence structure	2 times

Although these frequencies are only a small proportion of the whole sample, they are quite large for incidental references: there was certainly no evidence that English teachers were failing to urge on pupils' attention the importance of these matters. Teachers' views were not, however, the only influence at work: although Mrs Williams at Downtown School had clearly been urging the importance of thought in writing, one of her pupils, Marie, knew that it was really 'neatness that matters'. It is probably fair to associate with the salience of surface criteria the fact that two or three pupils who were intending to go into secretarial work said that they wished that their fifth-year course had contained some language exercises (which some called 'grammar'), though there was a notable lack of enthusiasm for them at New Suburbia where considerable time was expended on them. This suggests that teachers have failed to communicate to some pupils why they concentrate on continuous writing.

References to deep criteria, though only slightly fewer, tended to be more diffuse; here we are dealing with loose clusters of related ideas, not a clear-cut set of conventions as in punctuation, so it will be necessary to illustrate what was said rather than merely reporting frequencies. There were 17 mentions of the content of writing as a crucial element in its quality: 11 of these were references to 'ideas', which seemed to arise from particular teachers' presentation to their pupils of what was required. It was clear from the context of these references that the word 'ideas' was as likely to refer to original ways of handling stories as to lines of thought appropriate for discursive essays. One pupil who said that she often 'lacks ideas' went on to characterise them as an 'everyday sort of knowledge'; this fits with the perspective of others who spoke of 'knowledge of people' or who said that 'experiences from life' are more important for writing than reading or other people's ideas. Another added that 'the idea has got to be part of you', which matches with the remark that, 'More comes out of yourself than in other subjects'. These, of course, were all exceptionally articulate young people: most of those who we interviewed did not engage in such perceptive reflections.

There were nine references to thinking, but it is not clear whether this refers to something quite different from 'ideas' or whether it is just an alternative way of referring to a similar group of criteria. Certainly, thinking could refer to stories, though far less frequently than 'ideas' did. In some cases 'thinking' seemed to refer more to the process of writing than to its outcomes: for example, several pupils seem to have been advised to 'think carefully instead of rushing' into writing; one, who admitted that he often 'gets lost' when writing, acknowledged the value of 'planning in your head'. One made his preference for deep criteria explicit: it was 'thinking deeply, not technicalities' that mattered. We have referred in section 6 to English teachers' concern to pass on to their pupils certain rational procedures: only one of these appeared in a recognisable form, and this was when a boy said, 'It's really your opinion, so long as you can state an opinion and back it up'.

There were only two mentions of feelings, which is surprising in the light of the frequent references we had heard some teachers make in their lessons. One said, 'It's just feelings and how you express yourself', which conveniently leads towards the third cluster of criteria, those relating to expression.

There were ten references to expression, in forms such as 'putting words together', 'how to put ideas on paper', 'the way you express an opinion'. A slightly more sophisticated version referred to 'style' and the need to 'describe fully'; one teacher had clearly succeeded in communicating a criterion highly appropriate to fiction and certain kinds of personal writing. An even more striking insight into his English teacher's values was expounded by a boy in Mr Austin's bottom set at Smalltown School. John thought that good marks depended on 'neat writing' and on 'the way you put the words together to make it sound as if it is an expression, so when a person reads it he can actually feel the same thing that you felt when you were writing the assignment down'. One can almost hear Mr Austin saying it. (Conciseness and the avoidance of slang were mentioned once each, but have not been counted as belonging to this cluster.)

This section is summed up in Table 3.6:

Table 3.6

Pupils' references to criteria summarised

SURFACE	Orthographic conventions	26	
	Neatness	13	52
	Vocabulary and sentence structure	13	
DEEP	Content	15	
	Thought	9	32
	Expression	8	

Extracting these indications of what criteria fifth-form pupils are able to talk about reinforced our sense that most pupils find it difficult to formulate for themselves the goals they are aiming at, so it is appropriate now to move on to their views on what might be done to improve their performance. This we asked explicitly, and it was the replies to this question that often supplied the oblique references to criteria that have been analysed above.

It would not be unfair to say that a large proportion of pupils had no answer to this question, and that there was a general sense of powerlessness. Twelve pupils said they would have to work harder in order to improve. Not many of these seemed to know what they would work harder at, except that it would involve spending longer time on homework. (In two cases it involved listening more attentively to the teacher.) Perhaps these answers can be dismissed as the kind of acknowledgement of personal responsibility for academic performance into which the majority of pupils are well-socialised during the years of schooling. Nine mentioned the importance of the habit of reading, mainly — it seemed — because they were conscious of not having it. Perhaps that reply should be assimilated to the next group as an expression of their sense that there was nothing immediately to be done, that a radical change of interests and even personality would be required, but that is no more than surmise. Seventeen pupils attributed success to abstract qualities that seemed out of reach of deliberate change. Seven of them mentioned 'imagination' and left it at that; others spoke of 'flair', 'inventiveness', or said 'It's just a gift' or 'You can't work at it.... You've just got to know it'. The sense of powerlessness reached its apotheosis in, 'You can't dream up more than you are capable of dreaming up'.

There were few positive expressions of purpose to put against this overriding sense of powerlessness. There were two references to the importance of 'technique and practice', and the remarks about thinking harder which have already been discussed. Several pupils expressed their appreciation and even gratitude to those teachers who saw to it that topics were thoroughly discussed before asking them to write. There were sharp criticisms of a teacher who failed to do this; one boy said, 'I don't feel as if I know much about English, or the way I'm supposed to do an essay or a comprehension... Right through the school from early on we just get set an essay to do, we get marks, and then get set another essay...' It seems likely that this articulate pupil, whose written work was in fact of a very high standard, was putting into words a bewilderment shared by others, but each attribution of blame to the teaching was quite exceptional. Most pupils felt that responsibility lay with them, but were far from clear how they might exercise it; a few said explicitly that teachers cannot help.

Since the range of writing done in school is limited by the conventional range of topics, genres and rhetorical functions normally required of school boys and girls, it might be expected that some pupils would comment on the restriction. Only one boy did so. He had apparently amused himself over some period by writing dramatic sketches in the manner of Monty Python, and some of these had been performed at school and elsewhere. When the interviewer asked him whether any of these sketches were to be included in his coursework folder for assessment, he seemed surprised and explained that what external assessors valued was 'good, serious, well-written-out essays... not daft humour', clearly not resenting the exclusion. This unusual case can be used to exemplify the general truth that pupils tend to accept uncritically the school account of what constitutes writing, in spite of their sense of a mis-match between school English and the English outside.

Our last quotation comes from Sean, who was in the top set at Catchwide School: 'It's up to myself if I want to get better at English'. Asked what makes a good essay he said, 'It's got to have a good story-line, it's got to be fairly longish, good English, punctuation, spelling, paragraphs'. Is this the message that most young people receive from their English lessons? If so, it is quite inadequate, not merely in its concentration on surface criteria, but in the lack of any sense that writing in different situations and for different purposes gives rise to different criteria. English teachers might ask themselves whether their pupils could not be helped to have a better grasp of these matters by the time they are old enough to leave school.

9. The teaching of writing

It has been a common criticism of English teachers that they do not teach their pupils to write but merely give starting points and leave them to find the way for themselves. If we had asked teachers directly about this, it is very likely that they would have replied that by the fifth year pupils would have received a great deal of teaching; it would be misleading to ignore the many years of English that had gone before. As Mrs Sutton, head of department at Urban School, said:

> I would emphasise very very careful planning and checking at this stage with the fifth year. If the groundwork's been done in the third and fourth year one shouldn't need different advice in the fifth.

Mr O'Donnell, head of department at Catchwide School, appeared to disagree when he spoke of 'the basic competence which they have mysteriously acquired over the years that we haven't bothered teaching it to them'. (This does not necessarily imply sharp differences in the teaching received by pupils at the two schools but may result rather from differences in the two teachers' views of what constitutes 'groundwork' or 'basic competence'.)

During the initial interviews four teachers mentioned the planning of essays, two being Mr O'Donnell's two colleagues at Catchwide School, one being Mrs Sackville, a colleague of Mrs Sutton at Urban School, and one Mr Porson of New Suburbia School. These were the three schools most concerned about examinations, and also entering more pupils for examination papers rather than other modes. With the exception of that made by Mrs Sackville these remarks referred to less-able pupils. Mr Gilham, in his second year of teaching, spoke of 'telling them what to put into the essay' but seemed to be referring mainly to literature essays. Mr Porson gave details of his methods with 'weaker groups'. Asked about planning essays in class he said: '...to suggest we'd better do an essay now on "A Minor Injury" or something. What can we look at? Let's go through the various stages you might deal with. A little paragraph for each and here we are we've got an essay plan to work round.' He went on to lament pupils' impulsiveness in examinations.

Mrs Sackville spoke of giving pupils notes on essay structure taken from a textbook, and seemed to imply that she would go through them point by point with her pupils. We have only three classroom examples of teachers giving instructions for planning 'language' essays, though several teachers gave detailed help with literature essays for coursework folders. Mrs Sutton gave very general advice to her bottom set, before walking round and giving particular advice to individuals. What she said to the class, who were preparing for writing on two private topics, was:

> Now the first step, as usual, is simply to jot down some ideas in the back of your book, just to jot them down; don't attempt to put them into sentences or paragraphs . . . (omission) First step then just a list of ideas, please, that you might choose to use, and then we'll edit the ideas and cancel any that we don't need. . . .

These brief instructions seem to imply that on some previous occasion Mrs Sutton has worked on the blackboard with the class, collecting 'ideas' and then reordering and selecting them. Such a teaching method is likely to have the advantage of making available to pupils the methods and criteria used by the teacher herself in planning a piece of writing.

The second occasion when we saw help given with planning was during the lesson, described already on pages 126–28, in which Mr Austin constructed blackboard outlines from his pupils' suggestions, in preparation for writing a story. These included the list of 'people telling us what to do' and an itemised expenditure account for an impoverished family. These background lists, whatever their function, would not provide a shape for the story, so Mr Austin went on to suggest, or elicit from pupils, the members of the family, their names, ages, jobs and other characteristics, all the time writing these on the blackboard. The first part of the story, said Mr Austin, was to be an account of the family; and it was this they were to write first. (Later they would place a rebellious adolescent in the family and work out likely events.) This double period provided the only occasion when we saw a teacher demonstrating how to plan, and it is interesting to notice how tight a structure he provided for his bottom set.

Contrasting with this was the tendency noted earlier for many teachers to prepare pupils to write by reading a selection of works of literature on a related topic, discussing them cursorily if at all, and then leaving pupils to write. Such an approach assumes that fifth-year pupils are themselves capable of finding a shape for their work, and many indeed can, particularly for stories which are often very skilfully managed.

It is non-narrative writing that provides the sharpest problems both in collecting related material and finding an order for it, and indeed finding a subject to write about that will imply a focus, and a set of criteria of relevance and order. The mere injunction to write an outline is sadly inadequate for most young people of this age; one can only write down a meaningful sequence of headings when thinking about the topic has reached the stage of generating relevance and order. For many young people it is the ability to generate the criteria that is difficult: without them the jotted notes are nonsense. For example, one of Mrs Sackville's pupils was writing on the topic, 'Describe your memory of staying in a room that impressed you for some reason, pleasant or unpleasant', and her plan was:

1. Where room was
2. Why was in room
3. How got there
4. Who or what did sea (*sic*)
5. Using senses describe room (top set)

The girl who wrote these had been unable to imagine abstractly before writing what kind of structure might make sense for a task like this. Notes 1 to 3, for which she dutifully provided a paragraph, were essentially irrelevant, and weakened rather than strengthened what she wrote. Most other sets of notes that we saw, not only from Mrs Sackville's pupils, proved to be unhelpful to their writers. It is the processes of ordering thought that needs to be taught, and not its surface appearance in a list of headings. Mr Austin's attempts to show his pupils how to order their thoughts were more to the point than the outline in note form which Mrs Sackville appeared to have required her pupils to provide for every piece submitted.

Mr Saxon's requirement for pupils to list 'points' (p. 113) may have been helpful: his pupils produced work that was better than might be predicted from a bottom set. When he asked them to note a point this was in the context of a classroom discussion of the topic, so that whatever phrase the pupil wrote down would later point towards a hinterland of discussion instead of hanging in mid-air as did the empty phrases quoted in the previous paragraph. In spite of what teachers said about 'training pupils' thoughts', few seemed to be doing so as effectively in the lessons we saw as Mr Austin and possibly Mr Saxon.

Another teaching procedure we saw little of in these fifth-year lessons was the 'workshop' approach;[15] this procedure is not common at any stage in teaching, partly because of the organisational problems it can give rise to. Such an approach implies a more radical change of perspective than appears at first glance. We have already described 'preparing to write' lessons in which teachers read aloud passages of literature — perhaps significantly described by the term 'stimuli' borrowed from behaviourist psychology — and then after brief discussion set the pupils to write on a related topic. Such a teaching method suggests that the teacher's attention is more focused upon the product, the pieces of writing, than upon the process by which the writers will achieve them, this appearing in the first instance as a failure to help their pupils to relate the passages to their own experience, perceptions and priorities. It is typical of such teaching that the teacher walks around the room while the pupils write, cajoling some and supplying technical advice to others, but leaving each pupil alone with the task of generating and shaping a piece of writing. It would not be far-fetched to relate this to some of the preconceptions of romantic literature, where writing is expected to come almost unreflected upon from the private resources of the ego; if this is so, the pedagogy and the privatised view of writing are in tune.

The workshop approach is an alternative to this. At the centre of it is an essentially public view of writing in which the writers become consciously aware of the criteria for choosing and ordering content, and for adopting and maintaining a style or persona. The teacher's role then becomes that of encouraging pupils to read their own early drafts and those of their fellows in an analytical and diagnostic manner, thus becoming their own critical readers and editors. In this way more pupils would move towards the experience of writing that, for example, we have had in working on this book, and by learning to read more reflectively come to 'own' their own writing in a way that only a few can be said to at present. The emphasis would fall upon writing as a craft, with skills and criteria that can be pondered and discussed as well as practised. It would undoubtedly take a long time for many young people to learn to regard their writing in this unaccustomed way, and would require a very different pedagogy from what we saw in most classrooms. At the very least it would require more preliminary discussion of possibilities than generally occurred, the exchange and discussion of early drafts, and guidance from the teacher to elicit relevant criteria to match the emerging intentions of each writer. Such teaching would at first be very time-consuming but would offer enormous potential gains for the students: perhaps it is more likely to occur at a greater distance from examinations, though we have no great faith that this is so. Perhaps the workshop offers too great a threat to the teacher's traditional ownership of the criteria, which usually remain largely implicit.

Very little of this kind appeared in the lessons observed. Mr Austin took his bottom set very carefully through the process of structuring a story, building up notes on the blackboard as he went.

Mr Saxon seemed to be reaching towards a more reflective approach to writing, when he spent a considerable part of the writing lessons in reading pupils' completed stories and essays aloud to the class. Not all of the boys and girls liked this; the comments given by pupils were generally critical rather than helpful while Mr Saxon himself added little advice, but the procedure provided an audience more lively than a lone teacher is able to. Perhaps it was this audience, rather than the point-listing technique that raised the level of writing done by Mr Saxon's set.

One implication of a workshop approach is that by involving pupils in the discussion of the work done it helps them to reflect upon the criteria appropriate to different kinds of writing. It was shown in the last section that most pupils whom we interviewed were unable to say anything about criteria except those we have called 'surface', and that in general they had little conception of differences between kinds of writing or of how they might improve their work. To say that current modes of teaching writing give pupils little conscious insight into what they are doing, or into the qualities that distinguish good writing of one kind or another, is not to imply that there was once a time when English teachers did achieve this. It seems important to ask of our material how far teachers thought that awareness of underlying principles would be of value to 16-year-old boys and girls, and what signs there were in lessons of activities designed to help them to become aware. For pupils to become aware of these principles it is necessary for them (i) to have enough control over what they are doing not to be merely reproducing models; (ii) to engage in a diversity of kinds of writing, including writing for different audiences and purposes; and (iii) to have the time and incentive to reflect on this writing and to discuss it with one another and with their teacher. For those who are entered for an examination in literature, there seems to be little likelihood of the third condition being fulfilled; coursework assessment in English Language would lend itself to these methods, though we saw little sign of its being used in this way.

Hints of such values were detectable in some of what Mr Saxon said in the interview. Speaking of what he called 'thematic teaching', he said that he began by explaining the topic, then followed this with 'stimulus materials' such as films or tape-recordings, and then set up group discussions with 'certain questions to be answered and reported back on'. There might be input from members of the class: 'For instance, someone may say, "I work in stables on a Saturday", so I let them bring in implements for grooming a pony; I let them talk about that...' He concluded, 'There will be bits and pieces of writing all the way through, but because of the nature of the assessment it must be a well-rounded essay we move towards'. Although there are personal elements in some of Mr Saxon's lessons, he framed his central concern plainly when he said that what he wanted was to make 'better citizens...more effective operators in the outside world', which included a considerable emphasis on impersonal writing. In fact, he was not able to put this ideal model into effect, partly because of his not very satisfactory relationship with the bottom set he was teaching that year. Such an approach would fulfil the first of the three conditions enunciated in the previous paragraph, by throwing more responsibility on pupils to collect material outside the classroom and to find principles on which to order it; it also hints at the second condition, but ignores the third, though Mr Saxon's practice of reading writing aloud for comment suggests that he was not unaware of its importance.

We can contrast this with what Mrs Sutton called 'formal teaching'. She described herself as 'about the middle of the range, tending to formal', and when we asked her what she meant by 'formal teaching' she characterised it as:

> Very little interaction, the teacher giving a lecture and then the children getting on with the work . . . certainly very little group work . . . a lot of use of the formal language course from a book, very little picture work, or tape work, or film or television . . . a large emphasis on grammar . . . and very little thematic work.
>
> (A few explanatory phrases have been omitted here for simplicity's sake.)

It should be noted by readers not conversant with English teachers' current usage that 'grammar' probably refers to work on written conventions such as punctuation and to exercises on standard usage, and is unlikely to include syntactic analysis. 'Formal language' is likely to include 'grammar', and writing tasks — including what are called 'comprehensions' — carried out primarily in order to practise skills. This contrasts not only with 'thematic work' as described by Mr Saxon, but also with those personal approaches in which the main justification is the relevance of the subject matter to the learners' concerns, and improved skills expected as a by-product.

After a rapid survey of transcripts of the interviews with teachers we came away with a sense of frequent emphasis on individual teaching and advice, but closer examination showed that all of the ten references came from teachers at either Smalltown School or Greentown School. For example, Mr Tremaine said that as the examination approached he tended 'to organise activities as much as possible in which I can talk to individuals'. We asked teachers what activities they would wish to engage in if any extra time were made available and, as Lortie[16] predicted, most of the choices were of activities directly related to teaching. Mr Saxon explained his choice of individual teaching by saying: 'I always feel if I just had another three weeks in the summer then I could get the whole thing beaten at last'.

We must be careful not to allow the greater availability of data on class teaching to obscure from view either what teachers say to individual pupils while they are writing or what they write on pupils' work after it has been completed. Mr Austin of Smalltown School made a point of saying to us that he spent about half of the lesson time with his bottom set in talking to them individually as they wrote. When Mrs Brennan of Downtown School found one of us making notes of what she had written on pupils' work, she hastened to explain that what she wrote was mainly a reminder for herself, since she always tried to speak to every pupil individually about each piece of writing he or she had done. (We found on inspecting her comments that about a quarter of them included an element equivalent to 'See me', and that — more strikingly — half of them addressed the pupil by first name.) Our classroom materials include seven lessons in which teachers are 'going round the class' while pupils write general essays, and a number of others in which the writing being done is concerned with a work of literature. It is difficult under such circumstances to record more than fragments of what is said, but it is clear that much of teachers' efforts with lower sets is devoted to encouraging laggards to pursue the task, often by helping them to make necessary choices. Mrs Williams, for example, teaching the bottom set at Downtown School, approached a boy with, 'Well, Michael, what's it going to be?' Reassurance is important too: this includes giving help with spelling and lay-out, assuring a pupil that he or she can choose the names of characters, and making suggestions of possible content. Mr Austin, for example, replied to a question about how to begin a story by saying: 'I would suggest er perhaps a conversation, somebody saying something like, "What's for tea, Mum?" and that would lead straight into it. . . . ' On the basis of the evidence available, however, teachers appear mainly to give help with surface criteria such as spelling; help with content, or with the interpretation of the task seems less frequent. Advice to supply more detail or to 'work in your own experience' occurred only on isolated occasions. Mr Austin was unique, in that he was willing to talk with members of his bottom set about any topic they introduced which he thought important, collecting for Oxfam's Cambodia appeal and a television documentary on life in prisons amongst them; this was in line with the Smalltown department's desire to shape pupils' social attitudes. (All of these were of course different in kind from Mrs Brennan's retrospective comments on written work, which we do not have access to.)

Another aspect of the teaching of writing which might be undervalued is 'marking', the comments which teachers write upon pupils' work before handing it back to them. We were able to consider and analyse the comments written on over 700 pieces of writing; these included marginal comments as well as those written at the end, usually with a mark or grade. Some comments referred to the content of the writing, others to its organisation and style. More comments were positive than negative: teachers clearly looked for something to praise. Nearly every comment, however, could be read as an evaluative judgement, whether or not this was made explicit: marking functioned as a device for directing pupils' attention and for re-emphasising criteria.

For all teachers a considerable proportion of the comments — often more than half — referred to the content of the essay or story, or to its organisation. If the piece was narrative or descriptive, it would be approved or disapproved because it was or was not: dramatic, sensitive, amusing, varied, full of life, full of character and atmosphere, or exciting. The presence of detailed description was frequently praised or its absence bewailed. In the light of the personalising observed in lessons, it is interesting to note that the presence or absence of personal involvement, including the expression of feeling, were quite frequently referred to; pupils were urged to 'use your own experiences' or alternatively to 'get inside' their characters. Planning and organisation were frequently mentioned in connection with personal as well as impersonal writing: an introduction and a conclusion of a proper length were required so that, for example, the piece 'gets quickly to the point'; writing was to be 'well put together', not 'jumbled', and 'logically argued'. The style was approved or disapproved as: clear, accurate, colourless, attractive, fluent, verbose, vital or chatty. Most teachers, especially those teaching lower sets, referred frequently to written conventions in spelling, punctuation, paragraphing and sentence structure: there was no sign of any tendency to undervalue conformity to convention. (A number of comments also insisted that the writers should have conformed to the topic or genre that had been set to them.) A typical final comment, particularly from the more experienced teachers, would have two elements, as in: 'This essay is a curious combination of effective comments and inaccuracy. You do need to eliminate some of the errors'. This comment, written by Mrs Wood, typically praises the writer for positive achievements but also urges improvement; it is typical, too, that the achievement refers to content and the criticism to conventions.

It is not easy to estimate the importance for the pupils either of the teachers' written comments or of the individual advice given while pupils are writing. Our view is that, though individual attention is probably important in persuading some pupils to take writing tasks seriously, its value in advancing their understanding is less than teachers believe. The effect of teachers' written comments is likely to be severely weakened by the fact that they are not normally available until a week or more after the work has been completed, when the choices and criteria which informed what the pupil wrote have long disappeared from memory. Both are weakened because they depend upon the one-way communication of criteria controlled by the teacher; only a long-term use of 'workshop' methods, in which criteria are explicitly discussed and negotiated by pupils and teacher, would remove this weakness.

In the second section of this chapter we pointed out that pupils not taking a literature examination receive a very different version of English from those who were to do so, and that the kinds of writing done by pupils sitting an examination paper was likely to differ in emphasis from those done by pupils assessed via coursework. Since lower sets were seldom entered for an examination in literature, and somewhat more likely than upper sets to be assessed via coursework, this amounts to saying that different sets experienced different versions of English. We analysed teachers' entries in the diaries they kept of lessons taught to their fifth-year classes during two weeks in the second term. (The results of the analysis are more fully displayed in Chapter 2, p. 58.) The categories used in this analysis were not those used in Table 3.2 but instead they distinguished:

A. Classes being examined in Language and GCE O-level Literature
B. Classes being examined in Language and CSE Literature
C. Classes being examined in 'English' only.

These distinctions were designed to maximise the effect of literature on the versions of English taught. The percentage allocation of time in lessons for these three groups is displayed in Table 3.7.

Table 3.7

Percentage allocation of lesson time to activities (diary)

		Group A	B	C
Literature	- Reading	2	1	21
Literature	- Study and writing	66	30	2
	TOTAL	68	49	23
Language	- Essays and stories	10.5	42	46
Language	Comprehension exercises	17.5	9	17.5
Language	Practice of skills; oral work	4.0	0	13.5
	TOTAL	32.0	51.0	77.0

The 'C' category is composed of six classes, of which five are bottom sets. The version of English they experienced during that fortnight had three characteristics: the study (as opposed to the reading of) literature was almost absent; nearly two-thirds of their time was spent on writing (63.5 per cent); the practice of skills played a larger part than in other classes.

Differences could be detected between the experience of various classes who were preparing coursework assignments for assessment. Pupils in higher or lower sets would be presented with very similar titles, but the guidance they received would differ considerably. After introductory discussion the more able pupils would be relatively free to choose the treatment they would give to the topic, and would write without close supervision usually at home, whereas the less able would write during lesson time, often with a plan on the blackboard and with the teacher moving round the room encouraging and giving guidance. This reflects in a strange manner a difference observed in our analysis of examination tasks: the public tasks were relatively open, and the private tasks closely specified. In the classrooms we found a similar difference in tightness of control.

Some teachers held that the needs of less-able children for instruction in writing were different in kind, and this led, as was shown on pp. 117–18, to a wish to substitute 'functional' writing, writing tasks that pupils might recognise as having a possible context in the world of work. It also led in some schools and with some teachers to spending a large proportion of time on decontextualised exercises, some of them devoted to the practice of orthographic conventions, others to small pieces of writing. It would probably be misleading to link this in too simple a way with the needs of classroom control; many English teachers, as we saw in an earlier section, place considerable weight on the mastery of conventions, and believe it to be in the interests of those pupils who have not mastered them to be given exercises until they do.

One or two remarks by teachers threw light on their perceptions of less-able pupils; to these should be added the Smalltown perception of such pupils as culturally deprived. Mrs Brennan and Mrs Williams of Downtown School agreed that their pupils' lack of knowledge and interest was a major problem in teaching writing: the bottom set pupils have 'no interest in the news, not even the local news', said the latter. Mrs Brennan remarked that at Downtown School even the top set lacked confidence. Although neither teacher said so, it seems possible that this picture of their pupils accounts for the unusual stress on vocabulary teaching that was patent both in their lessons and in the syllabus, a stress that co-existed strangely with the personal development elements in them. At New Suburbia Mrs Harrison said that one of the difficulties of teaching less-able pupils is that they 'turn their nose up' at 'figurative language'. She continued:

> They see you as somebody fussy and on a different plane. I don't want to bring a class thing into it, but, 'Oh, it's just the posh English teacher wanting to use clever expressions. Why can't I just use what me and mi Dad say at home, what I read in *The Daily Mirror*?'

It is not surprising to find that teachers have stereotypes of pupils just as pupils have stereotypes of teachers; both seem an unhappy basis for English teaching and learning, since they are likely to shut off opportunities for more precise understanding of one another's perspectives and values. It is clear that many English teachers feel considerable frustration in teaching the less able, and the remarks just quoted throw some light on this. To understand this it is necessary to take into account the active part played by pupils in negotiating a *modus vivendi*. When discussing his use of a thematic approach with the bottom set at Greentown School, Mr Saxon pointed out that less-able pupils did not always favour the more open tasks which threw more responsibility upon them, and added: ‘Some colleagues have said how the less able love to do comprehension exercises or spelling tests, because they can have tick, tick, eight out of ten’. To reduce English to a competitive game that did not require personal commitment might well make sense to pupils who saw English as totally irrelevant to their future lives, and who therefore aimed to pass lesson time with the minimum of discomfort.

During the discussion with the New Suburbia department one of the investigators reminded Mrs Waterhouse of something she had once said:

> I remember your saying that if you gave them the kind of comprehension that they got in the exam they did hopelessly so you gave little things which they found they could do to give them the feeling of succeeding.

Mrs Waterhouse tacitly accepted this recollection and replied:

> You’re torn between trying to give them something which is more like the exam or giving them something they can succeed in so they go into the exam with an element of confidence and just be immediately shattered when they’re faced with two-and-a-half pages of tiny print.

The use of the coursebook seems to be part of an attempt to enlist the co-operation of less-able pupils – to maintain ‘control’ in the technical sense – by setting brief unchallenging tasks. Mrs Harrison, who also taught in New Suburbia School, said that less-able pupils prefer ‘structured’ writing tasks, probably textbook exercises not requiring continuous writing or personal involvement by the pupil. Putting these together gives a picture of a departmental strategy for the control of less-able pupils, which can be sharply contrasted with the strategies used by other teachers, notably Mr Austin, to enlist the co-operation of bottom-set pupils by moving towards their concerns, not avoiding them. Both are, of course, forms of what might be called ‘situational control’ — the establishment of goals and pursuits acceptable to teacher and pupils alike — in a way analogous to ‘social control’ at the macro level. Learning is likely to be considerably more effective if pupils accept the goals of the course as valuable, realistic, and relevant to their future lives; teaching that depends on compulsion is wasteful and ineffective. This is very like the way in which the larger social order depends on most people in society accepting the way of life as normal and proper, rather than on compulsion by judicial or more overt forms of force.

This section began with the question whether English teachers teach their pupils to write. They clearly do so. A great deal of time is given to illustrating for pupils the deep criteria which apply to the selection, ordering and presentation of the content of writing. In doing so, teachers are responding appropriately to examinations which give major rewards to this aspect of writing. In some schools, less-able pupils are likely to carry out many short pieces of writing — 'exercises' — which are primarily intended to reinforce their grasp of surface criteria though whether they do so is uncertain. What are not well taught are the principles, or deep criteria, which underlie the appropriateness of different kinds of writing to their various purposes; writing is practised but not reflected upon.

10. **The pupils' choices**

We suggested in an earlier section (pp. 131–32) that cultural changes in teachers' conceptions of the nature of writing — much influenced by models drawn from literature — have generated preconceptions about the relevance of everyday social experience, and placed a high valuation upon the use of writing for self-exploration. This account, however, treats as homogeneous the demands of teachers and examinations which are in fact various and, by placing all its emphases upon teaching, ignores the pupils' contributions to their own socialisation. As we have seen, pupils sitting for examinations attempt different writing tasks from those preparing coursework folders. Half of the writing done by the latter group was fictional, and another quarter was personal writing on a private topic, whereas nearly a third of the writing done by the examination paper classes fell into the more detached *belles lettres* category. It is difficult to tell how far such differences arise from the 'coursework' pupils being given greater freedom to choose the mode of writing. (Similarly we have no means of telling what pupils in the other group choose to write about in the examination room; one girl we talked to attributed her A grade in O-level English to a policy of always choosing descriptive topics.)

The point being made is that various modes of writing offer different opportunities and problems to different pupils, so that each appropriates those modes which can be best exploited, and avoids those which present difficulties. It will be convenient to consider the four modes — fiction, *belles lettres*, personal-autobiographical and public-impersonal — in terms of the availability to pupils of (i) appropriate knowledge, and (ii) a manageable voice or persona. Fiction and *belles lettres*, especially descriptive pieces, are the most available to the largest proportion of pupils. They depend on everyday knowledge, and appropriate personae are easily available, from teenage magazines for example, which do not impinge upon or threaten the writer's self-image. The personal-autobiographical mode is somewhat more threatening; like fiction it requires no more than everyday knowledge, but the adoption of an appropriate persona presents problems, which is why so many pupils, particularly from lower streams, do not like writing about themselves. Amongst the young people whom we talked to it was those from professional homes who moved most easily into a persona that allowed them to deal with personal experience without feeling at risk. This is not to ignore the fact that some pupils have good reason to wish to preserve the privacy of their lives, but to note that others are able to engage in successful personal writing without making public any vulnerable areas. Public-impersonal writing, on the other hand, faces young people with two problems: they may doubt whether they have appropriate knowledge of the topic, and their customary reading is unlikely to provide them with a suitable persona. The minority who read middlebrow Sunday newspapers with the support of family talk about public topics will be provided with both: it is perhaps even surprising that as many as a sixth of the boys and girls we interviewed said that they enjoyed writing on topics that enabled them to express their own ideas. This matches the proportion choosing to write on such topics. (See Table 3.2 on p. 83.) The middle-class minority amongst the pupils are thus able to choose and do themselves justice in any of these four modes, whereas the majority are most at ease in writing fiction or descriptive accounts. As we showed in an earlier section, there were few attempts to teach pupils to write in an impersonal way about public topics, even in those classes where such topics appeared relatively frequently amongst those set.

These opportunities for pupils to select strategies carry two sets of implications. How pupils experience the version of English presented to them will depend partly on the resources they bring and the strategies they choose. As we have seen, substantial groups of young people, particularly in middle and bottom sets, dislike writing about themselves and/or regard school English as irrelevant to practical life as they see it. Our material is unfortunately not of a kind to allow us to explore the implications of this, though such perceptions may have considerable influence on their success in English.

Furthermore, it is doubtful whether the values transmitted explicitly or implicitly as the *content* of lessons speak as loudly and persuasively to young people as the choices which they themselves make while negotiating their way through the demands and conditions of schooling. There was nothing in what the pupils said to us that suggested passive acceptance of their teachers' views of how the world is; quite the reverse, in fact. It seems more likely that it would be their strategies in response to the processes of teaching, learning and assessment that would in the long run ascribe or reinforce a particular stance in the face of experience.

CHAPTER 4

Language and Comprehension in the Fifth Year

by Stephen Clarke

The evidence for analysis of work in language and comprehension was drawn from the four syllabuses obtained from the six schools, from discussions and interviews with teachers, from interviews with pupils, from textbooks and from lessons. Six lessons were observed in which language was being taught and five in which passages for comprehension were studied. The lesson sample was small compared to that obtained from other areas analysed and we saw no lessons in either category in Downtown School or Smalltown School, but we found, nevertheless, certain patterns emerging from this limited body of evidence. What became of interest, first from the data on language teaching, were questions about how 'language' was understood and interpreted in teachers' theories, which aspects of it were taken as important to teach and to whom, and how far any kind of reflectiveness on language-use in general was encouraged. In the comprehension section the main questions concerned what kinds of texts and extracts were to be read, what models of the reading process emerged from the textbooks used and from the lessons and what range of possibilities existed for the encouragement of interpretative readings.

LANGUAGE WORK

1. Syllabuses and other theoretical viewpoints on language

Each of the four syllabuses differs in the extent to which it discusses questions about teaching and learning language, although there is between them a fairly uniform view that the purpose of study in this area is the mastery of clear expression and correctness in writing. Each has little to say about language under a specific fifth-year heading, so that most of the time we have to assume that general statements apply to fifth-year work as much as to that in other years.

Downtown School syllabus espouses a 'growth' model of language and learning and is concerned to show how different kinds of lessons in reading, writing and speaking can work together, each having a beneficial effect upon the others and leading to a broad improvement in language competence by pupils:

> The development of language will arise out of exploration in reading, writing and speaking.

The actual content items to be learnt comprise a traditional list of writing skills such as spelling, paragraphing and punctuation, as well as speech skills, but these are not to be imposed on pupils in a way that would make them seem an alien or culturally strange set of requirements:

> The aim should not be to alienate the child from the language he has grown up with, but to enlarge his repertoire so that he can meet new demands and situations and use standard forms when they are needed, a process which cannot be achieved overnight.

Put thus, it appears that pupils are credited with existing powers and abilities as language-users, abilities that have to be added to rather than erroneous habits that must be corrected. As we shall see, such a position makes a clear differentiation between the Downtown School position as given in the English syllabus and that of Smalltown and New Suburbia Schools, where a greater stress on the eradication of error is evident. In the Downtown School syllabus, Literature has a central role in language development for it has:

> virtue manifest in so many ways — not least as a means of exhibiting styles and structures.

There is also reference to the need for vocabulary books in which newly-met words are to be listed by pupils. This combination of a sympathetic attitude towards the existing language of pupils and an insistence on extending it by reference to literary models, written conventions and vocabulary lists not only provides teachers with a practical programme but itself composes a theoretical map which charts the relative positions of what is known already with what has yet to be learnt. Answers about what to teach, and how, may be broadly similar in all of the syllabuses, but only in Downtown School's case is the idea of individual development given such theoretical clarity. This is consistent with, and probably stems from, the following expression of a relativist position with regard to correctness and language-use:

> 'Correct' language varies in different situations and communities.

This entails, it seems to me, the idea that pupils are already 'correct' in much of what they say. Possibly also consistent with this relativist position is a general sense, difficult to define from any one quotation, of the pupils being subject to the same, or equal, language needs. Teachers are to take as optimistic a view as possible of pupils' life-chances and thus not to think in advance of restricting the scope of what language is taught to whom. Where clear error is manifest, then it should be corrected by grammar exercises given to individuals who need them. This does, arguably, place rather hopeful reliance on the instructive power of such exercises (gleaned from 'grammar textbooks fallen into desuetude') but it does not assume that whole classes will be in error.

A point of clear agreement between Downtown School syllabus and Smalltown's relates to how an improving grasp of correct writing should be learnt. In Downtown School's syllabus it is stated that:

> skills should be taught within the context of the shared experience,

and this points towards an instructive continuity in which there is as little isolation as possible of punctuation, spelling etc., as drills to be learnt, and instead a consideration of the usefulness of these things in relation to broader objectives. The Smalltown School syllabus tends to support this position with regard to fourth- and fifth-year work, for with these age-groups the teacher is instructed to teach correctness mainly by advice about actual mistakes made rather than by formal exercises, though these, especially in the lower school, are:

> nevertheless indispensable in making sure that the basic points about syntax, grammar, punctuation, etc. are covered by all pupils at an appropriate time in their school career.

If the two syllabuses agree upon the subservience of correctness to other aims in fifth-year writing lessons, then they differ signally in their more theoretical and general assumptions about pupil language and its value.

How different Smalltown School is from Downtown School has already been described but the distinct social and geographical locations seem significant in this context. From the inner-city school emerges both a general respect for present achievements and an expression of equal needs: from the ex-grammar school in Smalltown emerges a much greater concern with hierarchies, with distinctions about which ability group need what and why. Upper-ability pupils, for example, will need a wider range of language-forms than their less-able contemporaries: GCE groups are expected to cover:

> letter-writing, formal/informal invitations, thank-you notes,

whilst the others learn:

> methods of applying for jobs, filling-in of forms and routine letter-writing.

These statements are quite in accord with earlier remarks in the same document to the effect that the cultural poverty of the less-able must be enriched by reading. If Downtown School's syllabus had held 'correctness' as already existing, then Smalltown's offers a contrasting view:

> There need be no denigration of local accent, but THE can be spoken by all, aspirates given attention, final consonants sounded, statements completed. It is useful to structure for them a situation in which they *must* use clear speech (e.g. speaking to a deaf person . . . etc.).

Those who cannot speak (properly) must rehearse on those who cannot hear. There may be no denigration intended of those who come to school using the local accent but, despite the denial, many features of local speech are clearly held to be deficient. One particular segment of total pupil catchment is singled out and identified as being in need of correction. Seeking to 'improve' speech by insistence on standard forms is different from wishing to teach correct ways of writing, for it seeks to change language at a more personal level and a more fundamental cultural shift is thus involved. Statements like the one above, however, do not characterise the whole tone of the English syllabus at Smalltown School. In many ways it is a positive and informed document, strong in its support of a 16+ style of examining that fulfils the 'Comprehensive ideal'.

The English syllabus from Catchwide School shares with the two others already mentioned a concern for action which acknowledges the psychology of language development and for the interrelated nature of different activities. New Suburbia School's syllabus does not dwell at any length on the business of how language is learnt, though it is largely made up of lists of skills to be mastered as well as reading-lists. It is the most content-dominated of the four, and concerned to 'mount a concerted attack' upon 'particular weaknesses' as they arise.

Three of the syllabuses share the idea that learning an improving grasp of language should involve spontaneity, experiment and rehearsal, particularly when it is written language that is being improved, though there is rarely much detailed practical guidance on how spelling, punctuation and parts of speech etc. should be taught. Correcting errors during the marking of written-work is a commonly agreed method of instruction, but otherwise the lack of explanation of how to teach speaks of an assumed body of practice. Even in Downtown School's syllabus there is little that champions alternative models of language and language learning that might have been expected to go hand-in-hand with a revised view of pupils and their language. Where this syllabus differs from the other three in another way to those already mentioned is in its carefully constructed and presented ideas on the encouragement of oral work. Elsewhere the productive emphasis is so much on writing that this in itself excludes a range of possibilities, and removes from theoretical sight at least whole areas of language competence displayed by pupils in ways other than writing.

It is difficult to know what weight to put on syllabuses for their function for the average English teacher may be a very limited one. Is it fair to note the absence from the syllabuses of any statements that relate to raising the awareness of pupils to aspects of spoken and written language beyond those already given? For whatever reason and with whatever effect there is scarcely a glance at the language demands of the world of work or the kinds of issues concerning truth and bias in newspapers, or accents and social class, or any discussion on a basic matter like meaning being the use and the use being subject to change. Some of these sorts of things are taken up and developed by FE teaching; their absence from school syllabuses would suggest not that these things are not necessarily attended to in some lessons, but rather that they are not considered significant as ways of learning how to be a better writer, reader or speaker.

2. What the teachers said

Many teachers felt that it was wholly inappropriate to spend much time in the fifth year on decontextualised exercises to do with spelling and orthographic skills, partly because there was, as Mrs Sutton observed: 'so little transfer from it'.

As we shall see, it was almost entirely low-ability groups who were set to do punctuation exercises and this can be explained in terms of teachers' feelings about how such pupils enjoyed the satisfaction of right answers. 'Kids love *Clear English*[1] because they can get eight out of eight,' said Mrs Waterhouse, whom we saw teaching from that particular textbook. This book may well have been in Mrs Sutton's mind when she said:

> Now we're seeing a swing too far in the formal direction because the stuff that's coming out from publishers is a lot of very formal grammatical exercises which seem to be their answer to the creative bandwagon of the sixties and early seventies.

Mrs Sutton's criticism of the polarised positions assumed by publishers would appear to have been borne out by what we saw in language lessons, for there was a marked lack of alternative to drills except in the case of the letter-writing lessons in Catchwide School.

Some of the teachers expressed, in interviews, an interest in finding ground on which they could construct styles of language-teaching that enabled an insight into correctness and appropriateness and which could yet be free from the aridities of exercises. Mr Callaghan of Urban School said that he wanted to emphasise the idea of appropriate styles for different occasions, initially by reference to the language of chemistry. Mrs Sackville, from the same school, and Mr Saxon from Greentown School (from neither of which could we obtain syllabuses) both had considerable experience in work outside teaching, and they too expressed alternative perspectives about some aspects of teaching language. Their views, though on quite different topics, were critical of the limitations of what they saw as current practice. Mr Saxon's experience as a journalist may have influenced his views about the apparent lack of purpose in examination writing:

> The whole point is that the child is writing for an audience, not for Mr X

> with his big red pen or faceless TWYLREB or JMB but because he is communicating.

In this idea of the writer-communicator the individual pupil is perceived as one whose language and experience will necessarily link him or her to worlds outside school. The theory of writing expressed here is not our concern, but rather the theory of language-use which it carries with it. This suggests that Mr Saxon would wish, ideally, to teach by reference to communicative needs beyond those required for examinations. These could well be less literary than is commonly the case and less concerned with superficial correctness and they also seem consonant with some of the requirements Mrs Sackville had in mind:

> The first thing I'd want to do is consult a number of bodies of employers as well as universities and colleges of further education and find out what they need, then base . . . an examination . . . on their needs.

There could well be so little uniformity of view among these different bodies that Mrs Sackville would be disappointed but her position, like those of Mr Callaghan and Mr Saxon, represents the beginnings of a move away from — or outside of — the customary limitations surrounding language work. The three teachers seem to seek legitimations for an approach to language work that acknowledge a broader context of experience and needs than was found in most of what the syllabuses had to say or most of the lessons to exemplify. This raises the question of the sources of legitimation for language-work that operated generally. In passing it is worth noting that Mrs Sackville's opinions look similar to some of the communications ideas in further education colleges, as did the form of the passage she set for comprehension work, as we shall see. There remain a number of questions, still, to do with which language study is suitable for whom, and why, but they will be taken up in the final discussion, after some exploration of what went on in the lessons we saw.

3. The language lessons

Table 4.1 (p. 160) summarises the language lessons to be discussed in this section.

New Suburbia School's syllabus had referred to, 'language skills that can easily be taught in isolation from other work', and what we saw there were two such examples of isolated exercises, though with quite different sets, examinations and purposes and with different teachers. Mrs Waterhouse's bottom set were learning to punctuate via reference to unpunctuated passages from *Clear English* and, on another occasion, by teacher-dictation. In each of the two lessons the work on punctuation did not develop any considerations about its purpose or derivation nor was there any opportunity to practise further in any extended writing the points they had just been taught.

Table 4.1

Lessons on language topics

New Surburbia School			
Top set	(O-level literature class)	– Mr Porson	– work on 'images'
Bottom set	(CSE)	– Mrs Waterhouse	– punctuation work
Urban School			
Top set	(CSE)	– Mrs Sackville	– rectification of grammatical errors
Bottom set	(CSE)	– Mrs Sutton	– layout and punctuation of dialogues
Catchwide School			
Top set	(GCE)	– Mr O'Donnell	– writing letters
Bottom set	(CSE)	– Mr Gilham	– writing letters

As the observer noted at the time, the work was neither related to their own production nor justified by reference to their needs, though we have to note that the punctuation exercise that was dictated by the teacher in the second of the two lessons was drawn from *To Sir With Love*, the set reader at the time, and so the class would have been confronted with familiar material on this occasion instead of the unfamiliar examples taken from *Clear English* the first time round. In this book capital letters, and quotation marks for book-titles were taught and tested in entire isolation, and though the examples were quite random one pupil did in fact check that what the teacher and textbook were saying about capital letters was true by opening his desk and producing a copy of *To Sir With Love* and was pleased to notice as he did so that what he'd been told in theory was carried out in fact.

Punctuation played quite an important part in another class, this time a bottom CSE set in Urban School. The class had written 'draft conversations' and the lesson concerned an editorial task: 'I want you to swap books with a neighbour and correct each other's while they're still in draft, while they're still practising them', said Mrs Sutton at the start of the lesson. Several pupils seemed not to find this an easy exercise; the teacher had handed over to the class an assessing function and in a sense was thus helping to make explicit the significance to readers of punctuation and layout, that it helped to make clearer who was saying what in a conversation. However, the exercise was handled in such a way that while it drew several explanations on how to punctuate and arrange a conversation from Mrs Sutton, there was no discussion at all about what had been corrected, or why.

In the same school there was observed another language lesson with a top CSE set — a less than easily tractable group. Mrs Sackville was concerned to rectify a writing error: 'I noticed that many of you are not connecting verb and subject. With a singular subject you are using a plural verb and vice versa, it is something you must learn to do.'

The class then set to work correcting errors like the following from a textbook, *Themes*: 'The Queen, followed by her husband and children, were entering the abbey'. The teacher justified such work by reference to the class's errors, but the observer looking at the exercise books from nine of the pupils could find no example of either fault described by Mrs Sackville.

Both Catchwide School syllabus and Smalltown's had mentioned how a letter was important even to the lowest ability pupils. In Smalltown School's case it was 'routine' letter-writing that was required, and in Catchwide syllabus letter-writing was given as the only form of 'creative writing' that all pupils would need as adults. As chance would have it, we saw two lessons on the writing of letters in the same school, one with a top O-level group, the other with a bottom CSE set. Mr O'Donnell, with the top set, began at the beginning, the sender's address and how to indent it etc. and went on through to the correct form of subscription and signature. The lesson was given because a pupil had previously asked for some instruction. It is a significant lesson within the sequence of observed language-lessons because the teacher admitted large areas of ignorance and he also raised questions about the audience and function of this particular form (as did Mr Gilham also). There were times when the rules were quite definite but other times when ignorance was openly admitted:

P: Sir, where would you put the telephone number?
T: I don't know. (pause) Can you leave that and I will consult authorities about it?

Again, there were other occasions when Mr O'Donnell invited his class to see that 'rules' of letter-writing were not susceptible to definite answers because they were not simple, not consistent:

> Well, you see, this is the problem, I think that most of the letters we get, all the business letters we get, are typed and have a different code of behaviour, a different code of standards of writing.

Reference in the above quotation to actual letters, to models of language-use from the world outside school rather than to those in textbooks showed a willingness by the teacher to consider the varying forms of letters and he went on from there to consider the relationships between form and function:

> Let's not kid ourselves. Part of the purpose of this is to impress — to persuade an employer that you know what you're doing and how to set it down.

There were several remarks like this in the lesson, so that the idea of writing to affect someone else's attitudes and actions became a kind of 'given' in the proceedings. One of the effects of these strategies and explanations by the teacher was that the pupils contributed to an unusual degree:

> Sir, if you are writing for a job and you write down — well, wouldn't it be better to write down the job that you're wanting and your qualifications and then leave the rest until you find that they perhaps interview you?

Pupil contributions of that length, germane to the subject-matter in hand, were almost unknown in the other language lessons except in Mr Gilham's, where a similar idea to that expressed above became the subject of an extended debate.

Mr Gilham approached the task differently from his head of department. By using a textbook[2] specifically about letters he was able to provide his bottom set with examples of four different letters of application for the same job, and to discuss their relative merits. The class took eagerly to the work and joined in discussion about which two letter-writers should be invited for interview. Primary emphasis was on the content of the letters rather than their form, but many questions were raised about the function and effect of the particular examples by opening to debate questions about the criteria for a 'good' letter:

> P. The one that wrote that short one might be the best (applicant).
> T. Why do you think he might be?
> P. 'Cos he gets straight to the point, doesn't he?
> T. Yes, he gets straight to the point.
> P. You might think that what they've put in their letters, you might think they could do it, get used to it and all this lot. But when they come for an interview, like owt like that, they might be different.
> T. Well, that's true . . . you can't be certain . . . by reading the letter can you?

I am reminded by this of discussion in some of the further education classes, where criteria for interviews and appointments were made public in a similar way. In the textbook used by Mr Gilham's class there were two letters that seemed more explicit and full of relevant details than two others, yet here some of the pupils preferred a brief letter precisely because of its brevity and they did this partly by casting doubt on the validity of the more elaborated examples. Perhaps they intuited that any attempts of their own would more resemble the brief applications, but they were challenging in a perfectly articulate way (and in the local accent) the conventional bases for selection. Cultural preferences may have been involved as well as simply stylistic ones, but the responses of the pupils were, throughout the lesson, closely based on the texts, keen and sincere, and the participants' right of access to the language and to criteria for judging it were signalled and recognised.

It is difficult to know quite what significance to attach to two lessons but in these 'language study' began to resemble an examination of what is available to pupils through their pooled and public knowledge of language. Mr O'Donnell assumed that everyone had seen a letter before and that, in so far as certain rules were given, they were partly matters of taste: 'Personally I don't like things like "23.1.80", it looks more like a cricket average . . .'

At the time the observer noted that not only were there stronger expressions of pupils' viewpoints than in literature lessons with Mr O'Donnell, but that he seemed less authoritative than when talking about literature. Mr Gilham assumed that all pupils were able to have a valid opinion about a form of writing that they might soon be involved in and would enjoy experimenting with a 'privileged' assessing perspective that would not soon be theirs. These lessons provided evidence that language teaching in the fifth year can become something that relates to the pupils' experience of a world outside school whose linguistic forms and functions school can help to unravel. Letters are as rule-bound or taste-bound as points of punctuation are, and we can speculate that punctuation lessons could be based upon similar kinds of public documents that could be examined in such a way as to elicit and deduce what the governing conventions were. On the evidence we have it rather looks as if punctuation were a matter pertaining only to the world of classroom exercises. The classes doing punctuation were generally low in ability and were no doubt felt by their teachers to need practice so that they could improve a skill whose lack would be all too evident to anyone who read their letters, reports, exam papers, etc. Perhaps the teachers tend to underestimate the ability of such classes to work out conventions and rules and then apply them, but the boy who looked at *To Sir With Love* in order to verify what the textbook and teacher were saying was illustrating the possibility (no more) of working inductively from the printed word.

The remaining 'language' lessons were taught by Mr Porson to his top set who, at the time, were nominally doing literature work. The poems of Ted Hughes were considered two days after an initial lesson on images and figures of speech, but in this second lesson the literary discussion remained at a rather basic and literal level, suggesting perhaps that the class had not been able to utilise for critical and interpretative purposes the earlier work on similes and metaphors. In the first of the two lessons the class read a definition of imagery from the blackboard and were then told to substitute the literal phrases provided for imagistic uses such as, 'like a kick from a mule'. Ted Hughes's work was mentioned, but none of the images from his poems was quoted. In the second lesson the line:

The parrots shriek as if they were on fire...

from the poem *The Jaguar* became the subject of a dialogue between Mr Porson and one pupil. The debate was on whether or not the parrots looked as if they were on fire or merely sounded as if they were on fire. The pupil insisted that the line referred to sound only, and remained unpersuaded that any other possibilities about colour could have been applicable or intended.

4. The pupils' perspective:

'To be good at English you have to be a bit queer.'

This comment from one of the pupils we interviewed probably refers to more than just 'language' in its use of the word 'English', but it sums up the feeling that English in school attends to its own kinds of study yet the use of language outside school goes on normally and healthily. According to this same pupil: 'They (pupils good at English) won't be out in t'fresh air . . . they'll be sat down messing about'.

That it's a pupil from a bottom set who says this may come as no surprise. There was, among the other pupils interviewed, some correlation between their evaluations of the relevance of English in school and their position in the streaming system. Further support for the above view can be found in remarks such as: 'All you have to do (in a job) is write it, read it and talk it — you don't have to explain things'.

This last remark was from a fairly disaffected pupil in a bottom set. Other pupils in more prestigious groups held to the belief that school English was necessary in order to improve your language: 'You have to broaden your English a bit, because when you're outside you tend to use a lot of slang and that and you have to use language a bit more'.

Another pupil from a bright and well-motivated group saw certification in English as a kind of general intelligence score available to anyone, so that employers, to name but one group, can use English to, 'get rid of people that don't seem brainy enough'. These and other comments by pupils that show awareness of the links and points of disjunction between English in school and the language requirements of work and everyday life suggest the existence of a body of spontaneous reflection about language, however misinformed and unsystematic.

The days of traditional grammar teaching are largely over and in one sense a tradition of classroom attention to language (as often as not doing exercises) has gone and has not been replaced by any other. The time, we can surmise, that was spent on such things as clause analysis is now taken up with assignments or literature, with reading stories, poems and 'stimuli' and writing lots of essays or comprehension answers. Mrs Wood, in Smalltown School, felt that this shift had meant a raising of standards — that the demands on pupils' powers of eloquence have increased and their performance likewise. This could well be the case and if it is then English teachers would have cause to celebrate the validity of new approaches and the passing of the old tradition. There are, not surprisingly, residual elements from that tradition and they can be found in textbooks and syllabuses alike (in Downtown School as well as New Suburbia). Orthographic skills and conventions have obviously still to be taught and, equally obviously, they cannot just be left to 'grow' in a vaguely hopeful way. They are practically all, though, that is left of 'language study' if the lessons we saw represent typical practice. (I have to concede the dangers of generalising from a small number.)

5. School and beyond

Outside the work in conventions, there is little that has replaced 'grammar' as a way of studying language. This is not the place to investigate why this is so, nor should there be too conjectural a look at what kinds of language study could be undertaken. However, in so far as fifth-year English is considered by teachers, examiners and employers as not altogether irrelevant to work or further study, then it would seem appropriate to begin to question how far pupils are empowered by schoolwork to cope with the language demands that will confront them once the fifth year is over. Precisely what these demands are is, of course, a very difficult matter to decide. No teacher can predict quite what pupils will need in terms of language experience once they have started work, though the requirements for further study are much more familiarly known. In a very valuable paper[3], Mike Torbe has suggested that what fifth-year English can do is to prepare pupils for a wide range of possibilities: 'All that can be done is to consider the universals — those processes which are basic to all possible futures'.

This would suggest both rehearsal in particular skills that might well be required of a range of studies and occupations — like indexing and developing an understanding of specialist technical prose — and also studying language and its behaviour in such a way that a kind of general understanding is begun of more than just skills. What would be required would be the beginnings of a kind of reflective awareness of language that enabled the learners to grasp more than just the ability to perform correctly certain writing and reading conventions. They could, perhaps, begin to understand something of the linguistic contexts and social settings that both promote and constrain verbal communication. The areas to be examined are wide and could include any number of studies of speakers in particular settings and writers with particular purposes. Punctuation exercises etc. in school are concerned above all with correctness, but the notions of 'suitability' and 'appropriateness' could also come into play. Such study might well entail a broader look at a variety of styles of writing and speaking (via tapes) from more diverse sources than is, apparently, normally dealt with in the fifth year. School-based English lessons may do much to help pupils understand what they read and to become lucid at writing, but they don't aim to help pupils improve their understanding of what sort of phenomenon language is. Correctness in conventions is unarguably useful, but it doesn't enable much in the way of critical understanding of those conventions. As HMI said in 1977:[4]

> Paradoxically the deeper his understanding of the way conventions work, the more free the individual is to achieve his own purpose, to use the language appropriately as an individual but also with reference to the whole context. The best scientific and historical writing illustrates both the confident use of the conventions and the ability to bend them to make new meanings.

What is pointed to here is the advantage of using examples from diverse contexts, not only textbooks or literary passages.

A further point from Mike Torbe's paper that is usefully considered here relates to the forms to be filled in by young people once they leave school and seek jobs. Torbe found that many applicants were worried by the forms, particularly by the amount of space which they (properly) left blank when filling them in (because the forms covered such ground as experience in Her Majesty's Forces etc.). If such application forms had been looked at in school then not only might the pupils have later found the task of filling them in easier, but they could also have been led in some discussion about whether the form was in fact well designed. Such discussion might help pupils achieve an immediate end — the proper response to the questions — and could help them to feel a bit less helpless (or subordinate) when presented with other such forms by virtue of the fact that their understanding of the function of forms might have been improved by bringing into question both the point-of-view of those who design them and their intentions. The class could ask whether the questions were worded in the right way, could talk about likely reactions of those who read them and what sorts of messages about the fillers-in would be conveyed to the readers of the completed versions. This relates to Mr Gilham's lesson and at the same time brings us round to wondering whether thinking in class about the intentions of those who write things is in fact best achieved by reference to so much literary writing, where 'intention' is not held as problematic. Elsewhere we shall look at the nature of passages given for 'comprehension' work, but in this context we can note that in general terms so many of the examples of writing looked at in class are literary that the question of 'intention' is not as likely to arise as it might be if a broader range of examples of different functions of written language were available to teacher and pupils.

In interviews with pupils we found, as we said, that many of them had quite clear notions about the usefulness of school English. The girl who said: 'writing an essay, answering a comprehension... I don't see that that sort of testing is the sort of skills they're wanting' (employers), had been able to see or opine that for the world of work (though not necessarily for her own purposes) English was of limited use. Yet her perceptions about different language needs in different contexts were never required in class. It begins to look as if English teachers rely on the pupils bringing to the classroom feelings, experiences and knowledge which can be put to good use in essays but are not called upon in other terms that could well prove helpful towards building up a better understanding of language roles and functions. Concentration on literature and literary modes tends, perhaps, to filter out much of the developing 'folk linguistics' of pupils that could be fruitfully applied to their own ends. The pupil quoted earlier who talked about 'slang' as characteristic of out-of-school language seems to have accepted a deficit model of how people operate for most of the time. Could it be that the use of literature to enrich the given poverty is, while highly valuable, one way of ignoring much of what pupils are already good at as speakers and participants in language exchanges? However sympathetic teachers reveal themselves to be in their syllabuses towards a 'growth' model of language there is little sign in lessons that school English can help pupils reflect upon what language is and how much it has grown for them, how we come to have it and what we do with it to achieve our aims. Pupils are not for the most part seen as having ideas of their own about language, nor are they invited in any way to investigate how language functions, either within school or out of it. One of the two lessons in those looked at that seems to point in the direction of an open investigation that requires the existing knowledge of pupils is Mr O'Donnell's session on writing a letter and it is surely significant that once separated from the literary customs he did not know the answers, and yet was happy enough to cull some of them from the class.

COMPREHENSION

6. Introduction

Comprehension is one of the chief elements in examinations in fifth-year English, at both O-level and CSE (and 16+) and, despite the often literary nature of the passages set for classwork as well as for exam, is thought of as 'language work'. The passages used in class in our sample were of a literary nature rather than strictly literary or fictional, but of these more later. It is arguable that 'comprehension' is the least changed in style and assumption of any of the elements in O-level English Language. The change towards a syllabus D continuously-assessed O-level may have put traditional notions about essay writing to the test, but the comprehensions seem to continue as ever. Although in our sample of 17 teachers and 18 classes from six schools we saw only five lessons spent doing comprehensions, nevertheless we believe that in the fifth year most pupils will spend a fair amount of time reading what are to them randomly selected passages and answering questions about them set by a reader other than themselves or their peers. How far these enable a deeper understanding of the difficulties of interpreting and understanding the writer's intended meaning must to a certain extent depend on how they are taught. As we shall see, there was some significant variation in the extent to which 'comprehensions' were interpreted by teachers as either testing devices or occasions for instruction.

7. Syllabus statements

Generally the syllabuses say little on the subject of comprehension. Let us take Smalltown School's syllabus's statements first:

1. 'Some of their assignments should test their understanding and appreciation of the written word.'
2. 'To encourage and test understanding, an occasional comprehension passage (one complete short article or extract) should be studied in some depth and detail to counterbalance any tendency towards carelessness and superficiality such a course could produce. Subjects dealt with should be biased towards their own adolescence and their relationships (see 'Conflict').'

Quotation 1 is from a single A4 sheet concerning the 16+ English examination. Number 2, from the main syllabus, concerns fourth-year work, but I assume that this is not inapplicable to the fifth year. In this second statement there is an element of moral disapproval of what the young readers would do if not guided in other directions and yet also a recognition of the need for relevance to present lives (full of conflict?). Put in the terms quoted above, we can see that the teacher of reading (of English) in Smalltown School has lots of work to do because the pupils start from such a poor base. If in the fourth year carelessness and superficiality of reading are likely to arise, then little trust can be based on existing competencies.

Smalltown School syllabus shares with Catchwide School's the notion of the natural inclination towards deficient readings. In this latter document the phrase is 'haste and superficiality'. When two out of only four syllabuses produce such closely similar wording then I begin to wonder whether moral disapproval is seriously intended. Both documents use their respective phrases in connection with comprehension and perhaps the ideas function primarily as justifications for the slowness of procedure that a close look at a passage entails and there is also the possibility present of an implicit contrast with reading for pleasure. What distinguishes Smalltown

School's syllabus from Catchwide's in terms of comprehension is Catchwide's concern that comprehension work has more to do with teaching than testing, and that the work should be based on 'set texts' rather than passages selected for their relevance. In Catchwide School syllabus the ideas about comprehension occur under the heading 'Literature' as they do in Downtown syllabus also. This may be entirely logical, but is nevertheless unexpected, because 'comprehensions' occur on the Language paper and because their questions are often literal tests of initial understanding rather than the invitations to interpret subjectively more characteristic of literary study.

In Downtown School syllabus there is a substantial section on reading under the heading 'Literature'. There is practical advice of a detailed kind on how to handle literary texts and a section headed 'Reading Skills' which lists 1–12 as follows:

Suggested by Assessment of Performance Unit, 1979

Comprehension

1. Understand Word and Sentence Meaning
2. Find Main Idea and Related Details
3. Organise and Classify Facts
4. Perceive Sequence of Ideas
5. Draw Inferences and Conclusions
6. Understand Problems
7. Form Judgements
8. Predict Outcomes
9. Read Critically — distinguishing Fact from Opinion
10. Read for Appreciation
11. Understand Relationship
12. Follow Directions

It is hard to see how each of these could apply equally to literary reading. The list is followed by no discussion and no advice on practical teaching outcomes that might be entailed by it. Its significance within the four syllabuses is that it represents by far the most sophisticated model of what comprehension is or could be and is located within a section on reading that is by far the most useful as a practical guide, as well as being concerned to see reading as problematic at all. I get the impression from Downtown School syllabus that, despite the conceptual blurrings and omissions within and from the Literature section, there is a concern to link 'comprehension', reading and the study of literature in mutually beneficial ways. The syllabus that is most concerned with problems of the reading process, and difficulties of teaching reading is the very one least concerned to chastise existing erroneous habits among pupils though, ironically, it sees 'comprehension' as a possible source of boredom, and thus antithetical to good reading:

> Use the book for work sheets or language and comprehension, thus providing a purposeful context for such work. Do not overdo this however, as boredom may detract from enjoyment of the book.

In New Suburbia School syllabus there are some general statements on reading that are not age-specific nor are they related to any one kind of reading matter. They posit the notions (i) literal reading; (ii) deeper readings concerned with nuance and meanings arrived at indirectly; and (iii) deeper readings concerned with modes of analysis that enable readers to see how they are being influenced. They look like an interesting theory-behind-a-programme but there is no programme to follow them. The following sentence only, in New Suburbia School's syllabus, relates to comprehension at all: 'The formal comprehension as in the course-books should be done regularly'.

From all four syllabuses only in Downtown's is there any kind of breakdown of the nature of what is involved for the learner in comprehension. Even in this case the Assessment of Performance Unit list is left raw: there is no mention of whether comprehension is of 12 facets or only one. From the syllabuses as a whole it would appear that reading in school is problematic at the level of persuading all kinds of classes to enjoy a wide variety of fiction and literature. There is virtual silence on all other aspects of reading development in the secondary school. This silence is more noticeable since there is, in three of the four syllabuses, a detailed theoretical and practical section on the teaching of writing. It is as if the Bullock Report had been read very partially. We cannot know from the syllabuses quite what it is that 'comprehension' should test or instruct in, except perhaps in Downtown syllabus's case, but even here there is a kind of vagueness about the relationship between 'comprehension' and the part it might play in teaching of reading in general or (literary) particular. These things suggest that writing is more important than reading or, if this puts it too crudely, that it is harder to teach writing than reading. Analysis of the syllabuses above would strongly suggest that no English department had recognised that the teaching of reading could be as complex as the teaching of writing, nor had it detailed what might be done in the classroom to help pupils with various aspects of it. Broadly speaking, the model implicit in examinations was accepted as perfectly satisfactory. In other words, there seemed to be no theoretical position that challenged the concept of fostering reading abilities by reference to paraphrasing someone else's ideas of what were 'difficult' words, phrases and larger meanings in a passage on a topic that may or may not have been of interest to the readers.

8. The passages and questions

It may be useful to start with a brief table (Table 4.2) of who was doing what with whom:

Table 4.2

The passages set for comprehension study in class

Urban School		
Bottom set	– Mrs Sutton	– from *The Only Child* by James Kirkup
Middle set	– Mr Callaghan	– from *A Pattern of Islands* by Arthur Grimble
Top set	– Mrs Sackville	– from *A History of Yorkshire Houses* and other sources, written in part by Mrs Sackville
Catchwide School		
Middle set	– Mr Keegan	– from Lord Kennet's contribution to *The Character of England* – an essay against street-advertising
Greentown School		
Top set	– Mr Tremaine	– from a 1961 *Guardian* article 'The Night Riders' about motorcyclists

There's nothing obvious in this list to suggest why any one passage should be used with any one particular ability group. Possibly one might guess — if not already told — that the *Guardian* piece was used with an O-level set (because in that class in that school some might be already acquainted with the *Guardian*) but in fact the language of that particular report is no harder than that of, say, *The Only Child* which was used with a bottom set. There are no phrases in *The Night Riders* passage that are as carefully or self-consciously literary as this from James Kirkup:

> all these I studied with obsessional intensity until I knew every colour, every repetition, every convulsion of their extraordinary designs. (Carpets, plates etc.)

Nor is the overall drift any harder to grasp. If there is no apparent concern to match 'ability' of pupil and difficulty of passage studied, then neither are there any preconceptions at work that might try to relate subject-matter to pupil interest according to ability-group. The ton-up boys were read about in a top set in Smalltown School, not the bottom set in Urban School, and it is hard to imagine that Lord Kennet's concerns about the built environment echoed much in the way of spontaneous curiosity in Catchwide School. Arthur Grimble's octopus story is a gripping narrative, the kind of well-told tale that transcends its geographical and cultural distance from us and, as we shall see, provoked a lively response in Mr Callaghan as well as in some of his pupils. That story and James Kirkup's memories of childhood became, either in the textbook or in class, invitations to write at length as well as being passages to be studied. In that sense these last two may have been selected with a view to extended use beyond being simply the bases of questions about them, but otherwise it is hard to see that any particular selection processes were at work among the teachers who chose the passages they did. The passages are all virtually journalism or autobiography; none is given any contextual setting except as being the product of the professional writer seeking to engage the interest of the general reader. The *Guardian* report is, significantly, not a news item that could carry a sense of urgency behind it; it comes under the 'topical interest' heading, as does the only other journalistic piece (about the last steam locomotives) from the same textbook. School thus gives prominence to the residual elements of serious reporting. The style, tone and authorial stance of each passage studied in class assumes a fairly well-read audience wishing to know about non-technical, non-controversial[5], non-political experiences and points-of-view that keep it informed in a broad liberal way. Culturally it is roughly mid-morning Radio 4. Even in the *Guardian* report on the leather-jacketed boys in the Busy Bee there's a protagonist who spends his all on motorcycling and who yet advocates common sense, crash-helmets and speed restraint. Do 'comprehensions' seek to teach, among other things, membership of an audience?

As far as pupils are concerned, some of the passages may have related more closely to themselves and their concerns than others and some passages may have provided echoes of literary study in the fifth year — *The Only Child* passage, for example, is not unlike the ubiquitous and popular *Cider with Rosie*. For some teachers (like Mrs Sutton) the content could have a secondary function as a stimulus for pupil writing and it could become, as we shall see, a kind of instrument to help penetrate pupil lives. Most pupils, however, would not, I think, have found their own out-of-school reading matter or world views reflected in the passages and questions set them to help improve their reading skills. There is, for example, no forward look to the world of work, as there is for BEC styles of comprehension, nor a broader reference to what pupils read outside the classroom. Nor is there any context provided, except marginally in the *Guardian* piece, that enables reflection upon the relationship of writing to situation. *Seals of Approval* reminds us that:

> The social situation of the examination candidate is of crucial importance, since making sense of a passage requires some kind of orientation, some sense of purpose and situation.

How far the social situation of the pupils was acknowledged by the passages found in use by us remains in question.

The questions

> It is when we turn from the content of the passages to the questions set that the artificiality of the typical comprehension test is most striking.[6]

Bearing this in mind, as a comment about examination comprehensions, and bearing in mind too that elsewhere in this report it is suggested that typical English comprehension work in further education does not seek to engage the student's personal involvement or sense of reality, then we must look at what the questions set for the passages already given seek to do. We need to see what kinds of readings are encouraged by the questions set on our passages, which aspects of the text are focused upon and what assumptions about readers and reading appear to be made. First, it is useful to outline the form of the questions in each of the five books or passages in use. In four cases, (i) *The Only Child*; (ii) *Night Riders*; (iii) *A Pattern of Islands*; and (iv) *The Character of England* the pupils had to read one extract only and then answer some questions on it. In three of the four books in which the passages and questions were set there was further work following the immediate group of about 12 questions. These further questions were in sections whose titles implied a broadening out from immediate paraphrase and close reading to wider considerations raised. Titles used for this second section were:

i. 'Implications' (of the James Kirkup extract)
ii. 'Interpretation and Criticism' (of *Night Riders*)
iii. 'Techniques' (Arthur Grimble's way of writing)

Beyond these second sections are further questions and activities (not always in the same format as the first group of questions) that are broader still. A few examples from these third sections are as follows:

i. Write about either (a) your first experience of being away from home; or (b) your earliest memories of school.
ii. What must a journalist bear in mind when writing for newspaper readers?
iii. Write about two travel books that deal with expeditions in remote parts of the world or life in little-known and distant countries.

Passage (iv) from *The Character of England* has only a single set of questions attached.

This broadening out from very small particulars of literal meaning is clearly an attempt to give larger significance to the original passage studied. In one case, (i), the extract from *The Only Child* becomes an imaginative starting-point for creative writing by pupils (and used as such by Mrs Sutton). In another case, (ii), there's an invitation to think about journalism from the point-of-view of genre, purpose and audience (an invitation taken up by a pupil and then Mr Tremaine) and in case (iii), the original passage on the octopus hunt is viewed as having potential as a literary taster that might provoke further reading along the same lines. In each case the editors of the comprehension anthologies are anxious to have classes do more than simply answer a few paraphrase questions; it is as if there were a danger in leaving the extracts merely as one-off exercises and compensation for this danger can be made if they are personalised, broadened and viewed in a detached way, or extended. As we shall see, the teachers in most cases were concerned with more than simply evincing literal answers. Either in the book or in class there's an implication that a thorough understanding requires more than a simple single reading whose only function is to enable some fairly low-level questions to be got right. This basic element of paraphrase and brief checks on literal correctness is there, unavoidable, apparently, and fundamental to the rest but it is later enriched (not modified) by additions that involve either more criticality or self-involvement than is deemed necessary or useful at the first level. It could be argued that these different sections were not very consistent with each other since there's a tendency for them to presuppose or require different models of reading. It is worth noting in this context that only one teacher took the questions as themselves problematic.

The comprehension lesson with Mrs Sackville in Urban School was based on a somewhat different approach. Here the class had to read five extracts about an 18th-century house in North Yorkshire; the first, dated 1957, described its architecture and recent decay, the second gave an account of a ghost story based on the house, the third, 1971, was an auction advertisement for the place and, from later the same year, a newspaper report of its burning down. Then followed an extract of who was paid what in 1763 among the house servants, and a map. Passages and questions had been written a few years earlier by Mrs Sackville and a colleague. The readers had to (1) write an account of the story of the house; (2) describe the character of the original owner and then (3) do one of three different tasks, only one of which was based directly on the information given. This format was interesting in that the first question gave the reader a synthesising role, something quite unknown in any other passages and yet the kind of approach that simulates a likely role for comprehension tasks in the world beyond the fifth year. The reader has to make more complex choices concerning what is relevant in the writing of a single account based on evidence from several different sources than when answering briefly someone else's questions. Question 3, however, was very similar to the later section questions quoted above except that it followed their form without seeming to understand what else was involved:

> *3(b)* Can you recollect an occasion when you were snubbed? What were your feelings? What did you do? Did you deserve it? Use this experience as the basis for story, or play dialogue, etc.

This attempt to make the comprehending deeply personal is a stiff order for a 15 or 16-year-old in that it tries to make their pain, humiliation (or outrage) and moral self-evaluation available to a teacher in a raw form. What is more it relates only to a brief paragraph in the entire set of passages to be read:

> Legend has it that the original builder, Joshua Park, a man who acquired a great deal of money from trade, though many believed him guilty of 'blackbirding' — transporting slaves from Africa to America — disappointed that his house and his wealth did not give him entry to the high society of the area, went mad. One night in 1769, having, it is said, been snubbed yet again by a neighbour, Park took a pistol and a sword, and entering the stable buildings which adjoin the house, ran amok where the grooms and stable lads lay quietly sleeping. Before he could be seized, he had shot or stabbed four young men, all of whom died. Park escaped hanging through the influence of his liberal purse, but died three years later never having recovered complete health.

This hardly gives the reader-answerer of question 3(b) much to go on by way of guidance on how to answer. The question seems similar to that based upon *The Only Child* extract, but it is a formal similarity only. In *The Only Child* question the writing task for pupils mirrored the writing task James Kirkup had set himself. In this instance, 3(b), the pupil writer is not asked to undergo the same process as the adult example, but simply to start from an affective nowhere.

In Catchwide School Mr Keegan's class had had to read an extract from Lord Kennet's contribution to *The Character of England*. After that there were only nine questions set that required summaries as well as paraphrases. The passage was the only one from our sample of five that was concerned to argue a case — that advertisements ruin townscapes — but only one of the questions set addressed itself to the validity of the argument:

> In one good sentence, argue the case against the statement that 'Advertisements increase the cost of production (lines 14–15)'.

It is fair enough that this is a genuine invitation to refute part of a larger argument, but at the same time it is a bit constraining by virtue of the 'one good sentence'. One suspects that the quesiton is intended to elicit a simple answer along the lines of the virtues of open competition. Another question of interest from this passage is:

> The author admits that some advertisements are useful (lines 8–9). Mention briefly an advertisement you would put into this category, and justify your choice.

This is one of the few questions from the whole set of our printed data that asks the pupils to select from the ordinary world around them.

To return to the original concerns about the nature of the questions set, we can see that in many cases it was assumed that enlightenment about the meaning of a passage — understanding it better — was likely to begin by a concentration on selected sentences, words or details of imagery; generally speaking the parts are to be dealt with before the whole, the particular having precedence over the general. The exceptions to this lay in the synthesising nature of making one story out of three or four and the summary required by the first question attached to the Lord Kennet extract:

> In not more than 70 of your own words state the bad effects that public advertising has 'materially' and 'spiritually'.

Questions that require the learner-reader to summarise a whole argument or part of one tend to force a reading that (with any luck) will build upon a sequence of ideas rather than take a mere succession of randomly featured words. In other cases than the two exceptions mentioned, the composite and the summary, the questions focused the reader's attention on whatever details there were that struck the question-compiler as interesting or difficult (or both). This is not to complain that the questions were obscure or altogether lacking in relevance to what one might judge to be the spirit of the original passage so much as that it was not easy to see why one particular element was chosen from the original in preference to any other. An example of a type of question that selected a detail whose salience was not exactly obvious is the following:

> 1. What is the most distinctive feature of the appearance of these motor-cyclists?

the paragraph for reference being:

> Every Saturday night, from suburban homes all over Greater London, hundreds of black-jacketed, teenage motor-cyclists move off in groups towards the M.1. Among them is one from Kingston-upon-Thames; and one of the seven members of this group is Joe Williams. He is 21 years old, has an Adam Faith haircut, the distinction of a black jacket made of leather, and he works as a builder's labourer for about £10 per week.

The right answer — black leather jackets — may have been of significance to the author of the question but it is hard to agree that it is a particularly crucial item in terms of making sense of what is there, either in content or descriptive technique. This suggests that, had the rest of the questions been like this, the pupils' reading was being guided by what must have appeared random items and, further, that the reading encouraged was fragmented every bit as much as it was selective.

Teaching a close and careful reading must to some extent be a mediation of the author's intentions but even so that would not rule out a form of analysis that allowed for and acknowledged a more tentative approach that was more inclusive of a range of evidence and, possibly, able to allow the readers to have more say in identifying what was significant or insignificant for them. Something is needed that perhaps offers an interpretative possibility without pre-empting the reader's own powers of discovery. Conventional questions seem either to be in danger of carrying all the answers with them or being themselves a cause of difficulty when the original passage is well understood. From this point of view we can see that the advocates of such techniques as cloze procedure and prediction exercises are justified if their methods enable the readers to develop their own questions, and if those in turn create a more involved search of the whole passage. Properly handled, such reading-extension techniques may teach well but not be readily employed as ways of testing. The form of most of the questions on four of the five passages results in their seeming to be testing devices rather than fruitful modes of enquiry or analysis. There's an unhelpful circularity, for example, in the demand:

> Explain briefly what you understand by 'proprietary brands' (line five).

because if you do understand, then line five was unproblematic to you as a reader to start with and you are merely showing that it was, or, if you do not understand, then the question does nothing at all to help you discover the meaning from the rest of the text. The pupil reader in this instance is not apparently envisaged as one who is able to make progress; he or she is the purely static knower or not knower. Only the teacher's supplying the right answer after the comprehension questions have been already answered can understanding be increased. By that time anyway the right answer may be seen as a reproof every bit as much as a guide to an improving grasp of the art. As we shall see, pupil dislike of comprehension, where it occurred, involved the feeling that it was arbitrary. Not all the questions, of course, seemed to posit the knowing/not knowing pupil in quite the way as the one quoted above, but many of them, especially in the earlier sections, didn't credit the reader with being able to take in very much at a time.

Seals of Approval showed that there tended to be a split between O-level styles of examining comprehension and CSE styles, with the O-level papers relying predominantly on questions that ask for paraphrases and short interpretation answers, and the CSE papers (some of them) being more inclined to set broad interpretative and inferential tasks which test 'the broader capacity to construct meaning which the Bullock Report called for'. Only one class of those observed was working on a comprehension that was modelled on the local CSE approach which had no paraphrase questions and placed reliance on longer interpretations and imaginative or developmental questions. This was Mrs Sackville's class in Urban School. Mrs Sutton's class, as already explained, were also engaged in writing that used the original passage as a kind of jumping-off point but they did so only after work on paraphrase questions. The model of 'doing comprehension' that four-fifths (roughly) of the pupils in our sample of lessons experienced was based on a traditional O-level model that had in any case been outmoded by the JMB syllabus A paper, where only a minority of questions ask for paraphrase or short interpretations. As we shall see, the teachers differed in the extent to which they took the text and questions as problematic, and some were more concerned with 'right' answers than others.

It is clear that, on the questions looked at so far, there is little else available to the individual pupil as a product of their thinking other than a page or two of answers. Some of the questions in the comprehension passages set for the folder-work in Downtown and Smalltown Schools (not included so far because they do not relate to any lessons that we saw taught) are entirely conventional, but others do involve tasks that relate closely to the actual matter of the passage and yet bring in a wider range of pupil response, like evaluations of substance and content. For example, there was from Smalltown School a question on an extract from *Of Mice and Men* that asked whether the pupils thought it right that Carlson shot Candy's ancient dog. From Downtown School there was a question which invited the readers and writers to describe the hero from the point-of-view of his opponent who was also the butt of the author's satire: here the pupil was requested to display qualities such as a sense of fun combined with an ear for that character's idiolect, and the resultant answer could have been an amusing and pleasing piece of work in its own right — something that an answer to a question like: 'Explain the meaning of "punch-drunk" ' could never be.

Questions like the two given do not entirely fulfil the condition of giving the reader a clear point for their reading; they don't for example, entail any action beyond 'aesthetic' writing, but they do suggest that reading has a point beyond being a preliminary for someone else's test items. They don't, however, by any means characterise the comprehension work for continuous assessment in either school. This is predominantly based (a) in paraphrase and short interpretation items; and (b) in questions which look outwards from the text but can be answered without very much reference to it. A good example of the latter is a question set for the JMB English Language paper that asked the candidates to imagine that they were one of the crew of the aeroplane from which the first atomic bomb was dropped: 'Describe your experiences that day.' This task was set (an option, it has to be admitted) after a passage about the events in Hiroshima as witnessed and suffered by one Miss Sasaki. From reading about her individual experiences it would have been almost impossible to write about events on board an aircraft or the view from it. Imagination, and with any luck, historical recall, would have been far more helpful than any careful re-reading. (This JMB paper was reproduced for use in Smalltown School's folder-work.) It would be wrong to assume that these extended questions, for all their apparent lack of concern with reading, do not provide valuable writing opportunities for some of the pupils — the ones who mentioned when interviewed how useful comprehensions could be as aids to writing in their provision of a substance or starting-point. Of the several pupils referred to here the one who said that comprehensions were 'a good test of the imagination' can surely have had only these sorts of questions in mind.

9. The lessons and the issues

When we come to examine how the comprehensions were being taught — the actual classroom work — we notice a number of differences in approach towards the task by the five teachers concerned. These differences have to do with such matters as the attitude towards the text and the comprehending of it that was shown to the class by the teacher, and construals about what was the nature of the task in hand and the degree of attention given to explaining to the pupils how they were to cope with what they had to do. Any group of five teachers could be expected to pursue their work in different ways but the variations to be looked at here will seem, I hope, more significant than simply a range of pedagogic styles of the kind that inevitably distinguish one teacher's work from another's. The deeper differences have to do with such matters as the reading abilities that teachers credit pupils with, and the notions about reading itself that underpin particular classroom procedures.

Three of the five teachers, namely Mr Tremaine, Mr Callaghan and Mrs Sutton, showed in class a fairly evident involvement either in the text for study or the comprehension process itself, or both. Mrs Sutton began by reading through *The Only Child* extract, taking her class orally through the printed questions in the first section — the paraphrase and short interpretation section. After half an hour she set the class, a bottom CSE set, to work in groups answering the following four questions printed above the passage for study, and each group had to write down their collective answer;

The Home (Security and insecurity)

> For the most part we take home for granted — until something goes wrong. What sort of upset could most easily throw your home life into confusion?
>
> If there were a serious accident that upset your normal home life, how would this affect your work?

> What can you remember most vividly about starting school as an infant? Can you remember not wanting to go back to school?
>
> What do you still like best about getting home after being out all day?

In the last ten minutes there was some discussion based on the answers. In this double period Mrs Sutton was mainly concerned to press for answers to questions like: 'What does he mean by "anguish and excitement"?' and then move out of the process herself whilst making the class move outwards from textual considerations to the more personal ones listed above. In the next lesson, two days later, answers to the above questions were discussed again, the teacher leading discussion. It was in this second lesson that the degree of Mrs Sutton's involvement became most apparent. She was quite prepared to talk about her home background, to tell the class fairly close personal details as, for example, that she had recently been glad to borrow money from her mother. One is reminded by her willingness to reveal details of her personal life of Mrs Wood in Smalltown (see Chapter 3, p. 91ff). The comparison is apt in the sense that Mrs Sutton was here preparing the class to write about themselves (and used the comprehension passage as a stimulus). The involvement that was shown was not so much in the text as in the autobiographical matter and contemporary experience brought to mind by the four questions. By revealing memories of when she was younger, Mrs Sutton created a kind of parallel text to James Kirkup's autobiographical fragment:

> That was the first thing that I did when I got home, got out of uniform into clothes that I felt were more me and not like all the other people at school, so that was a symbol if you like of being free of the discipline of school.

By inviting the class to give their own responses to questions about upsets at home, further contributions were being gathered towards this parallel text. James Kirkup's memories were there in print; Mrs Sutton's were also made available orally and the class too were expected to contribute. It was, logically, their turn next to do the writing. Thus the original extract had become not an item for study, but an inspiration for further thinking. An extension outwards had been enacted, not a deeper reflection back into the text. 'Comprehending' becomes thus a wide term, inclusive of many activities but not those that equip pupils with skills to look back into and ask questions of the original text. Those in the class who were going to take the CSE examination in English would encounter in it a form of comprehension little concerned with short-fragment paraphrase and more concerned with a broader interpretation. The textbook which printed the four initial questions already quoted was, originally, intending them as pre-reading raisers of interest; in Mrs Sutton's lesson they had become pre-writing raisers of interest. Either way they were unable to function as guides to the carefully constructed extract from *The Only Child*, except in the sense that they suggested that in order to read someone else's experiences, you need first to remind yourself of your own. What were lacking in terms of matching examination demands were questions which had this wide inclusiveness and yet which could not be answered without any reference at all to what James Kirkup had written.

Mr Callaghan's personal involvement with the passage in hand (with a middle set also in Urban School) was not evidenced in quite the same way as his head of department's. She was bringing a parallel text to life; he was more concerned to respond to the original text. However, his interpretative commentaries were nothing like as extended as Mrs Sutton's memories and points-of-view. Like her, he read the passage for study aloud and, like her, he aimed for an oral answering of some of the printed questions before any written answers were started. Like her, too, he had chosen a passage that was autobiographical but the similarities end here because the autobiographical fragment concerned not childhood fear of school, but an octopus hunt. Mr Callaghan's introduction to the extract from Grimble's *A Pattern of Islands* began thus:

> Last Thursday we were looking at *The Snake*, one man's attitude to it — and now we're going to look at something which people find equally horrific and detestable and that is an octopus (murmurs). Now — certainly when I was younger and I used to go to the Saturday matinees, nearly once a month somebody would be diving for buried treasure and he's caught in the clutches of an octopus, and the passage we're going to look at today concerns young people who purposefully put themselves in an octopus's clutches — the better to kill it.

After this opening move the passage was read through, with Mr Callaghan interrupting himself occasionally to check that there was sufficient initial understanding of what amounted to a technical description of how to catch an octopus using a human being as bait. His own interest in the story began to be evidenced during these short question-sessions:

T. Why 'yellow' and not 'green'?
P. (reply inaudible)
T. Yellow is for cowardice. Yes, scared stiff. I think I should have been horribly green.

A few minutes later, having finished reading aloud the whole extract, he began questioning again, concentrating, as before, on feelings and emotions rather than facts of the text. As the observer noted at the time, he saw 'comprehension' as providing literary texts which could capture the pupils' imaginations as well as being passages whose literal meaning was to be worked out. Mr Callaghan questioned and led discussion for some eight minutes before he made any reference to the printed questions; in other words, the question items were of his own making and in that they continued to show his involvement with the text as something to which he individually had responded. In a sense he was providing his class with an initial 'reading' or interpretation via these questions; they enabled him to deal in considerations about the text that were evidently his own, to begin, if nothing else, to give priority to certain points:

> T. They flung it in his face when he was lying on the surface. I suppose it would feel like a slug. (Shudders and ughs.)

There were attempts, too, to move the incidents described into the world of his pupils:

> T. Just a game, just a bit of fun, bit of excitement on a Saturday afternoon.

This 'Saturday afternoon' reference was repeated once or twice from this point and it serves as an interesting example of a misleading idea stemming from the attempt to predict your audience's terms of understanding; Grimble says nothing at all about the day of the week, only that the activity of octopus hunting was not a serious adult one. One aspect of the otherness of Gilbert and Ellice island culture was in danger of being lost. It's a minor point, however, compared to other moves to bring things into the pupils' world precisely by ironic comparison to the otherness of the islanders' way of life:

> T. Why on earth should he be scared? What's wrong with being grabbed by an octopus on a Saturday afternoon? Nothing wrong with it whatsoever, normal thing, isn't it? Happens every day — you're walking out on a Saturday afternoon and you're grabbed by an octopus.

Still the Saturday afternoon references persist!

The third teacher, Mr Tremaine in Greentown School, with his top O-level set showed in the lesson observed not so much a high level of involvement with the text but rather a great involvement in the business of interpreting it. His primary response to the *Night Riders* passage was there, but as a kind of necessary subordinate or prerequisite to what was manifestly his overriding concern — making sense of questions that attempted to make sense of the text. In the whole double period he said nothing that could easily be quoted as his own direct response to the *Guardian* report. Instead, that response was implied almost continuously in his discussion about his pupils' answers to questions. There was no sense of his having to commend or sell the text, or grow enthusiastic about it, but instead there was a sustained critical evaluation towards it and everything surrounding it:

> Now Section C which I think is probably the most revealing and interesting one. If you ever get anyone saying to you (quotes from textbook), 'this is good journalism', don't believe them. Make your own minds up about any

> values that you're offered, and clearly, as one or two of you actually pointed out, whether you detect bias in a piece of journalism depends upon your own bias in the first place, to a certain sense.... Some of you indicated you didn't think the article was biased and some of you indicated you thought the article was biased towards the motor-cyclist. I slightly share that point-of-view myself and I was interested to see the arguments for both sides.

It's a long quotation, but throughout we can see (i) the critical evaluation of the textbook's assertion about good journalism; (ii) an acknowledgement of pupils' self-awareness as readers; (iii) an acknowledgement of the reasonable nature of differing viewpoints; and (iv) his own response to the original passage in terms of 'bias'. No other teacher approaches comprehension work in this way, taking the questions as problematic, and challenging their potential power to distort an interpretation. The fact that it's a top set is significant; it seems hard to imagine some classes being able to follow what's said here, but there's more than just 'intelligence' that the class is being credited with. Among the other elements that are assumed to exist already or are brought into being via such teaching are a great faith in rational discernment and a very sophisticated reading ability that interprets well before the notion of a 'right' answer becomes important. This was an unusual lesson in several senses, including the degree of critical and evaluative participation which it evoked from the pupils, but we shall return to it shortly.

Mr Keegan, in Catchwide School, was also, like Mr Tremaine, observed taking his class through their answers, but the comments that he made in a brief 20-minute session included no reflections of his own on Lord Kennet's contribution to *The Character of England*. Right answers and the demands of the examination seemed the guiding principles, the determiners of relevance.

Mrs Sackville, with her top set in Urban School, was introducing her class to the comprehension material but she, like Mr Keegan, seemed not to be personally involved in it. Her overriding concern was to make her instructions clear and to get her class writing.

The degree to which teachers are seen by their classes to be imaginatively or critically caught up in the text or questions for consideration was chosen as one way of elucidating some of the differences between the approaches of the five teachers in our sample. It was not taken as a measure of effectiveness. There is, of course, no reason why such personal responses, however clearly explicit, will necessarily help pupils comprehend what they read. Although 'involved' teaching can infect with enthusiasm, nevertheless it could equally be argued that an alternative strategy that kept the teacher's views and individual readings out of the proceedings until a late stage would at least avoid the danger of the pupil's interpretative work being done for them. The act of pupils comparing their own individual interpretations, however initially misguided, in an experimental atmosphere where failure carries no great stigma may well permit a greater degree of reflexive awareness than would be available via listening to a particularly persuasive account of what is there in the text. It is obvious that for the growth of reading skills more is required than good models of interpretation being offered, however significant these may be as items in a larger list. Other points of comparison between teachers that will follow are similarly intended, not as measures of instructive effectiveness but as further elements in our grasp of what was actually happening in lessons — characteristics that help definition rather than, primarily, judgement. It should prove useful to look next at:

i. Teaching devices used.
ii. The implied abilities of the 'readers'.
iii. What meanings can be attached to the idea of 'comprehension'.

We don't know in the cases of Mr Keegan and Mr Tremaine who, when observed, were attending to the answers which their classes had already written, what had happened by way of introduction to the text and the writing of the answers in previous lessons. With the other three teachers, however, we can see that there were variations in such factors as the urgency to have answers written and the amount of looked-for participation of pupils. In Mrs Sutton's class the initial group of questions were gone through one by one in discussion; Mrs Sutton had defined the questions in advance as 'straightforward', and the process of eliciting spoken answers to questions was similarly entirely business-like and customary. Good responses were praised and total ignorance was enlightened by a simple provision of the answer. Group work, which started after the initial discussion was over, drew a readier supply of answers when the time came for them to be submitted in the final plenary ten minutes. These answers were not, as already noted, textually based, but drew on the pupils' background experience. We can only speculate about what significance attaches to the fact that a different answering mode was employed to deal with a different content area. Possibly Mrs Sutton felt that the four questions given over to discussion needed by their nature a mutual reliance of pupils on each other, whereas the textual items first looked at, having right answers, were best kept under her direct management. It is worth noting that Mrs Sutton was the only one of the five teachers observed doing 'comprehension' who employed group discussion of answers, though Mr Tremaine had some experimental writing done in pairs.

Mr Callaghan's class spent the second half of their double period writing answers to questions that had been mostly dealt with in discussion in the first half. It is interesting to note that after he had dealt with his own questions in relation to the octopus hunt passage,

Mr Callaghan introduced the printed questions thus:

> Now look at page 173. There are a series of questions there. See how many of these we can answer together and then you can write them up.

This makes clear that testing-for-rightness is not perhaps, from his point-of-view, the chief purpose of the written answer. In the lesson there was no sense of a rush towards rightness for its own sake. There was time for discussion and re-reading and there was also an elaboration by the teacher of 'right' replies, as if they weren't the last word, but rather pointers to a deepening understanding whose nature could then be shown, by him. In this lesson Mr Callaghan urged his pupils (successfully) to deduce word-meanings from context (e.g. 'pellucid'), to look at certain passages for certain answers and to reflect further on the text for finer distinctions of meaning:

> T. 'Frightened'. Good. Would 'terrified' be too strong a word?
> P. No.
> T. Why not?
> P. Think he might have drowned.
> T. 'Think he might have drowned'. Yes.

In moves like this we see the encouragement of rational deduction based on an 'open' text that anyone may argue about. Elsewhere, however, in the same lesson there were tendencies towards a 'closed' text in which pupils were given less chance to explore. The difficulties were pre-defined, as were the elements that were easy:

> Number two is very simple there: 'Explain in your own words how the Gilbertese hunted the octopus.' Now, three, 'What was their attitude...?'

Despite careful checks on understanding during the initial reading-aloud of the passage that preceded this particular series of questions, it is hard to believe that it was patently the case that grasping the entire sequence of the events of an octopus hunt was 'very simple'. Question one seemed to have been answerable by reference to only two-and-a-half lines of text. Question two just quoted seemed to require a much more extended reading. Yet there was no indication provided of where to look, or how to summarise. As with Mrs Sutton, it is difficult to be certain about what significance to attach to a single classroom action — a phrase by Mr Callaghan — but it looks as if what he had identified as 'very simple' was an item that had become so for him, not necessarily so for all of his pupils.

For the most part Mr Callaghan was sensitive to the need for the careful reading that had to precede any writing, but at odd moments like the one above, his own prior understanding of the text may have prevented exploration of it. One is reminded at this point of Mr Tremaine's:

> What I want you to do is... to comment on any question you found

particularly difficult to understand or answer . . . or any question that you'd like to discuss at all for any reason.

It was as if Mr Tremaine were trying his hardest to overcome the inherent drawbacks in the very form of teacher-led discussion of his own or quasi-examiner's questions.

Mr Tremaine's lesson was not one of the three already mentioned where the passage and questions were new to the pupils, but reference to it here is valid for all that, because 'going over the answers' is, potentially, an instructive strategy like any other. Like Mr Callaghan's lesson, Mr Tremaine's ended in written work. The comprehension questions had already been answered, but the further written work was based on the idea of 'bias' in journalism — a point raised by one of the questions on the *Guardian* passage. The class were, 'to try their hand' at biased writing. (They found writing quasi-journalistic accounts of Anthony Blunt very hard, but that didn't seem to deter Mr Tremaine.) This experimental approach ended what had been the most investigative lesson of the five in our sample. By taking the questions as problematic Mr Tremaine had appeared to identify himself with a reader's perspective and not an examiner's. Potentially, at any rate, this move gave him a closer understanding of pupil difficulties and powers. The class responded well to his style and joined in the criticism of the questions — one pupil, for example, pointed out that a purely factual question was quite misplaced under the 'Interpretation and Criticism' heading. In other terms, too, he was successful in bringing pupil-thinking into the centre of enquiry. Contributions of this kind are quite unknown elsewhere in our sample of five lessons.

P. (boy) *My Family* — it's a very descriptive book whereas this (*Night Riders*) is solely facts and arguments . . .
P. It's not all descriptive.
T. Pardon.
P. (also boy) He said that it's all facts. He said *My Family and Other Animals* is descriptive, but that's also descriptive *(Night Riders*). Description is facts. (Laughter)
T. Well, someone against Andrew. Mark? (Laughter)
P. Journalism gives — it's an argument basically on two particular subjects. One subject, two views; one for, one against — whereas a novel or something like that is a plot — one plot going through in time.
P. (girl) He's sidetracked us a good bit now. Can't think what I was going to say now.

Comprehension has apparently led to literary theory! That the pupils have become as involved as this is not just a function of their being members of a top set; they have been credited with more than just 'intelligence' (as already noted) and are here exercising critical evaluations of the kind that they have, presumably, seen demonstrated often enough by their English teacher's habitual way of talking. He invited pupils to challenge one another, and earlier in the lesson had posed as referee, keeping score of points in a debate which he and the comprehension had begun but for which his neutrality was usefully preserved right to the last possible moment in any dispute about the 'rightness' of an answer. Thus a complex model was enacted of how meaning is gained from a reading. Throughout the double period observed Mr Tremaine seemed to do all he could to invite his class in on his own thinking as if they were going to catch by example (which some certainly seemed to do) the ability to read first, interpret next and then review the question in the light of both processes. Such an approach validates the purely individual act of reading without suggesting that subjectivity is all: a commonly agreed understanding was being sought in which pupils were asked to challenge or support each other by reference to the text. The passage may have been a journalistic one, but the procedure had an obvious heuristic direction to it.

How far such teaching could have been adopted with other classes in other schools can only be guessed at, but it seems that we could, on the evidence of the lessons, come very close to constructing a scale of the credit given to pupils as readers and comprehension-question answerers. Mrs Sutton's pupils were entrusted with discussing questions, but not those that reflected back on the text. Mr Callaghan did much to help his class see what was there and how they should answer, but there was little sense of mutual challenge or garnering as many possible diverse readings before seeking the best agreed one — in other words his pupils did not often see their answers given public testing for their validity.

Mr Tremaine addressed an audience that was assumed to have a fair degree of critical sophistication and wide cultural background, even if some members of it didn't. Again we must remember that what is being discussed here is not necessarily a matter of effective teaching; giving pupils the chance to make tentative readings, altering (or strengthening) them in the light of other pupils' views and generally holding off from explanation and judgement won't make for better readers in a simple manner and overnight, but it does at least offer the opportunity for everyone to see that meaning is made not merely got or lost, and that active textual strategies can be far more involving than a quick passive decoding. Mr Keegan's and Mrs Sackville's approaches are not difficult to define, but quite what can be construed about them is less easy to determine. It would seem that in Mr Keegan's case accuracy and the examination demands were put at such a premium that pupils asked, not about substance and reasons, but about marks. 'Nice smooth English' was given as a demand rather than taken as difficult. The meanings of phrases and words were asked for in a perfectly open manner, but there was overall the impression of assumed ability that needed testing rather than assumed ability that was able to question what it was doing and why:

> T. Trouble . . . you've been guessing . . . you won't get much credit . . . being a bit too imprecise. (From field notes.)

Mrs Sackville hastened her pupils towards right answers, but no doubt aware of the need for extended concentration that the form of comprehension that she had helped devise took. Mr Keegan as well as Mrs Sackville emphasised 'precise' answers and accurate reading but the evidence here suggests that the less keenly it is pursued as an immediate goal, the more likely it is to occur if only because accuracy, when it is seen as difficult, may be eventually arrived at because of the attention paid to reading, thinking and answering.

Notions about the kind of thing 'comprehension' is as defined by the actions of our sample of teachers are not easy to deduce because four of the five were working from textbooks that must have been in some way influential. Mr Keegan and Mrs Sackville both aimed for rightness, but on passages and questions whose demands were utterly different, so that the common ground may not be very significant. Mrs Sutton appeared to take 'comprehension' as being as much to do with evoking feelings and attitudes that might be similar to those of the author's as with learning to read in any technical sense, but difficulties abound in assuming that this was a binding or constant definition for her. She kept almost exactly to the procedures and spirit of the textbook and was working with a bottom set whose understanding of 'autobiography' may well have needed prior exercise in a similar way of thinking. Certainly the evidence from pupil interviews in Mrs Sutton's class suggested that there was no lack of close textual attention on other occasions. For Mr Callaghan 'comprehension' seems to have included a prior reading that was independent of any test-item questions, that sought as much as possible to evoke a felt response, a sense of the passage providing some sort of intrinsically worthwhile experience and beyond that any testing seemed, by elimination, to be concerned with how well individuals worded their answers. If any one single factor could characterise Mr Tremaine's construal of 'comprehension' it would be that it was an essentially evaluative process that taught young critics their business rather than kept pupils in their place as accurate and tidy scribes. There was evident concern to foster their textual strategies, to make them independently-minded assessors whose job was to establish their own position relative to the evidence. That the class could do these things at all within the framework of a conventional passage and questions format was the result of Mr Tremaine's ability to convey how he and the examiner were to be understood as quite separate figures; in other words, he transformed a testing mechanism to very instructive effect.

A residual consideration is the matter of how far the nature of the passage studied, and questions etc. determined the treatment given it in class. Two autobiographical passages, James Kirkup's and Arthur Grimble's were not treated identically, but they did both evoke a fair degree of spontaneous comment from the teachers that in each case served as a kind of subjective response to an individual experience. Would Mrs Sutton and Mr Callaghan have been so forthcoming in the face of an argumentative passage, or a descriptive one like the *Night Riders* piece? Mrs Sackville stood quite apart from the *History of Purk House* etc. and we think that, on admittedly sketchy evidence, Mr Keegan seemed unconcerned to enter the argument that Lord Kennet's essay presented and might have provoked. If, so far, there is some evidence to suggest that personal pieces produced personal (and extended) responses and that 'objective' extracts entailed an aloofness towards them and the process of answering them, Mr Tremaine's work is an entire contradiction to the rest of the pattern.

10. Conclusion

> It depends on how intelligent you are whether you can figure out what the answer is. (Terence — Greentown School.)

'Sir, what if we can't do the questions?' asked a pupil in one of the lessons observed. 'I'll never know what you find difficult unless you say so,' said Mr Tremaine to his class (from whom the asker of the question did not come). These two statements, juxtaposed as they are, appear to form a question-and-answer sequence. Such a sequence seems, for all its brevity, an apt summary of many of the issues 'doing comprehension' in school raises; the pupil can all too easily see him or herself trapped in a very helpless position with regard to the text — indeed as one of those we interviewed said: 'I never know what people want from me when I'm writing comprehensions'. The teacher may find it difficult to discover what the appropriate level is at which to discuss extracts and questions. The first pupil question above serves as a reminder, too, that comprehension exercises are likely to seem on each occasion like arbitrary testing devices unless there emerges from them some kind of generalisable skills or system of analysis or simply general confidence in one's ability as a reader. The boy from a middle-ability set who said: 'We just have to do the question and hope for the best and if we don't understand it's hard luck.' must have felt resigned to his own lack of control. Mr Tremaine's statement required an answer from a pupil, but spotting what is difficult and being able to give adequate definition to the difficulty may not itself be easy for all pupils in all fifth-year classes.

What is at the root of the problem of identifying points and levels of difficulty on both sides is probably the question of who, in class, owns and controls the text in hand. This matter of ownership and control may well be evidenced at the level of techniques, methods and classroom strategies, but at a more fundamental level still it has to do with whether the teacher wants to mediate the entire meaning and experience of a text or hand over to the learners most of the decisions about what the text says, how they value it, etc. Comprehensions are likely, in their conventional form, to be very much teacher-owned precisely because they arrive in class with a built-in control device — the set of questions — with which most teachers readily and uncritically identify. At certain points in Mr Tremaine's lesson we saw how a few pupils began to take over, in public, a debate about a part of the meaning of *Night Riders*. It was an interesting exchange of views that allowed one speaker to elaborate his own thoughts on the text and make a comparative judgement with another genre:

> Journalism — gives, it's an argument basically on two particular subjects. One subject, two views; one for one against. Whereas a novel or something like that is a plot — one plot going through in time.

What seemed to be happening here in terms of control was not the wresting of the debate from the teacher's chairmanship, but rather a contribution in answer to an invitation to refute someone else's that was unusual for its length and for the degree to which the speaker gave himself space in which to think out loud about an aspect of the text in which he had come to have an obvious interest. He added a new dimension, or factor, to the discussion, one which the teacher might well have employed had he allowed, or encouraged, at this point the discussion to continue. Contributions like the one above, with exchanges like that already given in the previous section, do not show that pupils are wholly in control of the text but they, with other aspects of the same lesson, suggest possibilities for greater participation. They also tend to counter any idea that might have arisen that the format of the comprehension is necessarily a certain predictor of what the experience of studying it will be like and that a conventional form cannot develop or allow for much except literal and very partial responses. It seems important to establish that 'control' is not dependent upon method; that it is possible to imagine proceedings that involve a high degree of pupil participation that start from and relate to an entirely conventional set of questions, however unlikely in fact. All the same, we are forced to acknowledge that the other lessons contained (as already noted) no such exchanges as those already referred to and in Mr Tremaine's lesson itself the number of speakers was not large.

What appears to be required by way of enabling more pupils to discover ways of examining, analysing and evaluating are the use not only of 'new' methods of comprehension (like the already-mentioned cloze procedure and prediction exercises) but in addition a greater awareness that meaning is more likely to be present where the readers feel that they have some stake in the proceedings about it. It is, from this position, arguable that the selection of the text should not invariably be the teacher's. Good teaching could come to include teaching the class how to select a passage that was worthy of analysis and 'analysis' could come to mean a great deal more than answering paraphrase questions. Passages from the repertoire of pupils' spontaneous reading are not always uninteresting; often, for example, there is a profusion of technical language which an initiate could demonstrate to the class as being more comprehensible than it first appeared and well-argued and well constructed in its own right. Handing over to the pupils some element of choice in what is meant by 'text' amounts to a small concession in a year's work and may do much, not only to widen the inclusiveness of who speaks, but to look forward to the world after school and the reading which will be required in that. Choice, in that world, may not be much present, but flexible reading strategies are almost certain to be required, both at work and elsewhere and on texts that are almost certainly unlikely to be of a literary nature. This matter of choice is not simple and I have to acknowledge that advocacy of greater width and occasional involvement of pupils as choosers is not an entire answer. The choice of texts unfamiliar in style and content puts the reader on the outside, trying to guess the rules of the game, but familiar texts, however useful as the bases of reading techniques, are in danger of failing to extend the pupil, of leaving him or her within a familiar cultural milieu. Perhaps the key to the answer is variation and a broadening of the idea of what an 'acceptable' passage can be like.

It is clear from our data that, ultimately, producing right answers to someone else's questions was the main preoccupation, however arrived at. Even if choice of text and question remained on all occasions something which the teacher wished to keep entire control over then there would still seem to be a need for the development of more items like that which Mrs Sackville was using in which, for Question One at any rate (see p. 174), the reading of the passage was more concerned with wholeness of grasp than with exact details. In addition, it gave the readers an opportunity for a more constructive result. It is perhaps significant that one (of only two) of those who thought that comprehension had a significance beyond school came from Mrs Sackville's class. She said, with specific regard to comprehension work:

> When you're reading the newspaper you can pick things out and analyse this and that.

Teaching reading in the fifth year seems on the basis of all our data to be preoccupied with teaching literature, and the teaching of literature seems preoccupied with knowledge of the texts (rather than reader-response). Comprehension work that was amenable to change could, in an otherwise unchanging context, come to have considerable significance as an aid to the teaching of reading, in the sense that it could at times attend to texts other than the predictable ones and could handle and develop analytic possibilities that pupils would find of use in their literature studies as well as in other subjects in the curriculum. Many of those pupils who objected to comprehension work did so on the basis that it was of little use. In the section on 'Language' I suggested that too little was done that helped pupils discover how good they already were at using language and that built upon some of their existing knowledge about language. In similar ways, it seems to me, more needs to be done to widen the concept of 'comprehension' so that existing competencies of reading are given a fuller scope on the one hand, and more instruction is provided on the other that would help young people develop independent ways of learning to cope with the reading demands of new material in new contexts. The teaching of writing in the fifth year is in many instances much concerned with the presentation and transmission of values. Pupils' lives and interests are not ignored, but they are subject to editings and revisions. Similarly, comprehension work is not unconcerned with the 'reading world' inhabited by pupils and does seek to bring some of their existing abilities into play. However, it seems to look upon itself as not, ultimately, an instruction in value-free skills that can be imported into other contexts so much as testing for acquaintanceship with 'right values' and 'right styles of language' not by any means habitual to the readers in the classes.

CHAPTER 5

Literature Teaching in the Fifth Form

Mark, in Mr Richardson's middle set at Downtown School, described English as 'reading a book then writing about it'. Our observations and teachers' own records bore out that this might pass as a fairly accurate description of English for the majority of our fifth-form pupils, particularly those in middle and top sets. Books were read as 'literature' which implied they were to be examined, or they were read as one of the preliminaries for writing assignments when they were not being examined. It was only if you were in the bottom group that you might read them without the writing. The picture that emerges from our fifth-form data is of the supremacy of literature.

Work based on literature accounted for 53 per cent of all the English fifth-form lessons we observed (almost 36 hours). If we restrict ourselves to those lessons which teachers and pupils thought of as literature, that is, when reading was not regarded as preparation for writing or was not being used for testing comprehension, the proportion fell to 42 per cent and it is that element, 55 lessons in all, together with the spoken and written statements we collected about literature teaching that forms the basis of this section.

We ought to examine why in the fifth form there is this heavy emphasis on literature, before we consider the three elements 'reading', 'books' and 'writing' which make up Mark's statement and discuss: (a) What is meant by 'reading'?; (b) Which are the books?; and (c) What kinds of writing follow? What is the philosophy underlying this idea of English? English was not always like this, as Shayer[1] shows in his historical account of English teaching. We could start with a series of quotations from contemporary influential writers and thinkers about the place and purpose of literature in English teaching, such as literature is 'the readiest vehicle for talking about moral seriousness' (F. Inglis, 1981)[2] or 'an essential function of novel reading (is) to imaginatively re-create for oneself the experience of the author' (Stratta *et al.*, 1973)[3]. But discussion of such quotations would lead us away from the evidence, for we never asked our teachers the direct question, 'Why do you teach literature?'; we accepted with them the English teachers' taken-for-granted world.

We can, however, examine the assumptions which came out incidentally and the statements that occurred in the syllabuses we saw.

Justification for teaching literature

In Malcolm Yorke's research (1977)[4] the objective most frequently chosen by teachers for teaching literature was 'that pupils derive pleasure from literary works' and that was brought out strongly by syllabuses and teachers. The first reason 'for asking a child to read' in the Catchwide School syllabus was 'To give him pleasure' and this idea was echoed in Downtown School's description of 'literature as a source of pleasure', and in New Suburbia School's aim of 'pleasure and to modify attitudes'. The last phrase moves us beyond any mere epicurean delights; in isolation it sounds almost sinister, but Mr Callaghan of Urban School might have been supplying a gloss on it when he said: 'What I like is to have kids who enjoy picking up a book; (we) pick up the book, read a bit, talk a bit and we can bring it out into its wider areas'. Pleasure may come first, but there are 'wider areas'; literature study was seen as a means of 'enlarging emotional lives' (Catchwide School), as providing 'situations and characters with which our children can identify' (reference to Hines, Barstow and Sillitoe in Downtown School syllabus). There was little reference to the factual information pupils gained apart from Mrs Sackville's statement that 'Literature should . . . expand their general knowledge', but she went on at once to talk of 'their understanding of other people' which was referred to even more explicitly in the syllabuses from Catchwide and Downtown Schools.

The justifications offered, therefore, were in terms of pleasure and the effect of reading on pupils' views of themselves and the world. We were thus led to expect that in literature lessons there would be talk about the issues raised as well as reading. We shall demonstrate later that talk about what was being read did, in fact, play a large part in most literature lessons, and illustrate the facets of the texts which were concentrated on. But there were other more instrumental reasons for reading, such as its influence in improving written English, 'a constant contact with good writing will have a positive effect on written English' (Catchwide syllabus), or the aim is 'to improve vocabulary' (New Suburbia syllabus). Mrs Sackville of Urban School similarly believed that 'studying set texts leads to an improvement in vocabulary' and, conversely, Mrs Brennan at Downtown School saw a lack of reading as one of the causes of deficient vocabulary. Only one syllabus stressed the critical and analytic. Smalltown School believed that they should 'develop appreciation of style and the ability to offer sensible, sincere critical comments', whilst Mr Tremaine, the head of department at Greentown School, as might be expected from what we saw of his lessons, spoke of literature enabling criticism of a different kind: 'making head or tail of political pamphlets and advertisements'. Only one teacher, Mr Saxon also at Greentown, declared that he was 'very sceptical about literature *teaching*'. He was not, however, questioning the value of literature, but he was doubtful about the strategies.

Justification for reading was never made explicit to pupils in any of the lessons we observed, but in three bottom groups reading fiction was presented as an alternative to less pleasant activities: 'a break from solid writing' (Mrs Sutton), 'an opportunity to ease up a little bit' (Mrs Williams), or it could be a reward for those who finished their exercises quickly (Mrs Waterhouse). These teachers clearly thought pupils would regard it as a relaxation.

Most of our teachers had a crusading zeal. 'Teaching English is simply a battle to get children to read. Once they look upon literature as entertainment, the battle has been won.' (Mr Gilham of Catchwide School, our youngest teacher.) 'Obviously I'm interested in that bit of paper . . . all I hope at the end is they want to go and read books.' (Mrs Brennan.) 'If they leave school and never open a book we stand condemned.' (Mrs Wood.)

Reading is seen as valuable in its own right, for it represents the teachers' stock in trade. Teachers are book learned. The way in which pupils accepted that reading of any kind was important for success in school terms was clear from the number of times they suggested it was the magic ingredient which would enable them to improve their English skills. The reading of novels, plays and poetry, however, seemed to be justified in terms relating to the quality of life — its goals were affective. 'Although some haven't understood what's expected of them in judging books, I think they've all gained something from the course.' (Mr Richardson.)

We have not come up either from syllabuses or statements with a neat set of justifications or even aims against which we can judge the practice. We have, however, the high hopes of some teachers and their belief that what they were offering their pupils was of lasting value. Many of our teachers when we first interviewed them talked of the impossibility of separating discussion of literature from discussions of living. But before we look at the evidence of the lessons to see in what way teachers tried to heighten their pupils' awareness of books and their place in the world, perhaps, we can look at which books are chosen to see if any pattern emerges.

Choice of texts

In our first quantitative analyses of how time was allocated we divided our sample into three groups: A — those classes taking O-level Literature; B — those taking a CSE examination which involved work on chosen texts; and C — those classes not taking an examination which involved writing about books. For group A the teachers had to choose texts from a list provided by the GCE board, whereas for groups B and C the school or teacher could choose what they considered most suitable. So a first distinction emerges; for the most able the choice is bounded by what the GCE boards permit, for the rest the choice is left to the teachers.

Pupils who are studying literature for GCE O-level are usually examined on three or four books chosen from a list of a dozen or so. An individual teacher's choice is, therefore, first limited by the board's list and then by internal school factors: there may be a departmental policy about which books are used or simply no money to buy new books so that the choice is restricted to what is in the stock cupboard. However, except in one school where the head of department spoke of the expense of buying new books being a limiting factor, teachers seemed to feel that O-level texts had priority and that they could choose what they wanted from the board's lists. Nor, with one exception, was there criticism of what the lists offered: it seemed that teachers were working with books for which they themselves had genuine enthusiasms.

Most of the school syllabuses laid down no principles to govern the choice of books from the lists offered. Smalltown School, however, stated 'that every effort should be made to choose texts wisely', — a bland statement capable of any interpretation. It might be that the pupils' reception of a book, or the teacher's enthusiasm for it or any number of premises was the basis of wisdom. In the case of Mr Squires, the head of department who produced the syllabus, his own enthusiasm certainly seemed to be important when he spoke of choosing O-level texts, for he referred to the advantage of a text being 'on the same wavelength' as he was, citing as examples Philip Larkin and Ted Hughes. Mrs Wood talked about choosing from the point-of-view of the class rather than her own, but this meant *Romeo and Juliet* 'not *Henry V*, terribly out of date, all this nationalism and whatnot'. Mr Austin thought it was relevance to him which mattered: 'The only way in which I think I can function is to make it clear that the text in hand, whether it be a "Topliner" or an O-level text, has a relevancy to me. It's not something that's sterile and dead and monumental; it's active and it's mobile and it has something to say now'.

When we look at the novels being read we encounter the familiar 19th-century names: Dickens, Charlotte Brontë, Hardy, and the not-so-familiar Wilkie Collins; the only 20th-century novelist represented was H. G. Wells. The collections of short stories and the two autobiographies which made up the prose list were rather more recent but, in the main, they were written or reflected life in the early years of the century. Drama at O-level usually meant Shakespeare, but for two of our classes Arthur Miller's *The Crucible* had been chosen instead. It is only when we look at the choice of poetry that work written nearer to our own time predominated. Although Goldsmith, the Romantic poets and Hardy appeared, by far the most popular poets were those who came into prominence in the fifties and sixties: R. S. Thomas, Larkin and Hughes.

Most of the 16 titles which teachers of the O-level classes in our sample chose are by writers whom they themselves could have studied as students and this, as we shall see, contrasts generally with the books they have chosen for CSE and non-examination classes. Three characteristics distinguish the O-level texts: they come from the established canon of English literature, they are likely to be set in a period or milieu far removed from the present day-to-day life of their readers, and they tend to be substantial enough to demand considerable perseverance. When we examine lessons and the way in which the books are studied we shall see what were the values and interests on which teachers concentrated, but it is significant to observe at this stage the cultural assumptions demonstrated in choosing materials from a particular corpus of literature. None of our teachers had specifically chosen books because he or she thought their pupils ought to read them. Their acceptance of Shakespeare and the 19th-century novel may have implied such a motive, a belief in the importance of tradition and the values of 'High Culture' but, contrary to the common assumption, they never asserted this. It was rather 'I choose a book because I think it will appeal to them'. Teachers' own preferences were, however, clear from remarks such as 'I love *The Crucible*', or 'I detest *Kes*' to Shakespeare providing the 'greatest satisfaction'. Mrs King at New Suburbia came nearest to the ideal that in English pupils should have the opportunity to share in their cultural heritage; she wanted pupils to be able 'to experience the classics', but it seemed even then that she had no distinct corpus in mind. She bemoaned her lack of success at fourth-form level with *Silas Marner*, but then rather guiltily acknowledged she was prepared to re-define the term 'classic' to 'anything that's accepted by the JMB or CSE'. To be labelled 'classic' must mean that there is consensus valuation of it by society and perhaps not everyone would accept the examination boards as the validating authority. Mrs King, incidentally, was the teacher who was most worried by the shift in reading habits. 'Fifteen years ago *Over the Bridge* would have been considered wonderfully relaxing and a break from the examination kind of text, now it's at the top range of difficulty.' She was not the only teacher who felt that her pupils were non-readers and she wondered 'if lots of people, like me, are coming towards the stage where we'll say anything, everything if they'll read it'. To sum up, it could be said that O-level fiction and drama texts were likely to be established classics which the teacher enjoyed and CSE texts the social realism of a generation ago. Only poetry was predominantly modern.

Probably the most appropriate place to consider pupils' views on the books chosen for them to study will be later in the chapter when we have looked at the effect of the teaching. In one or two cases they had been consulted: at Smalltown School Mrs Wood's class said the majority had voted to read *Great Expectations* rather than *Jane Eyre*, but generally it was assumed that it was the teacher who made the choice.

At O-level English literature is an accepted and established subject, but there was no Mode 1 CSE separate English literature as such available for any of our schools[5]. However, Downtown School and New Suburbia School each operated their own CSE Literature syllabus. The CSE boards maintain the indivisibility of language and literary study, requiring the study of no particular set books but stressing the importance of appreciating literature. One of them, YREB, offers a coursework assessment, English Studies, half of which must be literary based. The long list of suggested books which is provided remains virtually unchanged from year to year and, although there is no necessity to choose from the list, many of the books we found in use figured on it. Some of the O-level texts reappeared, but generally teachers were being presented with a different group of books to choose from. At a first glance it seems that this was a 20th-century list and that there was a good deal which was post 1950. These may not be the authors our teachers studied at college and university, but they were well known and familiar. 19th-century novels were replaced by those of the mid-20th century, to which their detractors attach the label 'kitchen-sink': Sillitoe, Bill Naughton and Keith Waterhouse rather than Dickens and Hardy. With their provincial non-standard language and working-class settings they seemed challenging and even startling a generation or so ago, but to 16-year-olds they are rapidly becoming period pieces, interesting as social history. Drama was no longer Shakespeare, but the competent successful three-acter with a serious purpose which was a theatrical success in its day and is ripe for revival by the National Theatre. Poetry was not so well represented on the lists and was never compulsory. Teachers in the classes we looked at were reading isolated poems rather than working through collections of poetry: a traditional ballad was as likely as Ted Hughes. Poetry reading was an occasional part of the course rather than a regular lesson.

Mr Squires, the head of department at Smalltown School, had talked of choosing O-level texts on his own wavelength, but for those not taking O-level Literature his criteria seemed to be different. 'We've got two, if you like, standard texts . . . *A Kind of Loving* and *Kes* . . . We thought those two throw up a lot of interesting questions and problems, many of which were related to their own lives or futures.' Teachers were choosing for O-level classes books they valued and for others books they thought relevant to their family and working-class backgrounds, but Mrs King was not too happy with this position: 'I don't like the way I sigh with relief when it's my turn for *Kes* or *Joby*... *Joby* within its limits is good and so is *Kes*... but they (the pupils) don't want to explore the emotions'. There was a suggestion of dissatisfaction with the texts, but it was rather a sadness that even on these books pupils were reluctant to reflect. Mrs King was presumably thinking of her pupils 'exploring' the characters in the book not, as Mr Squires implied, of the relevance of the situations to their own lives, but it is interesting that both of them emphasised the personal and private.

It was the choice of reading for these 'bottom' sets, where they had complete freedom, which most exercised our teachers. *Kes, Joby* and *A Kind of Loving* might appear there, for just as there was some overlap between GCE and CSE lists so some of the books which were read for CSE could be found being read in non-examination classes, but we became aware of a new corpus of books emerging, books written specially for teenagers. In the last ten or more years educational publishers have been producing special series aimed at this market. With colourful covers they often look like the offerings on railway bookstalls, but it would be an interesting study to compare the message between those covers. A number of teachers used the various paperback series, but not always with enthusiasm. Mr O'Donnell found it at times 'a painful teaching experience. I can teach *Animal Farm* twenty-five times and find it worthwhile... would say the same of some Barstow and Sillitoe, but not of *Us Boys of Westcroft*'. Mrs Sutton felt that publishers were irresponsible as 'the children at that level can't distinguish very easily between the good and the not good'. There was a strong feeling that teachers needed to exercise caution and should not rely on a series such as 'Topliners' being consistent. Mrs Sutton thought some, such as *The Pit*, were good, but others, and she instanced *Maybe I'm amazed*, operated at the level of the worst kind of magazine with stereotyped vocabulary and ideas. The reasons for the choice of books which should be read cannot be considered in isolation from the justification for teaching literature, but it seemed worthwhile to look at them separately because of the distinctions we observed in the choice of books for different groups. The distinctions we have identified were not exclusive, but if we were given the titles of two books that a pupil in any of our classes had read in class we would know in which group to place them.

What is involved in reading? — Progress into text

We discussed the choice of texts in terms of three categories of books, those which were suitable for O-level students, those appropriate for CSE groups and those for non-examination classes. Were there similar distinctions in the models of reading and response offered? There was a wide range of difficulty in the books tackled but this does not necessarily imply different treatment. A book which might be read without help by an experienced and fluent reader might present problems to one more reluctant or less familiar with its assumptions, vocabulary or style. Mrs King seemed to be emphasising this point about difficulty in the remarks we quoted. Another distinction between the groups might be in the number of books read in a term or year and the speed of reading that was expected. Here there did not seem a great variation. If we exclude the two classes where there was no shared reading of a full-length novel or play — that is two of the bottom non-examination sets — most teachers expected to read with their class two or three books in the autumn and spring terms of the fifth year. Lists of what was read appeared to vary in length but this was often because, particularly in CSE courses, study was spread over two years and also short stories were often listed separately. Most O-level classes did not begin their set books until the fifth year, although even here there were the exceptions. Mr Keegan's 'middle' set, which had the dubious distinction of being the only class preparing for three examinations (AEB O-level Language, JMB O-level Literature and CSE English Studies), spread the work on the chosen four books over two years. Mr Tremaine's class at Greentown School, who tackled six books from the list rather than the three they needed for the examination, also began their reading in the fourth year.

We might think of the teaching of a text as being the stages of a journey by which the teacher leads the class to a greater appreciation and understanding of it. In our discussion we can look at work which represents different points on that progress. Sometimes the lessons we observed would be when classes were starting on the journey, meeting a text for the first time; in other lessons they were at a second stage, thinking over the book after they had read it; a third stage might be when they were writing about it. With long or difficult texts the progress was inevitably slower and spread over a longer period of time. If the text is a short poem a teacher might hope to reach the destination of as full an understanding as is possible in one lesson. *Woman in White* or *Great Expectations* with 600 or more pages need to have a different route planned.

The activity which Mark described as reading we will therefore divide into different stages, and the first of those will be how teachers chose to introduce a text. What was the first step on the way? What was the nature of the first encounter? Was it the same for plays, novels and poems or did we observe significant variations? The role of the teacher as mediator between the pupil and the text will move us to the second stage of reflection, to the comment which was offered, to the facets of a text which were thought important. We will consider whether it was local details of meaning which were stressed or the larger issues of the impact of the work as a whole, its theme or its presentation of characters. It will be interesting to look at the treatment of extra-literary knowledge and experience, seeing how far study remained within the texts, and if parallels were drawn and outside references made, who drew and made them and what they were. These will be stages on the journey of 'reading': the final stage, as with Mark, may be writing but this may not always be the case. We have referred to the role of the teacher, to the qualities of the texts and hinted at the position of the pupils. In what ways are these young adults, in what is for many of them their last year of education, being enabled to become successful navigators?

The first encounter: novels and short stories

Novels and short stories were the most widely read of texts as might be expected. They probably constitute our most usual private reading. Sometimes, maybe, we read for long stretches of time, but frequently it happens in odd snatches which might be equivalent to a lesson or period in school. However, private individual reading such as this at one's own pace only took place in the classes which were not taking literature as part of an examination. All 'bottom' classes, except one, operated a system whereby on occasion pupils could read at their own pace from selected books, sometimes it was a reading period, at other times it was whilst they were waiting for the rest of the class to finish written tasks. It might be described as 'silent reading', but it could be set against a variety of distractions: the most extreme example was when part of an oral examination was going on at the same time. But in the majority of classes, that is those which were being examined in some way on chosen texts, individual reading never took place for more than a minute or two.

In 14 out of the 16 lessons which we saw when a class was reading a novel or short story for the first time it was the teacher only who read aloud; only in two lessons was the reading shared with pupils, one 'bottom' and one 'top' set. There may be sound reasons for this. Teachers are more competent readers than pupils: nothing can destroy one's interest more than listening to something badly presented. One teacher, Mrs Wood, expressed this point-of-view strongly, feeling that it was unfair to expect any fifth former to read an unfamiliar text aloud. But for some teachers it seemed there was no need to provide a rational explanation. They assumed that it was the obvious method of introducing pupils to any book which was being read. It became clear that it was not the effectiveness of presentation that was the criterion, but rather the ability to control the text. If teachers were the only readers they were more able to comment or ask a question in the middle of a paragraph or even in the middle of a sentence than they could do if someone else was reading. In these instances, when there was frequent interruption, the first encounter and the second stage of reflection became fused into one. We were interested to estimate the ratio of comment to text. In the lessons we saw with classes who were reading books for an examination, on average at least twice as much time was spent in commenting and asking questions as on the text itself and often the proportion was higher. Mr O'Donnell's lesson with his top set at Catchwide School may serve as a good example. After spending two lessons with this class of able pupils reading and going through the first few pages of E.M. Forster's short story *The Machine Stops* he said that he expected it would take him another six or seven lessons to reach the end. He actively discouraged the class from reading for themselves by commenting disparagingly on one boy's answer that he had read on two pages ahead. He assumed that it was his role as teacher to pace and control the first reading. The ratio of comment to text, however, was considerably less when books were not to be examined. Mrs Waterhouse, reading aloud *To Sir With Love* to her bottom set, considered that the book was rather a difficult one for them; in fact it probably presented more difficulties than did *The Machine Stops* to Mr O'Donnell's able class, but she nevertheless read lengthy sections without interruption.

An alternative to the teacher reading the book is for pupils to share in the reading. Mr Tremaine's lesson on *Woman in White* was an example of this. He was trying to get to the end of the novel — 'two more sessions to go . . . hope to cover the last eighty pages'. Each member of the class had been issued with a guide prepared by another member of the department. They had been reading on their own at home, but it was clear that a good deal of the reading must have taken place in class, as individuals had their own particular parts. 'Stephen, you can make your last grand appearance as Count Fosco.' Mr Tremaine concentrated on selected passages, getting members of the class to join in reading three or four pages. 'I don't want to stagger through all this, but I'd like you to get the atmosphere.' He interspersed these public readings with spells of private reading. 'Will you look now at page 593, you'll be faster if you read on your own, so five minutes from page 593 to 597 . . . would you make your own notes on anything that comes up.' Mr Tremaine remained very much in control, he was pacing the reading, he was asking the questions, but the very fact of handing over the reading to the pupils seemed to enable them to become more active participators. The sharing of reading may seem a relatively trivial matter but it implied an active rather than a passive role for pupils and kept separate the 'encounter' and 'reflection' stages. The conflation of those stages and the passivity of pupils in classes where only the teacher read had the effect of making pupils dependent on the teacher's exposition. Mr O'Donnell's pupils came to accept that they should adopt a receptive role whereas Mr Tremaine's were active.

We have only given three examples, but we must remind our reader that the slow progress of Mr O'Donnell was the most common practice at this stage. Before we move on to the next stage and look at the nature of the comment and reflection on the books we will see how teachers introduced plays to their classes. Like novels they were not designed to be presented in 35- or 40-minute instalments and some of them, especially Shakespeare, presented particular difficulties.

The first encounter: plays

In all the instances we saw when plays were being read, teachers handled them differently sharing the reading with the class. This may seem to be a natural result of their form, the only possible way of indicating different characters, and therefore may be regarded as insignificant, but it is worth noticing that in our sample of A-level lessons from the following year, two out of the six teachers we saw read all the Shakespeare play themselves and asked for no student participation. Mr Squires certainly shared the reading of *Romeo and Juliet* with his top set pupils, but his method was akin to that of Mr O'Donnell in reading *The Machine Stops*: he stopped the reading for explanation every few lines. 16th-century language presents a problem. Very few 16-year-olds can make much of Shakespeare without help and all our teachers who chose to teach Shakespeare plays were looking for ways of bridging the gap between their pupils and the text.

In Mrs Wood's class at Smalltown School the pupils' first introduction to the text came as they listened to a recording of the play. As Mrs Wood said: 'I think the first thing, the worst thing, is to get the story across and get to the stage where you can read the poetry for poetry because they already know what it means. So I like to read it very quickly or play it on records and then go through this awful business of writing it in pencil at the side'. Her method of using records was significantly different in two ways: her pupils heard a professional reading with all that that implies and Mrs Wood never interrupted to comment. The play was not heard as a whole: it was broken up by the lesson length but that was not in her power to alter. She introduced and summed up the storyline at the beginning and end of each period; she made it clear that she would be going through the play in detail later, but she was willing to trust her pupils to make something of that first encounter with *Romeo and Juliet* for themselves.

We did not see Mr Tremaine's first lessons on the set Shakespeare play *The Merchant of Venice* because, as we said before, he began work on the texts in the fourth year. We therefore have to rely on what he told us. 'I generally get into Shakespeare by some drama work which takes weeks and weeks . . . Universally they find Shakespeare very difficult . . . we act out the theme without books to start with.'

This activity had culminated the previous Easter in a 'big costume read-through with stage lights and an audience from other forms of their stream. They had, well, I had a sense of occasion . . . I think it gave us all a little thrill'. A first encounter such as this would not have been possible in every school. At New Suburbia which had excellent drama facilities and a separate drama department the only drama sanctioned by the head in English lessons was desk drama.

Three different versions of the teacher's role have been exemplified: Mr Squires as instructor, Mrs Wood as manager and Mr Tremaine as producer. All the classes would eventually have to grapple with the language, with the ideas and assumptions of a period remote from their own. In the first case they were receiving explanations from the start, in the second they were getting as near as they could in a classroom to the experience of being an audience, and in the last they were approaching the play from the point-of-view of the actors.

Modern plays do not present so difficult a reading exercise; generally an act or scene would be read with pupils and teachers reading parts. Interruption for explanation was usually minimal, an injunction to 'speak up' or some help with the pronunciation of a difficult word would be the most likely cause for it, but there was difference in treatment at the end of the scene. In most lessons, after a few minutes of comment, the next section would begin but some teachers again preferred to move more slowly. At the end of the first act of *An Inspector Calls* Mrs Harrison slowly recapitulated it: in the lesson we saw she spent 50 minutes going through seven pages. Almost every speech was summarised or paraphrased so that there were two parallel versions of the play, Priestley's and the one Mrs Harrison produced with the class. However, although she did not go on to the second act until the parallel version of the first had been produced, some of the class had been sufficiently interested to finish the play on their own at home and she clearly did not disapprove.

We should not like to give the impression that teachers underestimated the importance of seeing productions: no effort was spared to ensure that pupils had the opportunity to see the O-level plays. Trips were arranged to neighbouring towns, and even to Stratford. Mrs Wood's pupils would have seen three professional productions of *Romeo and Juliet* before the O-level examination. At one stage of our observation it seemed as though every lesson we saw began with an announcement about the costs of seats or the times of buses. But the plays had always been recreated in the classroom before they were experienced in a theatre, in no case was the theatre the initial encounter.

Comments and interpolations: large issues or local details

We have referred to the proportions of commentary and explanation to the actual text which we observed in lessons when lengthy texts were being studied and this is, perhaps, the appropriate place to say something of those occasions, particularly in bottom sets, when there was little or no reflection on what was being read. For example, in the regular lessons in Mrs Waterhouse's class when everyone was reading different books, the only time when pupils were expected to talk about what they had read was when they prepared a passage for their oral assessment. In other non-examination classes it seemed that there was little reflection on the silent reading which happened regularly. The pupils may have been exploring the text for themselves, but no attempt was made to discover whether they had found anything worthwhile. This, however, was not always the case and we shall consider later Mrs Sutton's attempt to persuade her bottom group at Urban School to reflect on their individual reading. We turn now to look generally at the nature of the comment which was made to see what it reveals of the second of our concerns: what teachers regard as important as they read. One of the distinctions we thought significant was whether they concentrated on localised details or on larger issues. There seemed to be some correlation between teacher as sole reader and a concentration on details. In the lessons where the teacher was the only reader, breaking up that reading with frequent interruptions, word meanings and paraphrase were often the focus. These were the occasions when text and comment became, as we said, fused into the single experience. Some examples may be useful as illustration.

Mr Tremaine, whom we have already met producing *Merchant of Venice* and finishing *Woman in White*, will serve as an example of a teacher who took up the larger issues. We shall look at the same lesson on that novel which had begun with his hope that the class would 'get the atmosphere'; a similar phrase occurred later when they were to read a few pages 'to get the tone'. He introduced another passage by saying that it was typical of 'all final acts . . . the upright young man versus the degenerate character'. He prefaced one remark about a device in the plot with: 'Any of you who are thriller readers will know . . .' He was suggesting to his pupils that overall impressions were a part of the author's purpose. Mr Tremaine was anxious to make sure that the storyline with its complications was clear, but many of his questions asked for an opinion. 'Why is it a good way to dispose of Fosco like this?' His questions often started by asking for factual recall, but slid into probing for interpretation. 'Yes, but what are the advantages . . .?' Many a teacher, and perhaps Mr Tremaine himself, would find it difficult to explain to his 16-year-olds exactly what he meant by tone; it is a term more likely to be encountered by older students, but his usage of such generalisations and abstractions and the range of his questions suggested to his pupils that there was a level of understanding beyond the mere recapitulation of events.

Mr Keegan, a colleague of Mr O'Donnell's, was also reading a text for the first time, going 'through the story then we've got it out of the way for a first reading'. It was rather different from Mr Tremaine's lesson as the text being studied, *Odour of Chrysanthemums*, was a short story, but as the lesson opened it sounded as though he would be concentrating on roughly similar issues, character and atmosphere, but we notice how quickly he shifted to the small scale, the meaning of individual words. 'We're going to be looking at the character of Mrs Bates in the story and we are going to be looking at the environment in which she lives. We are going to be looking at her children and her relationship with those two children.' He had thus given the class some pointers and after he had read the first paragraph he paused. 'Well, what's the purpose of that little passage, Elizabeth, do you suppose? (Pause) Its general purpose in the story, Ann?'

Is it significant of the teacher-pupil relationship that Ann's reply was a question? 'Does it describe the location — where it's set?' Mr Keegan assured her she was right, going on with careful phrasing and rephrasing of the question to ask which adjectives were important. Before anyone offered a suggestion someone asked, 'What does stagnant mean?' Mr Keegan explained, gave an example and then asked, 'Any other words?' The answer came, 'Tapering chimneys'. Mr Keegan was trying to involve the class but after one paragraph they were not in a position to know what was likely to be important in establishing the atmosphere. They knew, however, that individual words mattered and from the frequency with which word meanings were checked they liked to be sure that they had them written down. Mr Keegan spent six minutes in questioning before he began reading again and only read one sentence before pausing to ask, 'Diverging, Paul, what does that mean? (Pause) Caroline?' The words he had been concentrating on in the first paragraph were important in establishing the atmosphere, but this was not true of 'diverging'. Why did he ask about this word? Often teachers pause to ask questions when they are reading as a means of ensuring that everyone is paying attention, yet this could hardly be the case here. Attention would hardly have lapsed after one sentence. He started off by looking at words for a particular purpose, but it seemed now that there was a presumption that every single word must be understood. No English teacher would ever make such an assertion, knowing how frequently we can understand enough of the meaning of an unfamiliar word from the context. Do we assume that this is not the case for our pupils: that they are incapable of such deduction? Sometimes this may be true, but I think that the more likely explanation is that teachers are anxious to ensure that they have prepared pupils thoroughly for the examination. This presentation of the text concentrating on the meaning of individual words was very similar to the paraphrase and gloss in Mr O'Donnell's class. The teacher took charge of the reading, he interrupted the text frequently and was the sole arbiter of meaning.

The effect of examination demands and the way in which they determine teachers' concerns is one to which we shall have to return later. Our attention has been so far upon initial readings of fiction ignoring poetry although 12 of our 55 lessons were dealing with poetry. We will, however, consider one of these next, a lesson when the class were reading *The Deserted Village*, a long 18th-century poem where the problems of length and difficulty were similar to those presented by some of the plays and novels. We are moving to this next because it raises the question as to whether the treatment of extra-literary knowledge is significant.

Extra-literary knowledge and experience

Mrs Wood was the teacher who had strong views about asking her pupils to read an unfamiliar text so not surprisingly she chose to read the poem herself. Superficially her approach shared the features we have already exemplified from Mr Keegan and Mr O'Donnell. By reading herself she kept control of the text, interrupting frequently to check for understanding, although understanding a long poem written in the late 18th century is, perhaps, a different matter from understanding a 20th-century short story. In a space of 10 minutes there were 11 brief questions checking understanding of meaning in the 20 lines describing the village schoolmaster, but there was also a personal digression on the satisfaction of teaching, the information that Goldsmith, the poet, was a failed teacher and much more comment and elaboration. As Mrs Wood neared the end of the portrait she pointed out, 'This is the famous couplet,

> In arguing too, the parson own'd his skill,
> For e'en though vanquished, he could argue still.'

and commenting that there was a difference in tone between the portrait of the parson and that of the schoolmaster: 'Anyone like to stick their neck out and say what it is?' As the lesson proceeded, there was always more comment and elaboration than text: even though she kept directing her pupils to the text, to an observer her commentary made her seem the authority. But it turned out she was not the only authority; when she hesitated at 'The pictures placed for ornament and use', with 'I'm not sure what to make of that . . . it might be because he needed the rhyme', a boy quickly stepped in with an alternative explanation which was accepted. The expression 'barber's gossip' prompted Mrs Wood to make a remark about travelling salesmen which one girl interrupted to point out it still happened and to talk about her family and their experiences. Her anecdote was capped by the teacher's telling about her own grandfather being a travelling bootmaker. Smalltown School draws many of its pupils from neighbouring villages, but even taking that into consideration it would seem surprising that this text produced so personal a response if one was not aware of the general tenor of Mrs Wood's teaching. In our analysis of writing her lesson was used to exemplify the private dimension; it seemed that this acceptance of personal reminiscence was significant also in her literature teaching. Here was one of the occasions when the discussion of a text spilled over into a discussion of living, a discussion not at any profound level but in terms of everyday social reality. It seemed to place the poem in the real world and to strengthen its impact.

This reference outside the text did not always have the same effect. We noticed that a number of teachers drew parallels between the set books and current television programmes or films. The slow progress of *Woman in White* was compared with the television version of John Le Carré's *Tinker, Tailor, Soldier, Spy*. In the search for the word 'individualist' to describe Mr Polly, 'What's the word for someone who wants to do his own thing?', Mr Porson whom we have not encountered before in this section referred to *Quadrophenia* (an X film). 'Come on let's talk about it — not just chatter idly. What happens at the end of the film?' This digression retelling the story of the film produced the longest break in Mr Porson's reading of the novel, but eventually he made the link he wanted. 'The Mod revival is surely all about people wanting to be individualists. In a sense Parsons and Mr Polly are.' In neither of these instances of moving out of the text into everyday experience was the effect comparable with Mrs Wood's lesson: in each case it was a teacher rather than a pupil move and in the latter case, particularly, the effect was one of diluting rather than reinforcing the concerns of the text. We saw some similar unhelpful juxtapositions in the following year when Mr Peel attempted to use evidence from women gossiping in a laundrette to account for Hotspur's inability to trust Kate in *Henry IV*.

But it is in the non-examination sets that we would expect the extra-literary references to be of most importance. Mr Squires, the head of department at Smalltown School, had remarked that there he taught, 'literature, less analytically, less critically much more for enjoyment ... much more for any social matters that arise ... or behaviour matters ... trying to relate it to their own lives'. We observed him teaching novels to an O-level literature class and to a non-examination class, a middle-ability group, and it was true that there were rather more questions and explanations moving outside the text with the second class. In the particular lesson we saw on *A Kind of Loving*, however, more of the questions were about understanding than social matters or behaviour. 'Why is there so much glass in this particular part of the factory?' 'What's it called when the management close the gates?' Pupils were asked to be critical of the author's purpose and style: 'Any point in that word "she"? Why doesn't he give us Ingrid's name?' and 'Is this the kind of account you might get in a teenage magazine, for example?' Probably, a few weeks later when the class discussed early marriages in preparation for an assignment for their Language folders, use would be made of the incidents and characters of the story, but in the lesson we observed Mr Squires seemed to be treating the book in fundamentally the same way as he taught an O-level set text. He controlled the reading, checked that pupils understood and drew attention to the author's technique. The explanations and interruptions were fewer than when he was reading *Romeo and Juliet* or *Great Expectations* but they were not different in kind.

In the two instances in bottom sets when we observed a class reader being used, outside references and relation to pupils' everyday lives were comparatively frequent. When Mrs Waterhouse was reading *To Sir With Love* to her bottom set, missing out some sections because she thought the class found it difficult, we wondered whether her short breaks in reading were to make sure they were still with her. Whatever her reason, the questions were interesting: they were often personal — whether they had ever known school dinners organised as they were described in the story or whether they could imagine any of their teachers behaving in a similar way. They could also move out to everyday knowledge; in the same lesson there were breaks asking about when the school-leaving age was raised, the kinds of dancing popular in the fifties, the meanings of the words 'atheist' and 'demobilisation'. In another lesson she explained the workings of the Race Discrimination and Equal Opportunities Acts. The novel was related to pupils' own experience much more directly and there was no searching for the word to describe a character or to comment on behaviour which we noticed in the other fifth-form lessons in New Suburbia School. The questions, however, although they interested the class, seemed to be unconnected with the purpose of the reading. It was as though the novel provided an excuse for the teacher to talk briefly about topics she thought interesting and important, to provide general knowledge and information. It seemed to have the status of another anecdote, one longer and more carefully worked out than those which the teacher and pupils offered, but not essentially different. The reminiscences about their own headmaster at the Christmas party seemed, if anything, more important than the incident in the story.

Mrs Williams' introduction of *There is a Happy Land* was similarly unlike the treatment we had seen of O-level and CSE texts for, in the lesson when she began reading the novel, it seemed that she was to approach the text from a personal point-of-view. She began by asking the class to think about their own lives and what episodes in them they would choose if they were writing a novel about themselves. They thought and she questioned them for a few minutes; then suddenly she switched without any connecting link to reading the introductory note in the edition of the novel she had given out, an introduction clearly intended to be read by a different group of pupils. Perhaps it was because Mrs Williams was unsure of herself as a non-English specialist teaching a fifth-form class for the first time that she never questioned the authoritative voice of the editor as he warned readers 'that these northern children have their own special dialect'; it was a dialect which, in fact, the majority of the class shared. The introduction read, the novel began with pupils reading out a paragraph as their name was called. Whatever her reason Mrs Williams never interrupted, questioned or commented; the class never reacted visibly; they sat there passively letting the words flow over them. No parallels were drawn and there is no reason why there should have been, but this uninterrupted reading was in sharp contrast to the kind of reading that generally happened in top sets and was completely at variance to the personal exchange that the opening of the lesson had suggested.

The use of literature as a preparation for writing

The lessons when literature was most related to pupils' own experience were those when it was used as part of the preparation for writing assignments. Those lessons have been analysed in some detail elsewhere, but this may be an appropriate point to make some brief comments about the reading that took place. It was quite likely, for example, that texts or authors which were set for O-level Literature would be used in a writing lesson with classes of all abilities. They would be expected to understand and appreciate the author's intention with the minimum of explanation or exploration, yet the same work would be treated quite differently if encountered in a 'literature' lesson. We even observed a sixth-form A-level class spend a whole lesson on an Owen poem which was read and apparently understood immediately in one reading in a fifth-form class preparing an assignment on war. In one 40-minute lesson in Downtown School Mr Richardson's 'middle' group read and talked about five poems and ten pages from *Sons and Lovers*, a feat inconceivable if the same material had been used in a literature lesson. They were not expected to reflect on the meaning nor discuss the style and manner of the writing, but rather to recall similar events or experiences in their own lives. It seemed that when some teachers in our initial interviews said that it was impossible to separate discussion of literature from discussion of living that this may have been what they meant, for most found no difficulty in keeping within the text in a literature lesson.

Poetry: the first encounter

Our digression into writing lessons has led us to refer to the kinds of reading given to poetry. When considering short 20th-century poems (and 11 out of our 55 literature lessons were concerned almost entirely with modern poetry) we are not necessarily embarking on a long journey. The poem is short enough for us to move through all the stages of discovery relatively quickly. Did teachers act in the same way as when they presented novels? Did they ever, for example, hand over the initial reading to pupils or did they retain control themselves?

Generally they did the reading themselves, but sometimes they gave the class time to read the poem on their own first and prepare their own readings. We will start in this section on poetry lessons with illustrations from lessons with two top sets taught by teachers whose own enthusiasm was particularly important in carrying their classes with them. The first lesson is one of a series Mr Austin at Smalltown School devoted to reading poems by a local poet. The quality of reflective thinking in all Mr Austin's lessons with this class made them distinctive. The class had been given the bundle of poems a week or so before, but like most of us given documents to read in advance they had put them on one side and forgotten them. The first part of the lesson, therefore, had to be spent in private reading of one of the poems. Mr Austin pointed out to them that this was an unusual situation, usually he had the advantage of prior knowledge of texts, but this was different. 'At first reading your opinion is going to be equally valid if you can substantiate it.' This could be written off as the typical teacherly gesture, but after the class had spent ten minutes on their own with the poem he elaborated again on the responsibility of the individual to be a thinking person: a socio-moral dimension was added. What they were looking at was the work of 'an artist who works with words' a man who was thinking for himself. The field-notes quoting some of Mr Austin's words give an impression of his exhortation: 'Need to think for one's self never more urgent than today — problems pressing on us, fuel crisis — nuclear threat — global consciousness — we need to think — can't expect to follow traditions as in a tribal society — Professor Townsend's publication on poverty last week — if we don't think someone else will think for us.' He went on to link this with the poem. 'This is what this man is doing — not seeing the herring gull as everyone sees them, looking in his own way . . . How do I know the creative spirit is important in society? How do I know it's potentially dangerous?' With references to the trial of Czech dissidents, China and Plato he returned to the poem. It was a parallel performance to the lay sermon he had just delivered to the bottom stream, but to describe it in those terms sounds to be belittling its tone of high moral seriousness.

From that point Mr Austin changed his role and became the literary critic concentrating completely on the poem: 'Let's look at the poem'. He read it then paused, 'That's the first time I've read it aloud. Don't know whether it's right . . .' That tentative hesitation provided the keynote for the exploration. 'First question we ask ourselves, what's it about?' Together the teacher and class built up an interpretation of the poem.

T. What do you think about his way of dealing with the gull in the first verse?
P. He's not dealing with the gull. He's more on about metal aeroplanes.

The gull began to be spoken of as a symbol for man; one boy did not 'know why he uses the gull' and his speculation as to why the poet chose that bird led to a long discussion. Sean thought a falcon would be more apposite, but after discussion that was rejected. When the attention turned to individual words no-one knew the meaning of 'spelter', but someone consulted a dictionary: 'It's used in solder, that's liquid as well', referring back to mercury which had been mentioned. Pupils' contributions generally came prompted by Mr Austin's questioning, but in this exchange he did not even formulate the questions.

T. 'Viscera'?
P. Entrails.
T. 'Their human appetite'?
P. Is it comparing our appetite for striving to get on, to be successful, with their appetite for entrails?
T. You're on form this morning.

As the lesson drew to an end Mr Austin's contributions increased in length: he was gathering ideas together and he rounded off with murmurs of satisfaction, 'Very pleased — I hadn't done those — got a lot out with you'. Mr Austin demonstrated that he himself was struggling with meaning, that he had a sense of achievement when he felt he had got it right.

The same atmosphere might have prevailed in Mrs Brennan's lesson with her top set at Downtown School: she was able to communicate enthusiasm. She believed there was 'no right answer with poetry', but her less confident pupils were not so ready to articulate their own responses and she left them little elbow-room to talk things through. She asked her pupils to read out the poems, urging them to think of the meaning, reminding them that people went to public poetry readings. When a poem had been read she expected reflection to follow a protocol, that she had already established:

1. What is the poem about? (What story, who, what events?)
2. What is the mood?
3. What is the message? What does the poet want to convey to us?
4. How does he create these effects? (Use of language, figurative language, diction.)

The first poem was R.S. Thomas' *Welsh Landscape* and Mrs Brennan, by asking probing questions, built up a paraphrase with the class. But to her question, 'Can anybody add anything to this?' there were no replies. She tried to move on to the mood but after one suggestion, 'morbid', had been offered was content to leave that poem and go on to the next. Perhaps because of the slowness of response she began this time with a brief introduction, leading to a very skilful presentation of the poem: her varying of pace, volume and tone provided a model as to how a poem could be read. We noticed that although her first question had been exactly the same as Mr Austin's, 'What's it about?', the tightness of the structure for the later questions implied to her pupils that there was a series of right answers.

The teacher's ability to suspend an omniscient position seemed to be crucial. Mr Richardson, who taught the 'middle' group at Downtown School, succeeded rather better in achieving his aim of encouraging his less-able class to grapple with the meaning of two of Ted Hughes's poems: 'I want you to work out what they're getting at because it took me some time when I first read this'. The poems were being studied as practice for the unseen question in the examination but, although the class had the questions they would be asked, no attention was paid to them until an interpretation had been produced. It seemed, however, even in this lesson, to be rather a case of guessing where Mr Richardson's train of thought led him, and of his persuading the class to accept his interpretation — as this quotation shows. (Unfortunately some of the contributions are not clear.)

T. An ancient, yes, those are the important words. All right then now come out with your interpretation, Linda.
P. (Replies — long sentence.)
T. Yes, alright, perhaps.
P. It tells you that in all them years that there's only one been killed, because they are so smart they don't get . . .
T. They're so smart they don't get killed.
T. and P. exchange comments.
T. Perhaps so but I didn't see it like that. The word that gave me my interpretation was the word that Simon asked me about — staked.
Ps. (inaudible)
P. . . . is it on fence? — it's come down (fades)
T. You're thinking too literally in terms of crows. Remember he lies a lot this poet.
(various inaudible)
T. Well, I thought your generation would know what stakes were usually used for.
P. . . . vampires. (Laughter — noise — vampires repeated twice.)
T. That's it — let's go on from there then.

In summing up this section we can comment that focusing on localised small-scale details in the first reading of poems seemed to be enabling pupils to join in the formulation of a possible interpretation whereas this was not the case with plays and novels.

The later stages: reflection and writing

We will move now to the issues that were considered in the O-level and CSE classes after the initial reading. Were the same modes of response exemplified that had been important at the reading stage? In some instances this was clearly so. Questions were set which covered exactly the same ground, as is shown by this remark of Mr Porson. 'Now in future after we've discussed a passage that we've read out in class and talked about I may, in the following lesson, just set a short extract from it and set one or two questions' and a few minutes later in the lesson, after the class had finished copying notes from the blackboard, he did that. The text was *Twelfth Night*, the page reference was given followed by the questions:

Question 1 'What do Fabian's words roughly mean? What is explaining away Olivia's behaviour?'
Question 2 'Why does Sir Toby want Sir Andrew to stay? What is the reason, is it great friendship? Does he really admire, respect him, love his company, can't do without him . . .'
Question 3 'What do they persuade Sir Andrew to do preparatory to the duel?'

These could have been questions he was asking as the text was read. He stayed firmly within the text: paraphrase and the fictional facts, so aptly entitled 'ficts', were what mattered. We considered why this emphasis on paraphrase persisted beyond the initial stage where it could be considered useful or even essential for the process of understanding. As with Mr Keegan, who also set similar tasks, an examination demand seemed the determinant although, ironically, the examination Mr Porson was preparing for had no context question.

If the prevalence of paraphrase and concentration on local detail could be attributed to the context question it would be interesting to discover how important, in fact, the context question was in the examination? Most of the O-level classes (four out of seven) were preparing for JMB Syllabus A which asked candidates to answer one or two questions on each text. On the paper there were three questions set on each text, one of which was always a passage from the text followed by short questions. We felt we could not but attribute this close attention to minutiae to teachers seeing almost any page as a potential examination gobbet. Yet when we looked carefully at the actual printed examination papers we saw that close textual comment amounted at the most to one-sixth: candidates could avoid it completely, and even if they chose every possible question it could only constitute slightly more than a third of the whole examination. However, it appeared to have such an influence on a conscientious teacher such as Mr Keegan that when we saw him taking his class through *Over the Bridge* for the second time he was paying just as close an attention to detail.

As the possible context question was lurking behind each paragraph, so other examination possibilities influenced what teachers commented on. We have referred already to the commentary on *An Inspector Calls* which was produced in Mrs Harrison's CSE class. In this, as well as recounting the events in the play, she was alerting the class to points that would be useful, she was building up a vocabulary that would be invaluable in later work. '. . . when we come to the Inspector's character you'll want to comment on that.' 'Do you know a word with a hyphen which means you're always right, an old-fashioned kind of word?' In this way she drew from her class the 'good' words such as self-righteous, protective, self-conscious, remorse, that they could weave into their own work, and frequently these were words that could be used in descriptions of character. The habit of talking and writing about created characters as though they are real people is common enough whenever we discuss works of art, but it is the emphasis on character 'studies' or on 'useful' words to describe people which can be attributed to the examination. Sometimes, however, teachers seemed to be almost paying token recognition to the examination demands; they asserted their importance, but taught in a way which did not seem to accord with them. We saw one lesson when Mr Porson began by writing on the blackboard 'Mr Polly and the theme of conflict' with a list of page references; it was clear from their exercise books that pupils later developed this heading, but in the actual lesson the class concentrated on localised meanings and going through sections of the text. Paraphrase and the small details seemed to be regarded as a preparation for every topic, there was no direct discussion of the topic. As much of our lesson material came from the first half of the year, it seemed that it might be possible to detect changes in emphasis in individual teachers if we looked at the diary returns which were from the end of the second term. We were surprised to find that this was not apparently so. Mr O'Donnell and Mr Porson were still slowly going through texts in most, if not all, of their literature lessons and close study in fact accounted for 28 lessons out of the 63 literature lessons which O-level teachers reported.

English teachers frequently lay the blame for their use of a more restrictive pedagogy in the fifth-form upon examination demands, but here some teachers seem to have forged their own manacles since the examination appears (at least on the surface) to be more enlightened than the teaching. However, we must also take into account the tendency of GCE examiners to award a large proportion of marks for reproducing 'ficts', whatever the demands of the question: awareness of this may be substantially affecting the relative emphasis upon reproduction rather than critical response.

Preparing the courswork essay

An important factor governing the mode of response and not unconnected with the method of assessment often seems to be whether the class is to write or talk about a topic. If a teacher asks for individual writing without first helping pupils to reflect on it, it almost invariably means an emphasis on facts. The writing is another means of rehearsing the content, another device to aid memorisation. Reflection on the text usually means talking through the areas and topics which arise. But there are different kinds of talk: it can be the teacher explaining, it can be the pupils working in groups or it can be a class discussion. We noticed that the form of the examination often apparently had a powerful influence on the talking through. In three out of the four lessons which were exclusively concerned with the preparation of an essay for coursework assessment we saw pupils being led in guiding reins through a poem or short story so that they could write about it. The necessity to produce an essay was determining the reflective process. This method of teaching may have been the result of the teacher rightly or wrongly feeling that the task of reflecting on a text was not within his pupils' power. The pressure to produce a finished piece of work whilst the story or poem was fresh in the pupils' minds could not be resisted. Sometimes the teacher dictated a title and then summarised the relevant sections giving exact instructions into which paragraph details should be placed.

To illustrate this treatment we shall look at Mr Callaghan's lesson on 'Snake'. When Mr Callaghan reached the end of his reading which the class had followed with every sign of interest, he paused, then remarked, 'there are some very hard words, but basically before I ask you to read it again, how did he react?' It is worth commenting, in passing, that on this occasion there was no careful rehearsal of word meanings. Quickly he drew the answers about the poet's reaction from the class.

'He liked it.'
'He admired it.'
'He honoured it.'
'He was afraid as well.'

The fear of snakes and the reasons for that fear were explored; pupils offered some anecdotes:

P. A lad in t'other English has got one — it's only a little one.
P. Ugh, it's horrid.

Mr Callaghan summed up what he wanted to draw from the talk and led the class back to the poem, 'Snakes are very unpopular according to your education. He decided that he wasn't going to kill the snake. Was it as simple as that?' Pupils were again ready to answer — 'He daren't kill it' — 'He sounded lonely as though he wanted to be friends'. Teacher and pupils were talking about the poem, responding to it in terms of their own experience, but this did not last for long. Quite suddenly, Mr Callaghan told the class to read the poem again whilst he gave out paper and when the paper was given out he dictated two questions: 'How does the poet react to the snake? Why does he react this way?' He had told them to read the poem, but there had been no time for anyone to read all of it and some pupils had only glanced at it before recapitulation began. 'Remember it's a long poem so presumably he reacts in different ways at different times. What's his first reaction?' There were various replies, none of them exactly what Mr Callaghan was wanting, so eventually he wrote on the blackboard, in a column headed (a) 'He waits', and, under (b) 'as if the snake is a person'. The pupils gradually began to realise what was expected, answers were offered and as Mr Callaghan repeated and rephrased them he slotted the replies as appropriate into the two columns. The first column, which was briefly saying what the poet did, was filled quite easily, but Mr Callaghan found it more difficult to extract the reasons and as time went on the blackboard notes became more and more his version rather than a pupil's reply. By the end of the lesson everyone was rushing frantically to make sure they had it all down before the bell went, because the writing would have to be done the following day. What had happened in this lesson? Mr Callaghan had chosen a central topic, one which had interested the class; he had involved them in producing the evidence, but because he was anxious that they wrote an essay immediately he found himself laying down very precisely what they wrote. From the notes he had made on the blackboard, his pupils could have produced an account without referring to the actual poem again. The class had been very ready to speculate about snakes, to reflect on the poet's experience, but by the structure the teacher was offering they were confined to expanding two lists into a simplified narrative account with rational explanations for the poet's behaviour.

The production of a coursework essay may cause the teacher to lead the class hastily through a text, narrowing the focus to the topic he has chosen but this is not inevitable, as we see from the responses demonstrated in Mr Richardson's lesson. The class had finished reading *A Taste of Honey*.

> T. Final curtain then.
> Now I want to recap a little about the play before we start the discussion. We did yesterday talk before we read the last part of the plot. The plot is what the story of the play is and I don't think it's very difficult is it? Could we just recap it again for the benefit of anybody who was drifting last lesson . . .

It seemed that the familiar going through the text was to begin, but on this occasion it was not what the teacher intended. 'So what is, what does make the play? The story can be told in just a couple of minutes as Christine told it. What are the important things in the play?' It was a genuine class discussion, the teacher played an important role, but as one reads the transcript it becomes clear how much was contributed by the class. In chronological order these ideas and terms originated from them (the numbers in brackets indicate the page of the transcript):

1. Plays are about emotions — (not developed) (2)
2. Plays are about conflicts. (2)
3. Setting of play. ('Look at places they live in, all scruffy.') (6)
4. Technical definition of twilight area. (6)
5. 'Not a normal family.' (9)
6. 'Not generalisable like most plays are.' (9)
7. Jo 'not capable of loving'. (10)
8. 'It's material things she goes after she doesn't go after affection' (Helen). (13)

It was an impressive discussion, the lesson bell would have sounded its knell even if Mr Richardson had not. 'Well we've talked a little longer than intended, but I'll have to set you another literature assignment. Sorry about this . . . What I want you to do is take two of the relationships in this play . . . Write about how they affect the lives of those people involved.'

Various explanations can be offered why this class responded so differently. The play may have been easier, they were probably more able, certainly more confident: as it was a full-length play it could be that they were dealing with material they had been familiar with for a longer period of time. None of these, except the matter of ability and confidence, stands up to scrutiny if we look at other lessons with similar classes when the teachers are using different texts. Most teachers define very exactly in their coursework literature essays what their pupils will write about, but only in this one instance is there any considerable opportunity to allow any reflection on the text that is other than narrative. Perhaps it is significant that Mr Richardson's class had in addition to the folder a literature examination. Paradoxically it seems that the freedom to present work done during the course could mean that pupils were limited to the very narrow areas which their teachers had judged them to be capable of tackling and that perhaps the inability of teachers to control what individuals wrote in an examination might limit the degree of control which they felt it necessary to maintain during the course.

We have used this lesson to demonstrate the quality of reflective thought which pupils can achieve but it was significant that the writing task, even in this instance, did not match the talk. We can speculate why this was so: points emerge. It is no easy task for unskilled writers, as most of these pupils were, to capture the moment of exploration and present their insights in such a way that any but the most careful reader would appreciate. The nuances of meaning which hesitancies and fumblings may betoken do not transfer tidily to the written page. It would have been very difficult for any participant to pick out the points we have listed: we had the benefit of detached hindsight. It is easy to understand a teacher's lack of trust in the ability of his or her pupils to display their qualities for public inspection. Fear of the external evaluator can force a teacher into Mr Callaghan's close control or Mr Richardson's limitation of topic.

Thus, although we have been purporting to consider the models of response on which the study of literature focused, we are again touching upon the role of teacher and the question of power, a topic to which we shall return later. Even in Mr Richardson's class when there was a genuine class discussion, an exploration, the writing that followed was not closely related to that exploration. Mr Richardson was free to set what topic he chose, but his choice had been made before the lesson. During the lesson he was very sensitive to his pupils and their responses; he helped them to develop their own insights but he was bound by his preconception of what the writing task should be. Did we ever see any instances when pupils were given an opportunity to write on their own topics? Coursework folders were only prepared by the CSE pupils: was there more freedom in the literature essays written by the pupils in the more able GCE classes? If we consider writing on O-level set texts the answer has to be no. When teachers were dealing with O-level set texts they invariably decided what the question should be.

Questions and topics discussed

What are the questions most frequently met? In the table analysing O-level literature in *Seals of Approval*[6] a third of all questions related to thematic reading and a third to character. We were interested whether the range of topics which teachers and class were reflecting on in lessons followed the same pattern. We have instanced the assumptions of the character study which lay behind the questioning in Mr Keegan's lessons and the commentary in Mrs Harrison's lessons. In Mrs Brennan's lesson on *The Crucible* we saw pupils preparing a character study of Elizabeth, one of the main characters. Before they began to work together she provided an implicit model by reading to them a long quotation from a critical account of Miller's work: there were no other explicit criteria, but she was defining for them the manner in which they approached their task. The interest was being focused upon people and their motives for action by abstracting them from the narrative; the intention was perhaps to regard them as artefacts, but more often in the ensuing discussion it sounded as though they were talking of real people. Mrs Brennan wanted her pupils to learn to engage in literary criticism for themselves, and may have intended to follow the discussion with a written task. The lesson, however, was in our opinion of value in its own right as a serious discussion of events and motives. As in Mr Richardson's lesson on *A Taste of Honey*, also at Downtown School, pupils were offering details and interpretations and, in terms of the play, talking of serious issues.

We will turn now to look at the topics proffered by two other teachers — Mr Tremaine and Mr Austin. In the lesson of Mr Tremaine's, when the class reached the end of *Woman in White* (see this chapter page 202) 45 minutes of the session remained so he proposed that they discussed the following questions:

1. What do you find to like in the book (which bits particularly did you enjoy)?
2. Discuss carefully what you don't like, what you think are weaknesses.
3. Draw up a group report on the characters of Marian, Fosco and Walter Hartright. (Pin your opinion to a piece of evidence.)
4. Who is the hero?
5. What makes the thriller form so popular?

The work was being done in groups so that the instruction 'discuss' was a literal one and not merely an examination type convention. As they had just reached the end of the novel, this was their first reflection in class on the book as a whole. We notice that, although there was a question on character, the emphasis was upon producing a consensus from individual reactions, and the questions were not framed in examination terms. In the short reporting-back session Mr Tremaine was happy to accept Sean's 'Anything exciting tends to be spaced out . . . not clumped all in one place', to encourage argument about the 'wetness' of Laura, to allow pupils to use their own terms and expressions rather than orthodox literary critical terminology. At this stage he was not, it seemed, concerned with topics as likely examination essays, general exploration going in various directions was possible.

Mr Austin, perhaps, paid even less attention to the examination demands in the following lesson. His method was similar to Mr Tremaine's: he presented his class with a list of topics on *Jane Eyre*, divided the class into groups to discuss them, moved round joining in some of the group discussions and then took the chairman's role in the report-back session which followed. The list of topics, however, looked very different from the previous list we saw: the class had moved on to reflection at a much less immediate and personal level. One group was commenting on 'the relationship of the book and its social context in England of the 1840s', another on the Gothic elements of the novel, a third on why the skeletal framework of the plot is an inadequate explanation of the novel's effectiveness and so forth. The reports were couched in literary critical terminology and their points were taken up, questioned and commented on by Mr Austin. The lesson had the air of an undergraduate tutorial seminar as this quotation demonstrates. Pauline spoke to the class at length: what follows is considerably abbreviated.

> If Charlotte Brontë was to tell the story just as Karen has just told it — you wouldn't feel with the characters at all because it's just a story, has no human emotion in it. So firstly Charlotte Brontë has to turn this story into a true story, to make us all feel it's realistic. The first thing she does is to subtitle it an autobiography which makes us think the characters really do exist, they're true live people and so we start off feeling with the characters right from the word 'go' and then she takes the position of first person narrative because it is an autobiography and this means we're drawn into the novel . . . we feel much more than we would as an outsider . . . Charlotte Brontë by describing people's physical appearance, we're judging them straight away the way she wants us to judge them . . . In the book she joins together the governess which is a kind of school ma'am image — . . . and also the fact that the governess can be loved and fall in love and be emotional. She turns the book eventually, Jane from being plain Jane, unacceptable by anyone, she turns it into a love story which makes it more acceptable to the public really. 'Cos you like a nice love story to read.

Only one point was taken up by Mr Austin, the ending.

> T. Acceptable to the public, but — there seemed to be a question mark there — you said the ending had changed it into a love story really. Are you saying that's a good or bad thing? . . .
> Anybody like to offer an opinion on that? How satisfactory is the ending in the terms of what Pauline has said prior to that? Sarah?
>
> Sarah. It leads us through as Jane's plain, but in the end Charlotte Brontë undercuts what she's been saying.
>
> T. There was a slight betrayal.
>
> S. Yes.
>
> T. For the sake of . . .?
>
> S. It's for the happy ending.

Mr Austin was offering an opportunity for the exploration of ideas and an initiation into a way of talking about literature. These pupils were speaking from personal experience, their own engagement with the text: for many of the class one could sense the excitement of intellectual challenge. This was corroborated later in conversation with some of them. Rachel described the lessons this way: 'You feel very much in that class that he's trying to — you feel like a child that's made to think like an adult: it's a really rifling process'. Marcus introduced other ideas when comparing English with history: '. . . in history it's more why masses do certain things, mass feelings; in English it's individuals. (In history lessons) not very much in way of comeback from the class . . . more the teacher getting over an idea and understanding what it was about rather than taking an alternative interpretation'. Exceptional pupils, an exceptional teacher but, ironically, we observed later that they had not such outstanding examination results as one would expect. We wondered if these pupils had been given the chance to produce the essays they had written as coursework for assessment, if the results would have been different? From our evidence it seemed likely that this would have been the case. Whether or not this is true, for some pupils there was an opportunity for coming to grips personally with a text, an activity which we thought merited the term exploration.

If we consider the discussions we have instanced in Mr Tremaine's and Mr Austin's classes they exemplify the complexity of real responses to literature which are ironed out when teachers operate only in the conventional thematic and character modes. Mr Tremaine's class were not attempting to formulate their first responses in literary critical terms; their responses were not being forced into the character study mould.

The sections on the later stage of reflection and writing have dealt almost exclusively with O-level and CSE classes and this is because we found so little evidence of it in the other groups. Reading there was sharply distinguished between class and private reading: Mrs Williams' reading of *There is a Happy Land* and Mrs Waterhouse's of *To Sir With Love*, in lessons we have already referred to, show what class reading was like. Individual reading, unaccompanied by a teacher's commentary, also took place in the lessons of most 'bottom' groups. Sometimes the practice was to provide a selection of books, a book box from which pupils chose, returning the book at the end of the lesson, or there might be a library system which allowed books to be read at home. Whatever the system, reading was intended to be seen as a reward for work done or as a leisure activity and the books supplied had been chosen with that in mind.

Although it may appear that individual reading was often used as a filler, a convenient device to keep pupils occupied so that the class could move at the same pace, there was evidence that it was taken seriously by the teachers. Books for individual reading had been chosen with care to encourage a reading habit, but we have only one example for a lesson where reflection was taking place. In this instance from Urban School the teacher's values and purposes were clear. A series of lessons (and homework) was devoted to preparing and reading out passages, '. . . which you think others will enjoy and make them want to read it' (the book). Although Mrs Sutton stressed the importance of rehearsing the readings and of being confident, insisted on pupils standing where they could be heard, her comments and questions were more generally about content than presentation.

Their choices were approved, 'Yes it's quite an irresistible passage' or 'a very dramatic reading indeed, yes, plenty of interesting language there'. They were prodded to justify them: an ending was 'not just a happy ending'; the teacher pointed out it was more interesting because unexpected. The emphasis was on the pupils' enjoyment of the stories, but reasons for enjoyment were being suggested by the teacher: Mrs Sutton was encouraging reflection and trying to make reluctant pupils make and justify preferences.

This reference to prepared readings leads us to look at the use of books in the oral examination. We referred on page 201 to the lessons at New Suburbia School where pupils were reading out loud prepared passages for their 16+oral assessment. There was a standard procedure of introduction, followed by the reading and then the answering of some questions.

T. Tell us what book you're reading, tell us what the story's about, then introduce the bit you're going to read.
P. The book's called *Jaws* and it's by Peter Benchley. And it's about this killer shark, what — in this pleasure town. It's got a pleasure beach called Amity, it's called. And it's killing, it's feeding, this killer shark is feeding in this area . . .

The six-minute long fluent reading was brought to an end by the teacher's interruption and the rather formal questioning began.

T. Have you read the whole of the book?
P. No, about half of it.
T. Why did you choose to read that bit in particular?
P. Well I thought it were pretty good, how it described her being eaten by t'shark.
T. Did you find it quite an easy book to read? I mean is it interesting, does the interest keep going?
P. Yes it keeps going all t'way through t'book, what I've read anyway.

There were five more questions asking Gary whether he would recommend the book, whether he had seen the film and whether it remained close to the book. Some answers were very brief; the testing lasted barely two minutes. The specific purpose was to assess oral skill rather than, as Mrs Sutton's questioning had been, to suggest literary values but it seemed worthy of inclusion, although it was not a general practice, because it was a compulsory element in the 16+ examination this group were taking.

It was very interesting to contrast the set of values which operated in a class when books were read and talked about as part of the oral examination and when they were read and talked about in preparation for the literature examination. Mrs Harrison's class, also at New Suburbia School, could spend some minutes trying to find the right word to describe a character in *The Inspector Calls*; they accepted that the commentary on seven pages of that play lasted 30 minutes because that was a literature 'set' book. No-one in the same class expected the questioning and comment on seven pages of 'a book of your own choice' to last more than a couple of minutes; they were not transferring any of the practices of the literature lesson to their own reading, even when that reading was part of the examination.

We have demonstrated in our examples of the mode of progress through a text some of the models of reading which teachers were offering. It is interesting to see how far teachers were aware of these models. Did they feel that the 'set' book had to be taught in a particular way? As we have demonstrated, they were clearly conscious of examination pressures.

Although they wanted the validation of their English Literature teaching by GCE success, some of them expressed their reservations: Mrs Brennan wondered about the class teaching of O-level texts: 'I'm not sure whether that makes children love literature: in fact I'm very dubious about that.' Mr Tremaine commented that, 'The trouble of English Literature O-level is that it is so passable. I am quite cynical about preparing for exams.' But his position was such that he could say with some confidence, 'I hope they won't confuse literature with literature for exams'. It was important, he thought, that his pupils knew of his own valuing of books and reading in his daily life.

Before we went into his lessons Mr O'Donnell warned us: 'You won't see teaching, you'll see streaking . . . what you're going to see is some kind of cramming pressure to cover the ground . . . what we're doing for the examination is not necessarily the way to read a book, in fact it's *not* the way to read a book and hopefully they'll never do it again . . . much more to English teaching than unearthing the stones in three set texts . . . it's going to be pretty deadly'. Mr O'Donnell was not unaware of what he was choosing; he was either unaware that examination preparation could be otherwise or he was absolving himself by using the examination as scapegoat. His ideal, he claimed, was to mount a massive reading programme, 'twenty-five (books) is a slight exaggeration'. He bemoaned the school's choice of a JMB syllabus which can be examined on only three texts, saying he preferred the AEB syllabus with four. Yet his colleague, Mr Keegan, teaching for the same JMB examination was doing four texts. Mr Tremaine was teaching six texts for the AEB and surprised when we suggested most people only taught the minimum. Mr O'Donnell believed he wanted to teach a large number of texts, yet he had not the confidence to risk one more unless outside pressures forced him to do so. Mr O'Donnell's comments have led us full circle back to our starting point, the choice of texts; our examples from lessons have demonstrated incidentally the areas of experience which were dealt with but before we move to generalise about these we will consider the two antithetical models of teaching which our progress into text has revealed.

Initiation and transmission

In using the metaphor of a journey we spoke of pupils being enabled to become successful navigators, which can be interpreted as becoming able to operate within the value system lying behind the teaching of literature. We have identified two models of teaching, Initiation and Transmission. Initiation is the term for describing when the implicit or explicit principles that inform the activity are made available to the pupils so that they can operate them for themselves. Transmission describes the kind of teaching when pupils are expected to take over the values, when the teacher or book is to be followed without question: the source of authority is external. It seemed that we could locate teachers and lessons along a scale which at the one end represented transmission teaching and at the other end initiation, and certain practices seemed to place a teacher as likely to belong at a particular point on that scale.

The process of reading and responding to texts is a complex activity; at particular stages in that process, authoritative explanation and assertions may play a more important enabling role. In reading *Romeo and Juliet*, for example, no teacher can avoid the necessity to explain and annotate; what Mrs Wood described as 'this awful business of writing it in pencil at the side'. The meanings of certain words have changed: misunderstanding will help no-one. Transmission teaching is consequently appropriate. However, this is not necessarily the best method for all aspects of teaching Shakespeare: it may not, for example, be the best starting-point for the journey or the ideal conditions in which to evaluate dramatic power. Similarly, progress into some texts may be facilitated by facts about the author's life or by some historical background, but rehearsal of information does not ensure that information has been assimilated. Oakeshott defines knowledge as the synthesis of information and judgement[7]: that synthesis can only take place if pupils gain some insights into the principles of procedure, the premises upon which judgement is made. And it is the activities which enable that synthesis which we have labelled initiation.

By conviction or temperament some teachers consider it necessary at this fifth-form level to cast almost all their lessons and activities within the transmission mode. We have observed certain indicators which seem to characterise this limited approach.

The teacher's assumption of the role of reader in the first encounter with a text seemed likely to be one indicator of a transmission mode of teaching because of the control it implied, but we needed to look more closely at the nature of the comment and questioning before we decided whether it was crucial. Shared reading implied a looser control, giving pupils the possibility of making the first steps for themselves, but again we needed to look at the second stage; the proportion of commentary to text could be far more important than who did the reading. Concentration on small topics, word meanings and localised details in plays and fiction, often indicated that the teacher assumed the authoritative voice whereas consideration of larger issues permitted pupils to join in and begin to appreciate some of the processes involved. If larger issues were never introduced at the 'talking about' stage, but only introduced as possible examination questions or in the form of dictated notes, a transmission mode may be deduced. The willingness to allow less structured talking unrelated to examination constraints provided opportunities for focusing on process rather than product.

Our placing of lessons on this transmission ⟷ initiation scale may seem very obvious. Mr Keegan's lesson on *Odour of Chrysanthemums* (see page 206) would belong at the transmission end of the scale as did the double-period he taught on *Over the Bridge* which we will describe now. The teacher was the sole reader and he stopped frequently, usually to check that his pupils understood. The progress went like this:

T. 'Giving', what does that mean, 'the *formal* apple and orange in the bottom'?
P. Traditional.
T. Traditional, yes that's right — the standard kind of gift that always came at the bottom of the stocking.
T. (Resumes reading — half a page.)
T. 'It' came always after tea — what is being referred to here Michael? (Pause) (T. repeats question) — anybody? Emmett?
P. A kind of anti-climax.
T. A kind of anti-climax. Yes, the fall, the disappointment.
T. (Reads four sentences.)
T. Fiona, why does he put that expression 'the rolling English road' into inverted commas, do you think? (Pause) Paul?

Mr Keegan believed that his pupils found this a difficult book so he used the same method as he did with a Shakespeare text, but it seemed that even if they could not produce immediately acceptable meanings for individual words they had an adequate enough level of understanding. In this example we saw how frequently the teacher merely repeated in confirmation the meaning pupils had offered, but his repetition established that he was the authority. This was a common feature of transmission teaching. The other authority invoked in this lesson was the examination. After half-an-hour's reading following the pattern we have illustrated 'a context question' was written on the board:

It's the one you'll get in the examination . . . they give you a passage and set a series of questions on it. I'll put the marks for each question to give you some idea of the relative importance . . . The following questions are all based on Chapter 11.

1. Quote the phrase which expresses Tom Church's attitude towards English pianos. (1)
2. What reasons does the author put forward for father's objection to Klingman? (Use your own words.) (6)
3. 'Mother would not deny him a second time.' Explain this phrase. (2)
4. Describe Battersea as it was seen by the writer on his Boxing Day ride. (12)

The layout and mark scheme were very close to the typical examination question and, by chance, the following summer's context question was taken from this chapter, but ironically it is significant that there was a difference. Pupils were not asked to repeat what the book said: they were asked to be authorities themselves. Question (i) on the examination paper began: 'What impression do you gain . . .?' Question (iii) read: 'What is the effect of . . . ?' Candidates were being asked for their reactions, their interpretations, not the facts themselves.

Mr Tremaine's lesson on *Woman in White* we would place at the initiation end of the scale. The presentation of the text was a shared activity, a semi-dramatic reading, with pupils as characters and the teacher acting as narrator. The questions which were given when it finished (p. 220) asked for opinion and evaluation as well as for information. The list had the expected question on character, but the others were different asking for a point of-view. They enabled Mr Tremaine to place his pupils in the position where it was they who carried out the literary critical work, thus giving them at least partial access to the relevant principles and criteria. The examination did not have to be invoked to validate the activity.*

Those lessons when there was no further activity beyond the initial reading, when pupils were offered no sense that there might be value in reflecting on what they had read are clearly not initiation, but must be regarded as transmission at the lowest level. This however suggests another dimension of analysis according to the levels of organisation of response. Effective response need not always be written, as we have illustrated particularly in quotations from Mr Austin's and Mr

* We tried to estimate whether transmission teaching which stressed the authority of the examination was more successful in examination terms. In the six roughly comparable 'top' classes taking O-level Literature 77 per cent of the pupils taught by teachers who used a predominantly initiation approach obtained grade C or higher, compared with 58 per cent in the transmission-style classes. Mr Keegan's 'middle' set at Catchwide School would have made the contrast even more marked, but we have omitted them from the calculation as they were dissimilar in ability.

Callaghan's lessons, but this might be a good point to turn to the evidence from the written work we saw and perhaps relate it to some of our earlier headings.

Evidence from written work

Unfortunately we have an unbalanced selection of data concerning written work because of our decision mid-stream, when we felt we were becoming overwhelmed with scripts, not to collect more writing on literature. From two classes, Mrs Brennan's and Mr Tremaine's, we therefore have nothing, and from Mrs Harrison's only three short essays, but we looked at the pupils' exercise books in these classes and our field-notes commented particularly on the sheer bulk of writing. Mr Tremaine's pupils had one exercise book for each of their six texts; as he was the head of department who mentioned the need for economy, obviously he expected them to write a lot. Mrs Harrison's class similarly had a notebook for each text, one for *Kes* and one for *An Inspector Calls*, and it seemed from the ones we saw that they wrote notes on almost every page as well as character studies of the most important characters. The notes were written in class when Mrs Harrison went slowly over the scene or chapter that had been read, the character studies were completed for homework after being prepared in class.

From the remaining nine classes which were reading books for an examination we saw 314 literature essays, focusing our attention particularly on the topics and titles and the teacher's comments. All the writing on books we saw was part of some examination course. Those pupils who were taking a final examination needed to have practice in the kind of questions they were likely to meet, but the frequency of practice varied and the emphasis fell on different kinds of questions. The O-level teachers who took charge of the reading themselves, who concentrated on localised meanings and the production of a gloss, in fact those who favoured a transmission approach, tended in the lessons we saw to set questions asking for recapitulation of facts and this was borne out by the remainder of the written work. For example, 'Write an account of the plot against Malvolio and the motives of those involved.' (*Twelfth Night*); 'Describe the author's experiences in Higher Grade School and how he was affected by them. Do you think that they contributed to his character?' (*Over the Bridge*). Examples of selective narration and the concentration on character that we see in these two questions could be instanced time and time again. The teachers whose lessons fell most often into the transmission mode also expected their pupils to write to practise examination questions most frequently. In addition to regular writing on short passages, Mr Keegan's and Mr O'Donnell's classes wrote respectively six and five essays on *Romeo and Juliet*, and

Mr Porson's six on *The History of Mr Polly*.

In contrast, if a text was being assessed for the CSE English Studies folder only one piece of work could be submitted on that text and generally only one piece of writing was set on each text. There is rather more variety in the way topics are set for CSE; pupils may, for example, be asked to relate events through the eyes of one particular character, but it is virtually the same task of selective narration. The titles of work submitted for coursework assessment were often uninformative about the exact nature of the task, for frequently there was only the title of the text. Occasionally, however, a pupil copied out the instructions, so that we could see the boundaries and guidelines provided. One of Mrs Sackville's pupils at Urban School had written, 'Read the *Daemon Lover* and discuss the logic of the argument put forward by the daemon that his love should carry out her former vows to him and her arguments against his demands. In the first paragraph say what the poem is about. In the second paragraph discuss his argument. In the third paragraph hers. Lastly discuss how the ballad resolves the problem'. We had noticed how Mr Callaghan similarly structured the writing on *The Snake*; he said later how he 'was really shackled by that syllabus . . . had to get those essays out of pupils according to a particular formula . . . began to feel it was a bit of a travesty of what we should be doing'. Similarly, Mr Keegan said he led his pupils through their essays paragraph by paragraph otherwise, 'you simply get back pieces of work which, while they may be valuable as evidence of their attempt to grapple with something, in terms of their eventual folders, may not merit much of a grade'.

Very few questions for coursework or examination practice moved outside the text. Mr Callaghan's 'Who's who in *Animal Farm*: a straight comparison with Russian leaders' did so, but it was a move into another content area, historical knowledge rather than into interpretation. Mr O'Donnell's titles on *Romeo and Juliet* were perhaps the most interesting as they contrasted so much with the teaching we saw in his lessons. 'What do you find in the play to account for the fact that two inexperienced teenagers Romeo and Juliet have become universal symbols of romantic love?' or ' "The foolishness of the young at odds with the selfishness of the old." To what extent does this view sum up the play?' We did not see the lessons leading up to these essays, but they ask for a very different approach to the play from the 'slog, slog' which Mr O'Donnell used to describe the term's work on it.

We were asked by one colleague, when we mentioned that we were collecting written work, whether we found any evidence that in writing an essay pupils discovered or even learned any things they would not have done by other means. Our conclusion on the basis of what we saw would have to be that they did not. Essays were either practice for the final examination or intended for assessment in a coursework folder. Teachers had two models: what could be written in about 35 minutes under examination conditions and what could be substantial enough to provide at least 250 words or four or five coherent paragraphs. By the time we were looking at written work we had reached the position where we did not expect to see any individual work on literature; we knew everyone read the same texts and answered the same questions. But we were impressed that teachers hardly ever failed to respond individually in detail to their pupils' writing. Of the 69 literary essays we saw from Mr Keegan's class, only two lacked a final comment. Mr O'Donnell replied to all but one of his 47 with comments varying from a phrase to half a page. The remarks were often encouraging, combining a general evaluation with some good advice: 'A good effort', 'Not a bad attempt', 'Analysed with considerable maturity, understanding and capable expression'. Expression and technique were given a good deal of attention, especially the logical arrangement of ideas. 'Too much like a set of notes. You are expected to write a balanced essay on the subject.' 'A weak conclusion' occurred more than once in varying forms, as did 'Lacks an introductory paragraph'. Punctuation was commented upon, 'Watch your capitals', and spelling errors were generally corrected. This concern with appropriate presentation justified the claim teachers made of teaching essay technique via the writing of literary essays. To their pupils they represented their aim as examination success, yet they concentrated on paragraphing, introductions and so forth, knowing full well that these niceties would gain little credit in the Literature examination. They were by no means the cynical trainers for the examination that they sometimes asserted, although there was plenty of useful advice on the handling of content. 'You must make detailed reference to the play' or 'Give quotes please', 'Too much narrative' or more explicitly, 'this is supposed to be a character study. You should by now understand what is required'. Examples were given as explanation, 'Still far too much description of scenes, far too little comment of your own. Too much missed out, e.g. Lady Capulet "For blood of ours shed blood of Montagu". You fail to come to any conclusions about Lady C. which is what you were asked to do . . .'

Scrutinising the comments on 314 essays was a constant reminder of the considerate patience of the majority of these teachers. The remarks above come from the two teachers mentioned, Mr O'Donnell and Mr Keegan, but similar examples, some even more detailed, could have been culled from Mrs Wood, Mr Austin, Mr Callaghan or Mr Porson. Occasionally, in exasperation, someone spat out 'Rubbish' or sarcastically added, 'Finished or just tired?', but the bulk of the evidence showed teachers painstakingly reiterating the ideals of careful presentation, logical arrangement of ideas, the importance of relevance and argument based upon evidence, and the careful development of a thought-out point-of-view. Muddle may be endearing in Mr Polly, youthful dreams of romance significant for *Romeo and Juliet*, but for contemporary teenagers it was a balanced appraisal of evidence and a logical exposition of argument that was important.

In this consideration of written work we have paid more attention to the teachers' comments than to the questions that were set. We have given some of them incidentally, but perhaps we could treat them more generally as part of the taken-for-granted world which English teachers expect to explore.

Areas of experience considered important

The public and private models we have characterised in our consideration of writing might be useful to apply here, alongside the terms personal and impersonal which we used to describe treatment. 'The discussion that takes off from reading a literary passage' was one of the indicators for personal treatment that we used in the analysis of the preparation for writing, and we might therefore have expected many examples of the personal in literature lessons but, as we have demonstrated, this was not the case. However, Marcus' distinction between English and history is worth noting (page 221). The mode in which the topics are discussed and presented may be impersonal but the subject matter of the topics, the feelings of individuals, their progress through life, their relationships with other individuals — these concerns are private. The paradox is that what we loosely accept as fifth-form literature is in the main a public representation of a private world. And, again, although most of the issues receive impersonal treatment, it is not so much their treatment in lessons which is crucial but whether pupils are sharing in the creation of meaning; again the dimensions of transmission and initiation cut across the personal/impersonal dimension. The relationship of characters in *A Taste of Honey* sounds a conventional literary topic but the discussion which led up to it showed that the pupils were engaging with the text, comparing the family in the play with their own, trying to define what they meant by a 'normal family'. The treatment ranged from impersonal to personal and power was not lodged entirely with the teacher. The lessons which seem to typify most completely the transmission category are those which were presumably preparing for those examination questions which we labelled 'Close Textual and Selective Narration'. The emphasis fell upon accounts of events, upon 'ficts', upon paraphrase and gloss, and the public knowledge and information embedded in the text. The treatment was predominantly impersonal.

We have said that the literature used in fifth forms is almost exclusively dealing with the private world. It seemed that in the books that were offered, experience was privatised and depoliticised; this was in part because of the choice of books. Of the 60 or so separate titles we met only a handful which were not concerned with personal relationships and even in those few the public issues were rarely considered. If we consider a text set for O-level — *The Crucible*, which was intended by Arthur Miller to parallel and comment on the witch-hunt of communists in the McCarthy era — we notice that it was the characters and personal relationships upon which Mrs Brennan focused. In contrast, Mr Austin who was the only teacher using *Henry V*, another of the more public texts, described two lessons in his diary returns as 'Discussion based upon the text as to the sources and abuses of power'. Yet all the questions set in the final examination which his class took asked for almost pure recapitulation. 'Give an account of the ... scene ... and say what it reveals of the characters of Pistol and Fluellen.' 'Give an account of (a) Henry's speech before Harfleur and (b) his speech ...' '... what purpose is served by the Chorus ...?' His attempt at moving the text into the public arena was effectively discouraged by the examination board.

Although teachers in their choice of books for the CSE and non-examination classes referred to relevance we noticed how often this meant a stress on the personal problems of adolescent relationships and the avoidance of societal problems.

The topics which people discuss after reading are, of course, pre-determined by those with which the literature deals but, although teachers spoke of moving into wider areas, when this happened it tended to be into family and personal relationships. Some reference to a sequence of lessons we saw on a D. H. Lawrence short story may be useful here. The first was a double period so Mr Gilham had time to read the story *Strike Pay* without interruption to his bottom class at Catchwide School, then go slowly through it recapitulating to make sure they had followed the sequence and the details. Just before the bell sounded the class was given the writing topic for next lesson: 'Explain how the miners' strike affects the relationship between Ephraim Wharmby, his wife and his mother-in-law Mrs Mariott'. As we walked to that lesson the next day Mr Gilham told me that he had chosen the topic because the pupils tended merely to retell the story and that they found it easier to write about episodes when there was a quarrel or argument because the characters stood out sharply. In passing, two points stand out: the first, that if the only model which was being offered in the lesson was that of retelling the story it was not surprising that that was what was produced, and the second, that the question as it was phrased did not in fact ask for a sequential narrative.

The choice of topic, the area of experience focused upon rather than its presentation to the class, however, is what is of interest. Mr Gilham believed that people were what his pupils could write about rather than poverty or strikes and that governed the topic he set. If the only issues which can be considered after reading a story are those which can be easily written about, we are considerably restricting our reflection on literature. One wonders if by demanding writing at length from less-able pupils, as these were, teachers are forced to make the assumption that everything must be a story. Analysis and reflection are difficult to sustain, pupils will tend to slide into the narrative, so the teacher's job degenerates into making certain that they have the 'ficts' straight.

Mr Gilham spent the beginning of the following lesson re-reading parts of the end of the story and checking that the pupils had followed the events leading up to 'the blazing row'. They were expected to speculate about some of these for when one boy asked, 'Sir, do we have to describe the relationship before as well as after?', Mr Gilham suggested that they would have 'to describe the relationship before they get married and how they don't get on so well before you get on to what happens on the day in the story'. The only textual basis for this could be a phrase 'he hated her' and the implications of 'he was more helpless before his mother-in-law whom he feared'. Considering the class it seemed that strikes and poverty were just as close to their experience as the nuances of a relationship between a young man and his mother-in-law. Family relationships are the material of most fiction since the 19th-century; this is the model of writing and thinking about experience which English teachers find themselves most in tune with and it is what they expect their pupils to be interested in. A good number of boys, however, particularly from working-class backgrounds, regard stories and novels as part of a woman's world; at this stage they are anxiously asserting their masculinity and the opposition of the masculine world to domestic values was one of the things this story was about. Perhaps Mr Gilham was right, perhaps his pupils could not write at length about these issues, but it may be that they could have reflected on some of them. They had listened to the story attentively but their response to the questioning seemed apathetic. Would it have been less so if there had been the opportunity to consider wider issues beyond the recapitulation of 'ficts'? Mr Austin, by raising the question of why the heroine of *Jane Eyre* was a governess, provoked a discussion on the position of women in the early 19th-century, but even with able classes such instances were rare.

Consideration of the areas of experience which form the basis of most of the literature we encounter is beyond the scope of this chapter. It would be a weighty historical and psychological study but nonetheless must form some part of what will be one of the final concerns of our study: why so much emphasis is placed on literature in English teaching in the fifth form. Perhaps we should remind ourselves of some of the justifications and hopes which the teachers expressed — statements such as:

> 'All I hope at the end is they want to go and read books'.
> 'I think they've all gained something from the course'.
> 'If they leave school and never open a book we stand condemned'.

Were these borne out by what the pupils we interviewed said about reading? From our interviews with pupils we gained some insight into their reading habits and their attitudes to what they had read in class but, as with all such data, there are problems of interpreting what they said. An apparently bright and lively girl told us that she enjoyed reading, a few sentences later this was reinterpreted as reading horoscopes and eventually it emerged as 'I get a lot of my reading . . . because I have to read the pattern' (for macramé); a lad who spoke in a slow, rather laboured style told us that he was not reading much at the moment, but a probe revealed that he was merely having a rest from the 'heavies', but had just finished *Pattern of Islands* and *The Good Soldier Schweik*. We tried to find the criteria for 'a lot' and 'not much' by encouraging pupils to give titles and details and, to a considerable extent, we think we succeeded. But a more difficult problem was faced when interpreting the answers about books read in class, for although the interviews were private and informal our own status was ambiguous because we were there by permission of the teacher. Some pupils were guarded in their replies whilst others, although willing to talk, treated us almost as examiners replying, we suspect, with what they thought were the 'right' answers. Generally, however, we had the impression that the majority of pupils appreciated being asked for their opinions and welcomed the opportunity to be honest in their replies.

Reading habits

First we will consider what pupils said of their own reading habits and an interested reader might find it worthwhile putting this beside Frank Whitehead's findings in his survey of children's reading interests, completed in 1974.[8] Most of the group taking O-level Language and Literature could be described as regular readers, but the proportion fell to considerably less than half for the group taking CSE Literature and there were very few regular readers in the group not taking a literature examination. Our opening question merely asked people how they spent their spare time: we followed with a general probe about reading but the information, for example, about particular books was usually volunteered rather than an answer to specific questions. We have produced tables giving proportions for the group totals (%) and the raw scores, divided according to gender.

Table 5.1(a)

Reading habits (%)

	Regular	Occasional	Specific titles	Newspaper	Magazines	*Girls* Regular	*Girls* Occasional	*Boys* Regular	*Boys* Occasional
GCE O-Lit.	72%	11%	38%	13%	39%	76%	12%	67%	11%
CSE Lit.	38%	26%	17%	7%	33%	50%	36%	25%	20%
Non-lit. exam.	11%	51%	8%	23%	38%	7%	64%	15%	39%

Table 5.1(b)

Reading habits (raw scores)

	Total		Regular		Occasional		Specific titles or authors		Newspapers		Magazines	
	G.	B.	G.	B.	G.	B.	G.	B.	G.	B.	G.	B.
GCE O-Lit.	34	27	26	18	4	3	11	12	3	5	22	2
	(61)											
CSE Lit.	22	20	11	5	8	4	5	2	3	0	14	0
	(42)											
Non-lit. exam.	28	33	2	5	18	13	3	2	6	8	17	6
	(61)											

We expected that there would be variation according to gender, and it is true most girls think of reading as a leisure activity, but the most striking difference between boys and girls seemed to be in the reading of magazines; 63 per cent of the girls read magazines whereas only 10 per cent of the boys did. Most of the girls said that they read teenage magazines such as *Jackie* or *My Guy* (they were the main reading of the non-examination group), but many of them also read the magazines their mothers bought. A few boys, mainly in the lower groups, mentioned football or motor-cycling magazines, but as we see they were very much in the minority. It is likely too, from some of the remarks, that in the non-examination group a number of the boys whom we have put as occasional readers only glanced at the sports pages for football scores, whereas the girls in the same category probably read longer articles on fashion, social relationships or horoscopes. We gained a strong impression, even though the figures do not fully support it, that reading was a normal human activity irrespective of gender for the more able, but a peculiarly feminine activity in other classes, but we were interested that twice Tolkien cropped up as an author described as 'fantastic' or in similar terms by boys in the less-able groups.

It is difficult to produce in tabular form the attitudes towards the books read in class, first because, as we have described, there is the O-level corpus, the CSE corpus and the rest, and secondly because interview data does not produce neat categories. 'What do you think of the books you've read?' meant that some people said a sentence or two about two books and ignored the rest, or produced contradictory remarks such as 'I can't bear...' but then later, 'I liked that bit where...'. Our comments must consequently be hedged with qualifications.

Attitudes to O-level set texts

The tables on reading habits show that most of the O-level pupils were readers. The majority of them chose to read for pleasure; there were no marked differences, according to school, so on that basis we would expect them to be equally receptive of the books they read in class. Unfortunately we cannot compare their reactions to identical texts because of the diversity of choice, particularly in fiction. *Jane Eyre*, *The Mayor of Casterbridge*, *Great Expectations* and *The Woman in White* were all spoken of with enthusiasm. Comments included 'super' (*Woman in White*), 'very good' (*Jane Eyre*) and 'I really enjoyed it' (*Great Expectations*). None of these was a book we would expect to find 15-year-olds reading without encouragement and some pupils showed that the pleasure had been unexpected. 'I was surprised... it was quite entertaining' (*Woman in White*). Teaching method seemed to have affected response, otherwise we could not account for the patterning of replies. That short stories were 'a bit long' or 'dragged a bit' in one class seemed more likely to be connected with methodology than with actual length, especially when only one person commented on the length of *Great Expectations*. Novels received more positive remarks than any other genre: only six people expressed dislike and one of those was a boy who could 'not stand reading' in any form and four were from Mr Keegan's class reading Richard Church's *Over the Bridge*.

It was easier to compare responses to Shakespearian plays primarily because the problems of understanding were likely to be similar and also because three classes had actually read the same play, *Romeo and Juliet*. Whereas considerably more than half of the total had enjoyed their prose set texts, the proportion fell to just over a third and even then liking was often accompanied with doubts. 'Once you'd figured out what it was about it was a really good story' (*Romeo and Juliet*). Watching performances had clearly helped as people referred to productions or spoke of liking the film version more than the play or of both of them making it 'much easier to visualise'. The rewarding study of one play, however, had not always convinced: 'It was quite good, although you usually associate Shakespeare with boredom', and there were a number of ambiguous or contradictory replies. Approval of *Romeo and Juliet*, for example, by some pupils may not have been so much because it was enjoyable as that it was thought to be safe: 'That's really packed full of notes, it's great, you read your notes almost to get the other side of the story, sort of translated into normal language'. It clearly had not been the almost unqualified success that the alternative play, *The Crucible*, had been. Most comments on that were very enthusiastic and even the girl who had not liked it at the beginning 'couldn't put it down, I had to finish it' and the only one whose dislike persisted, 'The teacher is mad on it, but I didn't like it', seemed to have been influenced by a weak amateur production they had seen. Although Shakespeare might not have been appreciated wholeheartedly by the majority, there was not the widespread rejection that pupils felt towards the poetry set texts. Not only were the strongest attitudes of dislike manifest here, 'unspeakable' and 'pointless, I absolutely hate it', but also the greatest bafflement, 'I just don't understand' or 'sometimes when I read a poem I haven't the slightest ideas what it's talking about'. If we had excluded the favourable comments from Mrs Wood's group, the only one who had read narrative poems, the figures would have been even more biased against poetry as an examination set text. Three of the pupils in Mr Austin's class commented on their savouring of the challenge of the difficult poems by a local poet, but they were less positive in their attitude to Hardy, their set poet. Our general impression was that pupils were worried and unsure. 'It's alright just reading them but when Mr Keegan tries to get the hidden meaning you sit there scratching your head. You don't know what he's on about . . . He was asking about a poem by Edward Thomas: you had to write what you thought about it. Then he explained and it was completely different to what you've got . . . When we handed it in at the end of the class he marked it right, but I thought it was wrong. My ideas of the poem were completely different to his.' Despite Mr Keegan's honest encouragement and acceptance of alternative response this pupil had found it impossible to tolerate uncertainty: years of conditioning to a right/wrong view of knowledge prevailed. The modern poetry which was set was not particularly obscure; to literature specialists it was probably the most accessible of possible poetry texts, but on the evidence we gathered, studying it for the O-level examination was not likely to turn pupils into future poetry readers. The 'old-fashioned' 18th-century language of the *Deserted Village*, the rural settings of *Michael* were apparently more readily accepted, but we must not underestimate the effect of an experienced, sympathetic and authoritative teacher coupled with the security which the narrative offered.

Attitudes to CSE texts

The five CSE groups, particularly the boys, were less likely to be readers by choice, although all but one group would be considered by their school to be above average albeit only slightly in two cases. The texts they commented on were predominantly novels or short stories covering a wide range: their reading included *Lord of the Flies*, *Of Mice and Men* and *Animal Farm*, as well as *Kes*, *To Kill a Mockingbird* and *Cider with Rosie*. Only the least able form, the one from Catchwide School where the policy was examinations for everyone, was basing its work on relatively undemanding texts. It was interesting that, whereas there were a number of remarks about the difficulty of O-level prose texts, there were none from this group. It could be that because these quite demanding texts were being read for coursework essays for which there was careful preparation pupils were not finding them too challenging. Although a number of short stories were mentioned they were not liked more or less than longer fiction so there was no point in separating the two genres. The comments on the plays — *A Taste of Honey*, *Hobson's Choice*, *The Inspector Calls* and *Night Must Fall* — also followed much the same pattern as those on the novels. There was one girl who got 'all confused when we change round parts', but generally plays seemed to be accepted, although interestingly the least able group read none. There were few remarks about poetry, probably because it was read relatively infrequently and short poems tended to be less memorable than novels.

Our general impression was of vague likes and dislikes with few

Table 5.2

Attitudes to O-level texts

	Positively liked	Non-committal	Positively disliked	Comments on difficulty	TOTAL
Novels or prose fiction	37	23	6	5	66
Shakespeare	15	22	6	4	41
Crucible	11	1	1	0	13
Poetry	10	10	12	12	43

Table 5.3

Attitudes to CSE texts

	Positively liked	Non-committal	Positively disliked	Comments on difficulty	TOTAL
Novels or short stories	23	18	10	0	51
Modern plays	6	8	5	0	19
Poetry	2	1	2	1	6

reasons being given. *Hobson's Choice* 'weren't bad if you like that kind of book' or *A Taste of Honey* was 'OK . . . shows what life were like for those who weren't well off'. Occasionally there were glimpses of enthusiasm: *Cider with Rosie* was 'fantastic' according to one girl, but a boy in the same group dismissed it as 'boring'. One girl who was a reader on her own found 'these books really down to earth': her own choice was very different. There were no sure winners. *Kes* could be 'alright', 'good' or 'too descriptive. (I) like more exciting books'.

Reading for the non-examination forms

Kes leads us conveniently to the non-examination groups for three of the six groups had read it. On two groups it seemed to have had relatively little impact, only four pupils mentioned it: for two it was merely a title they remembered, for another 'OK' and only the last thought 'it very good really'. A more able non-examination group had enjoyed it, for there five people expressed positive liking and for the remainder it was 'alright'. As we have showed, these pupils rarely wrote about books and in many cases they had difficulty in remembering titles, particularly of individual readers. We interviewed Mrs Williams' class whilst they were reading *There is a Happy Land* as a class reader so were able to collect a number of comments on that. Most of the remarks were non-committal and somewhat contradictory. Dale thought it 'quite real . . . actually what kids would do', but for Michelle it was 'not like real life'. Darryl also thought it 'good' because it showed 'what it was like in M—— ages ago'. Teachers sometimes forget that books which they think comparatively recent comers to the literature canon — Waterhouse's book was published in 1957 — are depicting a way of life which seems very remote from that of their pupils. *A Kind of Loving* was as likely to be labelled 'old-fashioned' by these readers as was *Great Expectations* by other pupils.

As few texts would be acclaimed by everyone in the class, so attitudes to listening to a book or reading it for one's self varied. In Mrs Waterhouse's 'bottom' stream at New Suburbia School the boys seemed to like being read to whilst the girls wanted to read for themselves. Paula remarked, 'When I listen to Mrs Waterhouse I wander off and doze off, but when I'm reading to myself I get more interested'. We had observed Mrs Sutton's pupils giving prepared readings and again these seemed unpopular with the boys. Responses to individual readers, as was to be expected, were just as varied as those to class readers. It is worth noticing that unless book boxes were very carefully organised and pupils, as at Urban School, were allowed to keep books, it was very difficult to maintain continuity. There were various comments at New Suburbia School about a book started one lesson not being available the next.

Excitement seemed to be what boys felt school books lacked, the few they singled out for praise were approved because there's 'always a bit of action, something going on all the time' (*The Intruder*) or 'It's exciting, there's more fights in it . . . when it starts to drag it livens up by something happening' (*The Contender*). We heard teachers speaking persuasively of some of the texts, but reading for the majority clearly remained a school subject.

That may seem a depressing note on which to end our discussion of pupil attitudes. 'If they leave school and never open a book we stand condemned', said Mrs Wood. She had managed to convince her able O-level pupils but she would have been the first to admit that she found it another matter with the lower streams.

Although this chapter is based on the material we gathered at fifth-form level it was interesting to see whether a further dimension was added by what students in sixth forms and the further education colleges said a year later about fifth-form literature teaching. The majority, of course, were commenting on fifth-form classes we had not observed but their remarks, nevertheless, reinforced the overall impressions we had gained. The least able FE students who had been prepared for CSE English made few references to reading or books. From our evidence we can assume that they had read in class but it did not seem to have been memorable: their comments tended to be very general or about writing stories and doing comprehensions. There were some positive comments from more successful CSE students: the strongest approval came from a boy who had been in Mr Richardson's class whose lesson on *A Taste of Honey* we have commented on. The facility with which he could recall five titles that he had enjoyed was in itself unusual and it was interesting to hear what he had liked doing: 'Well with Mr Richardson we'd do a lot of revising on t'books . . . we'd read before.' *Taste of Honey* was one of the books he remembered and perhaps the lesson we saw would have counted as the 'lot of revising' he had enjoyed.

Most of the comments from FE students we had were, of course, related to O-level literature: ten of them expressed either dislike of the texts or boredom with the teaching, and six found something they liked. 'It was very hard . . . a bit boring . . . though they were good books', 'it was monotonous' and 'an O-level that was all'. One or two approved of the discipline — it had been appreciated as 'a straight sit down and learn lesson' — but Shakespeare was described as 'hard' or they were 'not keen on the poetry'. It is interesting to compare two comments from students who were taking A-level literature. The first was giving the reasons for her dislike of literature teaching at O-level. 'They don't give you enough to make you interested . . . you say how good this book is because that's what the teacher's told you to say, it's not 'cos you really feel that it's a good book.' The second was trying to explain why the O-level literature course had been good. 'The thing I remember from it and the thing that I enjoyed most was the Shakespeare, just the first Shakespeare that we did, where we did a couple . . . *Macbeth* and *Twelfth Night*, and I think learning to read books, a novel, in a different light . . . You're not really doing them very deep at all, but even so you're learning to read them in a different light . . . it gives me a lot of pleasure.' We did not know at first-hand what the lessons which had given rise to these contrasting remarks had been, but it sounded as though they belonged to the opposing poles of the transmission—initiation scale. It would be simplistic to assume that liking for a course can be a reliable instrument for evaluating it, but the terms in which people expressed their liking seemed to be a significant indicator. The consideration of students' and pupils' attitudes to literature has led us back to surveying fifth-form literature teaching as a whole, the starting point of this chapter. We began our analysis by setting out the high proportion of time spent in the fifth form on literature teaching and the insistence of the teachers that it is an essential element of an English course. Our examination in the main has been of literature taught as a separate entity because, despite the emphasis placed on a thematic approach in the Downtown School syllabus and the statement that the themes it offered could be 'starting points for language projects' in the Smalltown School syllabus, all the schools accepted the principle of literature as a separate subject with separate certification. The CSE English examinations were originally designed to foster a unitary approach and some of the topics in writing lessons were linked to what was being read as, for example, when Mr Callaghan used references to *Hobson's Choice* as evidence in a discussion of marriage which led to an essay on it. Mr Squires made a similar use of *A Kind of Loving*, yet when he was reading it with the class he seemed to have a different purpose in mind. There was a model of literature teaching lying behind 'reading' lessons, a model, perhaps, linked to the teacher's own experience which could not be escaped or denied. Mrs Sutton, speaking for Urban School, said that literature teaching was integral; she was 'not prepared to consider literature as an option', and Mrs King spoke of her fights to resist the Head's suggestion that it should become an option at New Suburbia School, but what they were speaking of was O-level literature — the separate subject with separate certification. It is because we experienced this separation that our treatment has been as it has.

Most of the teachers in our sample stressed the importance of literature teaching; for them there was no doubt that the experience of literature had an intrinsic value which was not simply translatable into terms of examination success. But, although some doubts were expressed about the constraints which examinations placed upon them, the teachers nevertheless accepted and welcomed the validity that examinations conferred and we have put it on record that they rarely encouraged serious reflection upon a book unless it was to be examined.

For most adults reading a book, whether it be for work or pleasure, is a private experience, yet reading fiction and poetry in school is a different matter. In almost all English classes at fifth-form level it was a public activity completely controlled by the teacher and in the majority of lessons the teacher was the only reader determining the pace of reading, the explanations necessary and the comments to be made on the book. Treatment of those books, however, as we have shown, divided sharply according to whether or not they were being studied for an examination. The progress through books which were to be examined in a final paper could be at a snail's pace: about 20 hours spread over six or more months was spent reading and talking about each book. (This disregards homework when much additional reading and writing would be done.) Of the six classes not preparing literature for some examination, two did almost no reading, two used books mainly in the preparation of general essays for their coursework folders and, of the two classes who read books generally, in only one did the teacher encourage pupils to think and talk about what they had read. Our data does not allow us to make generalisations about the speed of reading of books examined by coursework.

In the process of reading a book it may become irrevocably embedded in our experience, but on the other hand it may make no impact at all. In the classroom, books were abstracted from experience: they were often treated as facts to be explained by the teacher and reproduced by the pupils, as content to 'sit down and learn'. Yet even the limited selection of episodes quoted in this paper illustrates the variety of procedures for penetrating a text which are available, with a teacher's help, to young people of this age. The following list comes solely from these examples and is capable of expansion. Pupils demonstrated their ability orally or in writing:

To interpret local meaning.
To discuss the choice of words.
To discuss characters, their motives, and the reader's perception of them.
To relate incidents to the reader's experience.
To make judgements of verisimilitude.
To comment on the wider characteristics of a work, such as its setting.
To recognise the effects of the authorial voice.
To consider a writer's intentions and methods.
To generalise about a genre.

We have demonstrated that it is possible for all these responses to operate and are interested in what teaching enabled pupils themselves to become confident and critical readers. Even the least able students showed that they could go far beyond mere paraphrase and one top set engaged in many of the activities of sophisticated literary criticism.

The distinction we have drawn between transmission and initiation type teaching may be a crucial one. It seemed to us that when lessons fell consistently into the transmission mode — when, for example, teachers maintained the tightest control on the first reading, concentrated exclusively on details and localised meanings, supplied a para text and limited the topics discussed to those which were to be subsequently written about for examination purposes — they were handicapping their pupils. They might argue that through unquestioning acceptance of authority and frequent repetitions of activities pupils eventually internalised the principles and values of the teachers so that they could operate them for themselves, but when those principles and values involve empathy, the interrelation of perspectives and judgements of relevance, pupils were not having the opportunity to exercise these faculties.

At the centre of initiation is the idea that pupils do not merely reproduce another person's account of a text but engage for themselves in a range of critical procedures that can give rise to such an account. We have illustrated some of these procedures in this chapter. In some cases they lead outwards from the text, relating the literary work to lived experience; others remain within the text, attributing significance to it without explicitly justifying the interpretations by outside reference. Indeed, it seemed to the observers that at times the pupils' ability to interpret was being just as effectively validated by remaining within the text and operating implicit modes of reflection and commentary on literature. Our culture supplies a repertoire of procedures for reading and response, and literature teachers pass these on to their pupils when they engage collaboratively in reading and commentary. Such procedures are seldom made explicit or subjected themselves to critical examination but if learnt at all are learnt through apprenticeship. By sharing the reading of the text, allowing pupils to move at their own pace, to ask as well as answer questions, and to use their own ideas and experience as a basis for creating meaning, some teachers induct pupils into the repertoire of procedures for critical and reflective reading. Transmission teaching operated in almost a pure form in seven out of the twelve classes who were preparing for an examination in literature; whereas the initiation model operated consistently in only three classes and in some of the lessons of the remaining two. Only a minority of young people are given the opportunity in the fifth form of celebrating the values of literature teaching to which most English teachers pay lip-service.

Conclusions drawn from a small sample must necessarily be tentative. Our impression was that a good deal of the literature teaching was irrationally narrow in its range, confined mainly to paraphrase and commentary on the local meaning of texts, along with stylised account of theme and character. These activities did not seem a close match with what was required by the examinations being prepared for, and indeed pupils thus taught did not do well in literature examinations. This narrow range was usually associated with a transmission mode; it was made possible by treating the meaning of literature as open to authoritative pronouncement and by treating pupils as passive receivers. On the other hand, we were impressed by the range of activities possible at this level when an initiation mode was used. By the fifth form most pupils assume that reading is followed by writing, an assumption frequently shared by teachers. The conscientious teacher becomes anxious to provide evidence not merely for herself but for others that pupils have gained insights and understanding. The kind of writing which reflects and contributes to a pupil's often private and idiosyncratic struggles to make sense of a work of literature is not the same as the well-rounded public statement expected in examination answer or coursework folder. The fact that writing about literature is the only method of assessment envisaged, the only means of providing evidence that the teaching has been successful, increases the amount of tension between the two kinds of writing.

As a final note we should add that we have been writing as though the teacher is the sole deciding factor, yet although teachers are apparently in control of the classroom they only operate with their pupils' consent; for example, Mr Austin was conscious of the pressure from some pupils because they only saw the course in terms of the examination. He spoke of the 'delicate structuring . . . to make it obvious that . . . you're concerned with the examination, but you're concerned with other things'. So long as most fifth-form examinations are seen as the means of selection crucial for deciding which paths will be followed, most pupils will have an instrumental view of the education which is a preparation for them. The aims and justifications we quoted in our opening section may not be the pupils' reality.

CHAPTER 6

Versions of English in the Fifth Form

1. Five versions

The first question likely to be asked of this research is, 'What versions have you found?' If the questioner is a teacher he or she may go on to suggest either that because of examination pressures there will only be one version, or (alternatively) that there will be as many versions as there are teachers. Fortunately for this book, neither is true. Examinations do play a part in shaping the versions — as we have shown on pp. 79–80 of Chapter 3 — but they must be seen as an expression of a department's or a teacher's choice at the same time as a source of external constraints upon their teaching. When we counted the different examinations taken by our 18 fifth-year classes they amounted to the bewildering total of 14, selected and combined in different patterns. Within such variety a department would have considerable control over the bonds it chose to wear.

The versions described in this chapter refer only to the school fifth year; the sixth form and further education materials are presented in the two following chapters. To name and describe 'versions' is (in a partly arbitrary manner) to impose regularity upon the complex irregularities of real life, yet such simplification is a necessary part of understanding what is happening. The complexities have been described in the preceding chapters. Our account of underlying versions must take note of the difference between highly personalised approaches and more detached ones, such as the kind of writing we called *belles lettres*. It must note how the teaching of literature changes from one stream to another, yet literature underlies many of the assumptions about the nature of reading and writing. In contrast with this, the emphasis in some classes on decontextualised language exercises also needs to be taken into account, and with it the occasional occurrence of a more reflective and analytical approach to reading and writing. To represent these variations, we have chosen to posit five versions, five 'ideal types', which in our view represent five underlying models of English teaching. We have decided not to identify particular teachers with particular versions, though in some cases this seemed possible; it is clear, however, that a teacher may display co-existing elements of alternative versions, or move from one version to another when he or she teaches a different class. We label the versions: (i) cultural tradition; (ii) personal growth; (iii) *belles lettres*; (iv) basic skills; (v) public rationality. The labels are familiar but will attract more precise meanings, partly because of the discussion that follows and partly because they refer back to the materials already discussed in earlier chapters.

(i) *Cultural tradition*

Top sets spend much of their time studying set texts for English literature examinations, and teachers often justify this as giving access to high culture, which is a just description in some cases. (When literature teaching is confined to the teacher's commentary on set books it is an example of version (iii).) Although in the cultural tradition version the general essays set to pupils are likely to lean towards the personal treatment even of public topics, based upon fictional and autobiographical models, literature essays are couched in the impersonal modes expected in literature examinations, even when the subject matter (for example, the relationship of Jane Eyre to Mr Rochester) might be not far distant from some pupils' experience. In this version the pupils are offered not just knowledge of particular works of literature, but insight into modes of reading and of critical commentary.

(ii) *Personal growth*

This can be described as a modification for lower sets of the cultural tradition version. The central rationale is to enable pupils through reading and writing to change their experience of the world — from the inside, as it were — though, as we have shown, many are resistant to any such invasion of their privacy. Literature is for pleasure not for study; it can also provide what teachers call a 'stimulus' for writing. The reading and writing concentrates on private topics, especially close personal relationships, often set in a stylised urban milieu; language development is held to be inseparable from development in social and moral awareness. Much of the writing done is fictional, often in a naturalistic quasi-autobiographical mode that owes much to the novels of the fifties and sixties.

(iii) *Belles lettres*

This version, to be found in top and middle sets, is strongly influenced by examination requirements, and often accompanies the choice of examination by written papers. It differs from the cultural tradition and personal growth versions by not aiming to penetrate into pupils' experience: the pupils are expected to display competence in essays, comprehension exercises and in literature without necessarily involving themselves as people in what they are doing. Literary study is the learning of 'ficts', the contents of works of literature being treated as information, and not as an invitation to pupils to recreate those works on the basis of their own experience of the world.

(iv) *Basic skills*

This version, called 'functional English' by one teacher, can be seen as a descendant of the English taught in 'elementary' schools earlier in the century. It is the 'bottom-set' equivalent of *belles lettres*, sharing with that version the detachment of language from the user's purposes and experience. English is treated as a set of surface conventions and skills that can be separated from the purposes of the writer and from the content of what is written; these conventions and skills, seen as prerequisites to reading and writing, are 'practised' through exercises taken from coursebooks. Reading is represented by 'comprehension'; literature occurs only as a source for such exercises, or as a relaxation.

(v) *Public rationality*

This version is likely to occur infrequently, and usually in a 'top' set, so it can be seen as an alternative to the cultural tradition and *belles lettres* versions. The central model of language for both of these latter two versions is aesthetic; the public rationality version acknowledges both an aesthetic and a documentary model, in which language carries out transactions and is open to reflective analysis. The written work done includes a range of topics from private to public, and there is discussion of bias, appropriate style, and the relationship of writer to audience. Pupils may write about public topics with concern or commitment, yet at times they are required to simulate different kinds of writing or different personae. Discussion of issues is encouraged, both orally and in writing, and literature too is a subject for public exchanges.

There is some irony in the occurrence of personal experience and basic skills as the two versions most commonly offered to bottom sets. Teachers of lower sets in the fifth year face many pupils who have not found schooling very responsive to their needs — as they perceive them — and who are often highly sceptical of the value of low CSE grades. To engage their co-operation, teachers may select one of two sharply contrasted strategies; they may try to co-opt their pupils' participation by according significance to what they believe to be their pupils' interests and experience — the personal growth version — or they may treat that experience as irrelevant and offer a diet of decontextualised and undemanding exercises — the basic skills version — in the hope that pupils will accept them as potentially relevant to work, or at least be kept busy by them.

Some of the relationships between these five versions are represented diagrammatically in Fig. 6.1. Four dimensions are needed to account for the differences between the versions. Cultural tradition and personal growth share the purpose of penetrating deeply into the learners' experience and so are described as 'engaged', whereas *belles lettres* and basic skills are both 'detached', concerned with surface performances only. The public rationality version can best be distinguished from cultural tradition and personal growth by saying that its model of language gives more prominence to documentary than to aesthetic functions whereas, in contrast with basic skills, it is concerned with deep criteria, not only with the surface. As we explained in the previous paragraph, the difference between versions for top and bottom sets is not a single dimension, so it is represented by a dotted line; however, the personal growth and basic skills versions do have in common that they expect pupils to have only a restricted ability to use language for the close study of literature and for extended writing.

Figure 6.1

Five school versions of English

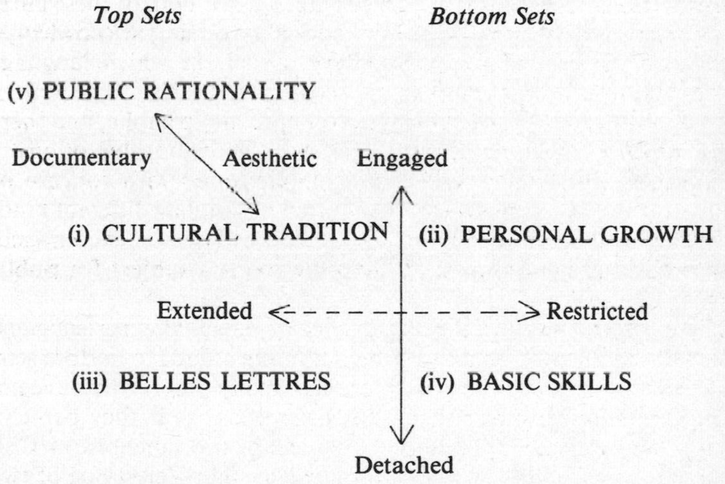

We can summarise the differences between the versions offered to top and bottom sets, though the reader should remember that these are idealisations; the complexities of reality have been illustrated in earlier chapters. Top sets are likely to be spending a considerable proportion of their time on preparation for a literature examination, which will for some of them lead later to an A-level in English Literature. Bottom sets will read some literature but will be given little or no help in deepening their understanding of particular works nor in developing more sophisticated ways of reading. Their other work may be strongly personalised, with much fictional writing of a quasi-autobiographical kind, or may remain in the impersonality of textbook exercises, usually unthreatening because undemanding. Some 'top' sets are expected to write predominantly on private topics in a personal manner; others are encouraged to write with detached elegance; a few, like those in Downtown School, will write mainly fiction because they are much more successful with it. But cutting across these patterns will be another, which corresponds to the mode of examination chosen. Those classes, top, middle, or bottom, who are sitting examination papers are more likely to experience one of the 'detached' versions, *belles lettres* or basic skills, whereas those assessed by coursework will probably experience one of the 'engaged' versions. School-based assessment encourages or enables teachers to set up learning activities that demand greater engagement of the learners' personal experience.

The effect of literature is pervasive, for it supplies a model of language activity that is unchallenged except in the public rationality version. It defines the aesthetic function as central, thus tending to prefer private above public topics, not only for general essays but in the discussion of works of literature (see Chapter 5, p. 233). In the cultural tradition and personal development versions, writing is normally either reflective or addressed to the undefined audience implicit in contemporary literature. What counts is truth to experience, 'language as being', as the realisation of self. Yet even for those teachers who decline to subscribe to ideas of personal development through English (see Chapter 3, p. 75), the curriculum is shaped by a literary model of reading and writing. Concern for context, for appropriateness and the match of manner to purpose and situation seldom appeared in the data except in the public rationality version, with the result that pupils had little or no opportunity to study models of writing on public topics or in an impersonal manner, except via the misleading simplifications of 'comprehension exercises'. The assumption that English relates solely to kinds of writing that, like literature, create their own context, narrows the rhetorical range and discourages reflection upon uses of language which are embedded in pre-existing context.

2. Who owns the language?

At this point we abandon the policy of descriptive neutrality to which we have adhered during the foregoing chapters (with the exception of some asides which we should perhaps have denied ourselves). In this section and that which follows we take the responsibility of expressing views about fifth-year English teaching as we found it and as we would wish it to become.

In Chapter 4 the question was asked: 'Who owns the language?' Pupils do not embark upon fifth-form English courses as empty vessels but as sophisticated users of language in many different situations. The great strength of the personal growth version is that this is acknowledged by attributing to pupils the ability through language to engage with and reinterpret important areas of experience: through extensive use they are to develop the linguistic and human competences they already have. An irony of this is that these uses are largely confined to written language: oral language activities for their own sake were almost entirely absent from the school data, yet most students may be said to 'own' their spoken language at a time when they are still groping for control of written modes. Much of the writing we saw in fifth-year classes fell within a narrow stylistic range, and almost all was addressed to the anonymous audience which is supposed (for example) by fiction. Yet outside the classroom the same young people must have found they needed to explain, to argue a case, to persuade, to criticise and to justify, in fact to engage in a far wider range of rhetorical acts than can be listed here. Of course, we are referring to speech, not writing, yet classroom speech was still more confined — usually to question-and-answer sequences which tightly constrained the pupils' participation. Pupils are directed away from the spoken language through which they negotiate and realise their day-to-day experience towards a limited version of written language.

It is not only speech and writing which is represented by inadequate models. Reading, too, is represented either as 'comprehension' — little more than low-level exercises in paraphrase — or as the study of literature, often with excessive emphasis upon local meaning and the learning of 'ficts'.[1] Much of the English teaching we saw was tacitly legitimated by the idea of language as the means by which the writer explores and reinterprets his or her view of the world. We are not wishing to dismiss this view but to put it in perspective. First, most of the writing we saw was not of that kind — examinations and the conditions of classroom production of 'work' ensure that relatively little self-exploration takes place — but rather fiction and *belles lettres*. Second, in our view, other kinds of talking, reading and writing are at least equally important. We are arguing the case for reading and writing in which writers engage with public topics as critical members of the community, and at the same time for the inclusion of situated assignments like those developed in further education. In our view, personal reflective writing should continue to have a place in the curriculum for those who can make use of it, but should not provide the dominant model of language use. Much of the reading and writing done is a poor representation even of the literary uses of language, and an even worse match for the talking, reading and writing required in adult life. As we have seen, many pupils, particularly those in middle or bottom sets, see English as irrelevant to real life because it is written and literary, whereas they believe the important uses of language outside school to be spoken and transactional. This may mean that for this substantial group of students the personal growth version for all its virtues is ineffective: much of the writing they did was a parody of self-exploration. It is worth noting that Mr Austin engaged his bottom set in oral discussion of emotionally-loaded issues but set them to write a story: personal issues were less threatening in talk than in writing. The continued emphasis in school English on written language at the expense of spoken, in spite of oral examinations, the Bullock Report and the decision of the Assessment of Performance Unit to test spoken language, is worth considering: who owns written language and who owns speech?

In literary study and in comprehension exercises we can reformulate the question as, 'Who owns the text?' In Chapter 5 we show how tightly most teachers control the reading of works of literature, taking pupils through them line by line, sometimes more than once, even when examination questions do not require knowledge of that kind. The teaching of literature to examination classes is relatively homogeneous, in spite of the distinctions we made in describing the versions earlier in this chapter. Works of literature are often treated as if they existed as objective information to be learnt; it is relatively unusual for the chosen pedagogy to acknowledge that each reader has to construct a meaning out of the cultural resources he or she shares with the writer, the teacher and the other pupils. 'Making the text one's own' is not just a liberal slogan but a necessary part of reading; from the point-of-view of teaching methods it would seem to imply a cyclic process of tentatively attributing meaning, trying this out on other pupils and the teacher, and reconsidering the result in the light of further readings. We saw this happening in a few lessons in the mode we have labelled 'initiation', but in many others — the transmission-type lessons — the teacher left pupils in no doubt that it was he or she who owned the text and its interpretation. More strange were discussion lessons in which a teacher encouraged pupils to explore a text, and then laid down authoritatively what they were to write about it, a phenomenon that can largely be attributed to examination pressures.

When it is applied to comprehension exercises, 'Who owns the text?' comes to mean something different. It asks: Why should it be this text rather than that? Why should it be Sunday-newspaper journalism rather than political pamphlet, travel description rather than technical manual, 19th-century rather than contemporary novel? Why should the teacher choose rather than the pupils? Could not examples be taken from life rather than from textbooks? (Some teachers do.) More important, however, is the control of questions by textbook and teacher, since — as every reader has experienced — the questions we ask as we grapple with a difficult text are our own, asked in the order we need them and they are different in kind from those asked in tests. Comprehension-as-test imposes its inappropriate framework upon comprehension-as-working-to-understand.

Something similar can be said of the teaching of writing. Our impression of writing lessons was of concentration on product rather than on process. Teachers provided elaborate starting-points and 'marked' assiduously to provide feedback after the event, but there was little or no sign of what are often called 'workshop' methods, where writers receive feedback while they are writing from other pupils and from the teacher. In a workshop the emphasis falls — as it does in most writing for publication — on a relatively extended process of reconsideration and rewriting. When teachers gave help in the lessons we observed it consisted mainly of suggestions for a starting-point, encouragement to laggards, and help with practical matters such as spelling. There seemed to be something of a pedagogical vacuum here: assessment by coursework, expected to free teachers to give more attention to process, seems not to have achieved this.

A little-discussed aspect of the pervasiveness of literary assumptions is that they often carry with them a high valuation of spontaneity as an indicator of authenticity. Yet it is not self-evident that reflection and discussion are destructive even of fiction or autobiography. Making process more visible must include the development of ways of talking about reading and writing, and even talking about talking. English teaching has not progressed very far in this direction: as we have shown (Chapter 3, p. 78), English teachers are not well provided with ways of talking even about different kinds of writing. In Chapter 3 we discussed the transmission of deep criteria to pupils in the course of preparing them to write; there seems to be every reason for making criteria explicit, even with those pupils whose capacity for such reflection is relatively limited. The language *should* belong to the pupils, and no service is done by denying them access to their teachers' and examiners' criteria — or to the possibility of rejecting those criteria. Literature is indeed one means by which we can generate hypothetical worlds, but any reader of a set of pupils' stories about 'Life in 50 years' time' will be aware that literature can be a trap as well as an open door. Without reflection and discussion we are not free to break out of conventions, to conceive alternatives, or to explore possibilities. English teachers have the opportunity of returning to children the possession of their own language, and part of this is finding ways of helping them to talk reflectively about it.

English teachers — we know from talk outside the research — often defend their emphasis upon private topics and personal presentations of experience by contrasting it with the predominance of other kinds of writing in the curriculum as a whole. If young people spend so long reading and writing about impersonal matters in science and geography, and even in history, is it not essential that for a fraction of the time available they consider life from the perspective of the personal? We concede the force of this argument. However, we take the view that the personal is not enough. What is wrong with the language of teaching and learning in the curriculum as a whole is not its impersonality alone, but its unreality; most school textbooks, far from being instrumental or transactional, are mere shadow-boxing. They offer simplified accounts of the world, accounts denuded of criticism, conflict and alternatives, and abstracted from the complex background noise of reality. Textbooks more than anything else deprive the young of their rights of possession in the language. It is important precisely for this reason that English should not confine itself to private topics. Young people should read and discuss writing on public topics that acknowledges variety and conflict in accounts of how the world is; such writing at its best is impersonal in the sense that its focus is well outside its author, but personal in that every phrase, every nuance of tone, acknowledges the author's responsibility instead of hiding behind a façade of unchallengeable authority. Experience of writing in such a way, and of discussing such writing, was not common, and it was to a large degree its occasional presence in one or two classrooms that induced us to give to 'public rationality' the dignity of being a version in its own right.

In our judgement current approaches to English teaching in the fifth year are too restricted. We acknowledge the validity of literature and of fictional and reflective writing as ways of making sense of experience, but wish at the same time to insist on the importance of other purposes for language. The personalising approach based upon literary models seems to imply that our sole moral responsibility is to those we meet face-to-face; and this goes with a restricted range of topics. English teaching to older pupils should, in our view, expand in five directions: by placing language in a social context, by grasping controversial issues, by looking for sources of material outside private experience, by including a wider range of rhetorical functions, and by giving a more active role to the learners. English should include attention to the contexts in which particular kinds of writing appear, and how people match what they write to their purposes and audiences. This would include analysis of bias and discussion of ethical issues related to *reportage* and persuasion, and could be related to simulated writing tasks. Second, there should be no shrinking from controversial public issues: the third world, weapons including nuclear ones, the role of the police, relationships between ethnic groups, and the quality of the environment we live in. One of the problems of all schooling is the detachment of what goes on in classrooms from the urgent concerns of the world: this is what justifies the third direction for expansion. Fiction has provided English teaching with both a model of how to write and an implicit definition of acceptable content, and in our view both, for all their strengths, are too narrow. There is much to be said for pupils going out into the world to interview, find documents, record what they observe, in order to engage at first hand in what might be called 'documentary', that is, writing which presents to a real audience an interpretation of reality that can be documented. Work on language and on reading should also be based on empirical data and not on the idealised inanities of textbooks. The fourth point is that we found too narrow a range of activities from the point-of-view of rhetorical functions: there was too much narrative and description, not to mention letters of application. Few teachers encourage their pupils to persuade, explain, analyse, criticise, plan, or justify in writing or speech. Pupils' contributions to classroom talk are limited to insertions into academic discussion controlled by the teacher; in the fifth year other oral activities hardly exist. In speech, in reading and in writing, pupils are too often shown implicitly that they do not own the language, that their task is to display competences, not to make sense of the world about them. English should put into effect Freire's dictum that education is 'the means by which . . . men and women deal critically and creatively with reality, and discover how to participate in the transformation of their world'.[2]

3. A future for English teaching

A question we have asked ourselves is what recommendations we should make to students planning to teach English in secondary schools and to their tutors. We hope that our display of teaching in action will provide a resource for discussion and evaluation, but we believe we should go beyond that. Such recommendations can, however, only be generated by our own values, not 'arise from the data' by some kind of auto-genesis. This is also to acknowledge that a close look at courses in schools and in colleges has changed not our values but how we think they should be put into effect.

We would wish to free young teachers from a simplistic antithesis between personal growth ('self expression') and basic skills. It *is* important for younger adolescents to talk and write about matters of immediate importance in language that they can use with ease because it belongs to them. But this should be a starting-point, not a final goal. By 16 years of age young people should be concerned with public issues as well as with private experience; some pupils need to approach public issues through private experience, but this is not true of all. Nor does all good writing need to be personalised: speech and writing can warmly acknowledge the writer's responsibility while engaging with its topic in a manner that displays its generality rather than its individual applications. Writing can be true to subjective experience without embodying quasi-literary self-exploration, which easily slips into manufactured 'fine writing'. We would want young teachers to recognise both the value of the personalising tradition and its limitations, and to possess a repertoire of teaching strategies for heading older pupils towards public topics and the mastery of a public persona, strategies which would include situated assignments as well as persuasive and argumentative writing.

The personal growth and cultural tradition versions of English are often accompanied by a 'deep-end' pedagogy; this is hinted at in the use of the word 'stimulus' for a literary extract used as a preliminary to writing. Perhaps pupils are 'stimulated' by momentary contact with literature before being thrown in at the deep end. Teachers who give a high value to the spontaneous expression of personal experience are often highly suspicious of the teaching of skills, whereas those who reject the personal growth perspective frequently describe themselves as 'formal' and turn towards decontextualised exercises. Young teachers need to be set free from this unreal dichotomy: there are valuable alternatives to both of these, ways of helping pupils without falling back upon exercises. These alternatives are not well represented in our materials, perhaps because we were looking at lessons for older pupils. We saw Mr Austin helping his pupils to construct a story at the blackboard, Mr Saxon persuading his class to note down 'points', and Mr Tremaine directing attention to biased reporting. In further education, but not in schools, we saw lecturers helping students to consider how a particular situation, audience and purpose can be used to generate criteria for talking and writing. Taken together these raise a central pedagogical question: how can a teacher best engage with pupils *while they are composing* — not before or after — so that they begin to grasp how an experienced writer sets about organising material and taking account of situational considerations.

The same pedagogical dilemma faces all teachers; how can one make available one's own skills and understanding without implicitly devaluing and discouraging the pupils' existing skills and understanding upon which all future development depends? Conversely, how can one allow the pupils to own the language, text and evidence, without abandoning them to their own devices? Teachers in training should be aware of the dilemma and be prepared with methods for dealing with it. One of these is the workshop approach which has been mentioned several times; most student teachers would probably need to begin by working as auxiliary to an experienced teacher in order to get the measure of the organisational problems implicit in the approach. They should understand the value of an inductive pedagogy, in which the teacher leads the class to utilise their existing knowledge to construct a set of usable categories. In our view, deductive methods, which potentially reduce learners to passive receivers, are acceptable only in the introductory stages of a new kind of work. Teachers should consider, too, the opportunities offered by coursework, which ideally lends itself to workshop and other innovative teaching methods, but which can sometimes degenerate into the mechanical production of standardised goods.

Literature, too, can be a trap in the examination year. Many teachers engage in a detailed exposition of literary texts which cannot be justified by the demands of literature examinations, and does not lead to impressive examination results. Fifth-year pupils do need help and encouragement in discussing what they read, and this should include non-literary texts. Neither the ubiquitous comprehension exercises nor the detailed exposition of texts provide this help; a few of the teachers in this study did show that they understood what was needed. Student teachers might consider these and work out other devices that aid the pupils to work on the meaning of texts and strengthen their confidence in doing so; they might also discuss what the written equivalents of exploratory discussion might be.

Literature, for all its value in offering to young people a means of exploring and evaluating their experience, has had a limiting effect upon the range of topics and rhetorical modes taken to form part of an English course, including the undervaluing of spoken language. It would be highly appropriate in the initial training of English teachers to look critically at the personalising tradition from the point-of-view of the rhetorical modes practised in schools, by considering what kinds of talking and writing are included and what tacitly excluded if teachers assume a literary norm. What we are able to say and be depends as much upon the other people we engage with as upon our reflective shaping of consciousness. It is important to devise ways in which talk and writing — used to persuade, argue, plan, criticise, categorise, evaluate and so on — can engage with real interlocutors about real issues, thus temporarily removing the barrier between schooling and life.

Comparison of fifth-year English with the work in further education which is described in Chapter 8 faces the experienced teacher as well as the novice with the question, 'Why does spoken English play so small a part in fifth-year English in schools?' Communications teaching, though at an early stage of development, supplies hints of what is possible. The underemphasis cannot be attributed solely to examination requirements: it is perfectly possible to choose examinations that include tests of oral English. It is all the more anomalous in the light of the attitudes of students in middle and bottom sets, who tend to perceive spoken language rather than written as important outside school. Discussion of this topic with young teachers might turn not only to teaching methods but also to the functioning of written language in the processes by which occupational status is achieved or assigned in our society. Indeed, all English teachers need to be aware of such social processes, since they affect day-to-day classroom decisions as well as larger patterns of cultural reproduction.

Finally, we suggest that courses for intending English teachers should discuss what part should be played in English courses by reflection on discourse. This is related to the traces of an alternative version which we called 'public rationality', but its possibility is brought into focus when communications courses are put side by side with school English. Descriptive linguistics was rightly banished from English more than a decade ago; 'rightly' because, although it is a valuable study in its own right, (like economics, for example) its direct contribution to understanding the *use* of language is slight. Since that time, no new form of reflection on language has taken the place of 'parsing and analysis', and we recommend that a reflective study of discourse should do so. This study would be carried out through an inductive pedagogy, which would help students to refine the intuitive understanding of communication that native speakers already have. We do not know precisely what part of the reflective understanding plays in talking and writing well; it is certainly of considerable importance in writing. Student teachers could benefit from reflecting upon their own awareness of language and discourse as a basis for building a programme for pupils. (The idea of a study of discourse is expanded in Chapter 9.)

CHAPTER 7

Literature after the Fifth Form

The central position of literature in English teaching is unchallenged in the fifth form. It is the touchstone against which everything else in the course is judged. But a year later the position has changed completely: perhaps the masses have been gentled; perhaps what the disciples of Matthew Arnold see as the civilising effects of a literary education are no longer needed. The new alignments are quite different: for the majority, literature disappears from the syllabuses, for the minority who are to go on and study English for A-level, literature becomes the whole of their English study. Overnight, or rather over the summer holiday, there has been a remarkable change in the definition of the subject. English in O-level and CSE was reading books or passages and answering questions about them; it was writing stories, letters and essays. English at A-level is literature, yet these are the very areas which English or Communication Studies in Further Education vocational classes avoids. It is a strange reversal of the picture in the fifth form. There was one exception to which we have already referred: at High Street College all the girls training to be shorthand-typists studied literature. 'We feel that if they are going into an office literature is very, very important', but as this was mainly O-level literature we will deal with that briefly later.

Although our sample of A-level literature classes was small, it forms the most homogeneous group in our second observation stage[1]. All four classes were preparing for the same JMB examination and spreading the preparation over the normal two years. Groups varied in size; the smallest at Downtown School had seven students, the largest at New Suburbia School had 18. Those two classes contained all the A-level English students in the year, but at Smalltown School there was another group and at High Street College three others. All the teachers we observed were experienced A-level teachers, two of them — Mr Underwood and Mrs King — being the heads of the English departments. The actual teaching was arranged in two ways, in Downtown and Smalltown Schools it was shared by two teachers; in New Suburbia School and High Street College one teacher took the whole course. We consequently interviewed and observed six teachers in all.

The first impression of the classes was that we had moved into a women's world: in Downtown School no boys took A-level literature; in New Suburbia and Smalltown Schools the ratio was four or five girls to every boy. It was only in our FE class that the proportion approached the national average with five male students to eleven females. Although many more boys stay on for post O-level education, in mixed schools, particularly, they do not choose to do English literature and this is not because the subject is predominantly taught by women teachers. A-level teaching tends to be given to those experienced university graduates who are in senior positions and these are usually men. Four out of the six heads of English departments in our research schools were men and the gender distinction was even more striking in further education. In our dealings with the colleges we encountered no woman who had risen above the lowest lecturer grade. These points may not be strictly relevant here, but it is significant that when boys can choose what subjects to study most of them avoid English literature even though they see that in the educational world it is a subject where the economic rewards and those of status go to the men.

Most of the students in the classes were studying English literature with two other A-level subjects, and conditions in the different institutions were remarkably similar: the actual teaching sessions varied in length from three hours to 40 minutes, but surprisingly the time allocated on the timetable in the schools only varied from four hours fifty to four hours forty minutes per week. In FE it was longer, but the two three-hour sessions were treated generally as four distinct periods with a different topic or text being studied in each period. None of the classes seemed to be working in ideal conditions: only the lessons at Smalltown School took place in rooms specially designed for sixth formers in that they were small, and furnished with tables where students faced each other rather than with desks in ranks. At New Suburbia School some of the lessons were in the Technical Drawing room. English A-level may be the subject which nationally had the highest number of entries, but it did not come high in any of the institutions when the allocation of facilities was concerned. It was particularly significant in High Street College that the General Education Department in which English A-level was situated was housed in a group of prefabs attached to an old church hall in the midst of a clearance area. The main site may have a library and impressive facilities — perhaps it has to reflect the values of the business world — but A-level students do not need carpets and potted plants. However, we have been sidetracked from our attempt to give the classes we are writing about a setting. If the reader imagines a large bare room with teacher and students sitting surrounded by empty desks it will not be too far from reality.

All the classes were working simultaneously on more than one set text, (sometimes this was inevitable because of there being two teachers) and the Miller plays were the favourite choice with which to begin. They were, in fact, the most popular choice, and would be studied by all four groups, whereas some texts such as *Dombey and Son* (New Suburbia), Keats (Smalltown), *To the Lighthouse* (FE) and *Revenger's Tragedy* (Downtown) seemed likely to be chosen by only one of the four classes. It may be significant that for Paper 2 the FE students were the only ones whose choice was restricted to 20th-century texts. The JMB syllabus stipulated the study of two Shakespeare texts, one long poem and four other texts, that was a minimum of seven texts. Some groups studied more; for example, the Downtown School class was studying an additional text and all our teachers expected their students to read more widely. At Downtown School each student was expected to give a talk on a modern poet, but although most teachers presumed that students would read another novel or play by the author of the text they were studying it only seemed to be in discussion of Arthur Miller, when *The Crucible* had been read for O-level, that teachers were confident enough of this background to refer to it. However, despite all these similarities of examination and books, of gender and working conditions, the experience of being a student in each of these classes seemed to be significantly different. Our purpose will be to explore the common experience and the significant differences keeping in mind the same concerns on which we focused when we looked at fifth-form literature teaching. However, all but one of our teachers and many of the students stressed the differences between O-level and A-level literature study so it will be interesting later to see, for example, whether the concepts of initiation and transmission which we delineated were still important.

Where to start examining the data is our first difficulty. Do we start with what the teachers said to us in our first interviews with them; do we start with the aims of the examination course and the syllabus they were all teaching or do we dive in, as it were, immersing ourselves in a lesson, sharing the student experience? In a logical sequence the drawing up of a syllabus would precede the teaching of a course, but in real life this is rarely the case. A-level literature study has evolved gradually: the present day syllabuses explain and justify practices which have developed over the 60 or so years since English literature was approved for study in Advanced courses for the Higher School Certificate[2]. Teachers rely on much unstated knowledge. Only one of the schools, Smalltown, produced its own sixth-form syllabus, the others presumably would fall back on the JMB's aims and its description of the abilities 'the examination attempts to assess'. The document from Smalltown School indeed is very close in spirit to the official statement so it may be simplest to quote from the JMB board.

A. THE AIMS OF THE SYLLABUS

The JMB recognises that the aim of a sixth-form English course is to present the subject as a discipline that is humane (concerned with values), historical (setting literary works within the context of their age) and communicative (concerned, that is, with the integrity of language as a means of enabling human beings to convey their thoughts and feelings one to another).

B. THE ABILITIES TO BE TESTED

Within this general context, the examination attempts to assess
(a) the candidate's understanding, in some depth, of works he has studied;
(b) the response to literature jointly affective and evaluative (i.e. his personal response and his understanding of the causes of his response);
(c) the ability to use his critical powers on unseen passages of verse and prose;
(d) the breadth of a candidate's reading;
(e) the ability to write organised, clear essays on literary subjects and to comment precisely on the use of language.

The JMB also recognises that a sixth-form course may develop the ability to write original works of literary merit. Since it would not be appropriate to require a demonstration of this ability under examination conditions, an optional test in creative writing is provided.

We now have a baseline from which we can measure the reality, but a second more careful look at the official document makes us question its value as a measuring instrument. The aims are a public statement, ideals which would probably be shared by many apologists for their particular subject discipline. This does not diminish, of course, their value as an affirmation of beliefs sincerely held by many English teachers. They represent a distillation from the writings of influential educational thinkers from Arnold onwards who have believed in the powerful and civilising effect of literary study. The problem for teachers comes, however, in translating a statement of beliefs into a body of practice; our problem as researchers is in identifying when this happens. The second aim of 'setting literary works within the context of their age' will be the easiest to isolate, the others we shall have to deal with incidentally. The acceptance of the values of A-level by English teachers depends on an elaborate set of unexplicated beliefs.

But before we turn to the practice, we should consider whether we found echoes of the examination board's rhetoric in what the teachers in our sample said to us individually and in their joint meeting. The teachers were ambivalent in their attitude to the examination. Mr Anderson referred 'to the conflicting requirements of the examination at the end and what one sees as the job of a teacher', yet none of them was dismissive of the instrumental use of their course. They appreciated that success and high grades were very important to their students in determining the next stages in their career, although they all spoke of a purpose beyond examination success. When we had a post-observation meeting with them it ended on a highly moral note. Mrs King was challenged for claiming 'no utilitarian value' for A-level literature teaching, but the challenge hinged on the meaning of utilitarian. Mr Underwood summed up by saying, 'There are still many of us who deep down would like to think that we're involved with the business of moral discrimination' and everyone agreed, an endorsement of the first aim.

In interviews, and as they told us about their courses, there were times when teachers referred to the historical which showed it was an aim that many of them thought they put into practice. Mr Underwood at Downtown School said he liked to start with Chaucer partly 'to get some sort of historical perspective'. Mr Anderson said he began by a series of lectures and talks interrupted by actually studying parts of texts. For example, before reading Arthur Miller's play *All My Sons* he had traced 'the history of drama from its beginnings in ritual, right through up to Shakespeare'. He was sharing the teaching of the Smalltown group with Mr Austin who, although he worked on the set texts from the beginning without preliminary lectures, wished for a less restricted syllabus. 'If you can break it down to periods and themes I think they get a much better sense of tradition and continuity in English literature.' Thus, from the evidence we collected, all the teachers we observed shared the first two of the JMB board's aims, but it was interesting that in their joint meeting at the end of the year their main concern was with the kind of literary experience which best prepared their students for the demands of the examination. How could they get students to read and think for themselves? 'O-level really is pretty easy for anyone who is average bright', said Mrs King of New Suburbia, 'whereas A-level seems to require a depth of personal response and commitment'.

A useful way to approach the lesson material might be to look at the modes of literary response which they exemplified and then consider how successfully they lead to a 'personal response'. We identified nine broad categories:

1. Paraphrase — Local / Recapitulation of plot
2. Re-creation of text
3. Commentary on local texture and rhetorical devices

4. Discussion of motives and actions
5. Description of character
6. Attitudes towards characters and incidents
7. Commentary on organic or thematic structure

8. Relation to own and others' experience
9. Relation to social/literary context

We have listed and grouped them in a way which moves the focus from the localised and particular to the larger and more general issues within the text: the last two categories deal with moves outside the text. We shall see when we look at individual examples that the categories do not imply a hierarchy of difficulty or abstraction; our concern in drawing up the list was with the content of the activity. Other dimensions, such as that of transmission and initiation or of the level of abstraction, will cut across the categories which are based solely on the models of response.

It is not possible to say that such and such a proportion of A-level literature teaching was spent in one particular mode of literary response. Some of the categories as we shall show overlap or the activities were embedded within others, but we can indicate the frequency and the relative importance of their occurrence. Some 60 per cent of all the lessons we observed were spent in activities which fell into the first three categories — that is, close textual study. This is not an unexpected finding; it is the traditional student occupation. At fifth-form level what it frequently involved was the teacher reading a couple of sentences, checking that meanings were understood, commenting on a particular word or phrase, and then moving on. At Downtown School, where 70 per cent of the A-level lessons came into these first three categories, Mr Baxter apparently came closest to this slow progress of teacher-going-through. He was a recent recruit to the department, on very friendly terms with the class, the youngest of our A-level teachers but by no means inexperienced. He had begun reading *Coriolanus* with the class in September and by February, after spending two or three periods a week on it, he had reached Act Four, Scene 6. He told us before the lesson that he had to go through line by line because the students found it so difficult. He was determined he was not going to tell them meanings; as sixth formers they must sort it out for themselves. 'Kids just don't seem to be trained to think', he had bemoaned when we talked to him in the first term. This is how, after some good humoured bantering, the work on the play began, some three months after that comment.

T. Right 138 please, Act IV, Scene 6. If you remember we had Sicinius and Brutus sitting round feeling very contented with life, whilst we knew Aufidius was coming closer. They'd just received the news that these raving, ravishing . . . Volsci . . . and at the bottom of page 138 we've got the citizens arriving. We've just got the discussion between Sicinius and Brutus and the Patricians.
(gives me a copy)

T. Menenius 'Here come the clusters' (repeats) — any comment on that?

S. Crowds.

T. Crowds yes. What about the word 'clusters'?

S. It sounds as if they were fruit.

S. . . . blackberries . . .

T. How does Menenius mean it? Does he mean look there are lots of people coming towards us?

S. Like a disease — a cluster is.

S. Poisonous berries.
T. Poisonous berries. What's the essential feature of a cluster?
S. Sticks together.
T. Sticks together right, so presumably that sort of picture.

His request for comment produced five possible interpretations of 'clusters' from the class; examples of a reflective awareness of local meanings.

1. fruit
2. blackberries
3. like a disease
4. poisonous berries
5. stick together

This kind of exchange was typical. Although all the reading of the play was done by Mr Baxter and he tended to speak at greater length than his students did, they were much involved; in this particular lesson the students' utterances outnumbered his. He had established a routine so that at times he merely had to read a line with a rising and questioning inflection for a student to offer a comment. There were only seven in this class, so that although two took very little part, and one girl contributed the most, it seemed to be a genuinely shared activity. Mr Baxter commented that an outsider's presence had put the group on their mettle. The researcher had chatted with the girls on previous visits and it was probably true that they were keen to impress, but this strengthens the fact that this was what they thought an A-level class studying a Shakespeare text should be like, concentrating on localised meanings, producing (in the margins) a paratext. It was a play for academic study, with the occasional reference to possible examination questions: no attempt whatsoever was made to bring it to life dramatically. In a later session however, Mr Baxter did do this and we will deal with that when we come to our second category of re-creation. In our fifth-form data this kind of teacher-controlled progress through a text was one of the indicators which characterised a transmission mode of teaching, yet the amount of student participation and the nature of their involvement prevents so simple a judgement here. However, we will delay our consideration of the transmission/initiation issue until we have discussed all the models of response.

Mr Baxter and his class were not alone in expecting that the first reading of a text should be to sort out in detail the meaning. In another classroom at the FE college in the High Street a somewhat larger group of students had been going at the same pace through *Antony and Cleopatra*. Again there was no shared reading; Mrs Lincoln like Mr Baxter did all the reading herself, but here there was a striking difference in that there was no student participation. Mrs Lincoln had described her methods in the first two terms as 'baby-sitting . . . I don't ask too many questions'. Whether her term 'baby-sitting' is an apt description readers will be able to judge from the following quotation, but it was true she did not break off to question. In the four-and-a-half hours' of teaching we recorded in the first term of the course only once was a student's voice heard. In a pause he asked a question, but Mrs Lincoln was clearly so taken aback that despite his repeating it twice she could not change track sufficiently to answer it. However, although the students did not join in, their participation or agreement was presumed. Mrs Lincoln co-opted their voices not only in her use of 'we' in 'we notice' or 'we recognise that', but even more in her rhetorical questions 'we all agree, don't we?'.

The quotation that follows comes from the first lesson we saw. Mrs Lincoln had decided to pause at the end of the second act of *Antony and Cleopatra* in order to prepare for the kind of context question students would have to face in the final examination in two years' time. The 'context exercise' was the pretext, but the lesson seemed to be a re-reading of and commentary on sections of the first act which Mrs Lincoln considered particularly important. Occasionally she read as much as 50 lines of the play without comment, but frequently the comment and quotation were so interwoven that to a listener who was not following closely from the text it became almost impossible to disentangle text and paratext. A brief quotation will illustrate:

> L. 'Good Enobarbus, 'tis a worthy deed. And it shall become you well to entreat your captain to soft and gentle speech'. Lepidus is concerned then that these two should be brought together and Lepidus, of course, flattering Enobarbus with the deed required, as a worthy person to perform it. It will be very fitting for you, Enobarbus 'to entreat your captain to soft and gentle speech'. And Enobarbus we have, of course, already had reason to understand his boldness and his statement of things as they are and no nonsense. 'I shall entreat him to answer like himself', in a manner of course worthy of him. 'If Caesar move him', that, of course means anger.

The Shakespeare text reads:

> Lepidus Good Enobarbus, 'tis a worthy deed,
> And it shall become you well to entreat your captain
> To soft and gentle speech.
> Enobarbus I shall entreat him
> To answer like himself: if Caesar move him, . . .

Mrs Lincoln was reading and explaining, offering her class the play in predigested form: it was interesting how often she used 'feeding' metaphors when talking of her teaching methods. Mr Baxter's and Mrs Lincoln's methods of presenting a Shakespeare text to their classes may have had some similarities; both of them thought their students needed a great deal of help, but whereas Mr Baxter expected his students to join in with him in worrying the bone to get at the meat, Mrs Lincoln offered it already garnished on the plate. Whereas Mr Baxter's primary concern was with local meanings, Mrs Lincoln seemed also to be concerned from the beginning with more general interpretation. Both of these teachers would have considered they were, however, working 'in depth', that favourite word used by students and teachers alike to characterise A-level literary study. 'You've got to go into a lot more depth' (Gaynor–Downtown).

The second model of literary response we entitled Re-creation of the text. At the simplest level this could mean a reading aloud of a text and this, in fact, happened with the Arthur Miller plays. Teachers and students shared in uninterrupted and effective readings as their first encounter with text. (Only once did this happen with the Shakespeare texts: the group at Smalltown School rushed through selected parts of *Antony and Cleopatra*, but it was not so much to get the flavour of the play as to sort out the characters and plot before they saw it at the theatre.) Generally it seemed that teachers thought that with modern plays, when the language was accessible, students should make their first encounter with a text in a dramatic form, but even then this might be followed almost immediately by detailed study, 'looking at it piece by piece'. We saw one session, however, which was not a simple reading: it seemed to have been primarily designed to bring out the dramatic force of a Shakespeare play. Some background information about it may be useful. During the first term Mr Baxter had been on two in-service weekends, coming back very excited about the ideas. More than once in conversation he referred to them and was very anxious that we saw a special session he was planning to have when he had finished going through *Coriolanus* with the class. The timing did not fit in with our arrangements: we were glad of the excuse as it would clearly be an atypical lesson and we were not wanting to record special performances. However, a combination of circumstances caused changes of plan and to Mr Baxter's surprise as well as ours our observer found herself not only observing but participating in the session. It seemed at first to be an initiation and training in reading blank verse: for more than half an hour Mr Baxter directed pupils and observer in turn as they read, mouthed or sang the 30 lines of a soliloquy. Ingeniously the activities were shifted to focus on the idea of the struggle within Coriolanus: there was much moving around and physical struggle recreating the tension revealed in the speech. Finally the students improvised two little scenes of their own based on a situation where a character was pulled in two separate ways. They said afterwards how much they had enjoyed the lesson and Mr Baxter was obviously pleased with their wholehearted involvement. The fact that a session quite clearly designed to introduce students to reading the play might be rather inappropriate when they had been working on it for more than six months seemed to occur to no-one: it was a welcome change from desk-bound, text-bound lessons. Mr Baxter seemed to offer it as relaxation, a 'one-off' lesson, a reward for being patient and hard-working in going through the play, not an alternative model of response.

It was therefore very different in kind from the other example that we saw of an attempt to re-create a text by dramatisation. Mr Austin's class at Smalltown School had read Keats' *Eve of St Agnes* and in a previous lesson one of the class had come up with the idea of acting it, so this lesson began with Sean's being asked to spell out the reasons for his proposal.

T. Let's have some ideas then. First of all let's go over why you want to do it. Sean it was your suggestion originally, I think, so defend your suggestion.
S. Well I thought it would be good fun first, instead of just keeping talking. I fancied doing a bit of acting myself.
T. Is there any justification for it, other than that?
S. I think it might help us to understand it more. I think we might get something out of discussing how we're acting it.
T. But why — but why didn't you suggest it say, when we were doing a chapter of *Persuasion*. Why didn't anybody suggest it?
S. It just struck me with this, with it being sort of a story. I don't know, I suppose you could do that just as well, but —
T. Well, I wonder — There is something in the *Eve of St Agnes* which lends itself to dramatic presentation — I wonder. Well we'll see this morning. Suggestions? How are we going to organise this? How are we going to organise the setting. Any ideas Elaine? (Although series of questions, put forward in very tentative style.) Well what shall we do? Shall we get the tables all to the back of the room and have a space here. What do you think?
P. I think it would make more room if we pushed them back to the sides then —

For the next 15 minutes attention was concentrated upon positioning and reading, with Mr Austin following the students' leads as they decided about the technicalities of sharing out the lines. Then he intervened with various suggestions so that for a while he became the director, but it was interesting how often his remarks were framed as questions that needed affirmation and he waited for that agreement before he moved on.

T. I'm just thinking we could get right through the poem in this lesson, but I'm beginning to wonder whether it might be better to work on a limited number of stanzas say —
P. The ones we've done this morning.

Further discussion was followed by another reading with the different voices taking part as they had arranged. Sean was the centre figure crouching, telling his beads. Everyone was caught up in the presentation, involved in ideas for improving it, eager to reread and to prepare for the next section. Attention focused on individual words and phrases, not in this instance on their meaning, but on their sound or visual effect. Changes in rhythm and pace were noticed and attempts made to incorporate them in the presentation. It was an enactment of what constitutes the third category in our models of response.

This third category, commenting on local texture and rhetorical device, also happened incidentally within the paraphrasing which went on, but we have isolated it because it was so often seen by teachers as a discrete activity. They talked of reading a novel or play, but they did something called literary criticism or 'lit-crit' when they presented their classes with some previously unseen poems or passages. We saw one session at New Suburbia which was rather different, when students were working on short passages chosen from *Coriolanus* which they had already studied. After they had spotted where the lines came from, discussed 'whether you think what is said affects the action . . . or illuminates a character', they were told by Mrs King to 'consider the language, the imagery, the verse'. It was, in fact, a first training session for the examination context question, but unlike Mrs Lincoln's lesson it was not a pretext for repeating the initial reading and commentary, it kept close to the task of answering the question. 'For instance, look at the following points: is it blank verse, prose or couplets? Is there any significance in it being whichever one it is? Are the sentences long or short, simple or complex, questions, statements or exclamations? . . . Is there any particular word that you pick out as requiring to have something said about it? What about figures of speech, do you recognise any? Why are they used, are they effective, what are they? Look out for metaphors and similes.'

Mrs King's list of instructions may sound as though they provided a straitjacket, but in comparison with the 'lit crit' lessons we saw they were open-ended. Two of the lessons drew their material from 20th century poetry and in the fifth form we had commented that lessons on modern poetry which was unseen, not a set text, sometimes resulted in genuine sharing; the 20th-century poetry lessons we observed with the A-level classes, however, were much more constrained. The poetry was being studied for one purpose only, in order to answer questions from a textbook. A topic was discussed by teacher and students, not apparently because of any intrinsic interest, but because this was part of the examination game. When Mr Anderson introduced the exercise at Smalltown School he almost dissociated himself from the activity: 'I'm not really going to pass any value judgements on the questions . . . in a sense it's an artificial exercise', but he carefully added, it 'is a good thing to do'. It seemed that the textbook writers set the teasers and teacher and students rather enjoyed the game. The first question on R. S. Thomas' *An Old Man* was, as Mr Anderson said, 'A nice technical question to start us off with':

What is the effect of the imperative of the verb as an opening word?

The second was to consider 'the effect of ending the second line with "trying" '. And so the class went through the poem, responding like puppets to the textbook writer's questions. This textbook (*The Language of Poetry*) was not an unusual one. In yet another lesson, when the Downtown group had had a tasting session in which Mr Underwood presented them with extracts which demonstrated different rhythmic effects in poetry, they were asked to go away and look at a series of questions on the last extract. The first was, 'Rewrite the poem and scan all 16 lines'.

Attention was directed to the technical, emphasis was placed on individual words: this was to be the first response, the model of reading expected. In a lesson at New Suburbia the class was using a book entitled *Comparison and Criticism* where the questions were more general but the tasks were very limited. The students were given ten-line extracts from two poems and then asked:

1. (a) In a sentence, say what you consider to be the situation in A.
   (b) In a sentence, say what you consider to be the situation in B. . . .

3. (a) There are two varieties of language in the stanzas of B. Indicate where the second variety begins in each stanza.
   (b) State, as exactly as you can, what each variety represents.
   (c) What adjective could describe the first?
   (d) What contrast between the people concerned is suggested by the contrast in the two varieties?

The questions in 1 may be rather more akin to a reader's natural response: our first concern is usually with what the poem is about. But in this book students were not even given the whole poem. Mrs King tried to remedy this by reading out the whole of *Exposure* and *The Naming of Parts*, but clearly the writer of the textbook did not consider this necessary. The assumptions behind question 3 'two varieties of language' seem far removed either from the syllabus' concern with the 'integrity of language' or even an informed understanding of the way in which language works.

None of this poetry was trivial or meretricious: it was worthy of serious attention, yet the paucity and aridity of the exercises were impressive. Presumably these experienced teachers considered this the best training they could give their students in preparing them for the examination; they would hardly justify such exercises on aesthetic grounds. However, if we consult the most recent examination question that candidates had tackled, the one set the previous summer, the question there read, 'Write a critical evaluation of the following poem referring to such matters as theme, feeling and tone, verse form and imagery'. The examination cannot be made the scapegoat; textbooks were not following the examination format. Their writers, and presumably the teachers who were following them, considered this to be an appropriate method of training students in judgement.

In the A-level lessons that we observed close study of localised detail and meanings was the most common activity and it tended to be closely controlled by the teacher. We move now to consider the next group of categories. It is more difficult to allocate whole lessons to each category and there will be considerable overlap. As our data was collected early in the course we are still dealing with initial encounters. But with modern plays, when the text had been first re-created in a dramatic reading, the model could be different from 'the going through'. When, at Downtown School, they were reaching the end of *A View from the Bridge* Mr Underwood's first question was not designed to check their understanding but to focus attention upon the characters: 'What was very noticeable about the reactions of Beatrice and Catherine?' Each character's motives and behaviour in the last scene were talked through briefly, 'Is it just anger or is it more than that? . . . Does he tend to show a great deal of fear, do you think, at this point?'. It is not merely a recapitulation of the events, but an attribution of real feelings to the characters. With younger students it might have stayed at that level, but the class went on to discuss their attitudes to the characters. Mr Underwood asked, 'What effect does that have on our reaction to Eddie . . . ?' and received the reply, 'Makes you feel some pity for him'. Finally, from a consideration of the function of Alfieri and his relationship to the structure of the play, Mr Underwood moved on to talk about the theme of justice. In a space of 35 minutes he touched briefly on all of the modes of response we placed in the middle range of response, the third to the seventh of the categories. Although we separated these activities, as would be expected in the lessons discussion ranged from the concrete to the more abstract, from a discussion of Eddie's motives via the students' attitudes to him, to the function of Alfieri and a consideration of the theme of justice. When Mrs King's group at New Suburbia School had finished the last act they were asked an even more general first question, one about the author's characteristics:

> T. Did you recognise anything in this play that made you feel, 'Yes this is Miller'? If you had a plain text without the author's name on it, is there anything that would have made you feel we've come across those concerns, we've come across those kinds of people before?

Most of the class had studied *The Crucible* for O-level and *All My Sons* recently so this was not so daunting a question as it may seem. Interest then narrowed to the particular play.

> T. What's your first response to the situations of this play and the characters in it? What do you make of those Sicilian Americans and their ideas and values?

(We shall consider the students' response later.)

Mr Anderson's class at Smalltown School had followed the same route. They had finished the play and begun talking about it in the previous lesson: the half-term break had elapsed so the teacher began, 'If we can just recap... we were talking, if you remember, about some of the things which would make the plays the work of a single author... Now can you think what Eddie and Joe have got in common? It doesn't have to be anything very profound, just anything at all'. It seemed that if a text was such that teachers considered students could understand the language the concern was much less likely to be with close textual analysis. The setting might be alien, but students were assumed to be in a position to have a point-of-view. It is significant that these Arthur Miller plays were clearly considered accessible since they were chosen in three out of the four groups as texts to be studied early in the course.

Was it possible to work in a similar way on novels? We saw two novels being taught — *Persuasion* at Smalltown School and *The Secret Agent* at High Street College. The methods were very different, but was the same model of literary response underlying them? In a lesson at Smalltown School the students were, in turn, commenting on a small section of *Persuasion* which they had prepared in advance.

T. Well, Sean, over to you.

Sean Here comes Anne. It's very much a pointer to Anne's character in the first paragraph because here's Anne who returns home to her very callous relations, Elizabeth and Sir Walter...

Sean's commentary with Mr Austin's and other students' additions lasted for some seven minutes and ended on a note of uncertainty.

Sean ... What I wasn't sure about actually is that Anne, Anne's satisfaction or Lady Russell's? Thought it was Anne's but I wasn't sure.

Sandra I think you've missed something. You know the paragraph that you've just said, she is saying that he was steady, observant, moderate, candid. I think that is sort of first impression we get of him possibly, but when you delve more into his character then you find out what we have found. I think... (inaudible) '... without interference.

T. Yes, it's interesting, without pre-empting the text I think it's very valuable for us to experience Mr Elliot as a new acquaintance and to try and work through that without kind of bringing in knowledge which we've acquired from later on, because we can't do this in real life can we, of course.

This was a slow progress: the students were finding their own way of coming to grips with Jane Austen. They were articulate and able to develop their ideas mainly at the level of discussion of character, but they were seeing characters as artefacts, as Sean's 'very much a pointer' shows. They were interested in how the author presented characters and not only in the characters as people.

The lessons which most strongly exemplified the approach via themes were those of Mrs Lincoln at High Street College: her commentary on *The Secret Agent* was remarkable for its high level of generalisation. From the first her students had been accustomed to this treatment, as the sheets of notes she had distributed to them when they began work on the novel illustrated:

> Conrad's intention involved a consideration of three levels of existence — the superficial one of official and unofficial action (the public), the personal one of private emotions and relationships; and the inner spiritual and psychological level which ultimately erupts into violent expression. For Conrad, the most important level is this last one, though it is the least apparent, and hence we have the undisturbed surface of the novel.

In the lesson we shall quote from, her students were nearing the end of the book and her opening remarks introduced the theme of blindness:

> T. We're going to start with the novel so we want to get on with that. Keeping that in front of you, those notes I've just put on your desks 'From a certain point-of-view' and you remember that discussion we had before about the different points-of-view and if I suggested, for example, a theme of blindness would it mean anything to you at all, Jonathan?

Within the space of the next hour she offered at least five other global statements about the novel.

1. The pivotal relationship of the novel is the relationship between Mr and Mrs Verloc.
2. The irony itself is the novel. (A set of notes had already been distributed on Irony as Theme.)
3. The city itself, for example, is the centre of the novel.
4. Obesity, for example, is a central motif.
5. This novel . . . is a discussion of conservatism.

Mrs Lincoln taught by directing her students' attention to underlying images and ideas, by suggesting interpretations, by emphasising memorable and quotable statements (those we have underlined), and by providing them with the exemplar of a literary rhetoric.

> L. You know I asked you to underline those images as we went along. I said references to eyes, and there is a sense, isn't there, where there is the eye of the beholder, the narrative voice which in fact calls for almost different points-of-view. That's something else which was suggested isn't it? An image which in fact derives from that idea would be, for example, isolation, a sense in which they are operating within their own little worlds and would you say that they come into that part of the novel which borders perhaps on the tragic, but be careful how you use that word. We'll discuss that — the idea of not only Mrs Verloc operating within her own little world, blindly as it were, and Mr Verloc operating within his and no communication between the two. There is

> a sense, isn't there, in which they have built a world which we call a domestic world which is a sort of façade. It's a sort of parallel with the shock, in a sense, do you agree with me there? There is a kind of domestic scene which they share and that brings us again, doesn't it, to the levels of awareness, consciousness and so on and then we had that discussion, of course, about the comparability, the idea, that we'd gone beyond that. There is no clear line from a particular disaster back to a person we could say is responsible for that disaster. Does everybody agree with that statement which came from the discussion?

The difference between Mrs Lincoln's way of talking about the novel and the way novels and plays were talked of in other classes is in its level of generality.

The model of response of relating literature to our own experience should perhaps logically have headed our list, for it is so often our initial response in penetrating a book. The first affirmation of our response is often a statement of verisimilitude, a recognition of the events and people. We compare them to what we know and have experienced.

In some O-level literature lessons a deliberate effort seemed to be made to find comparable situations in everyday life or in a television series. On very few occasions did we find this happening in the course of routine A-level lessons. It may be that our presence in the classroom constrained teachers and students and inhibited digressions. In the lesson on *Persuasion* we have already quoted there were two occasions when the class spent a significant time on peripheral concerns. The word 'snob' had been used to describe Sir Walter Elliot; a student had looked up the definition in the *Oxford Dictionary* and for some five minutes its usage was discussed. Then Mr Austin instigated a discussion on manners and morality concentrating on everyday instances of what people regarded as bad manners — barging into a classroom, keeping someone waiting — and this discussion lasted for more than a quarter of an hour. An instance of a different kind occurred in Mrs Lincoln's class at High Street college when they were studying *The Secret Agent*. In contrast to the lessons on *Antony and Cleopatra* when no student spoke, there was an animated exchange about the behaviour of Conrad's characters. Mrs Lincoln's comments remained firmly within the novel, but not so the students: they were interested in relating the novel to their own experience of life and of talking about the impact of the novel as they read it. One of them had complained that none of the characters was likeable, there were no hero figures:

S. My family's a bit like this (laughter) . . . (inaudible) . . . very violent physically — get into fights with each other. Mental cruelty as well so that's why I like reading this.

L. Yes.

S. Because it's representative of —

S. There's no hero in a bit of life in a short time, it's just going on like this —
L. You're saying that there's nothing real about it.
S. Yes (some confusion) (S. repeats.)
L. There's no hero in a bit of life — that's not real is it?
S. Heroes aren't real. You don't get 'em any more — Robin Hoods don't pop up now; they're all rogues.
S. To Robin Hood's sister Robin Hood wasn't a hero.
S. I suppose it depends on your own personality. If you're an optimist you can't associate with him, if you're a pessimist you probably can (some disagreement).
S. But it's a quality of life, Cynthia.
S. I'm an optimist so I can't associate with him.

(Perhaps it is important to notice that all the students who spoke in this extract were older, the teenagers took no part.) Here these mature students were testing the values of the book against their own ideas about society and also trying to establish why their own attitudes were different.

This acceptance by students of the possibility that texts were material which could impinge on their own and others' reality could be related to the examination syllabus' 'historical' aim which we noticed that teachers reiterated. Mr Baxter, for example, had elaborated his aim of producing 'intelligent thinking beings' by going on to say 'someone who can see the different opinions within the political climate of Rome and see the differences in the political climate of the Labour Party or the Conservatives'. His particular instance might have led us to expect some wide-ranging treatment of issues in *Coriolanus*. It may have happened in some lessons but the work we saw Mr Baxter doing on *Coriolanus* rarely moved beyond the text in hand, and on the occasions when it did it was not to a consideration of political issues. The lines

> Your soldiers use him as the grace 'fore meat
> Their talk at table and their thanks at end.

prompted some speculation about whether we call it grace after a meal. When Mr Baxter remembered sitting at junior school waiting after the meal had ended, Susan immediately chimed in:

> Thank you for the world so sweet
> Thank you for the food we eat.

But that was all. Later Gaynor's interjection in mock Western accents: 'This town's not big enough for both of us: it's either me or him', was countered by Mr Baxter, 'Notice Martius is the good guy and Aufidius is the baddy with his gun under his hat or down in his pocket'. The parallels that were being drawn were to elucidate localised meaning; they were as likely to originate with a student as with the teacher; further proof of how thoroughly this class had taken over the shared interpretation of meaning. They had already internalised Mr Baxter's belief 'it's the text that's important — because the text is what they'll get their exam pass from' (interview November 1980).

Another instance was when Mr Anderson talking about how 'America generally sets much more store by the family' digressed for a minute to the Kennedys and the importance of the image of the family in Presidential elections. We have not attempted to calculate exactly the proportion of time allocated to such parallels; generally, as these last examples suggest, they were so brief as to be insignificant.

All the lessons we observed and recorded were in the first two terms of a five-and-a-half-term course, yet even so early in the course there seemed to be little elbow room for any of the unstructured talking about a novel or a play which happens naturally when a group of people have just shared an experience. We noticed some about the Miller plays and also about *The Secret Agent* but there it was soon brought to an end; in general it seemed that students must be shaped immediately into the kind of literary critics who perform in the way expected in examinations. In the meeting we held with A-level teachers in schools at the end of the year, although the question was raised as to what should be the nature of literary experience, it was models of literary criticism which preoccupied them. Yet when they were concerned about models, they seemed to be thinking only of written comment in literary essays; whether students could understand an established literary critic and model their writing on this critic's, whether it was better for them to emulate the best in each other's work, how they could be trained to write essays. Away from the classroom they were talking as though their own presentation was unimportant, as if they were unaware that it was likely to be the most powerful influence, their implicit and explicit demonstration of the nature of literary criticism. Our analysis here has indicated the range of models they were offering in their lessons.

We started this chapter with references to the high ideals of the syllabus and the hopes of the teachers that they were fulfilling them. Perhaps we did not give enough prominence to their doubts about their teaching. Mr Baxter's, 'The learning process stops when it gets around to learning for exams, because that's a totally different idea' or Mr Underwood's 'the danger (is) if you adhere too much to wanting them to be students of literature, they may not be adequately prepared for the examination' were echoed by others. We have examined the models of literary response that were presented, often implicitly, in lessons; our next consideration will be of students' writing. The students in our sample were not unwilling to lend us their files or notebooks, but we were not in a position to question them closely about the contents. Some of the notes, for example, on *Antony and Cleopatra* from Mrs Lincoln's class were so similar to each other that they could have been taken down from dictation, but there were other indications which suggested that they were produced individually: because we collected them on our last visit we had no means of discovering how they originated. All the students annotated texts in class, but when they were actively participating in lessons they obviously tended to write less. Mrs King's class was the only one where 'Everybody is writing now' or a similar comment occurred regularly in the field-notes. Mrs Lincoln's students were expected to write notes, usually a summary of the action, on each scene in *Antony and Cleopatra*, but no-one else wrote a scene by scene or chapter by chapter summary. Mrs Lincoln's class probably had more notes both of their own and provided by her than any other class: the conscientious students, and most of them were, were building up their own versions of the ubiquitous *Coles' Notes* seen on many a bookseller's stand; indeed the style of Mrs Lincoln's handouts was remarkably close to that model.

In addition to their notes all students wrote practice answers to examination questions. Mr Underwood had remarked of his group that 'for many of them it takes two years just to get into the hang of producing a critical essay'. In the first two terms, in addition to answers written in the mid-year examination, Gaynor at Downtown School, for example, had written at least ten essays, all of which had received careful correction and comments. She had five essays on *The Franklin's Tale,* two on *All My Sons,* and three on *Coriolanus*. The teachers at Downtown School, perhaps because they were under less pressure with only seven students in the class, annotated each paragraph as well as offering general advice. This is a typical example of the comment at the end of an answer:

> A good summing up. However, your penultimate section should really have been your pre-amble. Then, you could have dissected Men (Menenius) in the light of it. You are too vague too often. Explain the P of the B (Parable of the Belly). Show his strength, his weakness, his collapse — in detail. Convince the reader you know what you're talking about.
> I think more precise planning is needed.
> Again, watch your basic English.

This was written by Mr Baxter, not by Mr Underwood, but it illustrates the attention they both paid to the techniques of writing literary essays, which were similar to those demanded in the final A-level examination.

Mrs Lincoln also expected frequent essays but it was interesting to observe when in early December, after less than three months of the course, the class took two formal three-hour examination papers how closely the questions were tied to her teaching preparation. She had handed out, as we instanced in this chapter on p. 273, five typewritten pages of general commentary on *The Secret Agent* in which salient statements were underlined. Four of these statements and the opening sentence appeared as the basis of questions: ' "Conrad's intention involved a consideration of three levels of existence..." Discuss.' The students did not, in general, reproduce or expand the notes since as yet they could not take over the tone or style of Mrs Lincoln's critical model. The exception was Jonathan's answer to the question based on the opening sentence. A tick was firmly placed against his almost word-for-word reproduction of the first four lines but even he, despite his careful memorising, found it difficult to sustain the idea of 'three levels of existence'. As he applied it to each character in turn (he had been a very successful O-level student and knew that individual character was what mattered) it became clear that he had not understood it. 'Surely Michaelis however has no three levels any more, but just the one, that is the private level of thoughts and emotions that he is stuck on, oblivious to any public image or any feelings which he may have had long ago, deep inside.' Mrs Lincoln did not dismiss his attempt; there was no comment but he was awarded 17/25, although his answer showed he was still in the process of sorting out the action and its significance, unable to move towards the level of generality at which the topic could be discussed.

All the school A-level teachers referred at some time, either to their students or to the observer, about the possibility of their students entering pieces for the creative writing option, but we saw no-one making it part of the course. Mr Austin was the only teacher who asked for writing outside the genre of the literary essay and, in contrast with the other teachers, he did not expect the fortnightly essay. He sounded in discussion to be questioning the value of too much essay-writing at the early stages, to be seeing it as a potential hindrance rather than a help.

> Don't you find the kids come back into a lesson at the back end of the first year and they've got a folder this thick? And you may well ask them a question and they're ferreting through because they know they've written an essay somewhere in the dim recesses of their past about this subject and they hope they're going to find it in this essay. So that in fact they're not actively or positively thinking, you know. They're relying — 'ah that's somewhere there' — because of this vast bulk of material which they think is usable.

He set the conventional essay topic such as ' "Keats is predominantly a narrative poet." Discuss.' But he had earlier given a more open topic by offering a quotation from Keats' letters as a starting point: 'The other day during the lecture there came a sunbeam into the room and with it a whole troop of creatures floating in the ray; and I am off with them to Oberon and fairyland.' Whilst reading *Persuasion* he asked his students to produce either a parody or a pastiche of Jane Austen's style. It is not surprising that, although the class enjoyed the challenge, they found it difficult. Sandra tried to produce a character study: 'Lady Russell was certainly the most compatible and respectable woman one could wish to meet. Her manners and conduct were all one would expect from a woman of the higher intellectual circles. Not once did she lose her sense of what was correct, for she was all sensibility, sensitivity and wisdom . . . ' Her choice of such words as compatible, sensitivity and wisdom and her attempts to reproduce an appropriate tone showed how much she had already assimilated. Amanda, in contrast, tried for a rather less felicitous modern version: 'Anne soon became bored with this monotonous meeting and suggested everyone should have a dance. She glanced across the room to Captain Wentworth . . . crossed the room and approached him. "Fancy a dance captain?" The reply was unawaited and no sooner had Anne stuck her chewing gum on the underside of the dining room chair . . . ' Both these attempts in their different ways showed students becoming aware of Jane Austen's assumptions and values. Seventeen-year-olds today frequently find it difficult to appreciate Jane Austen. Amanda, whose ambition was to teach games, told us how she was reading a lot including *Pride and Prejudice*, 'with us studying some Jane Austen you can pick characters which are exactly the same in the book and it's really amusing, you can see her style all the way through the book'. It seemed that these excursions into parody and pastiche could be a basis for an appreciation of style, an understanding of the choices an author makes in the process of writing.

In the preceding paragraphs we have not attempted to analyse the written literary responses expected in the examination and in coursework, although we could have done so on roughly parallel lines to the models offered in lessons. The context questions and 'lit crit' exercises, concentrating on close localised study, approximated to the first and third of our categories. There were questions dealing with character, at both a descriptive and analytic level, and questions on structure and theme which constituted the second group of categories (Nos. 4–7). There was a tendency for the more general questions to predominate. Topics which students wrote about always remained within the text; in the examination no background knowledge was required. With the exception of Mr Austin's class this was true for all the students: there was no writing falling into the last two categories.

In our study of writing and in *Seals of Approval* we discussed the emphasis on the Private; in our consideration of fifth-form literature study we commented that pupils were offered a depoliticised, ahistorical view of the world. Is this still the case at A-level? Students and teachers alike emphasised that although success at O-level came from 'knowing the story', at A-level much deeper understanding was necessary. The plays they were studying, whether modern or Shakespearian, were dramatically dependent on the clash between public and private values. Miller demonstrates in *All My Sons* the evil resultant from blind adherence to the profit-ethic; Shakespeare in *Coriolanus* shows the weakness of popular democracy and the follies committed in its name. The examination board's aims emphasised that English is a discipline concerned with values and with setting works within the context of their age. But it was salutory to notice the limited view of values that operated; time and time again, except for Mrs Lincoln's generalisations, the only values that we heard being talked of were those of individuals in domestic situations. Mr Baxter, when he set his students to improvise, gave them the theme of internal conflict. The speech in *Coriolanus* that they were concentrating on was the one when he was struggling to resist the importuning of his wife, mother and son, the moment in the play when the private virtues prevail. The impression left from the lessons generally was that it was characters and their motives for action that mattered even with the Miller plays. Miller may have intended his plays to be a critique of contemporary society, but it is striking how carefully that aspect is avoided in the examination topics. Two of the four most recently set A-level questions are an indication of this. ' "If Miller were less concerned with his message, these plays might make better theatre." Discuss either *A View from the Bridge* or *All My Sons* in the light of this statement.' (JMB 1977) or ' "Our sympathy and admiration lie with those whom Miller apparently wants us to dislike — Eddie Carbone and Joe Keller. They know the realities of life." Discuss, giving particular attention to the degree to which you find the climax and outcome of these two plays satisfactory.' (JMB 1976). It is not a conscious conspiracy to eschew certain areas of experience but, however unconscious the decision may be, the very act of concentrating on the individual, of avoiding the controversial, of placing the emphasis, for example, on stagecraft rather than message is a political statement, a reflection of cultural and social values, albeit implicit.

The consideration of the topics for writing has moved us to a wider area; we need to return to the students and the means by which teachers can ensure 'the personal response and commitment' which they thought important. In all but Smalltown School teachers referred to their students' lack of background. They were not apportioning blame, as Mrs King said, 'Whose fault is it but ours?', but accepting it as a fact. Mr Underwood and Mr Baxter at Downtown School had given out a list of supplementary texts which they were hoping people would read and they were taking their group on frequent theatre trips, but they recognised that for their students it was the examination which mattered. Mrs King at New Suburbia found her classes uneasy about any reading apart from the set texts and thought that English A-level was often chosen as a last resort — 'it's English or nothing'. Her sentiments were shared in part by Mrs Lincoln who because of this felt that 'a large part of my job (is) to open things up'. The only students who had impressed their teachers positively were those at Smalltown School. Mr Austin described them as 'very keen — you mention a range of ancillary texts around say Keats and they're scurrying away and getting them in the library'. Academically, on paper, he thought his was the less good of the school's two groups but 'they're interested, curious . . . will come good'.*

At Downtown and New Suburbia Schools teachers referred to their students' unwillingness to talk. Mr Underwood restated the opinion we had been given in the previous year: 'Kids at this school are not great talkers . . . don't have a lot of confidence'. Mrs King attributed her group's reluctance to join in oral work to a desire for authoritative statements: 'They really do want to be told what to think, don't they? They don't like things being left open'. Teachers are powerful influences, but they can only work within the framework accepted by their students' expectations. Even Mr Austin can describe it as a 'very frightening prospect how the examination system can dictate and force you to make moves which you really don't want to do' and Mr Underwood is all too aware that, 'at the end both they and I are being judged on how they perform in those three days'.

We started this paper with some of the claims for A-level literature teaching. We have tried to demonstrate what the teaching looked like from the teachers' viewpoints, from our observation in the classroom, and from students' writing. At fifth-form level we tested our material against two models of teaching, transmission and initiation. For many teachers the transmission mode seemed to be forced upon them by their experience of their pupils' needs and the demands of the examination. Our conclusions were that if examination success were the yardstick, these teachers were not increasing their pupils' chances by their methods. The markers of the transmission mode that we applied were perhaps superficial and simplified, and in any case could not be transferred en bloc from the situation of one teacher with 25 to 30 pupils to the smaller A-level groups. These A-level students, whatever their limitations, had made a deliberate choice to study English literature. They were the people who to some degree could exercise their own ideas about what they liked to do and were therefore likely to expect to develop their own ideas about the subject. Paradoxically, for most this choice seemed to imply that they were more rather than less ready to surrender their autonomy. Perhaps this is true of all post-compulsory education. Students now see conforming to the rules of a subject as functional: they are serving

* This reference to academic qualifications led us to check whether there were in fact differences between the groups, but our sample showed no significant contrasts. The average achievement at 16+ for the A-level sample worked out at 6·4 O-level grades (A — C) per student and the average for each group varied from 6 to 6·5. In fact the only two students with fewer than five O-level grades were Sean at Smalltown (4) and Richard at New Suburbia (2). Again, no group had a higher proportion of students with high grades.

their apprenticeship to their chosen trade whether it be that of motor vehicle engineer or literary critic so that they can operate as a craftsman. Our interest is in how far they were being given the skills to operate for themselves and for a real answer to that question we would perhaps need to meet these students in two or three years rather than after six or seven months.

But what of the evidence our material produced? Perhaps we should remind readers of the indicators we used to decide whether teachers fell into the transmission or initiation style of teaching. In transmission teaching, where the authority was to be followed unquestioningly, we found that the teacher often was the only reader of the text, supplied a paratext or dictated notes, concentrated on localised meanings rather than general issues, referred rarely to everyday knowledge and restricted writing to the practice of examination requirements. In initiation teaching the teacher, by sharing control of the text, by asking more open questions, by accepting pupils' everyday knowledge, made it more likely that the pupils could create meanings for themselves. As we have emphasised, the teacher in the A-level classes did not need to take a dominant authoritarian role to maintain social control of the classroom; relationships were informal and students could be treated much more as adults. However, because the emphasis had now moved from knowledge of the text to a critical response and evaluation of it, students were on less sure ground. Teachers were more likely to be manoeuvred, whether they wished it or not, into adopting a transmission mode.

Mrs Lincoln of our A-level teachers probably displayed more of the transmission features than any other teacher. She was the sole reader, supplied a paratext, distributed duplicated notes which were intended to relate to the examination demands. She believed that she had to hand over to her students a way of looking at and talking about literature. Her lessons differed from all the others in that in the first term the lecture was the only form of communication: with a brief break students were expected to sit through three hours of teacher-monologue. Was it a successful method? The writing which we saw later did not seem to show it was, but we noted an entry in our field-notes after a lesson in the second term. 'The students delighted in showing their paces as literary critics: they are obviously genuinely able to operate within the boundaries and with the terms she had provided.' Had the students really ceased to be a passive audience and become literary critics? The lesson which had impressed was the one which we quoted from on pages 274–75 on *The Secret Agent*, when the students had taken an active part. Closer attention to the recording, however, made us qualify that statement. We had, for example, observed the frequency of Mrs Lincoln's generalised, global statements about the novel, but when we looked at the students' comments we found that they were often different in kind. Their boundaries, in fact, were not the same. To give an example, when Mrs Lincoln commented that: 'the irony is all pervasive, there is no way of extracting one's self from it', Russell replied: 'There's too much of it'. Rosemarie then contradicted: 'No I think it's brilliant . . . I like it very much . . . it personally touches me'. They were wanting to give their own personal reactions: their replies were at a different level from Mrs Lincoln's statement. The comments about heroes on page 275 similarly were relating the novel to their experience. Once or twice students rephrased Mrs Lincoln's ideas giving them as their own, as when Shula towards the end of the lesson said: 'In my opinion the central theme of it is what can happen when people are so blind', which showed she had taken over the theme of blindness, but such occasions were exceptional and an ability to restate ideas does not necessarily mean they have been assimilated. The students had impressed with their confidence, with their obvious enjoyment in adopting a critical stance but, and this is significant, none of them was a teenager, all of them were older. In fact, when we checked through the lesson calculating all the students' contributions, we found that the 17-year-olds had spoken only 40 lines out of 261, 4 per cent of a total student contribution of 28 per cent in the lesson. If we exclude two long speeches amounting to 26 lines which Sylvia, one of the younger students contributed, there were only 14 lines spoken by the 17-year-olds (1·5 per cent). The mature students' contributions were at two levels. When they talked of the book either they talked of their feelings or they referred to actual incidents and events. Mrs Lincoln could make overarching statements such as, 'There is no clear line from a particular disaster back to a person we could say is responsible for that disaster', but they wanted to talk about Winnie and her predicament. At a general level, they were interested in exploring why they liked or disliked the book, what the difference was between reading a book and studying it, or what kind of a person the author was. They accepted Mrs Lincoln's rhetoric but their response was different in kind.

In Mrs King's class at New Suburbia we noticed a similar unwillingness or inability of the students to respond in general terms. Her question, for example, whether self-deception was an important idea in *A View from the Bridge* was met with silence. Then one girl asked, 'Does Eddie realise that Rodolpho's not really weird?' After Mrs King had answered, there was another factual question from a student and the teacher's original question was never considered. It was apparent from their exchanges later that these students had a good basic understanding of the action but they were anxious to have all their interpretations confirmed, they wanted to be sure that they had the facts right before they ventured an opinion. Eventually these sixth-form students were talking much more than their counterparts in the FE class: they seemed to enjoy rehearsing their knowledge, sorting out the characters and their motives but when Mrs King again asked for a response to the play as a whole, their replies were at the level of likes and dislikes and they were reluctant to elaborate.

> S. It never seemed to get going for me, it just suddenly finished.
> (Various comments from students agreeing with the above.)
> S. I didn't get any impression of any of the characters at all.
> S. I don't think the play's got anything very much about it really.

In the fifth form it seemed that discussion at a general level enabled students to participate; it was not so straightforward with these A-level classes. Perhaps it would be useful to return briefly to Mrs Lincoln. When she was describing her methods before we went into her lesson she had talked of 'feeding in all sorts of things', yet when we discussed the difficulty of some of the notes she had given, she spoke of the necessity for a 'ruthless exposure' to the language of literary criticism. Jonathan, who was a typical able sixth former, (he had come to the college because of a family move) talked of his feelings at the beginning of the year, 'it was incredible'. Even after two terms, 'I very often get lost completely lost. Although I try, I'm sort of half there and I can just about get there then I sort of fall back again'. He was a thoughtful and articulate boy who, despite his difficulties, could say: 'What I often find is when I'm writing an essay for her, all of a sudden something she said in one of the lessons pops up and I start thinking about it and then it's all there'. We saw in the essay we quoted that he was making use of some of the ideas even at the end of the first term: he valued the prepared notes but he wanted something more.

> We just sort of seem to read the book or the novel or Shakespeare, make notes, write essays. I don't know, in a way, you get the impression there's a sort of depth missing, maybe an area you could participate more yourself. I don't know if we tried acting out a few or reading parts. I've no real idea, but you just get the impression that sometimes you're not fully active in it and there's another depth you could be participating in.

He appears to be asking for an initiation rather than a transmission approach.

Those who have committed, or are in the process of committing, themselves as students of literature are not daunted by Mrs Lincoln's world. For a few hours they can leave their workaday roles and savour the pleasures of intellectual challenge. They may not know or understand all the words which their lecturer can use so easily, her rhetorical style may be unfamiliar, but they are being initiated into a world they want to share. For those who are more unsure, who need to be convinced by experiencing literature at their own level, it is more complex.

'Reading parts' may be a beginning, but it was not enough for Mrs King's students; they were still expecting their teacher to simplify and clarify. They were unwilling to make judgements and seemed not to relish intellectual challenge. 'Acting out' clearly produced a sense of active participation, but as we saw in the *Coriolanus* lesson it could be an isolated experiment, enjoyable in itself but unconnected with the work which preceded and followed it. The dramatisation of *The Eve of St Agnes*, when the initial idea had evolved from the class as they worked on a text and was developed co-operatively, when the activity seemed to be growing from and feeding back into the literary study, seemed to be the strongest example of initiation. It was not merely an enjoyable experience, it was a direct engagement with the text which produced critical insights. As the students were paying close attention to the movement of the verse, to changes in pace and mood the teacher was able by his comments to support and sharpen their perceptions.

> T. ... you've got a tremendous visual sense about that — the movement is certainly there in my mind's eye, not because it's moving up and down, I think Keats is really generating that vision. And then, of course, looking on the senses again with the noise of the doors opening and the trumpets. Very good indeed. Let's work on the next bit, then.

No profound thoughts were emerging, but the students were finding out for themselves how rhythmic effects created meaning. This is only one method of initiation, as Mr Austin said in the lesson, nobody had suggested it when they were reading *Persuasion*. We are clearly not envisaging it as appropriate to any and every text. Mr Austin, of our teachers, most exemplified the initiation approach. He talked of 'feeling your way through a text together without faking it... a tentative approach'. It accords with that philosophy that he considered, 'The most enjoyable A-level experience I've had was teaching Patrick White's *Tree of Life*, it was certainly a marvellous experience, left it until the upper sixth. It didn't seem to matter that they hadn't got the same width of reading that I've had or the number of years. It was an encounter for all of us with spiritual difficulties'. His own instance was of work on an unfamiliar text, but we saw how in a lesson on *Persuasion*, a book he knew well, he was trying to keep in step with his students' perceptions by handing over to them the task of making the first comments. In this way he was also trying to help them develop their own critical voice. It is difficult for a teacher who knows a text well to re-create his own sense of discovery, but he set out to avoid imposing a reading and seemed to be succeeding.

'A personal response', especially at the early stages of A-level teaching, will not always produce the finely balanced discrimination or the nicely turned phrase. We are reminded of a lecture that Professor Barbara Hardy gave in 1968 on teaching English[3] to young students. She distinguished between the teaching of literature and the teaching of literary criticism and questioned the value of teaching the latter. 'The process of judgment... is something I rather suspect is taught by not teaching it, taught by teaching literature rather than critical judgment.' And in that teaching of literature she argued that we should be prepared to accept irrelevancies and irreverences.

> The encouragement of personal response and the training of controlling intelligence need not conflict. On the contrary, where there is a lack of connectiveness, where there is a lack of demonstration and supporting argument, it is very often because what the student is explaining or demonstrating is not his own experience at all, but a second-hand response. Where the intelligence falls down is very often in this area of plagiarised or depersonalised response on which, not unnaturally, it is extremely difficult to build a demonstration and a supporting and sustained argument. If you don't start with your own experience, how are you to justify, how are you to explain?

That seems to be the final word for this chapter, but perhaps we should return to the context of our data and remind ourselves that the title of this chapter is 'Literature after the Fifth Form'. Immersed in the concerns of A-level English we have begun to accept that literature and experience should go hand in hand, but we have forgotten how limited that study of literature was. Most of the FE lecturers we interviewed said emphatically that they would not spend any time on literature. Mrs Brindley said that occasionally, 'I sort of slip it in because I think it's important. . . . the real stuff,' and went on to talk of how she had read one story, H. G. Wells' *Country of the Blind*, with her auto engineers but 'I feel guilty, if I use it'. Hers was an unusual position; Mr Davidson had no regrets that English A-level was no longer taught in the Business Studies Department. 'I used to find that a struggle because they had no interest in this literature: they only did it . . . to give themselves an extra A-level.' An A-level English course, however, was still being offered, although it did not fall into our sample as part of the secretarial course to those students who already had O-level literature. Interestingly, the lecturers chose not to follow the JMB syllabus we have described since they felt unable to include poetry because of their students' lack of background. They claimed that, although they believed no 'A-level course is complete without poetry . . . the schools are not doing poetry now' — a strange assertion as all their students had studied some poetry at O-level. It would be interesting to speculate why English literature was important for only one vocational group, the future shorthand-typists at High Street College. 'We introduce all our girls to Shakespeare . . . we encourage people to watch BBC rather than ITV' sounded to be equating studying literature with a certain set of values. Mr Wilkinson, with his own strong personal involvement in literature, would retort, 'I'm very wary about . . . the middle-class assumption that *they*, in a sense, need something like that'.

CHAPTER 8

English and Communications in Further Education Courses

1. Why include Communications?

In analysing the teaching of English in schools it seemed reasonable to make the initial assumption that fifth-year teaching was homogeneous, since at first glance English teachers in schools share a common ethos and a common rhetoric of justification. It was only when we matched the details of courses and justifications with examination requirements that the assumptions of homogeneity became open to question. No such initial assumption could be made in further education; not only is there an overt distinction between courses labelled 'English' and those labelled 'Communications', but there are marked differences within the latter according to the nature of the vocational courses with which they are associated, in part corresponding with the requirements of the examinations.

It is necessary to justify our decision to include Communications in a study of versions of English. Communications courses overlap with English in that they are concerned with reading, writing, talking and listening, but they differ in five respects that are of some importance for our purposes. In many traditional English courses writing tends to go on in a limbo without context, purpose or audience; many English teachers in schools try to deal with this by turning the writing inwards, so that ideally the pupils are writing for themselves, or for a sympathetic eavesdropping adult. Communications courses, on the other hand, explicitly place talk, reading and writing in specific contexts which, in the nature of things, are usually simulated not real. The second difference between English and Communications arises directly from this. Communications courses are often related to particular groups of vocations, and set out to integrate the development of students' competence and understanding of spoken and written communication with their developing knowledge and understanding of their present or future work in business or industry. Since writing and discussion are embedded in a work context — the decisions that need to be made in setting up a work site, for example, and the written and spoken communications arising from them — it is impossible to separate the discussion of the messages, the writing and talking, from discussion of the practicalities of the work task and from the social relationships relevant to formulating the messages appropriately and effectively. Thus, Communications leads directly outside itself to a discussion of practical concerns arising from the work and its social context; unlike school English, it cannot be confined to personal and domestic experience.

A third distinction is that, whereas English is primarily concerned to develop abilities in writing and reading, Communications claims to encourage not only the practice of skills but the ability to reflect on them, by helping students to analyse communication in terms of theoretical models. Whether this is in fact happening in the courses is, however, an empirical matter which must be dealt with when we look more closely at our data.

A very noticeable difference between the two lies in the role played by literature. Literature as starting-point, as model and as focus of attention, lies beneath the greater proportion of school English; in FE colleges literature plays a far smaller part even in English courses, and appears not at all in our Communications data. (The one GCE A-level literature course we observed in a college is reported in Chapter 7, 'Literature after the Fifth Form'; the one O-level literature course is mentioned later in this chapter.)

Since Communications is a new subject even to the lecturers teaching it, its aims, procedures and criteria have had to be highly explicit, and this contrasts sharply with many English courses that are traditional in the sense that they rely heavily on teachers' taken-for-granted beliefs about the nature of English studies, thus obviating any need for detailed statements of goals and methods. The establishment of situated assignments in Communications courses, since it cuts sharply across the 'English Language' tradition, has demanded not only plentiful examples but a framework of theoretical justification.

It will appear from this comparison that English and Communications, though based on two different rationales and celebrating different values, have enough in common to make it essential to include Communications in a study of different versions of English. They are in effect alternative strategies for carrying out a similar task — the development of older students' ability to use language and to reflect upon its use.

Various historical factors lie behind the development of Communications and we shall have to consider some of them separately, first looking at courses in the area of Business Studies. Until the late 1970s many professional examinations and most ONC (Ordinary National Certificate) and OND (Ordinary National Diploma) courses in the business area included a compulsory English element — the general essay and test of comprehension that we have labelled 'traditional'. However, during the 1970s changes had been taking place in some examinations and in some lecturers' thinking. We found it interesting to look back at what Mr Davidson of High Street College had said to us in 1979 in our pilot study when he was teaching the BEC module, 'People and Communications', for the first time. 'When I first came here (1967) all English courses were variants of O-level English Language and because students had had years of this at school they were bored with it obviously. I spent the first few years trying to get some new slant on how to tackle them. I read Fred Flower's book[1], that opened a door, that showed the way and ever since then we've been trying to build up what we'd prefer to call Communication rather than English.' Business Education Council courses became available in 1978, gradually replacing the ONC/OND and HNC/HND system: BEC offers awards at General level 'mainly intended for young people in 16–19 age group with few, if any, academic qualifications who expect to enter, or have recently entered employment' and at National level for students who are competent in English language and have formal qualifications, such as four GCE O-level passes at Grade A, B or C or CSE equivalents. (We can ignore the Higher National level as that falls outside the range of our study.) 'People and Communication' are core modules which all students must take and their aims, general objectives and learning objectives were set out in detail for lecturers in documents published in 1977 but, as Mr Davidson said recently, even after the courses have been running for some years some colleagues 'think Communications is just a posh word for English'. Although he was at pains to point out this 'fundamental misunderstanding' he acknowledged that 'Communications certainly contains English and to some extent is about English, but it's English plus a lot more'. The link between English and Communications in BEC is, thus, a direct one.

The Communications elements in technician and craft courses have a quite different history, however. The further education explosion is largely a post-war phenomenon: the apprenticeship system which grew up in small industrial units under the control of the trade and professional institutions has been replaced by an examination system for which FE colleges have taken over the training. This examining system has become valued by industry 'as a cheap training method with an inbuilt quality control element'.[2] But as training moved under the control of educational institutions there was pressure for more general non-vocational studies and Liberal or General Studies developed as an area offering both 'contrasting' and 'complementary' courses. The case for 'contrasting' courses is that vocational training is, by definition, limited to the concerns of trade, commerce or profession, so that General or Liberal Studies are required to make for a full and balanced education. Such General Studies frequently included cultural, social and political elements. They have often been characterised by students, technical lecturers, and employers alike as irrelevant, and resented by some as patronising and paternalistic, gratuitously attributing cultural deficits to adults and near-adults who have every right to choose for themselves. 'Complementary' courses, however, are intended to intermesh with vocational courses and to offer relevant background knowledge and competences: typical of these would be courses in English which set out to provide the language competences required of the student by his or her technical studies and on the worksite. (Language needs during the remainder of his or her waking hours would presumably be categorised as 'contrasting'.) As early as 1962 the Ministry pamphlet *General Studies in Technical Colleges* insisted 'that the development of the student's skill in using language must be a central concern of all Liberal Studies . . . '[3]. That English be *taught in the context of its use* was part of the practice and theory of many Liberal Studies departments whilst, at the same time, they provided opportunities for a wide range of cultural and creative activities which were more contrasting than complementary. The position of the complementary apologists was strengthened by moves such as the setting up of the ILEA Communications group (1973/4) to devise methods to help craft apprentices who were failing because of their inability to cope with the study skills and communicative demands of their courses. And with the establishment of TEC with its compulsory communications element of 15 per cent in the first year assessment and the setting up of City and Guilds Communication Skills examination, 'Communications' has come to figure on the timetables of all craft and technician courses. It is always envisaged as vocationally related and in some cases is completely integrated into a vocational assignment. Builders are no longer assessed on their ability to comprehend by answering questions about word meanings or by summarising a passage about prestressed concrete, but they are expected to demonstrate their deductive and productive skills in a simulation of the kind of technical problem which actually occurs in the construction industry. In other cases the integration is less complete but, as in BEC, it is rare that discrete categories such as the essay and comprehension are examined.

Formal descriptions of Communications requirements in BEC, TEC and City and Guilds courses appear to converge upon a common pattern of assessment by assignments, in which the students, alone or in groups, undertake clusters of reading, talking and writing tasks situated in an imagined context which supplies criteria for relevance and appropriateness. (These 'situated assignments' are described and illustrated later in this chapter.) In practice, however, we have observed differences, particularly differences separating BEC Communications from those courses directed to the other examining boards' requirements. We have included this brief survey of the history of Communications because it is important to realise that BEC courses are felt to have grown out of English courses, rather than merely supplanting them; in contrast, Communications in TEC and City and Guilds inherited an existing struggle between contrasting and complementary versions of General Studies, so that Communications courses are often perceived by lecturers as supplanting courses designed to make young people more aware of the social world about them. The teaching of Communications in these two contexts can be seen to diverge. Although in both cases situated assignments form the basis of the courses, these are interpreted in terms of historically legitimated priorities linked to English and business on the one hand and to Liberal Studies and industry on the other. For this reason we deal with BEC courses in separation from TEC and City and Guilds courses.

It is an appealing possibility to retell the heuristic voyage that we took in moving progressively towards an interpretation of these data, so as to take the reader with us, but the demands of time and clarity of focus forbid it. The issues which dominate this chapter were not — with one exception — those with which we began. We present these issues in advance in order to help the reader to find a route through the details that we discuss, and yet do so in the knowledge that it makes the report still more unlike the processes which led to it. In analysing and interpreting the data we are specially concerned with:

1. The sources of legitimation for each course. This is not just a matter of offered justifications but the source of observed values. Colleges, because they have to attract and retain students, are unlike schools, which are sheltered from the direct demands of the outside world. School curricula often seem to be self-legitimating, so that in our account of school English the teachers' justifications played a minor role. Colleges are vulnerable to the values of students and their employers so that legitimations have to be made more openly. We are, therefore, interested to discover what contexts supply legitimation to the various versions of English in colleges: the examination systems, which can act as autonomous sources of cultural norms; the world of business; the world of industry; values believed to be appropriate to everyday private life; perspectives on public issues drawn from political, social or economic analyses.

2. Pictures of the world offered to students. This relates for example to what in Chapter 3 was called 'deep criteria' for writing.

3. The boundaries of the subject. What content and what processes are treated as falling within the boundaries of each course? (This may or may not correspond with the specific demands of examination syllabuses.)

4. Student participation. This is more than merely whether students talk or are silent during lessons. Are they given access to principles which would enable them to make judgements? Are they given the experience of choice? Are they encouraged to engage in a range of communicative acts, including formulating proposals, and criticising

and modifying other people's arguments?

5. Penetration into the learner's reality. The metaphor of depth is used here to refer to the relationship of what is learnt to the private world of the learner. Are knowledge and skills presented mainly in the form of surface criteria, so the learner can adopt them at arms' length? When deep criteria are made available, does the learner have to invest personality and moral commitment in order to use them?

All five of these concerns will not necessarily be dealt with overtly in each of the subsections that follow, yet with greater or lesser strength they direct the analysis.

2. Four English courses in FE

The English courses which we found in colleges of further education are directed towards GCE O-level or the English language examinations of the Royal Society of Arts. (There are also occasional courses in literature for GCE A-level, one of which has been discussed in Chapter 7.) Students taking English in RSA courses will almost certainly also be following other RSA options that together provide initial qualifications for secretarial and business employment. GCE O-level courses in English are 'free-standing', in the sense that they are not compulsory elements in grouped vocational training, but those who sit them in FE colleges are frequently heading towards employment in business. Thus, in considering English language courses in FE, we are looking at courses organised within a set of priorities and preconceptions derived mainly from the world of business.

The examinations, however, have a life of their own which does not necessarily match the practices and values of the business world, so it is with the examination requirements that we begin. We observed four English courses in two colleges as follows:

Table 8.1

English courses observed

Lecturer	College	Examination	Time observed
Mr Pattison	Smalltown	GCE English Language	418
Mrs Sands	Smalltown	RSA English Language Stage I	200
Mr Peel	High Street	RSA English Language Stage I	149
Mr Peel	High Street	RSA English Language Stage III GCE English Literature (O-level)	206

Mr Pattison was teaching for the first time a version of O-level English language (JMB Syllabus D) in which the assessment was based upon a folder of coursework, internally assessed and externally moderated. As we shall see, he had not yet responded to the opportunities implicit in this method so that he taught his class as if they were to sit the same kind of examination paper that he had prepared previous classes for.

The RSA English language paper (Stage I) contains three elements: an essay, a test of comprehension, and a letter. The values and emphases of these papers are not unlike those of many O-level examinations. The essay tasks include descriptive pieces ('... a crowd on an important sporting occasion...'), autobiographical accounts ('My earliest memories...'), topics for discussion ('Discuss some of the ways... television.'), and fictional narrative. The passages for comprehension were varied — a *Times* article on left-handedness, 'Whose skull at Piltdown?' and a passage about spring on a Scottish island — only the last of these displaying any tendency to 'fine writing'. The questions required the paraphrase of individual words and phrases, and the identification and extraction of ideas from the passage. Only the letter referred to a business context, for example, a letter of application for a post. RSA Stage III papers are similar except that the passage for comprehension is more difficult — perhaps being taken from an academic source such as a textbook — and no letter is required. Apart from the letter, there is no indication that RSA examinations usually form a part of secretarial and business courses. The composition required is the traditional essay, writing about easily available topics for unspecified audiences and purposes: the model is once again an out-dated *belles lettres* journalism. The comprehension exercises, for all the interest of the passages chosen, hang likewise in a no-man's land; candidates extract ideas and explain meanings for no conceivable reason apart from that of satisfying an examiner. We are far away from the complex processes by which, in real life, we bring our existing knowledge, expectations and purposes to bear when we attribute meaning to what we read, and reshape and reinterpret when we try to explain it to someone else. We may ask ourselves why traditional English examinations are decontextualised in this way, what function is served by displays of writing and reading that — unlike most reading and writing — lacks situation, purpose and audience, except that of enacting a range of competences for an assessor, though we have become so accustomed to such tests in English that it is difficult to take the question seriously. One answer may be that amongst the competences being tested is that of being able to maintain certain proprieties of content and manner even without any cues from the situation; but that cannot be all. Another answer may be that as soon as we situate writing or talking in a social context we commit ourselves, if only temporarily, to the knowledge, priorities, purposes and styles appropriate to that context. Situated acts of communication cannot be separated from the moral and political imperatives normal to that situation.

Although none of the three lecturers who taught English courses would have denied the importance of seeing to it that his or her students gained qualifications, each of them asserted that the English courses led also to other goals. Mrs Sands said, in interview, 'There are some people who can really develop and become interesting ... and as a sideline get these qualifications ...'. Mr Pattison wanted his students 'to be able to read critically and be able to write well or so it could be understood, and also that they gain a qualification'. Mr Peel was more specific: 'I usually tell them that comprehension is most important because it is something we do the rest of our lives'. Most of his justifications related English to his students' future jobs: he wanted them to be 'aware of vocabulary' because it was linked 'with their future in shorthand and typewriting'. (He was perhaps making the reasonable assumption that accurate spelling goes along with understanding.) And again, 'I frequently give them my idea of what a sentence should be and say, "I want you to look at it carefully and see if you can spot any mistakes that you feel should be corrected" '. He summed up his views as, 'English ... is a working subject ... part of the tools of an employee'. Mrs Sands saw her work at RSA Level I as 'really remedial work', and mentioned spelling and punctuation. 'Until I came to teaching,' she said, 'I just didn't realise that people found English so difficult ...' These 'rather traditional' English courses (Mrs Sands) are thus justified on these grounds:

1. The need for a qualification recognised by employers.
2. Relevance to the skills required in offices (including remedial work on written conventions not mastered during schooling).
3. General relevance to life.

At High Street College all of the nine streams of students — almost all girls — who were preparing to be shorthand typists spent a considerable proportion of their English time on literature. The eventual aim was success at O-level, a marketable commodity, but even when there was little likelihood of achieving that aim, 'We do with these girls what we call non-examinable literature, because every group we feel very strongly should have some literature'. Mr Peel justified this by adding: 'They come to us only having read *Betsy* or something like that all their lives. You ask them for a book and possibly the last book they read was Enid Blyton. We feel that if they are going into an office literature is very, very important, not only does it broaden their outlooks, but in giving them literature it gives us the opportunity of talking about another age or social problems or something like that'. The belief in the importance of literature in the office has almost the air of the finishing school about it, a preparation for a genteel and ladylike world where people will expect typists to be conversant with established literature. We must thus add a fourth justification:

4. Literature as cultural preparation for office work.

Although these represent the legitimations which the lecturers offered to us and sometimes, it appeared, to their students, it would be unwise to take them at face value. It is particularly important to note that there was not a close match between the skills tested in O-level and RSA examinations and the skills required in secretarial work. Indeed, on more than one occasion a lecturer commented on a conflict between examination requirements and the practices found in real offices. For example, Mr Peel, discussing paragraphing, found it necessary to tell his students to 'semi-block' in spite of the fact that they were taught in other courses that it was now standard office practice to 'fully block' paragraphs. He explained: 'The reason for that is in semi-blocked you indicate paragraphs by indentation: if they're fully blocked you bring everything up to the margin . . . Very difficult for examiners in English to know whether you are really following a rule as far as typewriting goes or whether you've forgotten there's a paragraph'. On another occasion, when a student said that rather than writing a letter she would telephone, Mr Peel replied:

> Well, of course, as we've always said, when we're dealing with an examination situation we're dealing with a situation which is unique for an examination. In practice probably ninety per cent of the letters that we write in class are things where we would use the telephone in an ordinary business situation.

Incidents of this kind make it clear that where there is a clash between two sources of legitimation, the examination and the needs of the business world, it is the former that overrides the latter. To put it more generally, the functions of social reproduction — selection and certification — override the claims of vocational training.

The essay topics and the materials set for comprehension are far from the world of employment and business. The essay and comprehension exercise test the ability to adopt a persona and deal with content that are far removed from these contexts, though they also incidentally test concern for the details of spelling and punctuation. Neither GCE nor RSA examinations contain direct exercises in punctuation, nor in the use of words in made-up sentences, nor in synonyms and antonyms: such decontextualised exercises have long been discredited as a means of testing language competences. Nevertheless, the three lecturers spent class time on such exercises; in the lessons which we observed, Mrs Sands, for example, spent 12 per cent of the available time on them yet, when we analysed the details she gave us of her teaching throughout the year, the results indicated a much higher investment of time in the teaching and practice of written conventions, apparently as much as 40 per cent. Mr Pattison appeared to give most of the time to writing but we have reason to believe that part of his teaching time, too, was spent on exercises. What in Chapter 6 we called the 'basic skills' version of English is preserved in further education in the preparation of typists.

English language examinations such as these exist in a disembodied limbo of their own; they embody implicit views of the nature of writing and reading which would not nowadays be acceptable to psycholinguists, and detach these activities from most imaginable contexts, except perhaps that of the light journalism of past years. We can see, however, that this unreal world can nevertheless be used as legitimation for curricular policy, and continue to have a life of its own for many generations of students. This account sets aside, however, the function of cultural (as against social) reproduction, the passing on to young people of values and attitudes thought to be appropriate to the work roles that they had assumed, or perhaps would assume. We have already seen that one college incorporated some literature work in English courses for this purpose. We shall see, however, that the transmission of values — deep criteria — in FE courses is different in kind from what we have observed in most school English courses.

English was part of the secretarial course both at Smalltown and High Street Colleges. All the girls we saw were aiming at some RSA English qualification because it fitted in with their shorthand and typing. 'When an employer is looking at them he looks at their RSA qualifications in shorthand and typing and then will accept as a good qualification English, Commerce, Accounts or whatever it is at the same level.' (Mr Peel, High Street.) Their lecturers assumed that college English was likely to be very closely related to school English; in fact the number of classes at High Street College were such that students were placed according to their O-level and CSE English grades. A-level was the eventual target for the top groups, O-level for the next groups, and so on down to the ninth group which might be entered eventually for RSA Stage I at the end of its second year. We shall see how closely it matched the students' experience of school English as we look in more detail at the lessons.

In the paragraphs that follow, composition, comprehension and written conventions are dealt with separately; in so doing we lose some sense of each lecturer's identity as a teacher but gain in being able to focus upon different issues raised by the different activities.

3. Preparing to write in further education English

When the lessons which led up to written work in college English are compared with those in schools, a quite different attitude to the content of writing is evident. This attitude is not the possession of individual lecturers or an accompaniment to particular courses; it appears to characterise all FE English in contrast to school English, and thus to be a function of institutional differences. The contrast can be made most starkly in terms of the lecturers' relationship to what we are calling 'deep criteria'. Where the topic was a private or domestic one it was left almost entirely to the students; this contrasts most sharply with our school data. When the topic required the expression of opinion or analysis of a topic (the so-called 'discursive' or 'argumentative' essay), when it required description of a scene or person, and when it required the writing of a report or a formal letter, the lecturers tended to lay down the content clearly. They thus kept tight control of content, rather than trying to communicate criteria that would enable students to select, arrange and present material in a suitable manner, as the schoolteachers tended to do.

Mrs Sands, for example, teaching one of the RSA classes, unintentionally communicated her lack of concern with the topic when she said:

> A lot of people, I think, for example if there's an essay on (pause) 'My Hobbies' or something equally scintillating like that, after they've battled on loyally for about a page and maybe done a bit over the other side, they (omission) a bit and think, 'I've done enough work', and stop, bang a full stop down. You stop in mid-air and from the point-of-view of the person who's reading it, you're reading on thinking, 'This is boring', waiting for it to get a bit better; you turn it over and – ah well...

Here Mrs Sands is concerned to communicate to her students the importance of a telling last sentence; elsewhere in the same session she deals with length, presentation, interest, introduction, paragraphs, the ordering of ideas, spelling and punctuation. That is, her primary concern was with what we are calling 'surface criteria'. When she approached deep criteria — 'interest', and 'the ordering of ideas' was how she labelled them — like other teachers she found it difficult to say anything likely to be of value to the students. Mrs Sands says of 'interest', for example:

> Some essays about boring subjects can be very interesting... Can't think of one. I'm always... expecting an essay to be interesting.

Length — the surface criterion par excellence — for Mrs Sands is an important matter. Not only should the overall length of an essay be 300 to 350 words, but length also provides the criteria for paragraphing: '... Do try and write paragraphs that are longer than one sentence,' she urged, and in reply to a student who asked, 'What happens if it's a really long sentence?' she continued:

> Well, in that case I'd either write a shorter sentence or... It's difficult... to have a hard and fast rule. If it's a really very long sentence, well all right.

The topics which Mrs Sands eventually set in this session were typically 'private' ones of the type common in schools. (For example, one was: 'A word picture of yourself, including outward appearance and personality'.) She introduced them, however, with the dismissive 'We'll just look at the choice of essays — a bit boring'. Although this is consonant with Mrs Sands' usual strategy as a youthful lecturer of allying herself with student values, it also matches her emphasis throughout this session on surface ('skills and conventions') criteria at the expense of content. (We shall have occasion later to consider two occasions when Mrs Sands took up quite different relationships with the subject matter of some writing.)

We will now turn to Mr Pattison, who was preparing a class for O-level English language by assignments. (Eight of the 16 classes in the school data were being prepared for the same examination conducted by similar methods, so comparison is not inappropriate.) For Mr Pattison this was a first experience of teaching for examination by assessment of coursework, and he seemed to find it difficult to detach himself from the approach established during his previous years of teaching for conventional examinations. Amongst our data are three sessions in which he prepared his group for writing, one a personal essay, one a piece of writing about a work of art, and one an essay on a general 'public' topic. It is the first of these that I wish to refer to here. Mr Pattison began by saying, 'Part 3 of this assignment is concerned with another aspect of writing about actual events', and went on to make a distinction between 'writing an account of how to do something, mending a puncture in a tyre, stuffing or preparing a chicken' and 'an account of something you've experienced'. This session was to be concerned with the latter and Mr Pattison gave as an example 'The First Driving Lesson'. He went on to elicit from the students a series of suggested topics, including 'Holiday Alone', 'First Day at School or College' and 'A Skiing Holiday'.

In the context of 'The First Driving Lesson' Mr Pattison indicated what he wanted: '. . . where you were all clumsy and inexperienced, you don't know the driving instructor, it's the first time that you've met him, you're doing most things wrong or most things clumsily at any rate'. He continued, 'We're talking about a description of what you do and how it affects you, how the circumstances make you nervous and how perhaps you do things you ought not to have done'. And later he suggested that they should jot down two lists of notes, 'the sequence of events' and alongside them 'something about what you felt, what you thought'. Although this introductory lesson thus contained references to the students' feelings — which were used in the school section as an indicator of personal treatment — Mr Pattison's whole approach was radically different from personal treatment, as we saw it for example in Mrs Wood's lessons. In personal lessons in schools there is usually a far more elaborate indication of what is required, including some extracts from literature, and discussion of possible topics in a way that in part exemplifies the anecdotal-reflective emphasis. Mr Pattison tended to leave the subjective aspect of the experience to be written about to his students: he certainly showed no sign of what we have called 'socio-moral purposes', the desire to recommend a set of attitudes and values to his students. The essence of his purpose seemed to be to fulfil the requirements for various kinds of writing demanded of the students by this mode of examining. In this sense the examination, and its requirements as interpreted by Mr Pattison and his colleagues, was offering him a set of goals so that he did not need to look beyond them for purposes that might be drawn from elsewhere.

Thus Mr Pattison exemplified an 'impersonal' treatment even when he was dealing with 'private' topics. He clearly wished neither to penetrate into his students' private lives nor to make his own available to them. The same might be said of Mrs Stones' teaching (apart from one session that will be dealt with separately). For such tasks both lecturers tended to leave their students to choose and organise the experiences they were to write about. Here we have a sharp-drawn distinction between the students' private worlds and the purposes of the courses; in most school courses, on the other hand, the distinction was weak or non-explicit. With other kinds of writing, however, the college lecturers gave a great deal more attention to the content.

Under the rubric of an 'Argumentative Essay' another assignment was presented to Mr Pattison's students in the form of a duplicated sheet. This contained essay topics which concerned: television, happiness, smoking, full-time education after 16, the 1970s, manners. Listed like this, the titles look like a typical list from a GCE O-level paper of some years ago. But they were not presented merely as titles: most offered eight or ten lines of guidance to the candidate. This one can serve as example:

> In order to attract more young people to stay in full-time education after the age of sixteen, particularly those people who find it difficult to do so, it is proposed to offer grants to all students over sixteen. The level of grant will depend on the parents' income. What are your views on this proposal? How will it affect future careers? Will it persuade more people to continue in education? What does attract them to stay at school or college?

This task deserves our attention. It gives those students who find it difficult to know what to write some starting points for their thinking by indicating the kinds of issues to be discussed. In this respect the task is more elaborated than the mere title 'Education after Sixteen' would have been. On the other hand, there is no indication of the audience to whom the writing is to be addressed or the purpose it is to serve. There is no attempt to disguise what it is, a writing exercise to satisfy examination requirements, a decontextualised piece intended for assessment by the teacher and possibly by a moderator.

Mr Pattison prepared his class for the 'Argumentative Essay' topics by choosing television as his exemplar and taking his group through it step by step, indicating what they could write. The duplicated question gave this guidance:

> Television – broadens the mind
> stifles conversation
> makes people lazy
> befriends the lonely
> is politically biased
> encourages violence
>
> Write your views on the way television affects people's lives referring if you wish to the above comments.

He began with 'the proposition that television broadens the mind', and asked for 'positive examples of the way in which that may be so'. Students suggested various documentary programmes which he then listed on the blackboard. The mention of a *Horizon* programme on acupuncture led Mr Pattison to ask: 'Now in what particular way does that help to broaden your mind?' and by persistent questioning drew from the students that acupuncture implied sticking needles into somebody in order to 'overcome some injury, some stress', as one student put it. He then commented:

> So you could say if you liked that that programme was mind-broadening in the way in which it informed you about a different culture from your own. If you're sick you go to the doctor and you are cured by one of two methods: you take drugs or you undergo surgery — either of those two methods usually. Here we have a different approach to a medicine which is a study of the whole body, analysis of pressure points and the application of alternative pain to those pressure points. Right, a different approach, a way in which a different culture works; so that you can say is (writing on the blackboard) 'an example of a different culture', and it's an example of how other people get the same problems . . . (brief omission) They are the same all over the world; our different cultures have tried to deal with those problems in a radically different way. There are other ways of thinking about things, there are other ways of looking at things, other than the ways in which most of European – English – people do. You can say that that was one example of this: you get to know how other people live and think.

Mr Pattison went on to deal similarly with television news and drama as broadening the mind, and then turned to the next statement from the original question: 'It stifles conversation'. After an exchange with students about this, Mr Pattison again commented at length:

> So you could take that this is true, that people instead of talking are watching television but you can say that they are watching in groups . . .

and this commentary continued for several minutes.

> ... I just stopped in the staffroom up there. As soon as there are about four people there somebody says, 'Did you see so-and-so on television last night?' and it provides a subject of conversation that people have in common....

In this way Mr Pattison took his students step by step through one of the set topics modelling how such 'argumentative essays' can be constructed, a valuable mode of instruction for any students who have not learnt this skill at school. At the same time he provided abundant content that could be used by any student who wished to do so, and also illustrated an appropriate style of writing. If you cast your eyes back over the quotations from this session, the appropriateness of Mr Pattison's spoken style to this last purpose is apparent: 'the proposition that', 'the way in which this may be so', 'informed you about a different culture from your own', 'a subject of conversation that people have in common'. What he illustrated for his students was not merely an appropriate content but a linguistic (and conceptual?) style drawn from certain kinds of books and journals.

Although this procedure included many references by students to aspects of their lives outside the college — watching television, particularly — Mr Pattison's interest seemed to be directed entirely towards the requirements of the examination. For example, some students provoked an exchange about old people and loneliness, yet it entirely lacked the personalising and moral elements that it would have had in some of the school lessons we have considered. This sense of detachment from reality partly arose from the list of topics, which could be said to ask for uncontroversial controversy, since none — except possibly the one about continued education — would be likely to generate much concern. But Mr Pattison's approach was consonant with this. When he interacted with his students — and once or twice he seemed hardly to be listening — his attention seemed to be upon preparing them for writing, and not at all upon influencing their views, as we might have expected in many of the school lessons we have observed. The two or three occasions when the discussion shifted into exploration of a topic rather than the production of ideas for writing were provoked by students who had strong views. Since the students were to be examined in the same way and for the same award as many of our school classes, we have here an undeniable difference of values between college and school. Mr Pattison's approach is consonant with the approach in other college English courses, and not with O-level courses in schools, that is.

Mr Peel's teaching of writing will be illustrated from two lessons; one concerned with 'the descriptive essay' was taught to a group of students, most of whom had already passed O-level language or its equivalent and were about to sit for RSA Stage III. Mr Peel's method is the same with all of his classes, he told us. From an examination paper he chose one or two titles which suggested the type of essay he wanted the class to practise. 'We realised yesterday that this ("A difficult journey") was a descriptive essay and therefore we have to watch very very carefully that we don't stray over into the narrative because, of course, question seven is the narrative essay.' From the list (1) A difficult journey; (2) Choice; (3) A modern social problem; (4) Is domestic life necessarily dull and frustrating; Discuss; (5) Amusing oneself with no money; (6) The first day at work; (7) A story beginning with the words, 'It might all have turned out quite differently if . . .', he decided that (1) and (6) are descriptive essays but advises against their tackling (6) because 'you haven't had the experience as yet'. Having decided which essay they would try he went through preparing it paragraph by paragraph so that they had a rough draft of the whole before they started to write. The heading for the second paragraph was to be 'geography' and Mr Peel spent 35 minutes suggesting what they might include. He decided they must think in terms of 'going over uncharted ground and our lack of experience . . . The difficulty behind the journey is that we're going over uncharted ground and whether it is a walk up the Dales or whether it is into a tropical country (there is) the idea of looking at the map and being able to track and visualise some of the difficulties . . .'. It seemed rather a contradiction that the girls had been advised not to choose 'The first day at work' because of their lack of experience; now they were being told to think of journeys in tropical countries and, even more amazingly, a quarter of an hour later they were being told to decide 'whether you're going to take pack mules the next part of the way'. The journey was 'over uncharted ground', yet Mr Peel spent almost a quarter of an hour talking about map reading, and contour lines, and reminiscing at some length about rock climbing in Iceland. This strange blend of anecdote and information continued through the whole lesson, Mr Peel ocasionally asking questions which received at most the briefest of replies; generally he spent his time suggesting subject matter while the girls had their heads down apparently scribbling notes.

If we ask what implicit messages about writing are being conveyed by these lessons, the answers might include:

i. That writing falls into discrete categories such as 'narrative', 'descriptive' and 'abstract'.
ii. That narrative is inferior in status. (Mr Peel's lively anecdotes about treks in the Himalayas inhabited a different universe from examination imperatives.)
iii. Surface rather than deep criteria determine structure: an essay of 650 words should have five or six paragraphs.
iv. That it was not for a student to generate the content of an essay but to receive it: Mr Peel normally supplied the content he wished them to use (in spite of having said, 'Only tackle those topics with

which you are conversant').

v. Writing is for genteel display, not for exploring experience. We found amongst a pupil's papers a model descriptive essay which the lecturer had taken from a book and distributed. Its topic was 'The Local Flower Show', and the genre to which it belonged can be seen from the last two sentences:

> 'The merry clink of cups from tea-sipping ladies lent a more refined air to the scene as I made my way past to the judging stand, where, in about a half hour's time, the results of the show would be given. I looked around and felt a warm glow of pleasure at being a part of this typical English Flower Show, knowing that when once the rivalry was over, everyone would share the happiness of the occasion, with its fairy lights and dancing on the lawn.'

It seems that further education is offering a retreat to the *belles lettres* version of English, now far less common in schools than it once was. The essential quality of this version is its separation from any content or context which might give verisimilitude to acts of communication. It treats reading and writing as skills separated both from the purposes of the reader or writer and from any situation except the examination room. Stylistic and social values are implicit but never made explicit: the source of values is the examination and not a social context. This version avoids both the personal concerns we have identified in schools and the work contexts which legitimate Communications.

Mr Peel made few references to the world of business, mainly turning to the examination for the conventions and priorities he taught to his students. However, the RSA Stage I examination also required a business letter, so in one lesson he asked them to draft a letter in which they were to apologise for being unable to attend an interview for a job, and to ask for interview at another time. Mr Peel made lengthy references to the importance of letter-writing in business contexts, but particularly its relevance to obtaining interviews for jobs. The tone and emphasis can be illustrated from the first minutes of the session:

> . . . And this is why the letter that we've been asked to write is so important. You've got so far as being invited to an interview. If you just don't turn up then not only have you lost the chance of a bit of experience, because, of course the more interviews you can get on, even though you don't get the job, the greater the experience you are gaining of talking to people. As it were, selling yourself. Because that is what interviews are all about, is selling yourself . . .

The students had already attempted to draft such a letter; Mr Peel, rather than asking for their versions and commenting on them, chose to provide them with a version he had himself drafted. After some comments about layout he dictated this version to the students. (We reproduce the letter here without the comments which he interspersed within it.)

> Dear Sir,
>
> Thank you for your invitation for (to) an interview. I was more than delighted (thrilled) that you should consider (deem) me a suitable candidate.
>
> Since receiving your letter I have been informed that the time of the examination I was to take on the morning of that day has now been changed to the afternoon. It is a three hour examination and does not start (begin) until 2.30 p.m. This has placed me in a very difficult position as *both* are extremely important to me. At the risk of offending you, for the sake of my long-term future I have decided to take the examination.
>
> The post for which I was to be interviewed is one which I would dearly love (to have), and I am wondering if under the circumstances it would be possible for the time or day of my interview to be changed.
>
> Yours faithfully,

Mr Peel's purpose in providing this example seems to have been to provoke discussion about an appropriate style for such a letter, this accounting for the alternatives (given in brackets). Students objected to 'dearly love' and 'more than delighted'; and their *sotto voce* comments included such expressions as 'soppy', 'lovesick', and 'over done' to characterise the style he had adopted. One student said, 'Might think you're too weak for the job and cry easily, something like that'. Another said, 'You've got to crawl'.

Mr Peel's response to whatever he heard of these remarks was ambiguous. On the one hand he led one of the class to say that the style was not formal enough; on the other hand he appeared to wish to justify it. The following remarks were inserted by Mr Peel into a discussion amongst the students, some of whom were highly critical.

i. '. . . Put yourself into that position. We really wanted that job. We've built ourselves up to the idea of going for an interview; we've decided what colour eye shadow to put on, what make-up to put on; we've even got as far as pressing the dresses you're going to wear . . . '
ii. 'You have in fact got to creep a little bit, as you say, because . . . '

Soon after this Mr Peel went through the letter again, deleting one of the options in each case, but taking little note of students' comments. At the end one student said, 'It's a load of creep'. As if in reply Mr Peel added:

> . . . if you look at it from (the other?) person's point-of-view, that they've been invited to an interview and yet you're going to do something in preference. You see they might take this as an affront.

The clash of perspectives between lecturer and student was recorded in fieldnotes at the time: Mr Peel was speaking for the perspective of the employer, and attempting to demonstrate to future employees their relative powerlessness in such a situation.

It has not been possible to test systematically the impact of Mr Peel's advice on the letter-writing style of the students. However, inspection of four letters written soon after this session and supposed to be addressed to prospective employers — though not necessarily in response to the same task — show some attempt to converge upon the recommended style. A few sentences drawn severally from them will illustrate this.

i. 'After great consideration to the above post and taking into account all you have to offer, I am very sorry to say . . .'
ii. 'Having received your reply to my application, I was pleased to find . . .'
'I must stress my disappointment and apology that . . .'
'I regret my grief very much . . .'
iii. 'In consideration with the two firms I had to takc in all possibilities . . .'
iv. 'I was very delighted when i received this invertation . . .'

It seemed that these four students (at least) had received the message about the necessity for a high style, but had some difficulty in sustaining it; there was no comparable evidence that the message about subservience had been received and acted upon. (We do not imply that these messages came only from Mr Peel's lesson, or even from lessons generally, since they are available enough outside formal education.)

All of these lessons treated the English curriculum as separate from and irrelevant to the personal concerns of the students, so that the sole session with personal elements stands out sharply. Mrs Sands first read with her students a newspaper article as a preliminary to writing a letter to the editor in reply. Such a purpose might well have generated a lesson primarily devoted to examination criteria, but in fact it was dominated by Mrs Sands' interest in the subject of the article, which gave a counterblast to puritanical feminism by arguing women's right to be as indolent as men. During the discussion she made many references to her own private life: buying a house, the size of her table, dancing classes, and writing to 'Jim'll Fix It'. As she said during the discussion, 'It's interesting how you always get all your students' attention when they're finding out something about you'. Considerable attention was given to explaining difficult words ('sloths', 'fledglings', 'clarion', 'Mandarins') and phrases to the students, in the traditional style of the 'comprehension' exercise. Later she indicated to the students what layout was expected for the letter, and then they wrote. On this occasion what might have been a typical examination-oriented lesson was turned into something different by Mrs Sands' relish of the topic, and also by her tendency to personalise the work as a control device to hold students' attention.

But it should be noted that though Mrs Sands spoke of her own private life she did not expect the students to do likewise, while the written task did not require this either.

4. Exercises in comprehension and written conventions in further education English courses

In our sample of school lessons we saw relatively few dealing with comprehension; it may have been important, but it was not the work which teachers generally wanted us to see. In the further education English courses it was probably accorded more time proportionally in the course and certainly it was presented to us as typical by all the lecturers in our 'traditional' English classes. All the lecturers regarded it as important, but their treatment differed. At High Street College Mr Peel was prepared to devote the major part of three or four successive lessons (that is three to four hours) to the preparation of a passage and the questions from an old RSA examination paper. Students would then be expected to spend another couple of hours writing the answers. At Smalltown College Mrs Sands dealt with the same material much more summarily expecting the class to read through a passage and prepare answers to the questions in half an hour or so. Mr Pattison, who was preparing his students for JMB O-level Syllabus D (the coursework option), was nearer to Mrs Sands, relying on one careful reading with interruptions to check that members of the class were understanding, followed by a few general observations before the questions on the passages were tackled.

What kinds of passage were given? Though Communications courses in BEC and TEC follow a policy of relating all work to the students' interests, which are assumed to be connected with their future jobs, RSA, although predominantly taken by would-be office workers, does not assume such unity of interest. Two of the passages, however, that we saw Mr Peel using were ones likely to interest young adults. One from an RSA Stage I paper came from a *Times* article on left-handedness, particularly school prejudice against left-handed children, and another from a Stage III paper was a longer extract from a Schools Council Working Paper on Community Service and the School Curriculum. Other passages which we saw from the students' files that they had worked on were not so immediately relevant to their experience ('Whose skull at Piltdown?' from *Strange Stories, Amazing Facts* or a passage about the coming of spring on a Scottish island or the Cabinet system in the 18th century). But even when the passages were likely to arouse the students' interest no attempt was made to ask for their own opinions or ideas: the questions asked only for selection of facts and rephrasing of words or phrases. The RSA I syllabus refers to the purpose of testing 'understanding and judgment', but in so far as reasons were required in, for example, the passage on left-handedness it was merely a matter of selecting from the passage — as this quotation (less than a third of the passage) shows:

> It seems, however, that teachers are still reluctant to share in this enlightened attitude. A recent study comparing left and right-handed 11-year-olds from a large national sample of the population showed considerable and significant differences between teachers' reports on left-handers and the results of objective tests. Teachers reported a greater tendency among left-handed pupils towards poor control of their hands, 'bad writing' and speech which was 'difficult to understand'. The National Children's Bureau, which carried out this research, tested for the truth behind teachers' observation. Standard tests of attainment and general ability, administered by the same teachers, showed no significant differences in performance between left and right-handed pupils. Likewise, clinical speech tests administered by doctors gave no factual backing to the teachers' theories.
>
> (i) What complaints are made by teachers about left-handed children?
> (j) Are their beliefs correct? Give a reason for your answer.

Mr Peel took his class slowly through both passages and questions. In this extract he is discussing a part of the passage that deals with the problems of a girl who writes with her left hand:

L. There are two questions I'd like to have a look at with you — the first one is (a) and the next one is (d). Now I wonder if first of all we can start with (d). Can you remember what we said the word 'cribbing' meant?
S. Copying.
L. Copying that's right. Now can you tell where in fact we come across the word in the passage?
(A student indicated the whereabouts of the word and Mr Peel read the relevant sentence.)
L. So why was she thought to be cribbing?
S. . . . (Inaudible)
L. Yes.
S. They didn't have the right equipment for her to use.
L. That's right, yes. I think we can summarise what was said by the fact not having the right sort of equipment, everything she did was not quite as the other girls and therefore in order to be able to get her shapes, to get her writing . . . she had to follow them very carefully indeed. So how can we say that in one sentence. Now remember we haven't to use the words from the passage. . . . What else could we use instead of 'cribbing' by the way?
S. Copying.
L. Copying yes I think that might be a much better word. Now see if you can draw together those ideas in one sentence. '(d) Why was she thought to be cribbing?' Remember what Joyce said and what Marcia said. Just one short sentence. Remember there's only one mark for it so we don't have to write a great deal. So you can use the word copying instead.

Comprehension as he taught it was not a skill that might one day be used elsewhere but an examination technique: 'Remember the amount you have to write is guided by the marks... Remember we've got to be rather careful...we don't use the same material in answering both questions. This is something we *mustn't* do if we're answering a comprehension'. With his more able class who were tackling Stage III Mr Peel had developed a technique of 'technicolour crayons' to underline the facts relevant for each question; he introduced further criteria but these were still concerned with examination technique:

> L. Now as soon as you've finished, ladies, the important thing is to see that you have in fact followed what the question says. You have extracted from what we underlined the most important aspects and you have actually included those in your answer. Then the other thing to check of course is that what you've written reads smoothly, doesn't just look as though you've copied chunks out and you get a disjointed piece of work. And then lastly, of course, I see Helen doing that now, just checking the number of words.

The examiner's assumption of a passive reader was strongly reinforced by the attitude of the students in this class. 'I like being told', said one; 'the lecturer helps you a lot', said another and yet a third commented how much better this was than school because, 'before we had to work it all out ourselves'. Paradoxically these passages were ones on which the students in other circumstances probably had points-of-view, yet they were not exercising any powers of analysis or synthesis they might possess. The examination offered little opportunity, the lecturer so structured his teaching that even that little became less and the students colluded enthusiastically. To the observer such training seemed not to be an initiation into comprehension but an initiation into unquestioning acceptance of the written word.

These may be thought harsh judgements; in the other classes comprehension practice was treated in a much more cavalier fashion. It was concerned with relatively trivial affairs — the problems of taming a garden (Mrs Sands), 'The last of the Prize fist fights' (Mr Pattison) — and was not to be taken seriously: it was all part of the examination game to be played according to the rules. The passages given might prompt an anecdote perhaps about a film or a television programme; the lecturers might add some interesting facts or comments from their experience. It was a relatively diverting way of spending half an hour, although the students did not enjoy the written work which the lecturers seemed to regard as a necessary concomitant.

Comprehension seemed to be accepted as a decontextualised skill to be acquired for a very restricted range of practices presented in a peculiar way: supplying the meaning of six words seemingly selected at random, picking out the author's view on a number of topics and presenting them, if possible, in your own words. No suggestion was offered in lessons that this ability might have relevance to work or leisure: its justification was the examination.

Only Mr Peel of the three FE English lecturers showed us a lesson in which he taught the written conventions, spelling and punctuation in particular. He began lessons with his less able class of shorthand typists with a list of spellings.

L. Now five little words then, plus one for good measure. Same as usual, most of them are very easy to spell but not only do I want the spelling correct but also I want the meaning put in as well. The first one is a word which we frequently hear today and that is 'component'...

'Delinquent', 'efficient', 'gradient', 'proficient' and 'recipient' followed and a quarter of an hour was spent in writing out the words, checking the spellings, and finding that meanings had been more or less understood.

L. Now we come to the word 'gradient' (spells) — it means, looking again at the dictionary — incline.
S. What?
L. Incline.
S. Inclined?
L. Yes, or a rise.

Mr Peel told us in interview: 'I always try, probably every other lesson, to give them five spellings. Now that takes the form of giving them words, some of which are fairly easy, others are possibly new words they haven't heard of'. The girls are told to note the meanings as well and Mr Peel said he tried to refer to the words in subsequent lessons. 'I try to get them to become aware of vocabulary. I think this is something that is important in linking with their future in shorthand and typewriting because when they are having letters dictated to them they may come across all sorts of words which they've never heard of before. The idea is not to be afraid of them.' Meanings were explained, not always very accurately, and coinages such as 'restorate' and 'provocate' were approved and accepted. Mr Peel was encouraging some interest in words and the class enjoyed the exercise which took up at least a third of the lesson. They did not seem to be gaining much confidence, if one judges by their success, and no attempt was made to explain or work out spelling rules; it was a matter of getting it right or more often correcting when it was wrong. But Mr Peel believed it was useful training and more than one girl referred to it gratefully, 'We do spellings here... I want to get better at spelling'.

Mr Peel devoted 48 per cent of class time not spent on literature to comprehension and other exercises, and by the second term both his classes were working through a succession of past examination papers. He told us: 'By the end of the first term (we have covered) paragraph construction, analysis of paragraphs . . . the construction of sentences and getting them to know what a verb, or adjective is. I usually try to get the descriptive essay and the narrative essay out of the way.' The girls had worked through exercises combining simple sentences into complex ones, correcting grammatical errors, practising the use of direct and indirect speech and so on. The exercises were those familiar from old School Certificate textbooks. (FE has continued to have faith in the isolated exercise for much longer than schools, as such a relatively recent publication as *English* by Rosser and McClintock (1974)[4], demonstrates.) The exercises were accompanied by dictated notes which always provided examples of correct usage, but the C.V.s (correct versions) that followed in the girls' files seemed to have a fair proportion of the errors preserved. As well as exercises on correct usage Mr Peel spent some time on grammatical terminology. Whether the girls had learnt about parts of speech before or not varied, but most seemed to feel that what they were doing was useful although one confessed, 'It don't make sense really'.

Mrs Sands spent 40 per cent of her time with a parallel class in Smalltown College on decontextualised exercises that included work on: homonyms, antonyms, homophones, jargon, clichés, abbreviations, prefixes and suffixes, and words of foreign origin, as well as spelling and punctuation. To take words from their context and relate them to rhetorical, etymological and semantic categories abandoned by linguists has long been discredited as a method of teaching English. The best that might be said for it is that by making words the object of explicit attention their shape and spelling might become more consciously available to future typists, though even this possibility lacks empirical confirmation. (That Mrs Sands, who approved of BEC, was aware that her methods would be difficult to justify was suggested by her failure to include them amongst the lessons we were invited to observe.) None of these activities is included in either the O-level or RSA examination; spelling, punctuation and the layout of letters were assessed indirectly in the examining of writing.

5. Conformity to surface criteria: an interpretive summary

Although we are considering three teachers in two colleges who were preparing students for four examinations there is every indication that 'General English' bears with it a marked ethos of its own. Most striking is the peripheral role played by the overt values of the world of business; apart from an insistence on acceptable spelling and punctuation and occasional self-legitimating references to the lecturers' experiences at work, the whole weight of justification fell upon the examination, which defined the values and skills that were transmitted and partly controlled the use of time. It is worth considering, however, why it was that Mrs Sands spent so long on irrelevant exercises, and why Mr Pattison, freed by an examination based on coursework to develop a new course, chose to remain bound by invisible chains. These activities, however superficially irrelevant, seem to have performed some function for the lecturers.

When we compare these courses with most English lessons in school fifth forms what is most striking is the acceptance of artificial activities which are at a distance from the concerns of students in their lives. The examination defines the essay as a set of genres — description, narrative, discussion — which exist in a limbo without context, audience or purpose. School English teachers struggle to find topics that their pupils can take seriously because they relate to their concerns; in these FE English courses it is often assumed that essay topics will be boring and distant from life. A lecturer expects 16-year-olds to plan trips in tropical lands; there is little or no concern to tap the students' first-hand experience. This artificiality is not perhaps far distant from what we found in one of the school departments; what sharply defines the difference between FE and school English is the former's deep-seated lack of concern for private areas of experience, and avoidance of personal responses to the world. As we have seen, when a topic calls for personal experience the lecturer hands responsibility to his students, unlike most schoolteachers who try to mould their pupils' deep criteria, to change at some depth their sense of what is worth writing about and how to write about it. In the college courses, on the contrary, there is little or no attempt to give students access to underlying principles; when the lecturers do 'teach' the content of writing they do so by laying it down authoritatively, sometimes as duplicated notes, sometimes by building notes on the board during teaching. The role assigned to the learner is that of acceptance, of taking over the lecturer's model without criticism and without insight into the deep criteria that make it what it is. Similarly, in the comprehension exercises, the questions do not require the student to bring his or her existing knowledge and concerns to engage with what the author of the passage attempts to communicate, but asks only for the selection of details and the paraphrase of the surface meaning of 'difficult' words and phrases. Both in the choice of passages and questions the student's perception of the world is kept at a distance.

In essay, comprehension and letter alike what is required is surface conformity, not personal commitment. There is no attempt in examination or in teaching to engage with the student as a person or to change his or her sense of reality: the stress falls on length, layout, propriety of content and tone, and the personality and values of the learner are treated as irrelevant. Other ways of putting it would be to say that the courses assumed an other-directed rather than an inner-directed ethic, or that they looked towards situations in which the students would not organise their own actions but would be organised by others. Surface criteria are more important than deep criteria; linguistic skills are to be exercised and displayed in separation from intention, for the private purposes of individuals are irrelevant. One of the investigators recorded in fieldnotes during a lengthy session that the course was 'preparation for boredom rather than for work'. Students were not expected to engage personally with the tasks, so that their interest was irrelevant; they were expected to carry them out, interesting or not, as they would have to as typists in an office. The values of the workplace took effect after all, but obliquely.

From the point-of-view of many English teachers in schools, used to a version of English that prides itself on engaging with pupils at a personal level, the foregoing interpretive account of English in four FE classes may read like an indictment. It is important, however, to see that this insistence on surface criteria, this drawing back from engagement with students' personalities, is an artefact of the FE context. Such teaching is one response to the practical realities of English in FE, not the result of perversity or incompetence on the part of lecturers. To understand the nature and limitations of these courses is halfway to understanding why Communications courses have been so widely welcomed. Schools have a captive audience over a period of years, so that teachers take a paternalistic view of their responsibilities, which seem to them to include 'pastoral' elements which involve attempting to penetrate at some depth into pupils' values and even personalities in order to change them. This has been particularly true of English teachers, many of whom believe that the study of literature gives access to particularly urgent systems of value. Colleges have a quite different relationship with students, who attend courses for a limited period, often voluntarily, and who view courses in terms of certification or vocational skills. (Eggleston has suggested that on a dimension Commitment-based — Contract-based, schools would tend to one end and FE colleges to the other, and this appears to correspond with the assumptions on which pedagogy and to an extent curriculum is based, though not always with the students' perspectives.)[5] Students and employers have to be persuaded of the relevance of courses; the students are older and often see themselves as autonomous adults. All these forces make it unlikely that colleges could sustain a paternalistic, pastoral view of their responsibilities to students, yet these students require qualifications. One solution to this is to focus on surface criteria — behaviour rather than attitudes, skills rather than principles — while treating the learner as a passive receiver of these criteria. (In another section we consider Communications courses as an alternative response to the exigencies of the college situation.) English courses in FE cannot be accused of indoctrination; changing students' deep criteria is not part of the strategy.

6. People and Communication in BEC: syllabuses

In presenting examples of FE English it has been necessary to make comparisons at various points with Communications courses, so that they already have what is perhaps a somewhat shadowy presence in this chapter. It is now our task to present the version or versions of Communications courses leading to qualifications validated by the Business Education Council (BEC). The starting point will be the official requirements of BEC, before moving on to a description of what we observed and were told. These include courses at two levels, General (the lower) and National.

There are no formal entrance requirements for BEC General, though the course is intended for young people who have completed their schooling. Students taking the one-year full-time Diploma course are required to complete eight modules of which three are compulsory, one of these being 'People and Communication'. (We shall take the liberty of abbreviating the title.) Unlike O-level English, BEC Communications is thus embedded in a group of vocational courses, and is planned to take advantage of this. The other compulsory courses are (2) Business Calculations and (3) either The World of Work or Elements of Distribution. The options form a long list which includes on the one hand topics such as 'Audio-Typewriting' and on the other 'Consumer Legislation' and 'The Co-operative Movement'. BEC General courses as a whole are assessed by four concurrent methods:

1. A written examination.
2. Assignments, some specific to a module (e.g. People and Communication) and others 'cross-modular'. (This opens up the possibility of collaboration in improving the writing done in the other modules.)
3. An oral test, preferably in conjunction with employers.
4. A college-based assessment, moderated by BEC.[6]

The BEC courses are intended to emphasise 'student activity rather than the detailed exposition of subject matter by the teacher', an emphasis that seems particularly appropriate to Communication courses.

The Business Education Council lays down objectives for People and Communication courses at both General and National levels. The statement of general aims for the General Level course links use of 'the spoken and written word' with both 'personal development' and 'effectiveness at work', and these are made more explicit in a list of learning objectives organised under the following headings:

On completion of the course, students should be able to:

A. Handle and understand appropriate types of written communications within their area of the business environment;

B. write accurately and concisely;
C. adopt an appropriate tone in written communications and be able to consider the effect of communication styles upon others;
D. listen to and comprehend spoken communications;
E. speak clearly and appropriately to individuals and groups;
F. adopt an appropriate vocabulary and tone and consider the effects of these upon others;
G. understand the function of written communications and records within an organisation and consider the effects of these upon their own work;
H. understand the functions of spoken communications and the effect of these upon working relationships;
I. understand their own and other people's role and function in the formal/informal networks within an organisation. They will understand the contributions accurate communications make to efficiency.

It should be noted that four of these nine 'general objectives' refer to spoken language; two refer to writing, one to reading, and one (G) to both writing and information retrieval, thus implicitly proposing an equivalence between spoken and written communication. The last general objective refers to people and communication within organisations, though this context is also mentioned elsewhere in the list of objectives. The full list is too lengthy to quote here, so its range and emphases will be represented by quotation and summary. In A, the 'types of written communication' are specified; works of reference are to include 'dictionaries, timetables, catalogues, telephone directories, library catalogues, almanacs, year books, etc.' and the students are to 'handle and understand . . . memoranda, letters, reports, minutes, notices, printed instructions, forms, invoices, statements, etc.' Writing (B and C) is to include awareness of tone and style and 'appreciation of another person or group's point-of-view'. Students, too, are seen as having points-of-view, since in both writing and speech they are expected to 'express . . . their own ideas, opinions, appraisals, criticisms, etc.' The objectives for oral communication (D, E, F and H) mention group discussion, the asking and answering of questions, and include (in section D) 'summarise orally the main points of a group discussion'. Appropriateness of vocabulary and tone is mentioned, and awareness of the significance of non-verbal cues. There is emphasis upon the relationship of speech and writing to persons and situations, including (in section F) 'raise objections, make suggestions or express disagreement without causing hostility'. Section G includes the filing and retrieval of documents, and summarising the contents of a file.

Readers of these objectives familiar only with 'English' courses are likely first to notice the total absence of literary studies and literary models of language, and yet the presence of 'personal development', apparently by other means. The marked emphasis on spoken language is equally striking since 'English' examinations treat speech as a quite separate matter. In contrast with English in schools, the objectives propose a wide range of written modes, and suggest reflective attention to the details of face-to-face talk — 'non-verbal cues', 'appropriate questions' and summarising group discussions.

The Business Education Council provided in 1978 a substantial set of 'Notes for Guidance' on 'Teaching/Learning Strategies and Assignments'[7] which comprises a general introduction and suggested assignments, some of them appropriate to Communications courses. Several points made in the introduction help to define the precise nature of assignments; it is assignments which introduce into Communications courses some of the characteristics which most separate them from English, both in its school and college versions. An assignment is, for example: 'A set of materials, documents, data and information which gives rise to a task or a number of tasks'. Although mention is made of the possibility of requiring students to collect their own materials, the norm — as far as our evidence goes — is for assignments (at least at the beginning of courses) to be based on material *given* to the students. Although a successful assignment is described as 'a selection from business reality', there are only very brief mentions of 'simulation' and 'appropriate style'. It is of the essence of these tasks that the student is to become more aware of the constraints on what is to be communicated and how it is to be said or written, constraints which arise from the precise situation, including the knowledge, relationships and purposes of participants. And yet the college classroom is *not* the office of a firm: whether students do become more aware of these constraints will depend upon the lecturers' success in involving them in simulation. It is surprising that these issues are not discussed in the BEC document.

As the sample assignments provided in the Notes for Guidance differ considerably from one another there is some difficulty in representing them here; the assignment that follows has been chosen because it is the one most like those assignments which we have seen in use.

The Crucial Visit

1. *Activity*

   Students are required to correct a draft letter, use a timetable, write memos, perform simple calculations and use a telephone.

2. *Situation*

   Students are required to adopt the role of a clerical officer employed by Universal Chemical Supplies Ltd. of Solihull. On the basis of the draft letter attached as Appendix 1 and the timetable and hotel price list attached as Appendices 2 and 3 [not reproduced here], students are required to carry out the following tasks:

   (a) Make a telephone booking for a single room with bath and for the meals required using the information supplied . . .
   Charge to UCS account. Estimate costs. Draft letter of confirmation to the hotel.

(b) Correct any spelling, grammatical, punctuation, stylistic and factual errors in the draft letter... Rewrite it with all details included in (c) below.

(b) Letter Note 1, use timetable... to plan the journeys, allowing Mr Smith to leave Wisbech as late as possible.
Note 2, insert estimated time of arrival.
Note 3, 4, 5, confirm arrangements to Messrs. Johnson, Wilson and Place.

Decide the appropriate form of the message of confirmation and the medium used to convey it.

Give reasons for the choices in answering notes 1–5.

3. *Materials*
The only materials required are duplicated copies of the draft letter, the extract from the B.R. timetable, and the hotel price list. Task (a) involves a simulated 'phone-call, which should be made as realistic as possible.

4. *Procedure*
After appropriate explanation by the teacher of the particular skills and abilities required in the assignment, students are set the tasks indicated under 2 above.
With regard to task (a) it is suggested that the teacher take the part of the hotel receptionist in order to simulate the booking by telephone of the room and meals required.
In the case of task (b) it is recommended that initial guidance is given on the types of errors which the letter contains. Also, since in the case of some of the errors, the correct version is not clearly apparent (eg. in the case of the inconsistencies in the dates) the teacher should adopt the role of the Office Manager and answer any queries raised by students.

Unlike some of the other sample assignments this does not necessitate group discussion, though such an approach would be possible. The task appears to call for (i) everyday reasoning about arrangements for a visit; (ii) the critical reading of a draft letter to detect errors of fact and divergences from written conventions; (iii) the writing of a memorandum. The reading and writing necessary is inseparably embedded in thinking about the requirements and constraints inherent in the simulated business context; learning to do the one is learning to do the other. This is highly characteristic of the situated assignments central to Communications.

BEC National courses[8] are a more advanced version of the BEC General courses. The formal entry requirements can be satisfied by a BEC General award at credit standard or by four passes in O-level or in CSE Grade 1. The Diploma course, which requires two years of full-time study, can be seen as equivalent in status to GCE A-level. 'People and Communication' is again a compulsory module along with other compulsory and optional modules, 12 in all. The time available is thus considerably less than that available for an A-level option in school, perhaps as little as a quarter. The official handbook lays out aims and objectives in detail; here we indicate some major differences between them and those for the General Level course. A new element is added to the general aims:

7.1.4 Encourage in the student a sensitivity to the ideas and attitudes of others, an awareness of how these can be affected by the student and other people, and a preparedness to adapt to them where necessary.

This concern with awareness of other people is reinterpreted at both levels of objectives. The General Objectives are:

Informing:
A. obtain, select and interpret information;
B. exchange information;
C select and use correctly appropriate formats for transfer of information;

Persuading:
D. identify false argument;
E. formulate rational arguments;
F. respond flexibly to personal factors;
G. engage in constructive discussion;

Operating:
H. understand the communication system of an organisation;
J. select and use appropriate media of communication;
K. adapt messages to the needs of different recipients;

Co-operating:
L. understand the constraints and opportunities of group working;
M. respond constructively to the contributions of others.

It should be noted that this range of rhetorical modes is different from the (largely unwritten) norms familiar in English courses where they are limited (with a few exceptions) to the modes latent in fiction, autobiography and *belles lettres*. These four headings, and their 12 sub-headings, are used to organise the Learning Objectives which are more extensive and detailed than those quoted above for Communications at the General level. For example, the 'Persuading' section includes such objectives as:

D1 recognise the place of emotional and non-rational approaches in persuasion and argument;
E2 select and structure his/her arguments;
G1 help others to say what they mean, i.e. identify their difficulties in communicating and offer positive help in overcoming them.

A sub-heading of the 'Operating' section is 'Adapt messages to the needs of different recipients', which includes such objectives as:

K3 relate written documents to a variety of recipients in respect of formality or tone, and level of technical diction;
K4 tolerate revision and editing of his/her own writings.

In reading through the National level objectives one is aware not only of the greater detail but also an increase in the level of reflective analysis required of students; D1, G1 and K3 seem to imply the ability to analyse as well as to utilise in speech and writing the understanding potentially arising from such analysis. Aim 7.1.4, quoted above, referred to sensitivity to the needs of others. We have chosen to quote K4 to indicate how this sensitivity is embedded in a context in which the writer is not always in control of the fate of what he or she writes. It is interesting to contrast this with writing in schools, which usually assumes tacitly that the context is like that of the poet or novelist who launches what he or she writes upon the world in the hope that it will generate an audience. Communications courses reflect another model of the relationship of writer to social context, in which the writer (or for that matter speaker) is not a free agent, but is constrained with respect to content, or purpose, or medium, or audience, or style, or all of these, and whose messages may be modified by others and used for their purposes. The values of the former model may be autonomy and integrity, the values of the latter perhaps verisimilitude and engagement with the world of action.

The National aims have a section 'Strategy and Implementation' which has no equivalent in the General level document. In this section the Business Education Council commits itself to an important methodological principle: they assert that what they call 'mechanical competence in written English' (i.e. mastery of the conventions) 'can best be achieved through work on assignments themselves and through the motivation which this can provide,' and thus reject the routine decontextualised exercises which we found in English courses in FE and even in some schoolteaching.

Some other assumptions of assignment work are also spelt out in this section:

7.4.7 The assignment sequence should:

(a) taken as a whole, provide a range of learning activities e.g.

speaking	listening	
reading	planning	drafting
writing	revising	note-making

abstracting and obtaining information:

(b) present a range of business communications which the student is required:
   (i) to prepare or clarify;
   (ii) to relate to context;
   (iii) to relate to varied recipients;

(c) require the use of a range of forms and means of communication:

(i) oral formats such as face-to-face, giving directions, taking messages, etc;
(ii) written format such as note for self, note for file, telex message, telegram, summary of correspondence, etc;
(iii) non-verbal formats such as tabular form graphics, charts, etc;

(d) allow for a diversity of student and class activity, eg.

whole class exercises	small group work
simulations	role play
individual enquiry	simple case study

(e) include a range of different types of business and business-related situations and contexts.

These notes make clear that what is intended is sharply different from 'English' in the range of genres or rhetorical modes, including the importance given to oral modes, in attentiveness to audience and situation, and possibly also in the range of learning activities. We shall see in the next section how far some of these aspirations were carried out in the courses observed.

Specimen assignments for Communications courses at National level were issued. They are similar to the General level assignment already reproduced except that the material to be understood and interrelated is more complex, while the tasks are more lengthy, often requiring extensive writing in various modes, and expect more sensitivity to situations and to people's attitudes (as the objectives indicated). In some assignments there is provision for students to work in groups, each adopting a role in the simulated situation, thus providing a further basis for talk and writing.

7. Two BEC 'People and Communication' courses

In spite of the relatively detailed learning objectives laid down by BEC, departments have considerable leeway in their interpretation of those guidelines. In this section we discuss two courses, one at National level taught by Mr Davidson at High Street College and the other at General level taught by Mr Hemmings at Smalltown College. Mr Hemmings appeared to be a teacher in transition, caught between the values of the English courses he had previously taught and the values of BEC; Mr Davidson, on the other hand, had enthusiastically embraced BEC and its goals. For this reason, in reporting what was observed we minimise the difference between the two levels in order to contrast the lecturers' approaches.

The account that follows is based, as before, on all the material relevant to these courses. The classroom observation component of the material is summarised in Table 8.2.

Table 8.2

Classroom observation in BEC courses

Lecturer	College	Course	Time observed	Nominal length of sessions
Mr Davidson	High Street	BEC National	443 minutes	3 × 3 hours
Mr Hemmings	Smalltown	BEC General	252 minutes	5 × 1 hours

The total observation time amounts to over $11\frac{1}{2}$ hours; this is distributed unevenly between the two courses partly because Mr Davidson had three-hour sessions and Mr Hemmings taught for only one hour at a time. (When the research was planned we were concerned to follow as wide a range of English and Communications courses as possible, and had not foreseen that we would wish to report BEC separately from other Communications courses.)

Though a sample of the students' written work is externally moderated, Mr Davidson was able to say, 'We have complete control over the assignments: we set them and we mark them'. The content of Mr Davidson's classes is quite different from English: literature of any kind is utterly excluded and students are expected to write in quite different ways from what they had been used to in English work at school. One of their initial difficulties is in making this adjustment. 'They think English rather than Communications', as Mr Davidson puts it. In their first term, he says, they repeatedly try to write an essay when what they are being asked to do is to write a report which presents information in schematic form with diagrams, tables and so on: 'Now you practically have to stand them against the wall and hit them and while you're hitting them tell them you will not write an essay, because unless you do this they will write essays and they will not do what we tell them to do . . . ' In one of his classes, while explaining the form of the report they will have to write, he reminded the students: 'Now folks, don't write essays'. And he reinforced this soon after when he explained how a report will be read not from beginning to end but selectively and haphazardly: often the conclusion will be read first, hence the need for a clear scheme and accurate sub-headings. What they write, in other words, will in no sense be read as literature — as self-expression, drawing upon individual experience or feelings.

All three of Mr Davidson's sessions were concerned with preparations for a writing task, though this is partly misleading since the preparation gave occasion — as we shall show — for other learning as well. During the first session the students were working in groups analysing responses to a questionnaire about their attitudes and those of other students to the Communications courses; the questionnaire had been designed by the class in an earlier session. The remainder of the session was taken up by teaching about writing reports, as a preparation for writing up the results of the questionnaire. The second session took place a week later and continued and completed preparation for the report. The third session we observed two months later. The class was involved in a lengthy assignment, or group of assignments, called 'The Recruitment Project', and at this stage Mr Davidson was teaching about advertising as a form of communication, in preparation for the writing of advertisements for a vacant post. This superficial account, however, fails to convey the nature of the teaching and learning that was going on: to do this it will be necessary to display part of the lessons in some detail. We will begin with the third, though the others were not markedly different.

The session began with preparation for a writing task that was highly contextualised in the world of business, but turned into an analysis of advertising for its own sake rather than as a means to carrying out the writing. The students had already embarked on the Recruitment Project, the first stage of which involved the preparation of a job description and a 'Successful Applicant Profile' for the post to be filled, and the design and costing of an advertisement for the post. Mr Davidson's style of teaching can be characterised as deductive rather than inductive. For example, he began by showing on the overhead projector a list of the elements of a Successful Applicant Profile:

Age
Sex
Education, qualifications, experience
Character, temperament, demeanour
Any special skills or qualities
Career interests and ambitions

These ready-made categories were presented to the students for them to use, so that discussion centred on how to interpret concepts such as 'temperament' and 'demeanour'. The categories were authoritative; it was for students to apply them. In this sense they were *deductive*, in comparison with teaching methods in which a teacher begins with descriptive categories suggested by students, and works *inductively* with them to refine and sharpen the categories. This use of lists and definitions was a frequent characteristic of Mr Davidson's teaching. Besides the list for the Successful Applicant Profile, he also used the overhead projector to give detailed definitions of social class according to the Hall-Jones scale, and used minor categorisations such as 'Gutter press', 'Medium', 'Quality papers'. It seemed that inherent in his deductive method of teaching was the practice of a particular kind of rationality that showed itself in these tightly defined categories. (It is tempting to relate it also to his use of 'scientific' and 'efficient': the concepts and the methods seem to belong together.)

During the first hour the lesson we observed was a typical Communications Studies exercise, a group of spoken and written activities set in an imaginary business context, and mainly shaped by the requirement of writing assignments for the BEC examination. The spirit of this first part can be gathered from this summary which came at the end of the hour:

> OK. Your organisation has created the job. You know the kind of person you want. The next stage is to go ahead and advertise it, which is what you in fact do if you're doing it in real life. What we have done so far is necessary if you are going to make a successful appointment. You've got to have some idea . . . an exact idea of the nature of the job you're going to fill, 'cos otherwise you won't be able to answer the applicants' questions in the interviews. You've also got to have a good mental picture of the sort of person that you want, otherwise you won't know what you're doing in trying to make the decision. So all this preparatory work is important. . . .

So far Mr Davidson's presentation is typical of the Communication Studies assignment, in that the nature of the task and the criteria governing its success or failure are firmly contextualised in the world of business. Indeed the lecturer easily carries his students with him, since he can so readily demonstrate that the tasks he has set — job description and successful applicant profile — relate closely to practical considerations in the commercial world. However, in the very next sentence he moves on to something which is slightly but significantly different.

> . . . Now we'll find that lots of organisations don't do this appointing very scientifically; a lot of it's very . . . rule of thumb. But I think you'll generally find that the bigger the organisation the more efficient; the more modern the organisation, the more scientifically it goes about appointing its staff.

At this point Mr Davidson is no longer merely defining and justifying his assignment by reference to the world of business, but is presenting a value-laden account of the world, which becomes most visible in the concepts of 'scientific', 'modern' and 'efficient'. The succeeding part of this long session was devoted to an extended presentation of advertising which, though superficially justified by the assignment, went far beyond the knowledge and understanding required to carry out the task of drafting an advertisement (a task in any case sharply bounded by the well-known conventions of the 'classified' columns). The students were in effect receiving a view of the world, or at least of the business world.

The first hour had been devoted to preparing for writing an advertisement; the following three-quarters of an hour was devoted to an account of advertising, after which the students worked in groups designing and costing an advertisement. (The quotations that follow come from the beginning of the time devoted to advertising in general.) Mr Davidson analysed advertising according to a communications model which represented it as a technical problem of conveying a message from an advertiser through a medium to a target group.

> ... All sorts of ways in which he can do it but he *has to* use one language or another. But also very importantly he has to define the precise nature of his target group. Because... he has to define the characteristics of his target group in order to choose the medium — singular — or media — plural — (for?) his message: he wants maximum contact at minimum cost.

The tendency of Communications models of this kind is to reduce all communication to neutral techniques, ignoring both aesthetic and politico-moral issues, since considerations of power and access to media, and of the eventual value of the messages are normally excluded from the analysis. The world is as it is: the student's task is to learn to operate efficiently in this world. Such a view of the world is not really neutral, since under the apparent neutrality lie assumptions about what constitutes efficiency and about what is worth pursuing.

Mr Davidson was giving his students far more than a training in vocational skills. Let us consider an episode in the second session when he was showing them a range of visual means of representing information — in our view an admirable extension of the range of Communications teaching. He spent 40 minutes in conveying to the students the concepts 'subjective' and 'objective', leading to a presentation of the concept 'empirical method'. Via question and answer and detailed illustration he moved through the difference between statements of fact and statements of value, the former illustrated via exact measurement ('Fred is five foot eight inches tall'), the latter via personal prejudice ('Fred is a nice chap'). This distinction was carefully established by discussion and by emphatic and authoritative definition inscribed on the blackboard to be copied down in the students' notes. 'Objective' was 'having regard to the facts as established by investigation'; 'Subjective' was 'having more to do with feelings which can often fly in the face of empirical evidence'. (The writing down of formal definitions seems to ascribe an impersonal finality to the knowledge.) Later discussions, controlled by Mr Davidson, dealt with subjectivity as irrationality (refusal to wear seat-belts), as distortion of the truth by self-interest (witnesses in a court case, or opposing sides in an industrial conflict). 'So it's extremely difficult to be really objective', Mr Davidson tells them, 'because in order to be really objective you've got to be fully aware of your own personal hang-ups, biases, your prejudices, your conditioning, education, social background, etc. etc. To be fully aware of all those things, well not many people can manage to do that. So to be truly objective is extremely difficult and most of the descriptions that people make of things usually have some element of subjectivity'. Thus concludes a sequence of teaching. This attempt to generate concept formation is not central to the direct task in hand, is not necessary to write up a report. Moreover, the ideological priorities here are an inversion of the priorities of school English: personal experience, immediacy, subjectivity are treated here with ruthless scepticism; they are sources of prejudice which distort objective knowledge. Here and elsewhere Mr Davidson is offering a very precise model of the world: distrustful of the personal/experiential dimension, perceiving society as an arena of contesting individual interests, identifying decision-making as based on bureaucratic procedures rather than ethical imperatives, seeing language in a functionalist manner.

Mr Davidson was highly attentive to the uses of digression and a great deal of information was transmitted en route by this means. For instance, seeking an example to demonstrate the way of using a line-graph: 'If you wanted to do a line graph showing the rise in population of Britain over the last, say, 1500 to the present day. How would you do it?' There ensued a history lesson lasting more than seven minutes covering by discussion a range of topics including the effects of disease on population, rats and the pathology of plagues, gin-drinking in the 18th century, effects of the Industrial Revolution, medical improvements and so on. Other sources of illustration in classes were drawn from politics, the legal sphere, industrial relations, road safety, current affairs. At one point Mr Davidson discussed how advertisers choose appropriate target groups for their advertisements, and described different kinds of newspapers and why they charged different fees for advertisements; the discussion of the readerships of different papers led into disquisitions on social class and on how newspapers are financed. A short quotation will give the tone of this lengthy section:

> People in social classes A and B read the *Guardian*, *The Times*, the *Telegraph* more than other newspapers, therefore that's where advertisers have to place their advertisements if they want to reach them. That's why they can afford £10,000.
> (The charge for a full-page advertisement.)

He was offering a sociology of newspaper readership which was heavily value-laden: more than once the *Daily Mirror*, *Sun* and *Daily Star* were called the 'gutter press'. The *Guardian* by contrast, which Mr Davidson always carries around with him, was an occasional source of reference for relevant illustration. More significant, however, is the particular moral universe that is assumed within Mr Davidson's teaching. As we have seen, what is positively valued is businesslike, efficient, liberal, utilitarian, forward-looking, factual.

It will already be clear to the reader that the range of tasks required of Mr Davidson's Communications students was considerably wider than would be found in English, especially in school English. In the first half-term of their BEC Communications students do work on tracing and collecting information, how to use a commercial library, the 'new information technology', how to make useful notes, how to cite bibliographical sources; the second half-term includes how to write a business letter, how to draw up and use a questionnaire, how to write a report. One class was partly taken up by a lecture/discussion on the different forms of representing statistical information via line-graphs, bar charts, pictograms and so on. Another class involved a good deal of time on costing different newspaper adverts based on a complex scale of charges. Such detailed attention to formats for business letters, to a schematic structure for a business report, and to the elements of a job description — an approach based on a model of the business world — is alien to school English.

This is underlined by Mr Davidson's insertion of Communications work into a broader frame of reference. At several points the 'real world' of business practice was signalled. He introduced the technique of report-writing: 'Okay, In the great big world of work there are two forms of written communication' — and he wrote on the blackboard 'Letters' and 'Reports'. In another class advertising was carefully introduced via a model of inter-personal communications and as simply a broader commercial extension of 'Communications'. A second aspect of this is the insertion of Communications work into the broader curriculum of the students by reference to other BEC courses. At one point, explaining that the advertiser wants maximum contact at minimum costs, he asked: 'what's the posh phrase for that . . . Think of your Accountancy'. The students saw Communications as 'fitting' with their business courses. One student, Dawn, found an underlying identity to all her courses: 'They all tie in with the same thing with being the same course'. Paul also found Communications and his other classes 'fairly much the same': 'Every lesson we have sort of binds in with every other lesson. There's bits in Economics which will come into Communications . . . '

Another aspect of Mr Davidson's teaching came very close to 'English', however. There was some expectation among other departments that Communications staff would teach written conventions such as spelling. Though Mr Davidson saw Communications as involving a great deal more than English he accepted that to some extent he had to teach some of the 'basics'. This was conditional on the needs of his students: 'I think the main thing is that students should be good at English as a base, if they're good at English as a base then you don't have to spend all your time doing remedial English with them'. However, even BEC students — most of them with several O-levels — had particular weaknesses. Mr Davidson corrected their written work with the English teacher's attention to spelling and punctuation: errors were painstakingly indicated in red ink. 'Content and presentation good, but a *lot* of English errors' was the comment on one piece of student work for instance. And in class he commented on spelling. For instance, he points out a mistake in one of the groups' questionnaires: he asked the class how 'questionnaire' is spelt, spelt it out himself and observed: 'As in "legionnaire" — it's French'. Later, when writing on the blackboard, he halted and turned to the class:

L. How do you spell 'recommendations'? Paul?
Paul (hesitates) I can't spell.
L. I know you can't. That's why I asked you.

In another class, while dictating some notes, Mr Davidson asked the class how 'principal' is spelt and again pinpointed one student (who made a hash of it). Other students hazarded guesses before Mr Davidson said: 'Look, there's an easy way to remember it, a little mnemonic. Help you remember it. The Princi*pal* is a *friend* of mine'. This kind of attention to spelling, and the use of mnemonics, is recognisably part of the English teacher's repertoire.

In discussion we asked Mr Davidson and his colleagues whether their courses were likely to produce submissive employees. Although this appeared to be an unfamiliar way of looking at it, Mr Davidson was able to reply confidently:

> ... One of our aims is to get students to think for themselves, to discover evidence, to weigh up evidence, to make decisions and the way to proceed rationally, to do as the evidence appears to indicate, rather than do as somebody tells them to do.

There seemed to be a good deal of truth in this account, in that Mr Davidson's sessions included opportunities for the students to apply, individually and in groups, the productive and analytical techniques he taught; certainly he did not suppress their opinions. It was rather the whole framework in which these activities took place that was uncriticised, taken for granted. This is what would have most struck a schoolteacher of English: not only the 'public' topics, and their treatment as subjects for 'public' detached analysis, but the withdrawal from explicit value judgements, apart from those based upon ideas of effectiveness. In the case of advertisements what was most noticeably lacking were responses to the aesthetics of advertising language of the kind associated with *Culture and Environment*[9] — and any ethical criticism of a consumer society large parts of whose expenditure is individual and manipulated by industrial producers. The critical training offered by Mr Davidson — and we do not wish to question its existence — appeared to stop short of these aspects of the world.

Mr Davidson provided us with copies of the classroom materials that he planned to use during the year and these allow us to characterise the relative emphases he intended the course to have, though he may have made modifications in the event. The materials comprised the Recruitment Project — divided into seven stages including the one which we observed — and six other assignments, each likely to take up from two to four three-hour sessions. A large proportion of this work — more than three-quarters, that is — was related to simulated business contexts and tasks, of the idealised kind already referred to. Most of the tasks included written work, sometimes for assessment and sometimes not, though discussion usually played some part in the preparation for writing. The written modes required were various: notes for a lecture, a questionnaire for other students, a job description, advertisements, memoranda, a leaflet, reports, agendas for meetings, and letters written for various purposes to a diversity of recipients. Oral productions were assessed on two occasions: for one assignment the students were to work in groups to prepare and present submissions as if from interested parties to a public inquiry about a proposed by-pass; oral elements of the Recruitment Project (probably including the simulated interviews) were also to be assessed. Although three or four written pieces were assessed, it is fair to say that in this BEC assessment considerable weight was given to oral communication. In the teaching of the course oral elements were even more important: small group discussion and role play are mentioned in many of the assignments, though it is not clear precisely what the latter amounted to in practice; some of the sessions we observed included collaborative work between small groups of students on tasks which they had been given. Unfortunately we were not able to observe occasions when Mr Davidson encouraged his students to reflect upon their experience of group work, though this is mentioned in the materials. (It is interesting to note that extensive digressions, including the one on advertising described above, were proposed explicitly in the materials as a deliberate element in the course under the heading 'Spin-off Topics'.)

Besides these assignments, BEC National requirements include 'cross-modular assignments', which are assessed by a technical department for their content and by Communications lecturers for their effectiveness as communications. Mr Davidson's class completed three cross-modular assignments during the year, part of the time being provided by various technical courses. The second of these assignments concerned four alternative proposals for the use of a site owned by a local council: the students, working in groups of four, were to simulate a council planning committee by examining critically the four proposals, deciding which was in the town's best interests, and to make a prepared oral statement justifying the choice, supporting the statement with visual aids and written handbills.

(Information about the proposals and about the imaginary town was provided.) In this assignment the heaviest emphasis fell upon group collaboration and oral presentation; students were assessed both as a group and individually.

Mr Davidson is an experienced and successful lecturer: his lectures were admirably planned with nothing left to chance, ran smoothly and undoubtedly carried the students with them. They were also very complex events, made up of a variety of strands that it is not easy to separate.

i. The students learnt communicational techniques and conventions appropriate to their future work. The techniques and conventions were treated as a neutral methodology, though it did not seem neutral to the observer.
ii. All of the assignments were given contexts in imaginary situations, usually but not always in business, which led to consideration not only of appropriateness of content and style but also of other groups' interests and concerns.
iii. Along with the techniques, conventions and knowledge the lectures projected a preferred view of the world. This included elements highly relevant to business — advertising, for example — and more general assumptions. Integral to both of these was a form of rationality characterised by deductive processes based on authoritative category systems.
iv. The kinds of writing done were wider in range than would be expected in an 'English' course whether in school or college.
v. Considerable attention was given to oral communication, even though in the lessons we observed class-discussion and group-discussion occurred as means and not as a focus of attention. This included some reflection upon the requirements of collaborative work.
vi. Although there was little or no overt discussion of values, values were inherent in much of what was taught, particularly those values appropriate to middle and lower management.
vii. Students had considerable opportunity to discuss and choose within the given frameworks. Many believed that they had benefited in confidence or oral skill from the course.

We are able to confirm that this account is accurate since two years earlier we had carried out a pilot study in High Street College, observing 12 hours of a BEC National, and three hours of a BEC General course, both taught by Mr Davidson and his colleagues. Although the details of the assignments had changed, the structure, emphases and procedures had remained constant. As we have shown, Mr Davidson is a teacher who was well prepared by his experience and position for the introduction of Communications courses; he has accepted the values and procedures appropriate to situated assignments and, along with like-minded colleagues, has put them very fully into effect.

For Mr Hemmings of Smalltown College, BEC People and Communication seemed to be something much less clear-cut. In teaching at BEC General level he had collaborated with a colleague in preparing assignments:

> I've got a bank of these and I just pick out the ones at the time which seem to fit in or be relevant.

This contrasted sharply with the closely structured course taught by Mr Davidson at High Street College; when he was teaching Mr Hemmings often seemed to be improvising both content and teaching strategies.

During a discussion at the end of the course Mr Hemmings expressed a qualified approval of the aims and methods of BEC communications; after initial scepticism he had found that 'the aims behind it are quite good'. In an earlier interview he had said of his students' experience of English in schools, 'They've had the formal approach, written exercises that they had to churn out daily, and I think they eventually get fed up with that system'. Yet what he said on the same occasion about his teaching of the BEC course suggested that he was in two minds about this: 'From half-term until Christmas it's all basics — apostrophes, spelling, letter-writing'. (This was confirmed by a 'Record of Work' which he made available to us retrospectively.)

Although we have quoted above (p. 318) the passage from BEC National handbook which urges that written conventions be taught incidentally and as the need arises during work on assignments, this has to be set against a qualifying pronouncement in the corresponding BEC General handbook that 'formal exposition by the teacher is an essential prerequisite of much of this learning'. Mr Hemmings' teaching responded to the spirit of the latter rather than the former pronouncement; much of his teaching was informal exposition combined with note-taking and with assignments involving the students in 'practising' what they had been taught, rather than the larger-scale tasks recommended by BEC, which require students to solve a communication problem by taking into account the demands of an imaginary situation. Thus Mr Hemmings' interpretation of BEC Communications approximated more to the norms of college English courses than to the version of BEC that Mr Davidson exemplified.

'We are still teaching English', said Mr Hemmings, 'but we are teaching with an aim in mind — to fit in with their eventual job'. It is possible to estimate the relationship between his course and work in a business context by examining Mr Hemmings' Record of Work, the written work of selected students, and the records of classroom observation. The introductory sessions first deserve attention: 'In the first week, just to find out what their standards of English are, I show them a film, then give them a series of questions on it to incorporate into an essay'. Mr Hemmings had learnt that students 'tend to be more interested, give better results if they've had some input'. The film he chose is not perhaps surprising for a communication course; it was a piece of South African propaganda, *Land of Promise*. In the piece of writing that followed one student described South Africa's industrial and mineral wealth, its parliamentary system, its variety of languages, the excellence of its table wines and its weather. 'It is governed by Parlimentary Democrasy. The courts are independent and the press free . . . The attractions of Africa are 300 sunny days a year, the space of which it has a lot . . .' And after five paragraphs of eulogy, the student concluded, 'It also has its disadvantages like shortage of water and Industrial polution. I thought the film from which I gained the information was very one-sided and tried to show only the best side but as we know everything has a bad side.' Considering that the class went on later to look at advertising techniques it seemed a strange choice to use a film such as this as a source of information. Mr Hemmings seems not to have perceived the film as an act of communication with a political context, with an intention to change people's perceptions and an identifiable audience, though the film would have provided an admirable opportunity to analyse how material can be selected and presented in order to mislead. Instead he saw it with the eyes of the traditional English teacher, as a context-free statement that could be used to test composition and comprehension — or rather that unrealistic and decontextualised activity that passes for comprehension in English examinations. His 'English' perspective had deleted from awareness some of the central perceptions of Communications. There was no link with jobs in this introductory work.

Our next task will be to characterise each of the main elements in Mr Hemmings' course, and to consider their relationship to employment in business. (As far as possible we are using the lecturer's own terminology.)

i. Communication in the Future	5 weeks
ii. Spelling, Apostrophes, and Business Letters	9 weeks
iii. Oral work	3 weeks
iv. Memoranda, Report Writing etc. (Forms of Communication)	4 weeks
v. Examinations and Examination Practice	6 weeks

(The remaining seven weeks are described as: Introductory, Revision, Summary of Term, Diagrammatic Representation etc.; each 'week' refers to three one-hour sessions.)

'Communication in the Future' was described by Mr Hemmings in this way:

> In the first term I deal with communications from the business angle in the sense of all the different forms of communications and all the difficulties that can arise through communications. I show them one or two videos of people communicating.

After some practice in using the library, the class learnt about organisation in business, and made a chart of communication in an organisation (though this amounted to no more than lists of work-roles grouped in departments and arranged in a hierarchy). We can show something of the more general outcomes of this work by quoting from two students' notes. Under the sub-heading 'Forms of Media of Communication' one began: 'There are over 100 different ways, apart from direct speech, in which communication can take place in a large enterprise', and she went on to specify 'Written', 'Oral', 'Non-verbal', 'Technological' and 'Visual', listing a few examples under each heading. Her notes on 'Causes of Difficulty in Communication' were even more cryptic, but another student wrote at greater length:

> Policies are distorted, decisions are resented, and orders are not carried out as intended; supervisors feel that they are not a true part of management, and employees generally feel unimportant, insecure; and that they are not taken into confidence of the administration.
> Most of these troubles stem from the inefficiency of the communication between supervisors and those above and below them. It has been estimated that seventy percent of oral communication is bound to be distorted, misunderstood, rejected, forgotten, or disliked. The longer the time after communication before action is required, less is the likelihood of its purpose being fully understood and of it being carried out correctly.

These notes, composed by the students themselves, give some impression of the content of this part of the course. One student listed the assignments she had completed, including 'Library Work Sheet', 'Advertising in Communications', 'Pictures in Advertising', and 'Glossary of Communications', each with a separate grade. Inspection of this written work showed it to be very unlike the situated assignments proposed by BEC; most of it was either essays in a typical social studies mode or limited 'English' tasks. For example, some sessions on advertising culminated in an assignment which consisted of five short tasks, one of which was:

> (4) Alliteration is the use of words beginning with the same letter, e.g. The *s*ea *sh*immered and *sh*one in the *s*corching sun. See whether you can find any examples of alliteration in your adverts. Why do you think it is used?

This is not far from the exercises to be found in a certain kind of English textbook.

In conversation and in speaking to his class Mr Hemmings made a distinction between 'Communications' — the work described in the previous paragraph, for example — and 'English', which seemed to be mainly concerned with written conventions. He taught the class for three hours each week: six of the 34 weeks were devoted to spelling and punctuation, two to the format of business letters, and one to homophones and malapropisms. This amounted to more than a quarter of the whole course. As he had told us, 'From half-term until Christmas it's all basics'. His students were expected to work through a pocket guide which in its spelling section had long lists of words, and three of their BEC 'assignments' were spelling tests. Assignment 12, for example, was 30 words 'absence to intelligence', 13 was 'accidentally to mathematician'. (For some reason the latter part of the alphabet received scant attention.) The words were not obscure, they were all ones that students were likely to meet in everyday usage, but except for the fact that they were in alphabetical order there was nothing to make them particularly memorable. Punctuation generally received less attention, but Mr Hemmings' class had in their folders dictated notes on the use of full stops, commas, apostrophes, exclamation and question marks. It seemed strange that this was the lecturer who had spoken of students' boredom with 'the formal approach'.

In one lesson on the apostrophe he presented a notice which included the phrase 'to student's attention' when a number of students was being referred to, and asked for an explanation of the error. One student offered:

> Because it's students as a whole. There should be another 's', but instead he's crossed the 's' off and put the apostrophe.

Mr Hemmings rejected this account by saying, 'I don't think anyone is actually aware of the rule'. It was as if he had to establish the students' lack of understanding in order to have the right to correct it. Generally the students took little part in these lessons. During the year they completed 12 assignments, which were either spelling tests or exercises in correcting errors, and these all contributed to the final grade for the course. He himself characterised his approach in this way:

> I'm one for formal English . . . I'm one that believes there is a right way of doing things. The exam to a certain extent gets in the way of that, but it's not too bad. It's business oriented, but they still have to produce a decent standard of English, so I don't feel there's too much conflict.

It appears from this that Mr Hemmings' conception of standards in English were bound to surface criteria, and that he had not accepted BEC's implicit shift to a more relative value-system that responded to the changing requirements of purpose, audience and situation, and included deep as well as surface criteria.

The three weeks of oral work which took place during the second term showed a quite different relationship to the world of business. They had been preceded by two weeks during which the class prepared for job interviews by writing a job description, an advertisement, a curriculum vitae and notes on interviewing. The main purpose of the oral work itself appeared to be to give each student the experience of being interviewed. At first, the students were set to discuss in groups what questions they would ask of a candidate for the first post in question; their ideas about this were not discussed, for it seemed that the purpose of this was to allow Mr Hemmings some time (seven minutes) in which to brief the students who were to act as a panel of interviewers for the first applicant. Later, a similar briefing was given to two more panels, for there was time during the hour for only three interviews. After each interview Mr Hemmings first asked the students for comments, elaborated upon these, and added some of his own. It is these comments by lecturer and students which enable us to discover which aspects of the interviews were being brought into the focus of attention. In response to Mr Hemmings' invitations, one student criticised an interviewee for failing to ask questions. Another student made a point about the content of what had been discussed, and Mr Hemmings tried to steer attention by asking, 'What about the speech of the person being interviewed, oral effectiveness?' The reply to this, 'Too quiet', led to an exchange about demoralisation, which the lecturer concluded by saying:

> You can always bring up that point at the end... you can say 'I would rather like to tell you about such and such'. (omission)... Don't tail off because one question hit you like a thunderbolt...

The other points he made included:

i. 'Got to try and compose yourself....'
ii. 'I thought the introduction was very good, very clear... It set the candidate at ease....'
iii. 'Couple of questions the panel almost answered themselves while they were asking it.'
iv. '...could have elicited a bit more information from her about (her interest in?) current affairs.'

The lecturer's comments referred predominantly to the interviewers' strategies rather than the applicant's, in a proportion of seven to three. (A similar emphasis occurred during simulated interviews during different courses in other colleges.) In their comments the students referred equally to interviewers and applicant (three and three). Of particular interest is the help offered to interviewees, since this must have been a major purpose of the activity. Mr Hemmings spoke of 'oral effectiveness' and seemed to refer mainly to voice projection and clarity of enunciation. He suggested that interviewees should always ask questions and urged that they should not allow themselves to be flustered by difficult questions, while one student wanted longer answers than a colleague had provided during the simulation. Most of the discussion, however, referred to content, and not the speech itself. (An interesting strategic issue was raised by one girl: what should one say if asked whether one intended to marry?) In this oral work the relation to the world of business had shifted; the purpose was now to get students a job, not to help them to the skills needed to carry it out once they had it. 'Communication' here, as in advertising, becomes synonymous with 'impression management'. Yet Mr Hemmings, like other Communications lecturers, found it easier to advise the interviewers than the interviewee; no theoretical framework was available for discussing self-presentation, so he had to fall back on vagueness and commonsense practical advice instead of communication theory. Nevertheless, in comparison with other sessions concerned with oral communication in any of the college courses, this seemed most likely to be useful to students, and to come closer to reflective consideration of speech, though it could hardly be called systematic.

Apart from a substantial block of time devoted to examinations the other main component in Mr Hemmings' course was the time spent on topics which could be grouped together as forms of communication, including memoranda, telegrams, note-taking, reports, telephone, telexes, note-making and memorising. As the topic of memoranda was allocated two full weeks, the treatment of the others must have been somewhat cursory. To teach The Memorandum — a favourite Business English topic — Mr Hemmings gave the students seven pages photocopied from a textbook. The author of the book tried to make commonsense seem erudite by inventing pseudo-technical concepts such as 'supportive function', 'clarifications or confirmations, motivations or exhortations', and 'synthesis of theme'; such mystification is not helpful to learners.

The students took little or no part in the session on the memorandum; indeed, our transcript shows Mr Hemmings to have spoken for ten minutes without any student contribution during one part of the lesson. The style, however, was far from that of the formal lecture. He alternated quotations from the text with his own commentary. For example, he quoted:

> Such a definition emphasises the brevity of many memorandum messages . . . and focuses attention on their supportive function in helping personnel to report, to plan, or to act upon the flow of business activity.

Mr Hemmings' style of commentary can be illustrated by the following:

> Once again the contents, the style of the memoranda varies considerably. It depends on what sort of memo you're writing as according what style you use. OK, you use the style to suit the kind of memo which you are writing, obviously. So it says here, style of memoranda varies enormously. 'Directives, for example, from a Managing Director or a chief executive may be couched in formal depersonalised terms.' In other words, rather than to

'Dear Bill' it could be 'Sir'. Or there's an example which I thought was quite amusing in this college a few years ago. . . . . . .

And Mr Hemmings launched into a lengthy anecdote. He had told us: 'I don't formalise things, write it down beforehand, think out the night before what I'm going to do. . . . ' but the comparison of his improvisation with Mr Davidson's careful preparation is very much to the advantage of the latter.

It is difficult to estimate the function of this part of the course in relation to the students' future employment. It seems unlikely to contribute much to their competence as typists: they are more likely to type others' memoranda than to write their own. Nor is the combination of textbook prose with random gossip likely to contribute much to their understanding of business, though it might persuade the more gullible that there are erudite mysteries beyond their reach. The written outcome of this part of the course was (in the case of one girl) two pages of notes on Formal Letters, one on Memorandum, and a half on Letters of Application. Such notes do not seem likely to increase the students' understanding, not so much for example as the four business letters drafted in other parts of the course.

It is not easy to characterise this course because of its ambiguities. It came closest to the BEC norms in the work on interviews, which proved to be the part of the course most appreciated by the students whom we interviewed. Those parts of the course we have given the headings of 'Communication in the Future' and 'Forms of Communication' were far from the BEC expectations and only superficially related to preparation for future jobs in business. The didactic style of teaching allied to note-taking and essays are not unlike the pedagogy of traditional, content-oriented versions of history and geography. The knowledge being transacted was abstract, separated from the learner's experience, controlled by the teacher, and assessed in written form. It was related only via the lecturer's impromptu monologue to situations in which people choose to talk or write in this way or that; the students were not involved in simulated activities like the BEC situated assignments. The most substantial part of the course was that on written convention and here the content and pedagogy were precisely those of Business English. The emphasis was upon surface criteria which were taught through detailed notes, and practised by completing exercises. These assessed exercises were called 'assignments', though they entirely subverted the BEC requirements.

In Mr Hemmings we have a teacher in transition. He has had to accept the framework of BEC, but he uses that framework and its accompanying terminology with assumptions and priorities derived from an alien system, Business English. His practice is precisely what is intended by the phrase 'Innovation without change'. (It is not unlikely that as BEC courses are increasingly taught in schools similar pseudo-metamorphoses will occur, with the BEC label being attached inappropriately while the teachers continue to teach as before.) The BEC policy is to develop communication skills by setting to students problem-like tasks whose solution will help them to become more aware of how to shape what they say and write in the light of purpose and situation. Mr Hemmings' course ascribes a far more passive role to the learner, and focuses attention on surface criteria such as spelling and punctuation instead of upon the deep criteria that arise from the context.

During the three years that the course had been running, it had been inspected twice by external moderators nominated by BEC but on neither occasion had received adverse comment. Mrs Sands (whom we have seen as an English teacher) was collaborating with Mr Hemmings in the teaching of BEC General courses; she said during our discussion with her and Mr Hemmings, 'We've now discovered that provided you can justify yourself in BEC jargon you can do anything really'.

Our rather limited materials have nevertheless enabled us to present one course — Mr Davidson's — which fully exemplifies the BEC principles at National level, and another at the General level based upon quite contrary principles. It seemed to us as observers, however, that — in their very different ways — both lecturers were doing something rather different from the accounts which they gave to themselves.

8. **Communications courses in TEC and City and Guilds**

During the first pages of this chapter we made a provisional distinction between Communications in BEC on the one hand and in TEC and City and Guilds examinations on the other, pointing out that lecturers concerned with courses in the field of business studies provided a different cultural milieu to receive the principles of Communications from those who taught in the field of craft and industry. Whether these divergent cultural histories have led to radically different priorities and emphases in the Communications courses themselves is an empirical question to which we turn later; it is this that has persuaded us to report separately the data from each group of courses, even though this results in each case in a smaller corpus for analysis and exemplification. In this subsection we are reporting on six courses in two colleges; these are summarised in Table 8.3. In two courses students were being prepared for examinations controlled by the Technician Education Council, in one for an examination administered by the City and Guilds of London Institute for the Construction Industries Training Board (CITB), and in the other three either for the City and Guilds papers in Communication Skills or for equivalent college awards.

In considering these courses we first demonstrate the curricular range to be found within them. In so doing such issues as these will be in mind:

(a) Had the principles of Communications courses been accepted and put into effect, with situated assignments and some reflective analysis of the relationship between communications and their contexts?
(b) Or did traces remain of older perspectives such as social education or basic literacy?
(c) What theoretical structures — if any — were provided to aid students' reflections upon communication?
(d) What values were implicit in the courses? Were they like those in BEC?

In arriving at tentative answers to these questions it was necessary to consider each session separately, but for the reader's sake we shall not attempt to reproduce the heuristic sequence, which was extremely lengthy. Instead we present a set of 11 categories organised under five headings; these represent the 11 distinguishable curriculum emphases that we found in these sessions. First we identify and illustrate them; later we show their distribution in the various courses, and discuss some of the implications of this in relation to syllabuses.

In Chapter 2 of this report (p. 45) we quoted three definitions of the subject which had been suggested by Mr Davidson: (i) old-fashioned English based on the O-level idea; (ii) literature and liberal studies; and (iii) Communications. In characterising the observed choices of content and pedagogy it proved necessary to adopt a more complex system with more subdivisions. Our main headings are: (i) Communication and Context; (ii) Social and Life Skills; (iii) Liberal Studies; (iv) Content-oriented Projects; (v) Decontextualised English, some of these being further subdivided.

i. *Communication and context*

Classical 'Communications' activities, conforming closely to the model common to the syllabuses, occur in two forms. The first is the situated assignment, written or spoken, which is accompanied by some discussion of purpose and audience, and how content, format and manner might need to be adjusted to these. The second is an extension of the situated assignment in which the communication activities are so closely integrated with work and workplace that teaching the one involves teaching the other.

The situated assignment has already been well-illustrated in the BEC section by the description of the work on Mr Davidson's 'Recruitment Project', so that illustrations from this other corpus of data can be less detailed. None of the work done for TEC or City and

Table 8.3

Classroom Observation in TEC, City and Guilds, etc.

College	Lecturer(s)	Examination	Total Observation in Minutes	Timetabled Time per Period
City Road	Mr Turner and Mrs Fraser	TEC	468	1 hr. 35
Square Hill	Mr Benson	TEC	472	2 hrs.
Square Hill	Mr Wilkinson	CITB	271	1¼ hr.
Square Hill	Mrs Brindley	City and Guilds (Level 1)	387	3 hrs.
City Road	Mr Blackburn	College Course*	392	1½ hr.
City Road	Mrs Brown	City and Guilds (Foundation)	235	1 hr.

* This course was considered to be equivalent to City and Guilds Level 1, since successful students would be entered for Level 2 in the following year.

Guilds was so lengthy or complex in organisation as Mr Davidson's, the most lengthy being a set of simulated job interviews carried out in Mr Benson's TEC class at Square Hill College. The activity took up several two-hour sessions, and began with the drafting and discussion of requirements for jobs, advertisements, and suitable questions for interviewing. Students then wrote letters of application for a particular post, and these were duplicated so that they could be available to the whole class during the interviews, which were carried out by panels of students. Four 'applicants' were interviewed and Mr Benson waited until all four interviews were completed before he asked for comments. One student said, 'I think Richard asked too many difficult questions . . . ', provoking an uproar which the lecturer eventually brought to an end by saying, 'Somebody's style of questioning was a little bit aggressive; well, so be it. Some people are like that. . . .' No other (audible) points were made by the students and the lecturer soon closed the discussion by making a lengthy statement. (For brevity it is represented here as a series of extracts.)

(a) 'The chairman who introduced the job did it very effectively the first couple of times; then it got more and more tired. . . . '
(b) 'The first two: you dealt with their hobbies very effectively to try and draw out what similarity, what this says about their hobbies and the pursuit of their hobbies which is possibly transferable to the job you expect them to do. . . . '
(c) 'I thought the second candidate didn't get enough really supportive questions. . . . '
(d) 'The important thing is asking the questions which are open questions — getting them to explain things, getting them to describe things. . . . '
(e) 'I thought at one point you could have given some indication of the need for teamwork. . . . '

This constituted the whole of the discussion, which was thus focused entirely on the interviewers, and as much upon content as upon communication.

Mrs Fraser, an unestablished lecturer who taught a unit on Decision-making and Problem-solving to the TEC students at City Road College, provides another example. In one session she arranged for the class to simulate a public inquiry, and this came close to being a classical situated assignment, albeit not concerned with work-skills and entirely oral. Surprisingly the first half hour of the session was devoted to other activities, leaving only an hour for the Valley Gardens simulation. She presented the class with a sketch map purporting to represent a new private-owner housing development whose amenities were threatened by adolescents using the area as a short cut to a comprehensive school nearby. While explaining the task Mrs Fraser guided the students in making notes of the necessary information, and then she asked them to suggest likely problems. A brief discussion included anecdotes from lecturer and students before Mrs Fraser divided the class into two groups representing dwellers in the council estate and the flat-owners. They had a quarter of an hour in which to prepare a group statement for the public inquiry into complaints. Two students chosen at random spoke for each group. Unfortunately Mrs Fraser felt it necessary to complete the whole activity in the hour, so that the 'inquiry' was completed in 15 minutes without any time for discussion. It did seem that a valuable opportunity had been partly lost to give more experience of putting a case in public, and in discussing reflectively the considerations that might influence what one says and how one says it.

Our last example of the situated assignment is the Continental Journey, which had been a compulsory assignment for City and Guilds Level One in the previous year and which was used as teaching materials by Mrs Brindley and Mrs Brown who were teaching City and Guilds Communications in their respective colleges. The tasks provide a tight framework which requires the students (i) to calculate mileage and petrol costs for a lengthy trip by road; (ii) to write a letter about camping sites addressed to the French Tourist Office; (iii) to tape-record a complex message addressed to a camping shop and inquiring about the hiring of camping equipment; (iv) to answer questions that test understanding of an appropriate 'Terms and Conditions of Hire' document; (v) to complete the standard form of application for a British Visitor's Passport. Although the tasks are much tighter than those in the assignments described in earlier paragraphs, they provide considerable opportunity for the discussion of communication. For example, here is Mrs Brindley taking her Level One class through task (ii), the letter:

> Task Two. You were writing this letter to the Tourist Board and you wanted to find out information about camping. What points do you think these people will have to know?...

After some difficulty with a student who was still thinking about hiring tents, Mrs Brindley received the suggestions that it would be necessary to enquire about: places where camping sites are and their location within or outside a city, but had to direct the students' attention to the need to specify dates when asking about charges. The attention of the class was not solely directed towards the layout of the letter but, predominantly, towards interpreting the materials and deciding the practical matters implicit in determining the content of the letter. (We shall later have occasion to comment on such activities as alternatives to conventional 'comprehension' tasks.) Once again the context of this assignment was a version of everyday life, directed towards leisure not towards work; from one point-of-view, working-class boys were being introduced to a style of continental holiday they were unlikely to have experienced. As will become clear later, it would have been possible to include this work in a later category, 'Social and Life Skills', but it seemed important to counterbalance the two examples of predominantly oral assignments that preceded it.

The second sub-category within 'Communications' proper is an extension of the situated assignment, in which the communications tasks are so integrated into the concerns of work and the work-site that in order to make reasoned choices in appropriate messages it is necessary to take into account a range of technical and organisational criteria. In this case the teaching of communications becomes inseparable from extending students' practical and technical understanding. Not surprisingly, when the CITB syllabus is considered (see p. 359) the example of this is taken from Mr Wilkinson's class. At the beginning of the session the students were provided with a map of a small estate of semi-detached houses, accompanied by these instructions:

> Your employer has asked you to visit the estate and report back on what facilities (e.g. foreman's office, mess hut, lock-up store, toilet and washroom, etc.) will be needed, and where best to position them. He has also asked you to contact the Clerk of Works to the Council and obtain his permission for siting the huts.

The tasks included listing the necessary facilities, consideration of the criteria for siting them, writing a letter to the Clerk of Works, and writing a report for the employer. The lecturer, Mr Wilkinson, led off with:

> 'What we're going to look at today is (the) question of site security and job organisation. Really when we're talking about site security what we're talking about is storing materials on site, and this exercise is about what you'd need to do a job. . . .

The observer was impressed by Mr Wilkinson's confident first-hand knowledge of the practical considerations relevant to decisions about a work-site of this kind. The students had to understand the considerations implicit in a precisely defined work context, including such relevant criteria as the number of workmen on site, the requirements of the Health and Safety at Work Act, the likely duration of the task, communication and access, visibility as a protection against vandalism, and nearness to drains. When the lecturer told an anecdote it was not in order to personalise the discussion — as it always was in our school data — but to contextualise the issues more firmly in real life.

After this teacher-led discussion, Mr Wilkinson pointed out the two written tasks, reminding the students of work on business letters that they had done not long before, and supplying on the blackboard this 'short report format':

MEMO REPORT FORMAT

DATE

TO *Contracts Manager*
FROM A.N. Other

TITLE

1. Terms of reference
2. Main report
3. Conclusion

Then he gave some more detailed instructions:

> Then the main report you split perhaps into what facilities you need, then secondly where you've actually placed or where you intend to place the hut, and also that you've asked permission of the Clerk of Works, and lastly you can just sum it up by saying . . .

Mr Wilkinson's voice faded away so that students might continue.

While the class wrote, Mr Wilkinson walked round giving individual advice, about inventing names, about using a sketch map and about what should go under 'Terms of Reference'. He told one student, 'I think you've got to do a bit more explaining to Clerk of Works than you would to employer', and told another about a (probably apocryphal) student in another group who placed the hut in a garden because 'Mrs So-and-So made good tea' and who 'added to the sketch map the cigarette shop, fish-and-chip shop and pub'.

In this extreme case of the situated assignment it was not merely that a work-site provided the subject matter; it also provided the criteria for evaluating the writing, including criteria of relevance and irrelevance (the fish-and-chip shop) and stylistically acceptable formats for letters and reports. Thus, preparation for the writing task involved students in thinking about the considerations relevant to practical action as well as inferring from the practical context those criteria relevant to an effective piece of writing. Mr Wilkinson involved students in discussing criteria rather than presenting a ready-made scheme, though this was not true of the report format. It would be a mistake, however, to assume that in so doing Mr Wilkinson was training his students in skills directly relevant to their present work: in the real world apprentices are not required to write reports for management. A proportion of them might eventually move up to positions such as foreman, but this would be some years away. So what is the function of such contextualised work? It certainly aided control in the classroom by providing tasks perceived as realistic, relevant to the world where people make real decisions. Mr Wilkinson could see another function, however: after another session concerned with progress charts when he was asked whether this would be useful to the students in their jobs, he said that he had only ever used progress charts when he had been made charge-hand. He added that courses of this kind seemed 'to presume a more tolerant work-force if they understood the problems of management', which in his view had political implications.

The idea of context which is implicit in the term 'situated assignment' deserves comment. Normally writing can be said to have two 'contexts' or 'situations' — that in which it is written and that in which it is likely (or intended) to be read. As we have seen, it is not unusual in schools or colleges for students to be asked to address their writing to a simulated audience, yet a report supposedly written for an employer or an official will usually be read in fact by a lecturer or examiner. This results in three contexts: (i) the writing context; (ii) the simulated audience context; and (iii) the real audience context. When the terms 'situated' 'contextualised' or 'decontextualised' are used in this chapter and elsewhere they refer normally to the explicitness with which (ii) the simulated audience context (and its accompanying criteria) have been formulated for the students — or (more rarely) *with* the students. This is not to say that writing done for teacher or for examiner lacks a context: on the contrary, the teacher or examiner will tacitly assign it to one and — for the purposes of assessment — generate deep criteria from that context. In this case, however, the writing will be decontextualised for the writer, unless the lecturer has discussed those criteria publicly. (It is one of the ironies of 'personal writing' in schools that the educationist's theory holds that it is written for the writer him/herself or for a sympathetic adult, but because of the exigencies of assessment it will in fact be read and marked in a quite different context.)

ii. *Social and life skills*

The title is borrowed from recent initiatives to redefine the curriculum for less-able older students in terms of the skills, habits, knowledge and attitudes needed for managing life as an adult. This view of the curriculum is implicit in several of the courses called Communications as we saw them implemented. Two aspects could be identified, the teaching of competences and skills needed in everyday urban life in our society, and the transmission of the attitudes and values thought to be appropriate.

What has already been said about the Continental Journey assignment makes it an admirable representative of the former group, in that it gave to students valuable experience of planning their activities, and to that end reading lists and timetables, writing letters and planning telephone calls. With this belongs the letters applying for jobs which several lecturers included in their courses, and some work on telephoning that Mrs Brown included for her City and Guilds Foundation course. Indeed it would not be inappropriate to consider the simulated job interview which occurred in two courses — as well as in Mr Hemmings' BEC course — as examples of the category; there is no reason why any particular learning activity should not represent more than one element in a lecturer's curricular purposes.

Values provide the other element in Social and Life Skills. Mrs Brindley devoted one session and part of another to a determined attempt to persuade her students — all male — that violence of manner and behaviour is ineffective in normal face-to-face relationships. After recapitulating previous work on stereotyping she asked the students to work in groups on a task in which they were required to simulate a dispute between a bus conductor and a female passenger in which an older male passenger also becomes involved. Each group discussed what might be said, and then wrote down a possible dialogue. Then each group read to the rest of the class what they had written, thus enabling some discussion of arrogance, swearing, politeness, aggressiveness, and the effect of uniforms. Later the lecturer asked the students each to write two parallel exchanges imagined to take place in a bus, exemplifying respectively aggressive and conciliatory strategies being adopted by the conductor, and the results of each of them. This writing was intended to feed back into discussion, to encourage not very reflective young men to reflect on the likely result of their actions. Its purpose seemed to be to help them to be more aware of the impact on other people of their behaviour. The exchanges remained impersonal in treatment, although the topic was within the area we have called 'private' in our discussion of writing in schools: in this way the students' privacy was protected, so that they could take part in the session while remaining relatively detached from the experience and the interpretation of it offered by the lecturer. Like some of the schoolteachers, Mrs Brindley was deliberately transmitting values; since this is a course for young workmen, however, one cannot ignore the control implications of teaching them to avoid conflict.

Our second example is well contrasted with the first: Mrs Brown led a discussion of Problem Page issues without any apparent intention of promoting particular values. First there was discussion, led by Mrs Brown, of letters taken from the problem page of a magazine; something of the nature of it can be seen from this extract from fieldnotes. (Not a transcription.)

L. How do you think it is for people who are going out with somebody who is out of work? And what kind of effect do you think it has if you're going around?
S. If she's working?
(Students talking amongst selves — omitted.)
L. Even though she loves him?
(Student's reply omitted.)
L. How do you think she might feel . . . ?
S. He may not be able to take her out so much.

S. She might think it's her.
S. Frightened.
L. Just have a quick look at the other problems.

The session continued with discussion in which each student is required to offer advice on a socio-moral problem written on a card, but the comments given are not different in kind or even in length. This discussion has to be interpreted in context: it took place with a group of 13 girls whose previous education had not been notably successful, and who would possibly have rejected a more rigorous approach. Mrs Brown's intention seems to have been to encourage reflection on matters of morality and sensitivity in personal relationships; in part she achieved this, though without taking her class beyond the sensitivities and awarenesses of everyday good sense. She made no attempt to reach generalisations, and when she offered an opinion it was as if she were talking to her equals.

iii. *Liberal studies*

We borrow the name of Liberal Studies from some of the departments in which Communications is taught (when it is not distributed as a service amongst technical departments) and this is appropriate because all the sub-categories except the first represent strands remaining from the 'contrastive studies' tradition in Liberal or General Education, which we characterised in the opening pages of this Chapter. We call the sub-categories: (a) Communications theory; (b) Social studies; (c) Socio-political values; (d) Interpersonal relationships; and (e) Literature and the arts.

The first of these, *Communications theory*, has been generated by an attempt to provide a framework of concepts that would aid students in thinking about acts of communication in their own experience and in society generally. In this respect Communications is attempting something that English has almost always ignored: students are not only to develop their ability to communicate but also to extend their ability to think, talk and write about it. Potentially the area is immense, as diverse as the forms of communications and the range of contexts that occur in real life, but in fact certain topics recur. Like Mr Davidson, both Mr Benson and Mrs Brindley of Square Hill College gave time to the study of advertisements. In another session Mrs Brindley, while returning written work to students, touched on a range of concepts, including 'sender', 'receiver', 'effective communication', and 'non-verbal information', before turning to the main work of the session. Her purpose was, it seemed, to provide a framework and a terminology to facilitate future discussion. Other lecturers, such as Mr Benson, similarly made distinctions between descriptive and evaluative language, concepts remaining from earlier attempts to describe communicative acts. As we pointed out in the section on BEC courses, Mr Davidson made such teaching a substantial part of his course.

Mrs Fraser's lesson to her TEC class at City Road College was quite different in content, offering the students a theoretical frame derived not from communication theory but from social psychology. It was typical of her teaching that the lesson was filled with a diversity of activities for the students including an exercise in which the students, organised in groups, attempted to complete a collaborative task while sitting in different formations:

Figure 8.1

Patterns of group communication

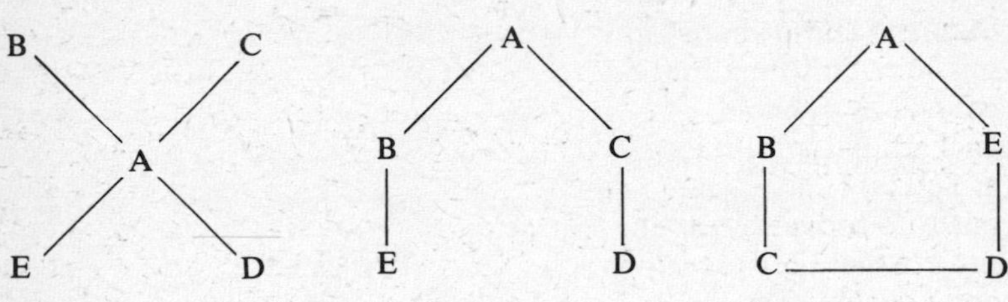

The students continued by writing notes on each pattern according to questions set by Mrs Fraser, and this led to an informal discussion about patterns of communication in business and elsewhere, and their likely efficiency. The students had been given some access to concepts in social psychology, yet without any explicit teaching of these concepts. A similar informality characterised Mrs Brindley's session on advertisements, in which she invited her City and Guilds I class to discuss television advertisements which had been video-recorded. The result had some of the qualities of social comedy, with the lecturer trying to lead the discussion towards concepts:

> So it's role reversal. The priest has stepped into the Teddy Boy role and . . .

and students offering contributions such as, 'They're . . . right watery when you put boiling water on'. Mrs Brindley's intention seemed to be to encourage a habit of detached reflection which her students found counter-intuitive; at times, however, she was willing to be side-tracked in topics such as the nature of yeast, as if she saw general knowledge to be part of her responsibilities. This brings us to the second sub-category.

Social studies, which at times amounts to little more than background information, has already appeared as an important element in BEC courses when we noted Mr Davidson's eagerness to include — even in the few sessions we observed — information about the social class of newspaper readership, the effects of disease on population, and the financing of newspapers. The central tradition of Liberal Studies sees itself as concerned with 'consciousness raising', giving students a wider knowledge of the world, and especially of socio-economic matters relevant to their future lives as workers and citizens.

It may be an artifact of our method of sampling lessons that we have relatively few examples of whole sessions devoted to these purposes, though it should be noted that brief references to matters of general interest are quite common in several of the courses, especially the City and Guilds courses taught by Mrs Brindley and Mrs Brown. It may well be that, asked to display the range of their teaching, lecturers chose more active and various methods than the transmission of information: this will need to be checked when we consider courses as a whole. The one substantial example of the teaching of background information is taken from Mr Wilkinson's CITB course at Square Hill College, and this is partly atypical since its purpose is partly to provide ideas about power stations that students can use in a project that they are to write. However, the series of lessons ranged quite widely over the set topics, and can be seen to be performing under the influence of the examination requirements the function of general education.

Whereas 'consciousness-raising' in some lecturers' hands becomes the quasi-neutral background information provided by Mr Davidson, in other lecturers' hands it can be explicitly concerned with controversial issues with the purpose of enabling young workers to look more critically at themselves and the world they live in. This is our third sub-category, *Socio-political values*, of which there are only two examples in the data. The shorter of the two occurred when Mr Wilkinson turned from descriptive statements about power stations to a discussion of the arguments for and against nuclear power. Like Mr Davidson, he presented to his students some of the technical and economic criteria relevant to large-scale industrial decisions; yet unlike him he was far from uncritical of the status quo. For example, he discussed the social implications of choosing to develop American pressurised-water nuclear reactors, which he said are, 'unsafe compared with ours but... cheaper to build'. The episode had, however, something of the quality of an aside.

It was Mr Turner, who taught parts of the TEC course at City Road College, who provided the most substantial example of consciousness-raising as social criticism; this was unexpected since his usual teaching style was a withdrawn one, asking questions to elicit student opinions without expressing his own. One of the units within the TEC Communications course at the college was called 'Commodities and

World Food Resources': the first session of the unit began with a short introduction before Mr Turner showed on the overhead projector a series of transparencies drawn from the radical monthly *The New Internationalist*. These presented in strip cartoon form various explanations for food shortages in third world countries. Successively, the cartoons gave evidence that shortages are not caused by under production, or by over population, and presented the view that colonisation had changed the pattern of agriculture in the third world, forcing farmers to grow cash crops that place them at the mercy of world markets, instead of food crops which would feed them and the indigenous population. Mr Turner took his students through these cartoons commenting on them and receiving a few responses. Although his presentation lacked emphasis, he clearly approved of the radical message:

> We tend to get the impression that we brought Africa and India out of the dark ages, out of the primitive period in their history, but the more you actually look at it you can see we only developed these countries for our own interests rather than in the interests of the people that lived there. In fact, if this (as it's called) 'colonisation' . . . if they went into Africa today, the headlines in . . . *The Times* would talk about 'invasion'. (Omission) It depends how you're manipulating words.

The materials, which had been prepared elsewhere in the department, presented a view of the impact of capitalist world trade upon the economy of third world countries, and expressed indignation about the injustice to people in the third world caused by the control of markets by wealthier countries. Mr Turner appeared to approve of these views, though he did not teach them with much conviction and — surprisingly — did not make them the basis for critical discussion. Nevertheless, this presentation and Mr Wilkinson's discussion of nuclear power make the point that within the Liberal Studies tradition there is the possibility of a critical approach to larger social issues.

The fourth category of Liberal Studies, *Interpersonal Relationships*, is the speciality of Mr Turner of City Road College who appeared in an unaccustomed role in the previous paragraph. In the list of overall aims which they presented to the Technician Education Council both colleges included 'Sensitivity and responsibility in personal relationships', though they translate this into very different curricula. Mr Turner, who has a degree in psychology, interpreted the aim by involving students in activities of the kind associated with 'T-group' or 'encounter group' approaches. We saw two sessions from this part of his course. In the first he began by asking students to think of an animal 'that you have some kind of affinity for', or that 'reminds you of yourself', and then to write down how the animal is spending its day. Later in the lesson these were read aloud anonymously so that students could guess the identity of their authors. Next they played 'Caterpillar', a game in which each person is passed in turn with eyes closed along the row formed by the outstretched arms of two ranks of kneeling colleagues. Mr Turner justified this to his students as finding out 'how much you feel you can trust the other people in the group'. In the second session a video-tape-recording was made of each student as she was questioned on random topics by other members of the group, and then played back, so that the student could comment. Our fieldnotes summarise the outcome thus:

> Group watch with some laughter and embarrassment. All agree that they look different, sound different, feel terrible, etc. Very shy girl doesn't watch her part at all, just sneaks one or two glances.

The purpose of these experiences seemed to be to help students explore their awareness of themselves and others. Mr Turner asked a few questions, taking a very unemphatic role by encouraging further elaboration or justification: 'Could you say more about that?' or 'Are you happy that there's always something to strive for?' He did not seem to have an agenda of issues to be considered; indeed it is difficult to see what the students gained from the interview experience since there was so little exploration of it. Mr Turner had told us that his 'hidden objectives' were to 'develop affective education which is something that is virtually ignored in our educational system'. For the most part he seemed content to allow the experiences to speak for themselves, and did not display a coherent technique for encouraging students to reflect. The students for their part were on the defensive; this socially adept group were not anxious to bare their own souls or to be made uncomfortable by others' revelations.

We cannot illustrate from our data the interpretation of Liberal Studies as the study of *Literature and the arts*, though we know that it has existed at least in stereotype, since during our pilot study the head of a Liberal Studies department in another college characterised the technical lecturer's view of Liberal Studies as 'a woman in green slacks playing records of Beethoven to apprentice panel-beaters'. The closest our material comes to this occurred when Mrs Brindley in an interview said that she liked literature and occasionally slipped a piece into her City and Guilds course, illustrating this with:

> My big thing at the moment is I do H. G. Wells' *The Country of the Blind*. It's a bit lengthy but they can usually manage it, and then I start talking about seeing . . . (omission) how they see things from their own point-of-view. And then I go back and talk about the Ptolemaic system of astronomy, how they thought the earth was the centre, that this valley that these people lived in was just like the enclosed system in the medieval age, and how people then were very secure and I believe this is what happened before the loss of religion, and people feeling insecure stems from Galileo and the telescope and I've had some good lessons off that . . .

It seems not unlikely that when literature does appear in Communications courses — and most lecturers explicitly excluded it — it will be used in a similar way to link with a range of issues outside the work itself.

iv. *Content-oriented projects*

This is a category which differs from the others in the pedagogy that accompanies it, as much as in the nature of the communication tasks and the content. Both of the TEC courses and the CITB course included in their assessment arrangements the preparation of a lengthy 'project', in which the subject matter was to fall within the concerns of the technical courses followed by students, and therefore to be relevant to employment. Mr Wilkinson went so far as to say that only the project had a substantial effect on the CITB students' final grade, which may be why he spent time providing content relevant to it. However, Mr Wilkinson's session is excluded from this category precisely because he taught it: one of its defining characteristics is that the students are working with no more than occasional attention from the lecturer. Projects occur at three points in the data: the later outcome to which Mr Turner's lesson on the economics of third world trade was directed was the writing of a project on that topic; most of what we saw of Mr Blackburn's course at City Road College was concerned with the preparation of a project; one of Mr Benson's sessions with the TEC course at Square Hill College was devoted to giving talks based upon the projects which they had written.

In presenting the task to his students Mr Turner echoed what can be found in publications on Communications:

> Project . . . can be something you put on . . . sound tape, videotape. Don't need to feel limited by normal forms. Do that in small groups or on your own. Don't need to feel project equals essay.

Our impression is, however, that most students in this course and others chose to do the kind of project they were familiar with from their schools, an extended essay based mainly on the paraphrase or transcription of material from elsewhere. And perhaps this was implicit too in what Mr Turner said a moment later:

> It's not as though a huge amount is expected, because you only have about six plus hours to do it in. . . .

The students were also given these written instructions:

> Using the information in the magazines and any other relevant material answer one of the following:
>
> (a) Explain the problems that face the small single commodity farmer in an under-developed country.
> (b) Discuss the relationship between the developed and developing countries with particular reference to trade in basic commodities.

(c) 'World Trade Kills'. Discuss the truth of this statement giving examples to support your argument.
(d) What are the advantages and disadvantages of the possible solutions to the world food trade problems?

We made oblique acquaintance with the projects prepared by Mr Benson's TEC class when we sat in on a session in which each student spoke on the topic of his or her project, the oral presentation being concurrently evaluated by Mr Benson in order to produce an assignment grade. (Using a standard format he gave a one-to-five grading for each of the following: preparation, presentation, clarity, fluency, response to questions.) They were based on 'library research' and were for the most part collections of second-hand information on topics such as: 'Space', 'Arms' and 'Local Radio'. One girl had chosen the topic 'Atomic War', and in the course of her presentation read the poem 'Your Attention Please'. Mr Benson's original intention had been that the students would prepare this oral presentation, but since the session began with a clamour for their written texts it seemed that most had not done so. Some students appeared at least for part of the time to be reading directly from the written text.

Mr Blackburn of City Road College wanted 'to make them (his students) as independent as possible' and gave them great freedom in the choice of topic and in the management of the work. He believed in freedom: 'We have the freedom in the General Studies section to do a great deal of precisely what we want to do with them'. For this particular course which, though held to be equivalent to City and Guilds Level One, led only to a college award, he was indeed his own master. After some preliminary exercises in study skills such as making notes and using the library, the students chose the topic for their project. Mr Blackburn listed on the blackboard all the materials used in the service industries to which this course was related. 'They can then choose any one of them, in depth, whichever they're interested,' he explained. The Notes for Guidance and the lesson in which Mr Blackburn discusses them both implicitly define 'the project' as a piece of writing concerned with the presentation of information, though the students are warned that 'Simply copying out whole chunks from a book is pointless, time-wasting and boring', the intention being 'to make brief notes so that you can rewrite them later'. The projects we inspected from amongst those completed by this class suggested that the notes, taken from secondary texts such as encyclopedias, had been full enough to be reproduced without much rewriting. There was no sign that the information had been made significant to the students by any radical reconsideration, comparison or criticism of sources, or interpenetration with the writer's first-hand perceptions or concerns.

Our impression is that 'projects' of this kind have been routinised so that they make little demand on the learners — or for that matter on the teachers. Those we have described are for the most part like the most pointless kind of content-rehearsing essay we all recognise from our schooldays, and thus in conflict with the central principles of Communications, which demand the simulation of realistic tasks written for realistic purposes and addressed to a realistic audience. (Mr Benson told us later that he concurred with this evaluation, and that for many years he had striven to point out to students the greater effectiveness of projects that are based on first-hand information and imaginative approaches. In the case we had observed, he said, a badly motivated class had retreated into sterile second-hand approaches — with the notable exception, of course, of the girl who had written about atomic war.) It is important to note that projects need not be like this, for we have previously encountered outstanding work in that form, usually when a group of students, actively led by their lecturer, have taken up an issue of real importance to them and have produced a communication intended to put a point-of-view to a particular audience and to support it with evidence. (Ironically one of these outstanding projects took place in a course in one of the colleges we have been discussing.)

v. *Decontextualised English*

Although work of this kind played little part in any of the courses dealt with in this section, this category is included for completeness, since Mr Hemmings showed that it is a very possible element in BEC courses. It corresponds to Mr Davidson's first category, old-fashioned English based on the O-level idea, and would include essays and comprehension tasks set out of context, and the exercises testing even more decontextualised conventions and usages which still appear in some textbooks and some lessons.

It may be of value to the reader to summarise these categories which can be used, we believe, to characterise the range and emphases of any curriculum in the area of Communications.

1. Communication and Context
    a. Situated assignments
    b. Integrated assignments

2. Social and Life Skills
    a. Competences and skills
    b. Values

3. Liberal Studies
    a. Communications theory
    b. Social studies
    c. Socio-political values
    d. Interpersonal relationships
    e. Literature and the arts

4. Content-oriented Projects
5. Decontextualised English

These can now be used in discussing the six courses.

9. Course by course: TEC, CITB and City and Guilds

It is not easy to provide a brief summary of syllabus requirements for the two Communications courses validated by the Technician Education Council, since it is TEC policy to require colleges or groups of colleges to submit schemes for approval. The official TEC handbook, which refers to the technical courses as well as to Communications, lays down the principle that TEC courses should not be concerned only with knowledge and skills, but with 'increasing the student's capacity to learn, to adapt to new situations and to communicate successfully with others, and developing his attitudes to responsibility'. The published guidelines for college submissions in General Studies and Communication Studies are brief, and unlikely to provide constraints. They include, however, an emphasis on 'studies which complement the technical and vocational content of the student's programme and broaden his perspectives'. The reader's attention is caught by the word 'complement': TEC Communications, it suggests, is to provide support for vocational courses, unlike Liberal Studies which were to provide a contrasting general education. Although colleges have freedom to submit their own syllabuses, the work of various national and local groups has ensured considerable common ground in Communication Studies, a cultural homogeneity that in effect embraces BEC and City and Guilds as well as different colleges' submissions to TEC. No national entry requirements have been laid down for TEC courses; they are held to be equivalent to BEC National, however, (not BEC General) so that one would expect entrants to have perhaps four O-levels, though this may not in practice be required by all colleges.

City Road College has made their submission to TEC on the basis of discussions within a 'network' of General Studies lecturers of the kind we have described. General and Communication Studies at the college was represented in the syllabus by a list of units: those relevant to the first-year course which we were interested in were called:

Interpersonal Relationships
Commodities and World Food Resources
Problem Solving and Decision Making
Trends and Developments (Economics; Statistics; Advertising)
Foreign Language (French)

We were able to see sessions belonging to the first three units. Though these headings make the course sound very unlike a version of English, the general aims given for all of them were more reassuring:

1. Reading
2. Writing
3. Listening
4. Talking
5. Order and presentation of information
6. Analysis of problems
7. Synthesis of solutions
8. Ability to work in groups
9. Ability to work independently
10. Sensitivity and responsibility in personal relationships
11. Awareness of standards against which sound judgements and consequent decisions are made
12. Adaptability
13. Understanding of the context of vocational work

The listed objectives for Communication Studies are clustered in seven sections, which refer to understanding and expression in spoken and written modes (including diagrams), thinking and problem-solving, and study skills. Objectives in the area of spoken communication include such relatively subtle matters as 'Identifies blocking tactics in small group discussions', 'Contributes to discussion in "exploratory talk" ', and 'Shows involvement in role-play/simulation situations'. Objectives for writing include: 'Recognises various appropriate styles of writing. . . . ' and 'Adopts appropriate report formats in given situations'; more surprising is: 'Writes expressively about personal experience'. These examples are enough to show that we are not far away from 'English', though the concerns identified are more diverse. The 'thinking' objectives include such matters as distinguishing fact from opinion, relevant from irrelevant arguments, and inference from assumption. (We do not share with the writer of these objectives the belief that such distinctions can be made on objective grounds.) This group includes also relatively complex processes such as 'Compares different theories about a specific problem'. These objectives emphasise oral activities and decision-making, and acknowledge an interest in interpersonal relationships and in study skills such as note-making, and the use of reference works and libraries. If we compare them with BEC objectives (see p. 317), it appears that they have much in common; the TEC objectives make more of the cognitive aspects of communication and do not mention communication within organisations. Surprisingly, the short section on 'Methodology' makes no mention of situated assignments, though it does presuppose 'that project and group work will be used extensively throughout and that students will be placed in a variety of situations requiring their active participation'.

Parts of the submission from Square Hill College were identical with that from City Road College, including the list of general aims and the sentence about teaching methods quoted during the previous paragraph. However, Square Hill College offers only one unit (called Communications) to the first-year students with whom we are concerned, and the submission includes a set of precise objectives concerned with oral communication, the abstraction of information, writing, comprehension of non-verbal displays, and the use of a library. The level of independent work expected of students appears at first glance to be lower, as in 'States a reasoned sequence of events for an assignment he has completed', though the oral section ends with 'Responds with appropriate arguments to a point put to him in a debate'. The sections on written understanding and production are similarly modest, as in 'Plans and completes written assignment for a specified audience'. 'Writes expressively about personal experience' occurs again, but there is nothing equivalent to the references to sensitivity to others or to cognitive goals that are so noticeable in the submission from City Road College.

Although the two TEC syllabuses are in some respects similar, the courses they refer to are very unlike. At City Road College the course was divided into units: at various times of the year we saw Mr Turner teaching first 'Interpersonal Relationships' and later 'Commodities and World Food Resources' and Mrs Fraser teaching 'Problem Solving and Decision Making'. The courses had been designed by Mr Turner's predecessor: there was an abundance of well-designed classroom materials available, mainly of the kind we are calling 'situated assignments'. (A typical one was the 'Valley Gardens' simulated public enquiry which has been described earlier.) Mr Turner, however, chose not to use these materials. He expressed to us a lack of interest in teaching students to write letters or to use a telephone, and thus in the 'Social and Life Skills' version of Communications, explaining that he liked 'something that has a little more mystery to it'. For Mr Turner, who has a degree in psychology, the 'mystery' was provided by a version of social psychology which included 'a lot of group dynamics and encounter games'. In this form the syllabus heading 'Sensitivity and Responsibility in Human Relationships' was put into effect. Mr Turner told us that the purpose of the Interpersonal Relationships unit was to 'draw people out so that they can — to use the American expression — "relate" to each other more thoroughly'. He said that students would come across similar activities 'in perhaps ten years' time when they are in a management position and off to country residences to do management training weekends,' thus attributing to his course the anticipatory socialisation of students for management, an account we do not necessarily have to accept.

In spite of differences between the units there were signs of a common pedagogy. In describing some of Mr Turner's sessions we have already pointed out that he tended to leave the experience to speak for itself; for example, after the video-recorded interviews he made few, if any, comments on what happened, contenting himself mainly with eliciting a few comments from the students. Mrs Fraser, too, after the simulated public inquiry called 'Valley Gardens', made no attempt to draw principles from what had happened. (This seemed to be in line with an emphasis upon gaming and other oral activities in the overall balance of the course: though Mrs Fraser set some written work, the project on food in third world countries seemed to be the only occasion when Mr Turner asked the students to write.) The implicit pedagogical principle seemed to be a reliance upon the learners and their experience of interaction, with the lecturer adopting a neutral stance, not supplying a conceptual framework (except Mrs Fraser's group theory) or even urging the students strongly towards reflection upon their experiences.

We found the students' comments on the course generally non-committal. Mrs Fraser's problem-solving unit was enjoyed and found useful: 'You actually find what the problem is . . . get it into perspective'. More scepticism was expressed about the personal relationships unit: 'I think that was a kind of silly subject,' and 'A lot of people say, "Stuff like that, you can't use it",' though one girl had appreciated the simulation of being blind. A significant comment was made on a project written during the unit on advertising: although the content was vocationally relevant a student said, 'We knew it was only a little project, and there was nothing that was going to come of it'. So much for projects when they amount to no more than information gathering.

It would not be unfair to say that the TEC course at City Road College embodied an interpretation of Communications as the Social Studies version of Liberal Studies — Mr Turner described it as 'General Education' in an interview — slanted towards what seemed to be an intuitivist view of people and relationships. At the same time, the syllabus emphasis upon oral work in groups was fully put into practice. The course was diverse rather than unified, so that the units we did not see may have been different.

In spite of the similarities in syllabus outlines, the TEC course at Square Hill College was quite different. It was one course, all taught by one lecturer, who gave us a course outline which was organised under the headings: Information Retrieval, Interpretation, Retention, Presentation, and Oral Accountability. The entries under these headings suggest a concern with writing, reading and oral work; writing and oral communication would involve exposition, summary, and argument, and the forms practised would include letters, reports, articles, interviews and discussions. Some impression of relative emphasis can be gained from the form for recording the course assessment from which it was possible to extract the allocation of marks to various activities as follows:

Table 8.4

Allocation of marks in a TEC course

Reports and letters	35%
Oral work	10%
Library	15%
Use of English	25%
Statistics	15%

The heading 'Statistics' probably refers to the interpretation of various forms of diagrammatic representation. 'Use of English' is more opaque: in an interview Mr Benson, who taught the course, mentioned exercises in 'punctuation, spelling, grammar' but attributed only 3 per cent of course time to such work. He described the course in this way:

> This particular TEC unit covers report writing, letter writing, basic use of library systems, it helps them to come to some understanding of different forms and structures in language, and especially in language which takes public form, like advertising, newspapers and so on. An important aspect of the year is giving them confidence in dealing with oral skills in a different range of settings. These boys are not yet employed; they are full-time students looking for employment ... I think it's important they should know how to handle interviews and that sort of thing. So this kind of interaction with peers and with people who aren't peers, like myself, is important. We also deal with a section of the work in which we take them into the complicated world of looking at information which is presented in different forms, like statistical form, and build up their sense of understanding of different ways in which information is presented.

It seems likely from the documents and from Mr Benson's account that the lessons we saw were not representative of the course as a whole. We saw two sessions of simulated interviews, one in which students told their peers about the projects they had completed, and one on persuasive language, in which Mr Benson presented to the students several different newspaper accounts of the same incident. On the basis of the mark-allocation and the classroom learning materials that we have access to, it seems extremely unlikely that the course as a whole places great influence on oral communication or uses small group discussion to any extent, though Mr Benson said that oral activities 'often bring the best out of students'. There is no evidence of any attempt to act upon the reference in the general aims to 'Sensitivity and responsibility in personal relationships' beyond what would be normal in any classroom. The classroom materials include exercises on advertisements, letters of application, the interpretation of diagrams, report writing, the use of a library, and arguments for and against. (The topics in this last case were fox-hunting and homework, which brings us close to our 'decontextualised English' category.) It is appropriate to describe these as 'exercises' rather than 'situated assignments': they tend to be brief, are structured into a tightly-controlled series of sub-tasks, and give the students little experience of matching messages to context, since the message is usually 'given' in the material. Although Mr Benson claimed that he wanted 'to lead them (his students) into an exploring attitude to the world about them' this was not reflected in the classroom materials, which seemed to match with the restricted level of expectation that (we thought) characterised the course objectives. Perhaps Mr Benson was thinking of his teaching style: on p. 339 we have shown something of his strategy in the interview sessions; the following exchange comes from the comparison of newspaper accounts in which he sought to increase students' awareness of persuasive uses of language.

L. (reads) 'When the Queen left the university she was again mobbed by demonstrators.' Notice there; what are they called? (Another newspaper had called them 'long haired, jostling drunken rowdies'.)
S. 'Demonstrators'.
L. They're 'demonstrators'.
Ss. (Many comments, apparently serious, including) Same thing . . . More civilised . . .
L. 'Demonstrators', yes. I suppose it's neutral . . . It isn't really . . . It's certainly an uncritical statement, isn't it?
S. It's just giving out facts.
L. Yes, that's right, they're 'demonstrators'. Can you see what's going on?

Later he summarised his main point by saying, 'You describe the incident selectively according to what you want to put over'. He had certainly tried to persuade the students to reflect on the reports, though he himself had made most of the substantial points.

As a whole, the TEC course at Square Hill College was devoted to a relatively limited range of verbal activities such as the writing of letters and reports, the interpretation of diagrams and the retrieval of information. These were taught predominantly by exercises which, although showing awareness of the traditional requirements of commerce and industry, were not — unlike the best situated assignments — likely to increase students' awareness of the adjustment of messages to purpose, audience and situation. In this they were not unlike traditional English exercises. Indeed, two of the students whom we interviewed said that the course was just like school English, though others approved of being given the opportunity to work independently. Two students expressed specific criticisms: one wanted to be taught to 'speak better' and the other thought there should have been more attention to spelling. Clearly Mr Benson had not succeeded in conveying to these two students the principles underlying Communication Studies. In effect, his course faced backwards in time (as did Mr Hemmings' BEC course) towards some kind of 'technical English' rather than towards Communications. Speaking of the attitudes to himself and other teachers of General Studies of colleagues in technical departments, he said that there had formerly been 'a tendency to look upon people in our business as subversive... (omission) but we're seen as conformists much more than we used to be'. There was certainly nothing in his course in the least subversive. He continued, 'I still believe in liberal arts, I still believe in a liberal approach to education'. It seemed as if, to Mr Benson, TEC Communications had made English into a servant when it should have been a critic — but that is our image, not his.

We turn now to the CITB course at Square Hill College, that is, the course assessed by an examination administered for the Construction Industries Training Board by City and Guilds. In the courses described above there is evidence of a wish to bring Communications courses into a closer relationship with technical courses; in the CITB course which we observed the two were indeed united. This course for young craftsmen was called 'Industrial Studies'; it was described under six headings, one of which was 'Communication', within which were specified: making reports on health and safety, knowing procedures for receipt, checking and security of materials and equipment, and making day-work reports and diary entries. However, the other sections included 'Planning' and 'Problem Solving', and the objectives used terms such as 'describe', 'select/reject with reasons' and 'state methods...' so that communicative acts were implicit in many of the technical activities. Their range, though, was severely restricted in comparison with the other courses we have described: there is no mention of speech or discussion, 'reading' refers mainly to diagrams, and there is no reference to interpersonal relationships. The version of communication implicit in this CITB course is much more restricted, and shows no concern for making students aware of the considerations involved in matching messages to audience and situation. Although situated assignments are not mentioned in the syllabus, the sample examination tasks which accompany it are not unlike them. For example, one assignment requires the students to answer a number of questions related to construction work in a hospital; each question corresponds to a section of the syllabus. The one headed 'Communication' runs as follows:

> Whilst drilling fixing holes from an aluminium step ladder at ceiling height, the electrician with whom you are working falls from the ladder receiving an injury.
> (a) Write an accident report of the event, describing what happened and what YOU consider caused the electrician to fall.
> (b) Briefly suggest ways of preventing a similar accident from happening in the future.

Besides these set assignments, which are completed during the course under test conditions, each student is given nine hours in which to complete a 'project', an extended piece of writing. Three topics are given — the one concerned with nuclear power appears to have influenced one of the lessons discussed earlier in this chapter — and the students are told in some detail in the rubric what aspects of the topic they are to deal with. Although their 'powers of initiative in collecting . . . information' are mentioned, this initiative is to be exercised within a very tight framework. This is worth noting, since although 'projects' occur in the TEC courses, and indeed in the lower level course assessed by City Road College, none of them confines the student within so tight a framework as do the CITB requirements.

It is no accident that our example of the 'Integrated assignment' came from this course: the CITB syllabus ensures that whatever communications work is done relates to a vocational topic and usually is set in a work context. In the case of the course at Square Hill this was increased by the limited time available: during a conversation amongst some of the Communications lecturers from Square Hill College, one mentioned 'race relations' as a possible topic, but Mr Wilkinson, who taught the CITB course, clearly did not see this as possible, and said, 'There's hardly any room for communications skills work sometimes'. He had explained in an interview that the Industrial Studies course of which Communications formed one part had made it impossible for these students to have courses in General Studies or in English. The insistence on integrated assignments had thus driven out what we have called 'Liberal Studies' either as background information or as socio-political values, as in the case of a topic such as race relations. Mr Wilkinson clearly resented what he called 'this lack of flexibility'.

As the syllabus indicated, there was no time given to group discussion or to interpersonal relationships. The only oral work arose in the discussions led by Mr Wilkinson; apart from that the work was entirely individual. Yet though the subject matter was always related to the craft and its industrial background, which (in Mr Wilkinson's words) 'sugars the pill' for the students, it did not by any means exhaust the lecturer's values and concerns. The syllabus said nothing about encouraging a critical perspective in the students, yet Mr Wilkinson undoubtedly had this amongst his aims. He felt that the lecturing style of colleagues in technical departments militated against useful discussion in his own lessons yet, as we have seen, he involved his students in considering the siting of power stations and was willing to embark upon controversial issues such as nuclear power. He had admitted to one of us after two lessons on progress charts — diagrams on which a contractor can plan the sequence of work and the dates when materials and subcontractors will be needed — that he had used such a chart only when he was a charge-hand. He added that the City and Guilds syllabus carried political implications, that it seemed 'to presume a more tolerant work-force if they understood the problems of management'. When we reminded him of this later, he said that such courses were 'double-edged'. Teaching basic skills (such as report writing?) was 'neutral'; whether the course carried messages about submissiveness 'depends on our way of teaching'. On an earlier occasion he had talked enthusiastically about a session in which his students, looking at a Central Electricity Generating Board pamphlet on nuclear power stations, 'sussed out for themselves that the statistics were very very selective, that they weren't taking the cost of the power station or the actual running costs. . . . ' which hinted at the kind of pedagogy he preferred. Thus in talking about the potential function of the course in producing either a more submissive or a more critical work force, he shifted his emphasis from the content of the course to the pedagogy; and this is a dilemma to which we return later.

We saw Mr Wilkinson teach two sessions about the use of a progress chart, one session in which students carried out simulated planning of work on a site (described on pp. 341–42) and one on power stations (p. 347). In describing the assignment situated on the work-site we made the point that the work context provided not only subject matter but also the criteria for the selection, format and style of the written tasks. Teaching about communications was teaching about work, and vice versa. This tight association between the industrial context and the practice and discussion of communication was the central characteristic of this CITB course. As the assignments — apart from the longer project — tended to be split up into tightly defined sub-tasks this might have led to a transmission pedagogy but for the effects of Mr Wilkinson's values. His concern for his students, his wish to help them to gain confidence in writing and in speaking to people with middle-class accents, and his perception of the 'political' implications of what he taught, led him towards a pedagogy that was more critical and which encouraged participation by the students.

Next come two courses directed towards Communications elements in examinations at Foundation Level and Level One of the City and Guilds of London Institute[10]. Foundation courses are taught at a relatively elementary level; the general statement of aims includes such phrases as 'to provide a broad educational base', 'to encourage the student's personal development' and 'to improve skills in literacy and numeracy'. Although each Foundation course is nominally linked to a particular area of employment (Community Care, for example), the aims show that the purpose of the course is to further students' general education, including — as we have seen — their 'personal development', goals very like those of typical school courses. The objectives for Communication Studies at Foundation Level are divided into three sections:

A. Written and Spoken Communications
B. Numeracy
C. Graphical Communication

'Communications' in this case includes kinds of learning that can hardly be claimed to belong within 'English'. The objectives for Written and Spoken Communications include not only the reading of technical material such as forms and notices but also 'Consumer Information' in such areas as House Purchase and Newspapers. Information retrieval, the writing of letters, reports and summaries, and participation in discussion are also included. The activities listed are predominantly practical but as much concerned with students' everyday lives as with vocational skills.

The City and Guilds Level One course in 'Communication Skills' does not specify entry qualifications, though it is implicit that Level One is higher than Foundation Level. At this level 'Numeracy' is a separate course, not part of Communications: communication in 'graphic and tabular forms' though mentioned is given less emphasis. Apart from this, however, the objectives for the two courses are very similar, including receptive and productive skills in oral, written and graphic form. The 'Media' suggested for the application of these skills cover a wide range: the list for 'Receive and Interpret Information in Written and Graphic Form', for example, includes 22 items, including books, instruction manuals, schedules, safety notices, memos, sketch maps, and histograms. The oral objectives give the impression of being more concerned with efficient 'messages' than with two-way contingent discussion of the kind more normal in our lives, yet this must be unintended since a later section of the syllabus stresses interpersonal skills, including: size of group, degree of shared knowledge, gesture, tone, and 'degree of personal responsibility for communicative performance'. This latter impression is reinforced by one of the main statements about teaching strategy:

> The word 'skills' has been used in the scheme not to imply that communication is made up of discrete mechanical skills which may be practised and mastered in isolation but to stress that the objectives of the scheme relate to the use of language in a wide variety of contexts. The aims of the scheme are most likely to be achieved by assignment work using real-life situations in which the four skill areas of reading, writing, listening and speaking are grouped together, and not only by exercise-based lessons. The emphasis throughout should be on real-life contexts which relate to the student as an individual, as a student, as a worker and as a citizen.

What are intended are situated assignments of a similar kind to those in BEC: the twin emphases on student activity and on real-life contexts are unmistakeable. Assessment both for Level One and for Foundation courses is by a multiple choice paper and by coursework. (The multiple choice test deals mainly with comprehension of forms and statistical tables, but includes items requiring students to distinguish opinions from facts, to use an index, to correct common errors of spelling and punctuation, and so on.)

The courses taught by Mrs Brindley at Square Hill College (Level One) and by Mrs Brown and a colleague (whom we were not invited to meet) at City Road College (Foundation Level) were very similar to one another. This appears not to result from the activities of a professional network, but from similar interpretations of the purposes and possibilities of general education to students whose experience of schooling may not have been very encouraging. It may also be relevant that both had been trained for teaching in schools, and that at the time of the research both were unestablished and (technically) part-time, which means that they were at the bottom of the college status hierarchy. (Neither said much in discussions when other colleagues were present.)

Perhaps what most sharply distinguished them from the TEC and CITB courses was the way in which the lecturers perceived their responsibilities to their students. Mrs Brindley of Square Hill College told us:

> What I would aim to do is to give them some skills to get by . . . how to talk, how to conduct yourself at an interview . . . (omissions) They just don't know how to behave, and people judge youngsters on these . . . They're all right inside, these lads; it's just that they haven't got the polish that they need . . .

She went on to say that she wanted to train them 'to present a better image of themselves', and added, 'I'd do anything for them just to give them a chance'. At the same time she saw them as needing structured work and being incapable of carrying the sustained effort required to complete a 'project'. In discussion with Mr Benson and Mr Wilkinson she appeared to value this personal function of the course above such cognitive skills as writing a report, summing up her views in: 'I think the individual counts as a person'. Mrs Brown of City Road College also saw her responsibility in personal terms. Asked what she hoped to achieve by the end of the year she said:

> I hope the ones who find it very difficult to speak orally will be able to contribute, that they'll know how to cope in a work situation, they'll know where to go in their lives, to different social agencies. Just that I hope they'll make the best of themselves.

And later she added, 'It's more building on their personality'. Thus the teaching of competences needed in everyday life was moralised as the development of personality. In this Mrs Brown and Mrs Brindley came close to the personal and moral interpretation of English teaching that we had met in schools, yet without the basis in literature. In neither of their classes were students expected to write or talk about themselves explicitly; Mrs Brindley, for example, dealt with the control of aggressive behaviour by asking her students to write little scenes, and the discussion of these scenes was general rather than anecdotal. Mrs Brown, however, had her class writing a letter about 'Looking after Granny' and said, 'It was the feeling that was important'. Here we are very close to the private/personal version of school English.

In line with these aims it is not surprising that much of the teaching we saw in their courses fell into the category of Social and Life Skills. By chance we saw both lecturers use the 'Continental Journey' materials which gave the students experience of obtaining information about and planning what might be thought a middle-class leisure activity. The social skills element in the course was also represented by Mrs Brown's sessions on using the telephone and on applying for jobs. Both lecturers attempted to encourage their students to reflect on communications in their lives — Mrs Brindley's discussion of television advertisements has already been mentioned — and offered them elementary analytical concepts such as 'effective communication'. The discussion of values tended to go on incidentally during their teaching; for example, Mrs Brindley was willing to turn aside from her television advertisements to discuss with her students such topics as sex-roles:

L. All right, Simon. Do you think older men should cry?
S. In public, no. I think it's . . .
S. It breaks a man's pride when they cry in front of somebody.
L. Yes, you've got an image of a man that he's tough and . . . Yes?
S. If he were to cry here I'd think, 'What a softie!'
L. If he were to cry because something had happened which was dreadful, say . . .
(Omissions)
S. If his Mam had died and it was summat like that I'd feel sorry.

As we have seen, Mrs Brown devoted a whole session to talk about everyday experience provoked by Problem Page letters, talk of an essentially similar kind though from the perspectives of girls not boys.

In her session on aggressive behaviour Mrs Brindley was willing to engage in the direct transmission of values, in a manner consonant with her desire to help them present a better image. Speaking of the problem of persuading a group of students to work for three hours on a non-technical subject, she said, 'In the end you have to teach them to conform because that's what life's about really, isn't it?' It would perhaps have been illegitimate to treat this aside as an indication of a value position were it not that later she said:

> There's been too many intellectuals gone in and thought these students could cope with concepts, and they've stirred them up talking about trade unions, when it's really harmful because they are dependent on the trade they've got, and I think it can harm a student to give them too liberal ideas.

This is coherent with Mrs Brindley's aims for her students.

> What I would aim to do is to give them some skills to get by, the social skills if you like, the basic life skills: how to talk, how to conduct yourself at an interview. I mean tomorrow we're doing how to dress for an interview, and we're going to do mock interviews and things like body language....

Mrs Brindley wishes to do the best for her students within the boundaries of the status quo; her interpretation of social and life skills is thus the antithesis of the radical criticism of society that is one strand in the Liberal Studies tradition.

Mrs Brown was considerably less explicit about her values; when she talked to us she tended to explain what she did without justifying it except in terms of student interest, in a manner not unusual amongst schoolteachers, in contrast with college lecturers who usually were ready to justify their work in general terms. It is possible, however, to analyse the written work done by her class during the year — some of it taught by the other lecturer — and so gain an impression of its emphases. One student whose work we examined had completed 31 short pieces of written work during the year. Some of these were concerned with the self ('The person I am'), some with social issues ('Do physical and mental affected People have the right to live?'), some with issues specifically related to communication ('Non-verbal communication'), and others with social skills ('Opening a cheque book account'). The emphasis was as follows:

Table 8.5

Emphases in a City and Guilds course

Awareness of self and others	15	
Communications	6	N = 34
Social skills	10	

At the same time all of the work, which had been carefully 'marked', was providing practice in writing. It must, however, be acknowledged that written work in a course with an avowed concern for oral expression cannot be more than a crude guide. The marked emphasis on awareness of social issues does seem to be typical of Mrs Brown's teaching, for in the interview she mentioned work on abortion and rape. Some of the published material she took into lessons was intellectually demanding; for example, a very penetrating analysis of the rhetorical devices by which nurses manipulate their exchanges with patients in hospital. Mrs Brindley thought effective communication more important than insisting on the correction of all errors of spelling.

Inspection of written work from both courses indicates a predominance of exercises — draft letters, completed diagrams, brief notes on topics in communications, short answers to questions. Only two situated assignments appeared in each course. Mrs Brindley insisted that her course was 'not English'; 'We're concerned with effective communication...They do written work every week but they do very few essays; it's more communications, not stringing a lot of sentences together'. Both Mrs Brown and Mrs Brindley accepted responsibility for teaching written genres such as letters and reports, but less enthusiastically than they embraced their socio-moral goals.

It will be remembered that the syllabus for the City and Guilds courses gave some prominence to objectives for oral communication, and that the Level One document specified a range of interpersonal skills. The oral work in the two courses was far from achieving the kind of sophistication suggested in that document, yet both lecturers gave importance to spoken language. Mrs Brindley said: 'I do a lot of role-play with them', but did not invite us to a session in which this was going on. We had the impression that most oral work was teacher-led discussion. Mrs Brown spoke of enjoying discussions with her very lively group of girls, and described her aim as:

> Basically I would say getting them to actually talk, put their ideas into a sort of logical framework, to talk about things that are going to be relevant to them in the future, in hospitals or whatever....

This matched what we observed of her lessons.

It should be understood that the academic level of students in these two groups was low. None had achieved more than a Grade 2 CSE in English at school, and many had been ungraded. Two of Mrs Brown's students had come from overseas, and were having considerable difficulty in managing the norms of written English. In spite of this, when we talked to the students we found their attitude to the courses was a very positive one: they recognised that Communications was different from school English and thought that it was more useful. In spite of the fact that at times Mrs Brindley had to struggle to hold their attention, several of the boys in her group particularly appreciated the amount of time given to discussion. The relevance of written tasks to the real world was recognised by some students; one boy had a strong sense of his inadequacies in writing, and another thought that people who were good at English were 'snobby rats' who lived 'in the posh houses'. (Another, however, wrote song lyrics for pleasure.) Mrs Brown's group were also following a course labelled English, taught by the Mr Turner whom we met in another context: from what the students said this appeared to consist mainly of reading and exercises in written comprehension, though one did say, 'Most of t'times we just talk'. One of the girls thought that the Communications course had helped her a lot:

> ... to deal with other people, how to talk to them, convince them to do things, how to go around their sorrows. You know, say if they've got a sorrow you just sort of talk to them you know, get it off....

Undoubtedly these two courses had far more satisfied customers than the TEC courses had, though it is unclear whether this can be put down more to the nature of the courses or to the expectations the students brought to them.

These two courses at two different colleges illustrate perfectly the aspect of Communications we have called — as did the lecturers themselves — Social and Life Skills, which we characterise as (i) further instruction in written modes relevant to everyday life; and (ii) the transmission of moral and behavioural norms. They shared with much school English a kind of moral paternalism — though perhaps in the light of the lecturers' styles it should be called 'maternalism' — yet this influenced only the discussions, and seldom spilt over into the reading and writing, which tended to be relatively impersonal even when it dealt with topics of the kind we are calling 'private'. Issues in Communications played a relatively minor role. Both lecturers taught with an easy manner that encouraged students to participate, though they did not hold back from trying to influence them by various means including contradiction. Where group work was used it was carefully controlled, and both lecturers seemed to favour class discussions in which they could teach by guidance and criticism. Their success in this was testified to both by the students' appreciation and our observer's approval registered in the fieldnotes.

The final course to be dealt with was taught to a class at City Road. We were not given any statement of aims; since students at the end of the second year might, if successful, be entered for City and Guilds Level Two, the course can be assumed to be equivalent to Level One, so it is possible that the Level One syllabus was thought to apply. At the end of the course the students were to be assessed for a college certificate in Communications. One or two students held no better qualifications than did those students mentioned in the foregoing paragraphs; others were well qualified including two girls with five O-levels. The course was entirely unlike those we have been discussing, and this may have been a reflection of the lecturer's preferences, not a departmental decision.

Mr Blackburn, who taught the course, said that his aim with these students was 'to make them as independent as possible', capable of studying, finding jobs and dealing with bureaucracy. 'I'd like them to be able to use information, find information and exploit it for their own ends.' At the same time he acknowledged a responsibility to teach 'basic survival English with study skills' and also 'basic computation skills'. Of the second year course leading to the City and Guilds Level Two examination he said: 'There's very little work involved, very little learning. It's more concerned with process than content, which is I think very good for them'. Mr Blackburn spoke of having taught notetaking and the use of the library at the beginning of the year, but what the observer saw was mainly directed towards the writing of a project. The topic was chosen by each student from the area of the vocational course he or she was following, but the choice was confined to an account of one of the raw materials used in the industries in question. Mr Blackburn did not make any comment on the way in which this limited the project to the reproduction of second-hand information; it is possible that these topics had been imposed by the technical departments concerned.

Five one-and-a-half hour sessions were observed: one the students spent in copying out from trade journals and reference books six addresses of firms to which letters asking for information about the project topic; one was devoted to drafting those letters; and one to writing a list of headings for the project. (The other two were taken up by a computation exercise and by an end-of-term game.) Very little time was expended upon teacher-class exchanges; students were left to continue while Mr Blackburn encouraged or advised individuals. One exchange occurred when one of two girls working together said she could not continue because the other was absent; Mr Blackburn replied gently, 'I suggest that you probably can'. He went on to insist that he wanted separate projects, and ended, 'So I'd like to see *your* plan; it's you responsible for it as well as Caroline'. Much time was also spent in helping and encouraging the least able members of the class. Mr Blackburn's *laissez faire* pedagogy did not prove very successful: our observer, an experienced English teacher, recorded in fieldnotes: 'Students respond to (Mr Blackburn's) low expectations of their responsiveness and ability by apathy, inattentiveness, indifference'. Students chatted or wasted time; by the third session one girl had not copied out six addresses. Even in front of the class the lecturer gave no clear lead, but shifted from one thing to another, distracted by students and by changes of focus in his own thoughts. It was clear that students do not develop independence when left to themselves without a framework to work in, especially when they are carrying out a meaningless information-gathering activity, culminating in a piece of writing addressed to no-one in particular.

Most of the time available to this course is, we were told, expended on the projects. We were able to inspect some of the more carefully done pieces. The continuous prose was frequently copied verbatim, and often contained technical expressions which the student was unlikely to have understood. In some cases passages had actually been photocopied from encyclopedias. The projects which the lecturer thought 'best' did show signs of selective paraphrase. ('Several hundred years later, Venice became the main entrepot (best place) for sugar trade and the centre of refining sugar.') These pieces of work did not match the rationale which Mr Blackburn had offered, and failed to justify the expenditure of time. With careful planning and thoughtfully-chosen topics, a project can provide an appropriate culmination to a Communications course, by providing an occasion to utilise and extend understanding that has already been partly developed; but projects can equally be a waste of students' time, a piece of writing that entirely negates the principles of Communications by being detached from any conceivable purpose or context.

Communications represents an unusual attempt to generate a radically different alternative in a curriculum area firmly occupied by English, a relatively long-established subject. This survey of six courses — or eight, if the BEC courses are included — shows that the new approach is still in a state of flux. The diversity of possible modes — our 11 categories — indicates health as much as uncertainty; much has still to be worked out. The differences between courses for the same award is more puzzling, however. In some cases lecturers may be clinging to a former perspective: this is true of Mr Hemmings (BEC) and to a lesser extent of Mr Benson (TEC). The other version of TEC (Mr Turner and Mrs Fraser) is more surprising, partly because of its unintegrated units but also because of the underlying reliance upon unreflective experience. More coherent and purposeful were Mrs Brindley and Mrs Brown's City and Guilds courses: quite independently they had arrived at a common perspective on the needs of less able students. Mr Blackburn's course, confined almost entirely to unguided project work, was extraordinary in a college (City Road) that prides itself upon its theoretical grasp of Communications. Most coherent in plan and execution was Mr Davidson's BEC course, which also came closest to carrying out the principles of Communications.

Lecturers teaching Communications courses have still to work their way through a number of issues and problems.

i. The place of situated assignments: are they essential to Communications?
ii. What conceptual frameworks aid students in understanding how they and others communicate.
iii. How far at various levels Communications should concern itself with encouraging conformity in behaviour and attitudes, or seek to encourage a critical habit of mind.
iv. Whether courses should continue to aim at increasing students' understanding of the social, industrial, economic and political contexts of their lives.
v. The conditions under which independent work on 'projects' is useful to students.
vi. The pedagogies that will offer students a clear direction and an acceptable framework, and yet encourage active participation.
vii. The levels of intellectual demand appropriate to the different courses.

The future history of Communications courses will deserve study, particularly as some are beginning to find a place in the upper forms of schools, where their values will directly challenge those we have illustrated in earlier chapters.

10. Situational influences on English and Communications courses

The purpose of this section is to inquire how far the characteristics of courses may be related to their institutional contexts. Whereas English courses are homogeneous, the subject 'Communications' is being competed for by alternative paradigms. Within the BEC courses which we observed, there was competition between Communications based on situated assignments and the still powerful pressures towards traditional English. The patterns in TEC and City and Guilds were more complex since five paradigms could be traced — situated assignments, General or Liberal Studies in one form or another, traditional English (though in a much weakened form), content-based projects, and social and life skills.

The characteristics of English and Communications courses can in part be related to the vocational courses to which many of them are linked. In departments preparing students for the world of business, future typists are likely to follow a traditional English course with an emphasis on forms of writing and comprehension based on values drawn from the examination rather than directly from their future work. The emphasis in such courses falls upon the student's acceptance of external norms for presentation and accuracy, irrespective of personal interest in the topic. Some of these women students follow additional courses in English literature or in speech with little direct reference to the skills valued in work. In the same departments, more academically qualified students — now with a number of males amongst them — follow BEC courses which may project a version of the world of business but may equally reflect the characteristics of the English courses which they replaced. These courses are said to offer anticipatory socialisation into the perspectives of business management.

In departments preparing students for industry — including future craftsmen and workers in service industries and in the social services — a wider and less predictable range of curricula appeared. TEC Communications was less likely than BEC to transmit the values and perspectives of management; the Liberal Studies 'contrasting' tradition was still alive in social studies of various kinds, some related to communication and all directed towards raising students' awareness of the social milieu. It was the CITB course, the one most strongly shaped by examination requirements, that most clearly drew its content and criteria from the world of work, though there were traces of this in other courses. The City and Guilds courses which we observed were mainly for less well-qualified students, and derived from a view of the students as socially rather than only vocationally inadequate. Interwoven with all of these was the decontextualised project, which was a strange hybrid bred from technical content — probably under the influence of technical departments — and a view of writing that negated the values of classical Communications, but was often justified by a reference to student autonomy. Taken as a whole, these courses showed less influence from the values and perspectives of industry than might have been predicted.

Nowadays it is commonplace to distinguish the 'intended curriculum' — to be found in syllabuses and other statements of intent — from the 'observed' curriculum which can be described from observational and other data[11]. We might expect the latter to arise from the interaction of four clusters of influences: examinations, business and industry, departmental values, and the students; these are discussed in the following paragraphs. The influence of examinations varies considerably. BEC is centrally controlled and requires 'communications skills in the context of working with other people'[12]; TEC offers more autonomy to the colleges, where its aims are interpreted in the light of a Liberal Studies tradition which set out formerly to 'redress the balance' of courses dominated by instrumental goals. In both business and technical departments, ambiguity has resulted from the interplay of Communications with earlier traditions, but because of the relatively loose requirements of TEC and City and Guilds examinations these courses have more cultural space within which the tradition of 'raising awareness' can survive, though in a greatly restricted form.

The relative influence of departmental values, pressure from employers mediated by technical departments, and the wishes of students also varies in a complex manner. When Communications is taught as a service by lecturers assigned to a technical department and not in a General Studies department, for example, it is unlikely to display a predominantly Liberal Studies approach. If they are to survive, college lecturers have to persuade students, and often their employers too, of the validity of their courses. This is achieved partly through examinations: students following higher status courses are more likely to accept the content as valid because of the potential contribution of certification to future careers. In these cases the examination manages classroom control for the lecturer, and does so very powerfully. Alternatively, the necessary confidence in the course is created by reference to business or industry as interpreted via the requirements of Communications examinations. Though in some courses this has led to the projection of idealised managerial perspectives, this is far from reducing the effectiveness of the course in co-opting the support of students. Students attend courses with their own preconceptions about what is useful or enjoyable: the sharpest control problems are faced by those lecturers who teach courses which are both low in status and only loosely related to the world of work. These lecturers dealt with potential disorder by one of two strategies. Some gave to their students tasks explicitly situated in everyday life, and were willing to turn aside from what they had planned in order to exploit students' expressed needs and interests. Another dealt with the problem by taking a neutral stance and leaving the students much to their own devices: this was possible because the course was assessed by a single content-based project. It was clear that assessment by projects gives considerable autonomy to lecturers, thus enabling some outstandingly original work (not in this data) as well as some unsatisfactory teaching.

The status of students had its own implications for the curriculum. College lecturers do not usually face conscripts: the very existence of some courses depends upon persuading students and their employers that either the curriculum or the qualification is worthwhile. The implications of this were clearest in the comparison of school English with college English. It was not merely that the examinations were protecting a version of English now largely discredited in schools. More noticeable was the relationship of the curriculum to the students' own experience. Whereas schools for the most part, by the choice of literature and writing topics, implied that English should engage the learner's unique personal experience of the world, the college courses — as we have illustrated — treated domestic experience as private, and did not invite personal engagement with the subject matter. The school curriculum aims to penetrate deep into the learner's sense of reality, and even into his or her personality; the college curriculum maintains a stronger division between the private worlds of students and the cultural norms enacted in the classroom. One implication of this division is that students can succeed in set tasks without necessarily committing themselves more than temporarily to any values implicit in them. Another implication is that students are expected to work assiduously at tasks that bear no personal urgency for them; this seems to prefigure their relationship with work as employees. The college student's private reality is his or her own, to be respected and ignored; the college's responsibility ends with the completion of the task, which belongs to the public arena of outward appearance and performance. The students did not, however, perceive this; for them the most salient difference between college and school was that in college it was their responsibility to 'pace the work', thus allowing their relationship with lecturers to be more 'friendly' and more 'adult'[13].

This withdrawal from the students' private realities does not imply, of course, that the college sector eschewed values. The values their curricula embodied or assumed usually belonged to the public domain, however. Mr Davidson's teaching about advertisements, for example, projected a preferred view of the world of business; in Mr Wilkinson's view the purpose of the CITB work in completing reports and progress charts was not merely to teach useful skills but to introduce workers to managerial perspectives. But these were for students who were more academically able — who had some O-levels, that is. For the less able students taught by Mrs Brindley and Mrs Brown the emphasis fell upon communication as an aspect of personal development; yet this included learning the value of self-control and conformity, and gaining some insight into middle-class patterns of leisure. In each case the learning of communication skills seems to carry with it the learning of cultural perspectives. There seems to be good reason to describe these aspects of Communications courses as 'cultural reproduction', since their function seems to be — to a greater or lesser extent — the anticipatory socialisation of various groups of students into different roles.

In contrast to this is the tradition of Liberal Studies in technical and industrial departments, which cannot be accounted for by referring to the need for legitimation. No course was entirely given over to Liberal Studies; several contained elements which found their rationale in a wish to inform the students about aspects of the larger social context. As we have shown, these were not always devoted to values that could be seen as preparation for work, or as acculturation into employers' values. One of Mr Turner's TEC courses, for all his reference to management, seemed to treat encounter group experiences as ends in themselves; and the other was overtly devoted to presenting a political analysis of world trade. The lecturers appeared to be acting upon perceptions of their students' needs — though this was not a word they used — which did not refer to the world of work. Mr Turner and at times Mr Wilkinson saw their students as needing to understand political, social and economic issues: in this they were supported by the remaining tradition of contrastive studies and by their own values drawn from education and other past experiences.

With the less able students who attended the City and Guilds courses, attention was confined to a more domestic range of topics; even in Mrs Brown's session with the Problem Page issues, however, the emphasis fell upon 'what people do' or should do, rather than upon 'what I did' as in the more extremely personalised lessons in schools. The contrast with the Liberal Studies tradition became overt with Mrs Brindley's explicit rejection of those lecturers who try to make students aware of their trade union rights (p. 364). To find a perspective which offers support for this interpretation of students' needs we must turn to the emergent perspective called 'social and life skills'[14], which has been generated by government financing of courses for potentially unemployed young people. It is also relevant to remember that both lecturers had been trained for schoolteaching, and had thus been introduced to more paternalistic attitudes to students.

It would be unrealistic to ignore the activities we have called content-based assignments, for they occurred in many of the courses. Since they were usually concerned with collecting information relevant to some aspect of industry, they were acceptable to the corresponding technical departments and probably to any employers who cared to ask their apprentices what they were doing in college. Although such information-gathering and paraphrase was antagonistic to the principles of classical Communications, lecturers tended to defend the allocation of large periods of time to projects by talking of cultivating students' independence and autonomy, while many students told us in interviews that they appreciated the greater freedom to manage their work. Such projects thus were legitimated in the eyes of key reference groups, such as lecturers in technical departments and the students themselves, and at the same time released the lecturers from much of the pressure of class teaching.

In sum, each of the patterns of activity (pp. 337–52) observed in the teaching of English and Communications can be accounted for as the result of interaction between: students' requirements for certification; the pressure coming from students, employers and technical colleagues for content and attitudes congruent with business and industry; two ideological formations, the Liberal Studies tradition and the newer Social and Life Skills perspective; and the lecturers' need to co-opt student attention without excessive nervous wear and tear. The precise combination of each of the patterns to be found in a particular course is not entirely predictable: examination requirements are more persuasive in higher status courses, as are the exigencies of student-management in lower status ones. Apart from that it appears that the combination rests upon departmental tradition and individual lecturers' preferences, though with the proviso that some examinations (such as TEC) allow more elbow-room than others do.

Although situated assignments are prescribed as the main method of teaching in BEC and City and Guilds, and are implicit in college submissions for TEC, they did not dominate the pedagogy in many of the courses we observed. From the point-of-view of lecturers, situated assignments solve some problems but create others: they create faith in the course by their reference to a putative social reality, yet they require careful classroom management to maintain the simulation. From the point-of-view of lecturers brought up in the Liberal Studies tradition, they appear to be an instrument for socialising students into an uncritical acceptance of perspectives in commerce and industry. In contrast some Communications courses contained elements which harked back to the decontextualised practice of literacy still to be found in RSA English; Mr Hemmings' spelling and punctuation exercises, and Mr Benson's rules for making notes are examples of this. We have already noted that decontextualised English avoids penetrating into the students' personal ordering of experience, and this impersonality clearly appeals to some lecturers as well as to many students. Moreover, the teaching of conventions via exercises, though often ineffective, raises fewer problems of classroom management than teaching them retrospectively when an assignment has reached such a stage that the conventions become obviously necessary. In contrast with English, the situated assignment in its very nature commits the lecturer to going beyond the mere manipulation of words to a concern with the criteria which govern what is communicated and the adjustment of the message to purpose, audience and situation. From this came Mr Davidson's involvement in the efficient appointment of employees, Mr Wilkinson's expert discussion of what has to be taken into account when setting up a hut on a new work-site, and Mrs Brindley's analysis of what a camper needs to know in choosing a campsite. Indeed, Communications courses as a whole were distinguished by the wide range of content dealt with, either as a result of situated assignments or because of lecturers' desire to raise students' consciousness of the world. English courses, in contrast, attempted to separate communication from content and situation by treating it as a set of context-free and content-free skills.

How far is it true that situated assignments offer to students an idealised view of the world of work? Mr Davidson's BEC course went furthest in this direction; for example, by implying that people in business are like Mr Davidson, able to give a rational account of everything they do. The tasks the students are set are at times glamorous caricatures, not the highly specialised, mundane and repetitive tasks they are likely to encounter at work. Mrs Sands acknowledged this by mocking BEC assignments as: 'You are chairman of a multi-national. . . .' The assignments construct a fictional world of business: individuals are engaged in a creative process overarching the whole firm or the firm is a caring institution concerned with the welfare of individuals. In one BEC assignment the student had to imagine himself or herself as the manager of a television rental company — Rentaset — writing letters to five individual customers each of whom has a particular problem which needs careful handling: the students are provided with detailed information on the personal situation of each customer, down to very specific aspects of their personality. They are also provided with a list of constraints, such as the fact that the firm has to make a profit on each hire contract within each 12-month period and the company is subject to keen competition. Thus the student does have to be cognisant of certain realities. Nevertheless, though the task is ingenious and a serious test of ability, this piece of writing offers the student an ideological model of the commercial world: the brutal exigencies of the market place, where people confront each other as strangers and abstractions, and problems may be handled briskly via standard bureaucratic procedures, are fictionalised into a comfortable set of personal relationships. Yet assignments are not necessarily biased towards management values. Students could be asked not only to deal with complaints on behalf of management, but equally to formulate requests, dissatisfaction and complaints in the roles of customers or employees, thus extending their ability to gain their rights as citizens. Assignments are not necessarily biased, but many proved in fact to be so.

Students following such courses can fairly be said to be learning to manage conflict, to be sensitive to tones in spoken and written language, to use tact and suggestion to manipulate relationships, all of these being sensitivities and skills likely to be valuable to them as well as to their future employers. Geraldine Lander[15] argued that BEC Communications fosters, along with particular management skills, a disposition to identify personal aspirations with the aims of the organisation. If this is so, BEC plays a part in the occupational socialisation of lower managers: BEC Communications assignments require the student to identify himself or herself with the perspectives of the manager, the advertiser, the personnel officer, and not with those of customer or worker. But many students will never reach managerial positions, yet — as Mr Wilkinson suggested — the courses may, nevertheless, function to make them less critical of their employers' decisions. Such surmises are impossible to prove or disprove; they have been presented here in relation to BEC courses, yet they can be applied in one degree or another to most of the Communications courses discussed.

The content of courses is not the only aspect of curriculum relevant to understanding the relationship between Communications courses and the world of work. Gleason and Mardle[16] suggest that lecturers in technical departments tend to import into colleges hierarchical relationships drawn from industry and commerce. When students told us — as many did — that they were treated in college like adults, this did not refer to consultation but to orders given as if from chargehand to worker. Relationships in English and Communications classes were certainly not repressive; one of the marks of Mr Davidson's excellent teaching is that his students made energetic criticisms of what he said and he responded seriously to these criticisms. In English classes and in TEC Communications the relationship was more frequently that of expert to beginner, but even Mr Wilkinson — expert indeed in his practical knowhow — was eager to encourage discussion. In the City and Guilds classes students did not suffer from inhibitions, often shouting contributions that cheerfully ignored classroom conventions. There is a pedagogical paradox here. What we have called a deductive pedagogy — lists on the overhead projector — was common; many of the written tasks, particularly from CITB and two of the City and Guilds courses, were highly structured in a series of sub-tasks; and content was usually provided. Yet at the same time several of the courses spared far more time for oral work than any school English course we saw. Both in speech and writing, students had to assume a wider range of communicative roles than the essay or the story writer of English. The evidence seems to point at once to more autonomy and to less. One aspect of this paradox is the greater explicitness about deep criteria. Situated assignments turn the focus away from the surface criteria important in college English courses towards considerations about whom one is addressing and why. Such considerations were not always dealt with in a systematic manner; for example, most lecturers seemed to lack a suitable framework for discussing spoken language. Nevertheless, students were given some access to the principles on which acts of communication can be evaluated: even Mrs Brindley's class showed they had some sense of what made for effective communication. For students to gain some conscious awareness of these principles — these deep criteria — is itself a major gain; English, both in its traditional and its more recent 'personal development' version, has generally failed to make them available to students' conscious awareness.

Was Mr Davidson right that, well-taught, Communications courses will help students to think for themselves, to weigh evidence and choose rationally (p. 326). Will it, in our terms, give them access to deep criteria? Will it enable them to undertake a wide range of rhetorical modes: expounding, inquiring, persuading, encouraging, and so on; and at the same time a range of cognitive functions: categorising, supporting with evidence, detecting inconsistencies, summarising, and so on? It seemed that students most readily undertook these roles in oral work. The syllabuses all made much of oral communications, and the lecturers mentioned in interviews an impressive range of oral activities, including role-play, simulations, oral presentations, drama, and group discussion. The oral work which we saw was, in contrast, disappointingly limited.[17] Of the five sessions that were devoted to oral communications for its own sake, four were concerned with interviews while the fifth was the simulated public inquiry described earlier (p. 339). To represent the range of rhetorical modes by those inherent in interviews is reduction indeed. Moreover, there was a noticeable lack of a conceptual framework for helping students to reflect on their uses of speech, and to relate its characteristics to purpose and situation in the manner central to Communications. On the positive side, however, the proportion of time devoted to oral communication, though limited, was considerably greater than the proportion in school courses. (See Tables 2.10 and 2.15.) Although several lecturers, notably Mr Davidson, made extensive use of small-group discussion, a much greater proportion of time was given to teacher-led discussion as a means to other learning. The discussions were much appreciated by the students, a quarter of whom mentioned with approval the increased opportunity to take part in college lessons. This contrasted sharply with the dismissive attitudes of one group of students to a course in Spoken English. They approved of the Communications approach to spoken language because it 'helps us to notice what other people are like . . . to be able to communicate with them and realise what they are doing'. Some were aware of the relevance of speech to other people's evaluation of them: 'You can't be right rough on t'telephone if it's customer', said a boy from a TEC course. Lecturers tend to overestimate the value to students of participation in teacher-led discussion, which may increase confidence in an academic context but offers practice in a severely restricted range of rhetorical and cognitive modes. In spite of this qualification, it seemed that the pedagogy adopted in many of these courses would go some way towards strengthening the students' ability to think for themselves. Mr Blackburn said, 'If you give people skills which might make them good employees, it also gives them the skills to be more independent', and he may be right. The messages to students about their roles in college and elsewhere transmitted by the pedagogy were quite different from the messages transmitted by the content of the courses.

Situated assignments in their very nature commit the lecturers to engage with some version of social reality, and the traditional relationship between further education and commerce/industry has seen to it that this version has usually embodied managerial perspectives. But Communications curricula are very recent and capable of further development. One possible direction of change is represented in our data by some aspects of what we are calling the social and life skills approach, in that these courses set out to develop communication competences and awarenesses that are not tied to particular vocations but are capable of being generalised to various contexts. It seems probable that similarly flexible courses could help more able students, too, to understand the social milieu and act upon it in a principled way, whether at work or elsewhere, thus retaining the advantages of situated assignments while avoiding their use as vehicles for managerial perspectives.

CHAPTER 9

How it Seems to Us

1. Situations and people

It would be misleading to treat curricula as if they were mechanically determined by the institutional structures in which they occur. Like other cultural phenomena they are constituted by the purposeful actions of individual people, but to take this as indicating an idiosyncratic lack of pattern would be naïve in the extreme. The teachers (and the students) whom we met during this study were able to tell us with greater or lesser explicitness about their aims, but were not so able to consider the constraints and influences that helped to shape their actions; none of us find it easy to question the taken-for-granted social realities that provide the groundswell upon which float our purposes and actions. The nature of their work with older students gives perceptual salience to examinations and to students' capabilities, and pushes into the background the effects of the social and institutional milieu in which the teaching takes place, which is not to say that teachers are entirely unaware of it.

A traditional account of social action would be likely to emphasise the 'unwitting regularities amongst groups and categories of individuals, of latent controls and limitations of action, of conventions and observances which can hardly be said to rise to the surface of articulate expression.' Such an approach directs attention to 'the institutional framework of social behaviour, the implicit, unthinking and inarticulated code of norms which govern or influence individual conduct.'[1] The earlier chapters of this report have provided examples of many 'regularities' in the content and processes that represented English as a subject of study; how far these regularities were 'unwitting' or based upon 'implicit, unthinking and inarticulated . . . norms' might well be challenged by some of the teachers who took part in the study: there were marked differences in awareness and reflectivity amongst the teachers and lecturers. Nevertheless, it was from the beginning of this study part of our intention to relate the observed distribution of versions of English to institutional variations and to the students. In a quasi-ethnographic study like this, the word 'relate' means something quite different from what it would mean in a correlational study; what we can attempt to do here is to link observed regularities with accompanying conditions that on the face of it seem likely to be at least contributory causes. Indeed not to do so — merely to content ourselves with describing the patterns we have observed in English curricula — would be to shirk responsibility. If we wish to change educational practices — and some of those we saw were in our view ripe for change — we have to understand the purposes, constraints and compromises that create and maintain those practices.[2]

The first two sections of this chapter are devoted to a discussion of how the versions of English — insofar as we found anything we can call 'versions' — can be related to their institutional situation and to the purposes and strategies of teachers and students. In this section we adopt an informal mode for considering the structural and contextual variables; in the second we attempt a more formal account of the control of curriculum variations.

Empirical reality in education is chary of lending itself to simplification: the teaching we saw varied in complex ways which could not all be accounted for. Although in schools we were able to locate five tendencies which we called 'versions', few teachers could be allocated unambiguously to one or another without misrepresentation. In colleges the difference between English and Communication was unmistakable, and fully recognised by the institutions themselves. Beyond that we had to be contented with identifying five groups of activities (see Chapter 8, p. 352) that appeared in various combinations in the Communications courses that we had observed. In the course of earlier chapters, each of these versions and activities has been related in detail to its context; in this section only summary references will be possible.

In designing the research we chose institutions and courses so that, by contrast with one another, they might throw light upon differences in curricula that are related to contextual differences. We planned to be able to make a range of comparisons (see Chapter 1, Table, 1.1) of which the following have proved most fruitful:

School/College
English/Communications
College departments concerned with business/technical courses
Schools in city centre/suburbs/small towns
High/middle/lower status pupils (by 'streaming', for instance)
Social standing of parents' employment

Alongside these differences came the nature of the examinations being taken. These partly follow from the contextual differences, but are also influenced by teachers' and students' choices. Of particular importance are (i) the tightness or looseness of examination requirements; and (ii) the relative weight given to assessment by examination paper or to the assessment of coursework. These contextual variables provide a programme for this section. The effects upon English curricula of differences between schools and colleges and between vocational courses for business and for industry and craft will be a major concern of the following section.

We expected that in schools there would be differences in the version of English experienced according to whether a pupil was in a high, middle or low set. The social status of parents' employment matched remarkably closely the school sets their sons or daughters belonged to for English. (See Chapter 2, Table 2.3.) If this is generally the case — and we have no reason to think it is not — to discuss differences between sets is to discuss the differentiation of 'English' according to social class. It will be remembered from Chapter 2 (pp. 59–62) that work on literature dominated the courses for top sets but decreased for middle sets and became very small for bottom sets. Conversely, coursework writing in class increased from top sets to bottom. Some departments chose to examine all sets by coursework or all sets by examination paper and this tended to modify the pattern. In general, however, there was evidence of lowered intellectual demands being made of bottom sets, and a prevalence of 'personal growth' and 'basic skills' approaches. Indeed, it seemed that at fifth-year level only bottom sets spent time practising written conventions. As we saw in some school syllabuses (Chapter 4, p. 156), there was a tendency to conceive more narrowly the needs of less able pupils, with an emphasis on conventions and low-level instrumental competences such as form-filling.

Colleges of further education too have 'streams', though the lecturers do not speak of them in those terms; in High Street College, for example, there were nine groups, carefully graded on the basis of school examinations in English, and all preparing for RSA examinations. It was difficult to discover, however, how students in business departments were channelled towards English or BEC Communications. The former, almost all girls, wished to become typists, and the latter aspired to management or to self-employment. Gender played an important part in this differentiation, but their existing qualifications did not seem to be a major influence, since many following RSA courses had better qualifications than students preparing for BEC general. Thus the students' own choices played an important role in selecting for them an English curriculum, either 'decontextualised English' or Communications with its implicit socialisation into managerial values. In technical departments there appeared to be a clear divide between the less academically qualified students who experienced the kind of course we described as 'social and life skills' and the others whose courses, though diverse, pointed generally towards the work context. It is important to recall, however, that these differences in college courses cannot necessarily be interpreted as dividing young people from different social backgrounds, since a large proportion of those from working-class homes had already been 'cooled off' by their school courses.

In the original research design we aimed to compare schools in a city centre, in suburbs and in a small town, and in each context to select one school thought to be of higher status and one of lower status. Although the differences by status have not proved to be related to differences in the English taught, the differences by social background do deserve comment. However, since we observed no more than six schools, we can venture only surmises about the effects of school background upon the English curriculum. It was striking that Smalltown and Greentown schools, the two with by far the highest proportion of parents in higher status employment, displayed the most innovative teaching, in lower stream as well as top stream classes. It may be that a large proportion of middle-class pupils in a school give teachers the confidence to encourage critical thinking and other forms of active participation in learning, and to place more responsibility upon pupils by teaching in the 'initiation' mode. They also were more ready to treat English as intrinsically important as well as important for qualifications, an unsurprising finding. The other schools seemed more overtly concerned with instrumental goals, though this did not necessarily lead to impressive examination results. Teachers at Downtown School, with the highest proportion of working-class parents, adopted cautious methods but had considerable success in achieving good examination results through teaching that respected pupils' experience but gave them careful support in meeting examination demands. Our subjective judgement was that the unity and stability of a school staff — a quality shared by the otherwise contrasted Smalltown and Downtown Schools — contributed greatly to the quality of the English teaching.

It would not be appropriate to offer a similar commentary on the four colleges. Not only did they serve much wider and more socially varied areas than the schools, but it seemed that it was the department and its position in the college which defined the ethos of English and Communications teaching, and not the college as a whole.

When college and school curricula are considered together, something approaching a common hierarchy of versions of English appears. The study of literature occupies the heights, probably because it is related to well-established university courses which provide powerful reference points and a supply of graduate teachers. Courses which, like the various versions of Communications, look at language in its context of use, hold a middle status; they offer fewer opportunities for specialism at higher levels. It might also be surmised that the position of Communications in the 'applied' sector of education puts it at a disadvantage in comparison with English Literature's secure place in the 'pure' academic sector, though a Communication Studies A-level now exists. In both schools and colleges, the lowest status is held either by courses focused on basic skills (such as RSA English) or by courses directed primarily towards personal and social education. It is an interesting paradox that courses which lay claim to economic usefulness occupy the middle ground, whereas both high and low status courses offer a more general education legitimated typically by reference to intrinsic values such as personal development or literary sensibility.

If it is asked what way of life each of these several courses is preparing young people for, no simple answer is available. Some theorists[3] have suggested that there is a correspondence between pedagogy and the future social roles of different groups of students: future professionals, expected to be inner-directed, would be given autonomy in setting goals and organising their work; students heading towards the supposedly more limited responsibilities of lower management or self-employment, would be initiated into self-control within a given framework; future unskilled or semi-skilled workers would be confined to repetitive tasks enforced by their teachers. The reality in schools and colleges is a great deal more complex, at least in English. In schools, some top sets were held firmly to examination routines while others were expected to think and take responsibility; bottom sets might be controlled either by a focus upon their interests or by a routine of undemanding tasks. These differences seemed to be more related to departmental values and school morale than to the top or bottom stream. It was the middle sets in schools whose experience approximated most closely to the production line, for it was held necessary to give them routine practice to achieve the best examination results.

Different patterns appear in the FE colleges. Business departments seem to exemplify the correspondence theory mentioned in the previous paragraph: courses for typists are characterised by close, routine control of external features of their work, but the more insightful assignments given to BEC students aiming at lower management require them to internalise managerial values. Technical departments show no such pattern, however: the City and Guilds and TEC courses we observed required active participation by students, while it was the CITB course which provided a very tight structure for the group of future craftsmen. In these cases the curricula seemed primarily influenced by examination requirements and the lecturers' priorities.

In schools, however, there may be a relationship between students' social background and the content of the English courses, via the parallels often observed — and repeated in our sample — between school streams and social class. This relationship is not a very tight one; moreover, it is modified when all the streams in a school take the same mode of examination which, as we have seen, partly determines the curriculum experienced by pupils. The differences are mainly related to the importance played by literature in the course. After the fifth year, the differences between one student's experience of English and another's are partly competed for — the result of failure or success in examinations — partly determined by the students' career-directed choices, and partly by the student pressures placed on teacher or lecturer. Success in the fifth-year examinations opens a wider range of options, including A-level English Literature and BEC National courses. Eventually, through the combined effects of streaming, examination success or failure, and choice of career, students fan out into a range of courses, each marked as differing in status from the others.

At one level, the influence of examinations upon curricula is too obvious to need discussion: O-level English Language papers require essays and comprehension exercises; Communications courses require situated assignments; Literature examinations require knowledge of literature. In each case the examination powerfully urges upon the teacher a model of what constitutes writing, reading, the study of communication or the study of literature, and urges these models at the expense of possible alternatives. But the examination demands are not so powerful as teachers often imply, for there are sometimes several alternative strategies which would satisfy them, particularly when assessment by coursework is possible. Teachers choose amongst these strategies on various bases which are not always accessible to inquiry: amongst them are their own values, their sense of vulnerability to criticism, the exigencies of controlling pupils, and the desire to husband their own time and energy. Of particular interest were those occasions in schools and colleges when we found teachers pursuing routine activities which were not required by the examination: it was not clear whether this was the effect of a cultural timelag or an unwillingness to abandon an effective control device. Teacher-controlled assessment — coursework folders in schools and projects and assignments in college — provides an opportunity for teachers to exploit students' strengths and commitments by increasing their responsibility, and this may come into conflict with habitual procedures derived from preparation for examination papers. It also provides the opportunity to widen the range of talking and writing to include modes not tested in traditional examinations, but many teachers and lecturers were not fully exploiting this. Sometimes this could be put down to the regulation requirements — the rush to complete 12 pieces of writing, for example — and sometimes to teachers' failure to escape from their pedagogical preconceptions.

In other contexts we have heard teachers — not those we met during this research — assert that teaching is 'all a matter of personality'. This is clearly untrue: there are skills that can be learnt and improved and, as we shall show, some versions of curriculum correspond to situational constraints as well as to teachers' individual preferences. We began the research with an interest in estimating the contribution of an individual teacher's preferences to the characteristics of the course he or she teaches. As we were studying the two years when the influence of examinations was highest, we must have been observing the teacher's freedom of action when it was at its lowest. The teaching we observed differed widely in content and style: consider, for example, Mr Austin persuading his top set to be literary critics, Mrs Brennan involving hers in a discussion of literary characters as if they were living people, and Mr O'Donnell marshalling his class through the details of a set text. Or, in colleges, compare Mr Hemmings' and Mr Davidson's interpretations of BEC Communications, or Mr Benson's and Mr Turner's TEC courses. Yet beneath these differences of style lies much common ground constituted by shared culture and common institutional imperatives. The literary-personal-moralising strand that runs through much school English, and the interest in effective communication through the analysis of situation that — in a rather uncertain fashion — runs through much work in colleges, cannot be treated merely as the choices of individuals in isolation from the context in which they teach. Teachers do differ. They differ in the strategies they adopt to cope with conflicting demands, but they do so in ways shaped by the professional culture[4] into which they have been inducted during education, training and early teaching experience. If we see a Mr Austin or a Mrs Wood as original and idiosyncratic, it is because their originality is supported by the school they teach in and by the culture in which they were raised.

Another of our interests was the part played by students in the shaping of curricula. Our account here is mainly impressionistic though we did find clear evidence that, whereas students in school top streams tend to accept school versions of English as valid, those in middle and bottom streams tended to see it as irrelevant to the real business of life. College students, half of whom come from middle-class homes, expressed mixed views about the English courses they had experienced in school, but were predominantly enthusiastic about Communications courses. (The exception to this were students from two courses who — with good reason — could perceive little difference between the school and college courses.) It seems likely that school English, like other subjects, plays its part in the cooling-off of many pupils from working-class homes who see little value in it, though others from similar backgrounds achieve some success. Colleges are more successful in co-opting their students, partly because many of the disaffected have already dropped out. Students' perceptions of a course are open to being shaped by a skilful lecturer's presentation of it, so that 'students' influence' is partly created by their teachers. College courses are perceived as valuable not only because they are legitimated by examinations or refer to the world of work; as we have seen, the world they refer to is a highly idealised and sometimes misleading picture. Equally important is the FE course as a symbolic acknowledgement of adulthood, a rite of passage; it is this rather than increased autonomy for students that makes a contract-based relationship possible in colleges. Ambitious high-status students may accept an examination as adequate justification for the curriculum; others, in spite of the rite of passage, need to be wooed. It is through the negotiation of classroom control that students in school and college have most influence over courses.

In the course of collecting this material we came to ask ourselves whether there were differences in the versions of English experienced by girls and by boys. Whenever literature was an option, it tended to be chosen by girls rather than by boys. Girls predominated in A-level Literature classes and even in two O-level classes (Downtown and Greentown schools). Nearly all of the students following RSA English courses were girls: this followed from the gender-linked choice of typing as a career. For some of them, too, the reading of literature was thought to be appropriate, this time as a cultural preparation for their future work. It seems that literary culture is seen as a proper accompaniment to the female role, where it is linked with a valuation of insight and sympathy above conflict and power, and perhaps also linked with private or domestic milieux. We might surmise that because girls usually internalise these gender-typifications they will be more at home with the literary-personal approach to English than boys are, and to an extent this is true, since more girls than boys expressed enjoyment of the subject and chose to continue with it. Nevertheless, many girls were as sceptical as boys about the public usefulness of English as it had been experienced in schools, and many in the lower sets expressed a dislike of writing about themselves and their families, just as the boys did. In schools boys and girls share the same English courses: there is no deliberate differentiation by gender, though there may be differences in their attitudes to the courses. In general, gender in college courses is related to gender in the outside world: RSA English stressed surface conformity for future typists; the CITB course deals with communication as an adjunct to a craftman's practical knowledge. But this must not be taken too far: it does not apply to the TEC courses, for example. The City and Guilds courses are differentiated for another reason. One group we saw was entirely male (Square Hill College) and the other entirely female (City Road College); the lecturers' need to find material that the students would take seriously led to marked differences in the courses. In these lower-level courses the gender differences were thus primarily determined by the students. In sum, we cannot pretend that we have identified a clear pattern of gender influences either in schools or colleges.

2. The control of curriculum: a comparison of schools and colleges

This section is devoted to a formal comparison of what we found in schools with what we found in colleges, as far as possible relating the curricular differences to (i) the characteristics of the institutions; (ii) the sources of teachers' values; (iii) the requirements of various examinations; and (iv) the perspectives of students. To do this it will be necessary to take for granted the reader's recollection of what has gone before in earlier chapters.

Two aspects of institutions will be referred to: relationship with students, and the reference group — or rather reference context — from which curricular values are drawn. We describe the schools' ideal view of students as 'commitment-based' and the colleges' view as predominantly 'contract-based': some implications of this are explored below. English teachers in schools turn towards university English courses, dominated by the study of literature, for their ethos and values; college lecturers are necessarily more dependent on values deriving from the commercial/industrial contexts from which their students come, though that is not the whole story. On the basis of these two sets of institutional distinctions we deal first with schools and then with colleges, bringing in the effects of examinations and students' perceptions as they become appropriate.

Because their students constitute a conscripted audience, schools are able to take a paternalistic view of their responsibilities, requiring of their pupils some degree of commitment to the official values of the school. That some pupils — perhaps many pupils — reject such commitment does not negate the fact that the school's ideal pupil internalises school values as well as conforming to expected behaviour. This ideal conception of the school/pupil relationship has to be placed beside the model of English drawn from university curricula and practices, in order to explain the versions of English found in schools. The study of literature occupies the commanding heights of the subject, GCE A-level[5] and university English courses; English teachers' own academic experience has normally been based on literary criticism, and this profoundly affects school English curricula even though they include kinds of writing unlikely to occur in university courses. Taken together the commitment-based view of schooling, and the preconceptions of a literary criticism still (in schools at least) deeply influenced by the Leavis tradition[6] have led to an ethical interpretation of the English teacher's responsibilities. In essence, this is the culmination of romantic individualism, the cultivation of personal vision as a private achievement as if separated from the social contexts which nurture it. In this rhetoric, reading is the individual's unique response to a work of literature, writing the opportunity to generate and explore a unique vision: for a few pupils the rhetoric is made real. By writing this we are attributing a central position in school English teaching to the private-personal perspective, though this is in practice modified by other influences. Literature has to play an ethical role linked with teachers' 'pastoral' responsibilities. Writing has to be an act of self-realisation, subordinating skills to intention, and is addressed to the undefined general audience to which literature itself is addressed. Spoken language can find little place except as means to some other end. English must be 'committed' — but committed to the values of the private domain not to public political values.

Across this dominant ethos cut the effects of certification. English qualifications are required for higher education and for many kinds of employment so that examinations cannot be made light of. Yet departments have some choice amongst different modes of examination: some constraints are chosen not ascribed. We have shown that the choice of assessment by examination paper can be related to a more 'detached' view of English, which qualifies the personalising rhetoric by accepting a relatively external display of skills and values, and eschewing a high degree of personal commitment. Examinations present literature as knowledge rather than experience, for example. (Nevertheless this detachment is only in relation to other school courses; far greater detachment occurs in college English courses.) Such examinations, particularly the more traditional forms of O-level and CSE, constitute a threat to the private-personal perspective that dominates most school English, completely subverting it in some fifth-year classes. This results in the evaluation of personal values in writing and literature through examinations which reward detached performances and inert knowledge of books, a strange paradox. In contrast, assessment by coursework lends itself to the private-personal perspective, by enabling teachers to co-opt their pupils' private concerns as part of the motive to do well. This is no mere 'coping strategy': most English teachers are committed to a version of the work ethic, and value in themselves as well as their pupils the will to work hard and excel, since it is the basis of their self-respect and their standing in the school system. Moreover, it is our impression that coursework assessment does lead to better writing, since it increases the pupils' sense of 'owning the language', of attempting tasks they can do well. At the same time it increases their dependence upon the teacher's deep criteria, which are likely to include a stress upon authenticity (realistic detail) and commitment (the expression of feeling). In this way, the choice of examination by paper or by coursework tends to accompany a polarising of courses along a dimension that can be called 'detachment-commitment'.

To explain this we must introduce the pupils and their requirements. Most top stream pupils accept O-level as a reasonable goal linked to career aspirations; most saw school English as in some vague way necessary as a background to their future lives. Bottom stream pupils are much less persuaded that low CSE grades are worth having. Whether or not they have enjoyed English in school, many see the private-personal versions as irrelevant; in their eyes the practicalities of life require a spoken language on public topics whereas school provides a written language on private topics. How these attitudes express themselves depends on the mode of examining. Success in traditional written papers depends upon the candidate internalising the largely unspoken deep criteria, and — to a lesser degree — the surface criteria too. Coursework assessment leaves the candidate much greater freedom to capitalise on strengths, to select topic, genre and persona that they can best manage. (It is this that produces higher average grades not soft-hearted teachers, as is somctimes suggested in the press)[7]. The effects of coursework assessment are both to make the results of teaching more visible, and to give to pupils the opportunity actively to influence the version of English they experience by their pressure for topics and genres at which they can excel.

To sum up the argument so far, the version of English experienced by particular groups of school pupils results from the interaction between (i) the paternalistic-pastoral interpretation of schools' responsibilities to pupils; (ii) the domination of English teachers by an ethos derived from the study of English literature in universities; (iii) the examination choices of school departments; and (iv) the strategies adopted by pupils to maximise the effect of their existing competences, or alternatively to make their enforced stay in the classroom less painful. Now we present a parallel account of the versions to be found in English and Communications courses in further education.

Further education colleges have to persuade their students — and often their students' employers — that the courses are relevant to their needs at work. One result of this is that the college view of their relationship with students is quasi-contractual: the college courses are to satisfy students' requirements for knowledge and skills seen as public and external to the students. For this reason it is external conformity that is pursued, not a change of values or personality. Co-existing with this idealised relationship, however, are groups of lower status students with whom — under circumstances to be outlined — the college will assume a more paternalistic relationship. This does not lead to personalised versions of English like those to be found in schools because of interaction with other factors.

The ethos of further education is characterised by the opposition of the 'complementary' and 'contrasting' perspectives, either of which may predominate. They differ because they derive from two different sources. The complementary studies perspective derives from views mediated by the technical departments in further education colleges and attributed to employers, whose views in practice often prove to be somewhat different[8]. This perspective points towards a concentration on language activities which are related to simulated commercial and industrial contexts, and which derive their criteria from them. Conformity and efficiency are central values, while personal experience is treated as irrelevant. The contrasting studies perspective is probably derived from the academic social sciences. It points towards attempts to raise students' consciousness of public issues (political, economic, social); although not concerned with personal experience in private contexts, its aim is to change the students' view of the world.

Which of these perspectives shapes the English or Communications course experienced by a particular group of students depends partly upon the vocational courses they are following and partly upon their existing qualifications, since these two together determine what examination they are being prepared for. We must therefore distinguish business from industrial courses, and high status (post O-level) from low status courses. In business departments, higher status students tend to be working for BEC Communications and lower status students for English qualifications. The English courses, like those school courses we have described as 'detached', focus upon written rather than spoken language, surface rather than deep criteria, and conformity rather than commitment, but they carry these tendencies considerably further than any school courses do. In technical departments, both high and low status students follow courses called 'Communications' but these differ considerably in kind. All Communications courses attribute greater importance to speech than school courses do; the implicit model of communication on which they are based refers to talk, writing and reading that draw their criteria from a known situation, purpose and audience, which is quite unlike English in colleges, and even more unlike school English with its assumptions about self-exploration through literary means. In technical departments, lower status students follow courses more related to communication in everyday life than to the specific language demands of work; 'everyday life' is here, however, treated as a public domain, with a focus upon social competence rather than on self-exploration. This is not to imply that values are not transmitted in the college courses too, but that their adoption as deep criteria is not so obviously a condition of acceptable performance.

At this point the students have to be taken into account. Because of their quasi-contractual relationship with students, lecturers face problems of classroom control. By 'control' we refer not necessarily to disorder but to the need to persuade students that the classwork is worthwhile, and thus co-opt their collaboration. With higher status students this is achieved partly through the validity that examinations confer upon curriculum content, and partly through frequent assertions of relevance to work. This probably places a limit upon how far any lecturer, however radical[9], can go towards consciousness-raising without risking rejection by the students. With lower status students, neither examinations nor reference to their — often non-existent — work can provide a basis for control. For the lecturer this is a major incentive for moving the curriculum towards everyday concerns that the students recognise as worthwhile. At the same time, it can be seen that these courses are influenced by values such as conformity and efficiency rather than by authenticity and commitment, as with school courses.

As a result of these interacting influences, FE students with low qualifications experience distinctly different versions of English according to whether their vocational aspirations relate to business or industry. Students with higher qualifications follow Communications courses which simulate for them managerial perspectives drawn from an idealisation of work; in the industrial–technical area this is more likely than in business courses to be modified in the direction of contrastive studies. Lecturers can be seen to use what autonomy they have — and this varies from one examination to another — partly in choosing curricula that contribute to classroom control, and partly in response to their own espoused values, which in some cases concur with those drawn from business or industry.

Thus the version of English or Communications experienced by college students is influenced by (i) the quasi-contractual interpretation of colleges' relationships with their students; (ii) the influence upon lecturers of conflicting sets of values, one derived from commerce and industry and one from academic social science; (iii) the differing demands of examinations linked with various vocations; and (iv) the various ways in which students perceive their own interests. These correspond to the four variables proposed above in the account of school courses: they are conflated in Table 9.1.

We are not putting forward claims for the generality of the model of curriculum control outlined in Table 9.1: one of the characteristics of the interaction of culture and social structure is that situations display unique configurations. We believe that we have isolated the major processes through which versions of English and Communications are defined at this level of education at this moment in time. It would be interesting to have parallel analyses for other subjects, for example.

The nature of this analysis should not be misinterpreted. If we took one step further back in the chain of causation it would be possible to offer an equally valid account in which the central terms included: the permeability of the subject to outside influences (as with literacy at primary school level for example); the effects of teachers' pursuit of career interests; the activities of key persons within networks of deference and influence; the access of institutions and intra-subject pressure groups to resources. This would lead to a different kind of account, more open to generalisation but less able to account for the particular characteristics of this curriculum or that.

Table 9.1

Direction of the four middle-level variables in schools and colleges

Variable	School	College
i. Ideal relationship with students	Commitment-based	Contract-based
ii. Reference group/source of values	English literature at universities	(a) Commerce/ industry (b) Social sciences
iii. Examination requirements	(a) Paper v. coursework (b) Literature examination	(a) English or Communications (b) Tight/loose
iv. Student strategies	(a) Maximise value of competences (b) Level of commitment to school English	(a) Vocational choices (b) Pressure for qualification or relevance

3. Teaching methods

When we began this research we hoped that it would be possible to locate each course upon a three-dimensional grid according to its characteristics. The three dimensions hypothesised were: (i) the content of the course, whether it was predominantly concerned with skills, values or knowledge; (ii) the level of explicitness with which principles were formulated; and (iii) the location of control over content, that is, the degree of participation by the learners in shaping what was learnt. The content dimension was quickly abandoned as unhelpful, and the other two have in practice amalgamated. The third dimension, location of control over content, has been represented by three categories: transmission, initiation and exploration. Exploration has appeared infrequently — mainly in small-group work — so that the most significant distinction has been that between transmission and initiation. In initiation, the principles underlying the teacher's choices and evaluations are made available to the learners, so that they too can criticise and choose; in transmission the learners are able only to accept and reproduce what they are taught, with no opportunity to reinterpret or generate understanding for themselves. Explicitness (ii) and control (iii) have united in various references in the foregoing chapters to the importance of reflective study of communication, for example, in the discussion in Chapter 6 of the 'ownership' of the language, and in the recommendation of workshop methods for the teaching of writing, all of these being directed to giving learners some access to principles.

We did not find any clear-cut pattern of distribution of transmission and initiation pedagogies. In school fifth forms there was a tendency for initiation methods to be more common in the schools with a larger proportion of middle-class parents. The examination of English Language by coursework did not always lead to initiation teaching, particularly when English Literature was being examined by a traditional paper. Indeed, one of the more depressing aspects of the fifth-year lessons was the predominance of transmission methods in literature teaching. In FE colleges, transmission methods seemed usual in English but to be much less common in Communications courses. The choice of teaching style — and thus of students' access to underlying principles — does seem to be largely in the hands of individual teachers. Some teachers choose a transmission strategy which enables them to maintain control of their students' attention by simplifying content and excluding the students' from participation; teachers adopting an initiation strategy seek to co-opt their students' attention by bringing them in as active participants, which results in greater complexity and more explicitness about criteria. We have no doubt of the educational superiority of the latter.

Owning one's own language is not just a matter of speaking, reading and writing it: we can be trapped within our taken-for-granted culture. Choosing what to say and how to say it requires not just the use of language but reflection on situation, purpose and content, as well as on the language itself. In the fifth-year English courses which we observed pupils were not required — with one or two insignificant exceptions — to reflect on talking and writing as acts of communication nor helped to relate them to their contexts. In contrast, the Communications movement encourages the explicit discussion of principles, though we noted in Chapter 8 that it was possible for a course (TEC Communications at City Road College) to engage students in active participation without requiring them to reflect upon what they were experiencing. Giroux, referring to teaching in any area of the curriculum, writes:

> If it fails to encourage self-reflection and communicative interaction, it ends up by providing students with the illusion rather than the reality of choice: moreover it ends up promoting manipulation and denying critical reflection.[10]

Part of the purpose of the study of communication is to help learners to be more critically aware of their responses to what others write and say as well as to be more responsible for their own talking and writing. It is the importance of such reflection that led to our interest (in Chapter 3) in the availability of deep criteria, and in the students' access to the principles which inform the teacher's contributions and judgements. The ability to understand and control talk and writing will for young adults develop most rapidly from an interaction between their attempts to make sense of their experiences as users of language and the interpretive accounts of talk and writing offered by teachers and books. Such interaction is more likely to take place in a context of use and reflection of the kind we have called a workshop. The versions of English that we found in school fifth forms were weak in this respect: apart from traces of a 'public rationality' version, reflection upon talk and writing played little or no part in the lessons, and reflection upon reading was sharply constrained by preconceptions drawn from the testing of literature and comprehension. Communications courses in further education had moved some distance towards a more reflective approach to the teaching of English, but were often guilty of reflecting a managerial perspective which ignored the concerns of the students when they were using language for their own purposes and not those of their employers.

We view education as more than an instrument of social reproduction and economic policy, and believe that schools and colleges should be means of cultural transformation as well as cultural reproduction. Students need both to understand the imperatives and opportunities available in the social contexts they live in, and to be capable of choosing and acting within them. The kind of English course we have in mind seems close to that described by Terry Eagleton in a recent paper in which he developed proposals for 'a study of the ways in which discourse works upon and produces ideology, the social relations within which it is produced and received, its articulation with other discursive and non-discursive practices'. He went on to explain that ' "ways" includes readers' positions, codes and expectations', and concluded: 'the reason why we want to analyse discursive effects . . . is to oppose them, nurture them, utilise them, transform them or — most importantly — discover in them ways of producing our own effect'[11]. He thus justified the study of discourse — a term that seems to be in this case effectively interchangeable with 'communication' — by reference to the learner's discovery of how to use it to his or her own ends. Use without reflection is not enough; nor is a course on communication detached from use.

In Chapter 6 we asked the question, 'Who owns the text?' and this points to another aspect of the conditions likely to encourage an informed and reflective autonomy in students. In schools and colleges alike, most examples of discourse that were studied turned out — when they were not literary — to be idealisations manufactured for the classroom. It is worth considering why it is not thought appropriate for students to deal with real letters, real speech, real advertisements and real business documents. If one compares textbook letters with real letters, for example, it becomes clear that the former not merely simplify but misrepresent linguistic practices, interposing a linguistic myth between the student and the world. There is every reason why students should have some responsibility for collecting linguistic evidence, spoken and written, relevant to issues that have been jointly defined in class. Such 'linguistic evidence' would at times include fiction, verse or dramatic texts. In contrast with this, courses such as the BEC National at High Street College leant towards what we called a deductive pedagogy which gave the lecturer control both of materials and of analytical categories. Though this might be necessary during the early stages of such a course, it is hard to justify later. Unless the learner has some opportunity to 'own' the texts, the study of discourse, however well taught, amounts to no more than the induction of the learner into a closed system, not initiation into a framework for critical thinking.

The four A-level English Literature courses which we observed cannot be reckoned an adequate sample. However, it is worth saying that in three of them the students seemed to be given even less part in interpreting the text than they had in the fifth-year courses. Ironically, they seemed to be willing collaborators in this, as if in choosing to follow English Literature at a higher academic level they had undertaken to surrender their autonomy as readers. In the majority of lessons the teaching conformed to an unbroken transmission mode: the pupils were passive receivers of instruction that transmitted a single interpretation of set books, and the teachers did not treat that interpretation as negotiable nor set out to teach a model of literary criticism which would equip the students to be readers of other works. The influence of the A-level examination was omnipresent: written tasks set in the very first week or two of a two-year course conformed to the pattern of typical examination essays. In our opinion as experienced teachers of English at A-level, this is neither necessitated by the examination nor an effective way of introducing students to literary critical procedures. Even within the values and preconceptions of literary criticism, the teaching of these three courses cannot be seen as a healthy state of affairs.

In most English and Communications courses the subject matter of most of the talking, reading and writing is neither language nor discourse. Courses can in principle deal with any topic, though we found strong boundaries in schools and colleges, boundaries that were mainly unperceived and uncriticised. We talk and write because we have something to say, organising discourse in ways shaped by our purposes. This important insight has played a major role in the rationale of the personal growth and cultural tradition versions of English and we must not lose hold of it, though it has often carried with it the less acceptable dictum that 'something to say' should have arisen from the speaker or writer's first-hand experience. (The earlier traditions which we have represented by the phrases 'basic skills' and '*belles lettres*' have, of course, continued to exist alongside the literary-personal traditions that have dominated published writing about the teaching of English.) A counter-truth is embodied in the Communications movement: what we say or write is often tightly bound to a particular context, the 'something to say' being generated by publicly available issues rather than by private experience. This has led to situated assignments and the presentation to students of simulated purposes, conditions and constraints. At its best this work offers a wide range of rhetorical modes and abundant opportunities — not always well taken — for reflective discussion. It also has the limitations of any simulation: the students own neither the content nor the problems. In our view, both of these perspectives have some validity: the study of English and Communications should acknowledge that speech and writing owe tribute to both private and public domains. There is every reason for courses to attend to both sources of criteria.

Some kinds of work combine the strengths of English and Communications; one of these was referred to at the end of Chapter 6 under the name 'documentary'. Documentary work involves reading, talking and writing; students are actively productive but have to reflect upon the communication they are engaged in; topics can be chosen to include both public and private elements, and to refer closely to real concerns in the students' lives.[12] Working alone or in groups the students collect evidence relevant to an issue in order to prepare a document — which can include visual and spoken elements — for a specific audience and purpose. Under such circumstances, the discussion of communications refers not to a simulated context but a real one. Such work requires careful tutorial support to ensure that discussion is relevant and critical: *laissez-faire* of the kind we found accompanying so-called 'projects' in one college class amounts to a betrayal of the students. Forms of assessment based upon coursework should provide opportunities for this kind of work, but — for varied reasons — it appears to be infrequent in colleges and non-existent in schools.

In this last chapter, as in Chapter 6, we have taken the liberty of expounding our own views. We believe that school English and further education Communications should move closer to one another. English in schools should no longer be based upon literary models of discourse to the exclusion of others. Talking and writing about public topics should take its place beside the exploration of private areas of experience. The English course should — at least by the fifth year — take place in the context of a study of discourse based upon reflective examination of the use of language rather than upon the transmission of academic knowledge, though the latter may provide pointers for the teacher. Courses in further education are already moving away from an exclusive concern with particular vocational skills towards generalised competences, and this in itself brings the concerns of college lecturers closer to those of teachers in schools.

The Further Education Unit of the DES, in a booklet of advice to colleges planning courses of vocational preparation for school-leavers, proposes a range of aims which well exemplifies the movement towards general competences. The sub-aims include:

> (The students should) 'Experience and practise various kinds of verbal encounter, and evaluate their own strengths and weaknesses.'
> 'Formulate their own codes of behaviour in relation to certain issues and dilemmas, coping with clashes of principles.'
> 'Participate in planning and creating an example of a particular form of communication, matching the form to the purpose.'[13]

Goals formulated thus make it clear that reflection upon one's own experience, and the ability to make principled choices, is part of each person's general social competence. Communications courses should not be vehicles for managerial perspectives but should offer competences needed in all areas of adult life. Education is unavoidably ethical: it presents to young people pictures of how the world is, and at the same time constrains the roles they can play in the classroom. For some students, the pictures are presented as real; for others they are represented as hypothetical constructs, open to revision. For some pupils, their education also suggests to them where they are likely to find themselves in the pictures, and the roles open to them in living. We want all students to have some access to the principles on which the pictures of the world are based and to see them as open to change. And like the authors of the Further Education Unit's document quoted above, we see their ability to reflect upon themselves and their own actions as a crucial part of their ability to participate fully in the life of our society, and their ability to join with others in changing not only the pictures but the world.

Notes and References

CHAPTER 1 *The Project: Purposes and Methods*

1 Williams, R. (1961) *The Long Revolution*; Chatto & Windus.

2 Lawton, D. (1973) *Social Change, Educational Theory and Curriculum Planning*; University of London Press.

3 Weston, P. (1979) *Negotiating the Curriculum*; NFER.

4 Squire, J. and Applebee, R. (1968) *A Study of the Teaching of English in Selected British Secondary Schools*; US Department of Health Education and Welfare.

5 Shayer, D. (1972) *The Teaching of English in Schools 1900–1970*; Routledge and Kegan Paul.

6 Mathieson, M. (1975) *The Preachers of Culture*; George Allen and Unwin.

7 Ball, S. J., 'A Subject of Privilege: English and the school curriculum 1906–35', in Hammersley, M. and Hargreaves, A. (Eds) *The Sociology of Curriculum Practice*, Falmer Press (forthcoming).

8 Inglis, F. (1969) *The Englishness of English*; Longman.

9 Inglis, F. (1981) *The promise is happiness: Value and meaning in children's fiction*; Cambridge University Press.

10 Abbs, Peter (1976) *Root and Blossom*; Heinemann Educational.

11 Paffard, Michael (1978) *Thinking about English*; Ward Lock.

12 Sharp, Derrick (1980) *English at School: The Wood and the Trees*; Pergamon.

13 Dixon, John et al. (1979) *English 16–19: The Role of English and Communication*; Macmillan.

14 Adams, A. and Hopkin, T. (1981) *Sixth Sense*; Blackie.

15 Young, M. F. D. (Ed.) (1971) *Knowledge and Control*; Collier Macmillan.

16 Karabel, J. and Halsey, A. H. (1978) *Power and Ideology in Education*; Oxford University Press.

17 Woods, P. (1977) 'Teaching for Survival', in Woods, P. and Hammersley, M. (Eds) *School Experience: Explorations in the Sociology of Education*; Croom Helm.

18 Hargreaves, A. 'The Significance of classroom coping strategies', in Barton, L. and Meighan, R. (Eds) (1978) *Sociological Interpretations of Schooling and Classrooms*; Nafferton Books.

19 Parsons, C. (1981) 'The Schools Council "Geography for the young school leaver" project: a case study in curriculum change', unpublished Ph.D. thesis, University of Leeds.

20 Willis, P. (1977) *Learning to Labour*; Saxon House.

21 It is not possible to extract the figures directly from the annual *Statistics of Education*; we have used the approximate figures of 35% of 16–17 year

olds in schools, 10% in full-time FE and 18% in part-time FE, supplied in Bailey, W. *et al* (1978) *One-year Pre-Employment Courses for Students aged 16+*; Garnett College.

22 *Statistical Bulletin* (12/81); Department of Education and Science.

23 Rogers, E.M. and Shoemaker, F.F. *Communication of Innovations: a Cross-Cultural Approach*; Free Press, New York.

24 House, E.R. (1974) *The Politics of Educational Innovation*; McCutchan.

25 Galton, M. and Simon, B. (1980) *Progress and Performance in the Primary Classroom*; Routledge and Kegan Paul.

26 Barnes, D. and Seed, J. (1981) *Seals of Approval*; University of Leeds. (A survey of 1979 O-level and CSE English examination papers.) To be reprinted in Ball, S. and Goodson, I. (Eds) *Defining the Curriculum*; Falmer Press (forthcoming).

27 Becker, H. et al. (1968) *Making the Grade*; John Wiley.

28 Hamilton, D. (1973) 'At classroom level: studies in the learning milieu', unpublished Ph.D. thesis, University of Edinburgh.

29 Delamont, S. (1973) 'Academic Conformity Observed', unpublished Ph.D. thesis, University of Edinburgh.

30 Lacey, C. (1970) *Hightown Grammar*; Manchester University Press.

31 Ball, S.J. (1981) *Beachside Comprehensive: Processes of Comprehensive Schooling*; Cambridge University Press.

32 Morton-Williams, R. et. al. (1970) *Sixth Form Pupils and Teachers*; Schools Council Sixth Form Survey Vol. 1, Books for Schools Ltd.

33 King, E.J., Moore, C.H., and Mundy, J.A. (1974, 1975) *Post Compulsory Education* Vols 1 and 2; Sage.

34 King, R. (1976) *School and College*; Routledge and Kegan Paul.

35 Vincent, D. and Dean, J. (1977) *One Year Courses in Colleges and Sixth Forms*; NFER.

36 Dean, J., Bradley, K., Choppin, B. and Vincent, D. (1979) *The Sixth Form and Its Alternatives*; NFER.

37 Dean, J., and Steeds, A. (1981) *17 Plus: The New Sixth and F.E.*: NFER.

38 Hirst, P. H. (1980) 'The logic of curriculum developments.', in Galton, M. (Ed.) *Curriculum Change: the lessons of a decade*; Leicester University Press.

39 Lofland, J. (1971) *Analysing Social Settings*; Wadsworth, quoted in Hammersley, M. (1978) 'Data Collection in Ethnographic Research' in *Research Methods in Education and the Social Sciences*; Open University.

40 Bott, E. (1971) *Family and Social Network*; Tavistock.

41 Elliot, J. (1978) 'Classroom research: science or commonsense?', in McAleese, R. and Hamilton, D. (Eds) *Understanding Classroom Life*; NFER.

42 Keddie, N. (1971) 'Classroom Knowledge', in Young, M.F.D.; op. cit.

43 Strivens, J. (1980) 'Contradiction and Change in Educational Practices', in Barton, L. et al. *Schooling, Ideology and the Curriculum*; Falmer Press.

44 Hammersley, M. (1980) 'Classroom Ethnography' in *Educational Analysis* 2:2, Winter 1980.

45 Hammersley, M. (1978), op. cit.

46 Woods, P. (1979) *The Divided School*; Routledge and Kegan Paul.

47 Anderson, D.C. (1981) *Evaluating Curriculum Proposals*; Croom Helm.

CHAPTER 2 *Institutions, People and the Use of Time*

1 Rutter, M. et al. (1979) *Fifteen Thousand Hours: Secondary Schools and their effects on Children*; Open Books.
2 Dean, J. and Steeds, A., op. cit.
3 Venables, E. (1974) *Intelligence and Motivation among Day-Release Students*; NFER.
4 Hordley and Lee's research is described in Young, G. M. and Macdonald, M. F. (1975) 'F. E.: An Alternative Route Reviewed'; *Educational Research* 17:3.
5 Grace, G. (1978) *Teachers, Ideology and Control*; Routledge and Kegan Paul.
6 Walsh, J. H. (1975) *Teaching English*, Heinemann Educational.
7 Flower, F. D. (1966) *Language in Education*; Longman.

CHAPTER 3 *Preparing to Write in the Fifth Form*

1 Bourdieu, P. (1966) 'The school as a conservative force; scholastic and cultural inequalities?', in Eggleston, J. (Ed.) (1974) *Contemporary Research in the Sociology of Education*; Methuen.
2 Dixon, J. (1974) (Third Edition.) *Growth through English*; Oxford.
3 Britton, J. N. et al. (1975) *The Development of Writing Abilities*; Macmillan.
4 Barnes and Seed (1981), op.cit.
5 Bernstein, B. (1975) 'Class and Pedagogies, Visible and Invisible', in Bernstein, B. (1975) *Class, Codes and Control*, vol. 3, Routledge and Kegan Paul.
6 Inglis, F. (1975) 'Against Proportional Representation', *English in Education* 9:1.
7 Barnes and Seed (1981), op.cit.
8 There is no clear evidence that pupils do indeed score more highly if they choose fictional tasks in examination or coursework. Rosen found that there was a narrower 'spread' of impression marks for fictional and private topics than for public. (Rosen, H. 'An Investigation of the Effects of Differentiated Writing Assignments on the Performance in English Composition of a Selected Group of 15/16 year old pupils', unpublished Ph.D. thesis, University of London, 1969.) The Assessment of Performance Unit report that in their assessment of writing at 15 years of age 'the tasks did not differ significantly in terms of their overall ease or difficulty'. (DES/Welsh Office: Assessment of Performance Unit *Language Performance in Schools: Secondary Report No. 1*; HMSO 1982.)
9 Bourdieu (1966), op.cit.
10 The passage presented for comment was: 'The "poetic function" is the capacity to explore and perceive, to come to terms with experience by the exercise of the whole mind, not just the intellect. Nourishing the poetic functions is the most important thing an English teacher can do with less able children – the free, informal, imaginative and often pleasurable work of creative English.' This is a paraphrase of a much longer passage in Holbrook, D. (1964) *English for the Rejected*; Cambridge University Press.
11 For the CORT procedures see de Bono, E. (1976) *Thinking Action*; Direct

Education Services Ltd (who also publish the classroom materials).
12 We have been unable to identify the 'exercises' referred to.
13 Grace, G. (1978), op.cit.
14 Willis, P. (1977) *Learning to Labour*; Saxon House.
15 We owe to Margaret Gill the observation that such classroom procedures were missing from the lessons, and the incentive to consider the implications of this.
16 Lortie, D. C. (1975) *Schoolteacher: A Sociological Study*; University of Chicago Press.

CHAPTER 4 *Language and Comprehension in the Fifth Year*
1 Finlayson, D. and Smith, T. (1956) *Clear English* (Final Stage); Nelson.
2 Wood, K. and Forsyth, I. *Writing a Letter*; Nelson/Post Office.
3 Torbe, M. 'Communication Skills in the Young School Leaver: Some Notes towards Research', in *International Journal of the Sociology of Languages* (forthcoming).
4 Department of Education and Science (1977) *Curriculum 11–16* (section entitled 'Language' pp.20—23); DES.
5 Lord Kennet's piece is mildly controversial — at any rate there is a clear line of cultural criticism which informs it.
6 Barnes, D. and Seed, J. (1981), op.cit.

CHAPTER 5 *Literature Teaching in the Fifth Form*
1 Shayer, D. (1972), op.cit.
2 Inglis, F. (1981), op.cit.
3 Stratta, L. et al. (1973) *Patterns of Language*; Heinemann Educational.
4 Yorke, J. M. (1977) 'An Examination of Teachers' Objectives in Teaching Literature to the 9–16 Age Group', unpublished Ph.D. thesis, Sheffield.
5 In some other areas English Literature is available as a Mode 1 CSE subject.
6 Barnes, D. and Seed, J. (1981), op.cit.
7 Oakeshott, M. (1967) 'Learning and Teaching', in *The Concept of Education*; Routledge and Kegan Paul.
8 Whitehead, F., Capey, F. C. and Maddren, W. (1974) *Children's Reading Interests* Schools Council Working Paper 52; Evans/Methuen Educational.

CHAPTER 6 *Versions of English in the Fifth Form*
1 The term 'ficts' is used in Whitehead, F. S. (1966) *The Disappearing Dais*; Chatto and Windus.
2 Freire, P. (source unknown).

CHAPTER 7 *Literature after the Fifth Form*
1 The lesson data we are using amounts to 19 hours 35 minutes, observed and in most cases tape-recorded in the first two terms.
2 For a brief account of this see S. J. Ball's paper 'A Subject of Privilege', op.cit.
3 Hardy, B. (1968) 'The Teaching of English: Life, Literature and Literary Criticism' in *English in Education* Vol. 2:2.

CHAPTER 8 *English and Communications in Further Education Courses*

1 Flower, F. D. (1966) *Language in Education*: Longman.

2 From a lecture given in 1981 in Leeds by G. Montford of the City and Guilds of London Institute.

3 Department of Education and Science (1962) *General Studies in Technical Colleges*: HMSO.

4 Rosser, G. C. and McClintock, T. (1974) *English*; Pitman.

5 Eggleston, J. (1977) *The Sociology of the School Curriculum*; Routledge and Kegan Paul, draws a distinction between 'commitment-based decisions' relevant to school courses in which students are expected to internalise official values, and 'contract-based decisions', which are seen as characteristic of further education.

6 Business Education Council (1977a) *BEC General Awards: Course Specification*; BEC, Portland Place, London.

7 Business Education Council (1978) *BEC General Awards: Teaching/Learning Strategies and Assignments*; BEC (cyclostyled).

8 Business Education Council (1977b) *BEC National Awards: Course Specification*; BEC.

9 Leavis, F. R. and Thompson, D. (1933) *Culture and Environment*; Chatto and Windus.

10 City and Guilds of London Institute (1981) *722—Communication Skills*; City and Guilds, Portland Place, London.

11 Stake, R. E. (1967) 'The countenance of educational evaluation', *Teachers' College Record,* Vol. 68, pp. 523–40.

12 Business Education Council (1977a), op.cit.

13 In response to a general question about the difference between school and college, 24 students (out of 61) mentioned pacing their own work, 13 mentioned adult treatment by lecturers, and 9 the friendliness of lecturers. This can be counterbalanced with the subjective judgements of the three observers, all former English teachers, that greater intellectual demands could often have been made on the students, more than half of whom had already passed English Language at O-level or its equivalent. FE lecturers, unlike schoolteachers, do not assume responsibility for individual students' examination results.

14 Further Education Curriculum Review and Development Unit (1980) *Developing Social and Life Skills*; Department of Education and Science, London.

15 Lander, G. (1980) 'The Language of BEC', in *The Social Science Teacher* Vol. 10.1, p.28.

16 Gleeson, D. and Mardle, G. (1980) *Further Education or Training*?; Routledge and Kegan Paul.

17 This part of the data has been discussed separately in, Barnes, D. (1982) 'Finding a Context for talk', in *Spoken English*, Vol. 15:2, pp. 6–14.

CHAPTER 9 *How it Seems to Us*

1 Burns, T. (1967) 'Sociological Explanation', in Emmet, D. and MacIntyre, A. (Eds.) (1970) *Sociological Theory and Philosophical Analysis*; Macmillan.

2 See Brown, S. (1980) 'Key issues in the implementation of innovations in schools', *Curriculum* 1:1, Spring 1980, for a framework for analysing the immediate situation of teachers.

3 Bowles, S. and Gintis, H. (1977) 'Capitalism and Education in the United States', in Young, M. and Whitty, G. (Eds.) *Society, State and Schooling*; Falmer Press; Anyon, J. (1981) 'Social Class and School Knowledge', *Curriculum Inquiry* 1:1.

4 Lortie, D. C. (1975), op.cit.

5 Since 1978 there has been an A-level in Communication Studies available from the Associated Examining Board.

6 Ball, S. J. (1982) 'Competition and Conflict in the teaching of English: a socio-historical analysis', in *Curriculum Studies* 14:1, pp.1–28.

7 Wood, N. (1982) 'Exam marks influenced by "halo effect" ', in *Times Educational Supplement*, 20 August 1982.

8 See Torbe, M. (forthcoming), op.cit.

9 Gleeson and Mardle distinguished lecturers on the basis of what they said, using three categories: 'liberals', 'radicals', and 'cowboys'. These distinctions were not, however, visible in their teaching because 'confronted with disillusioned and poorly motivated students, the Liberal Studies teacher must adopt a variety of strategies in order to survive'. (Gleeson, D. and Mardle, G. (1980) *Further Education or Training*?; Routledge and Kegan Paul.) Our observations suggested that lecturers have considerably more room for manoeuvre, perhaps because of the introduction of Communications since Gleeson and Mardle completed their study.

10 Giroux, H. A. (1981) *Ideology, Culture and the Process of Schooling*; Falmer Press.

11 Eagleton, T. (1982) 'The End of Criticism', in *English in Education* 16:2, pp.48–54.

12 'Documentary' work is illustrated in Schools Council Project English 16–19 (1978) *New Directions in General and Communication Studies*; Bretton Hall College; and in Gill, M. 'Three Teachers: Defining English in the Classroom', in Arnold, R. (Ed.) *Timely Voices: English Teaching in the Eighties*; Oxford University Press (1983).

13 Further Education Curriculum Review and Development Unit (1981) *Vocational Preparation*, DES/HMSO.

Appendix I (a): Teacher Interview Schedules

We have tried to group these in categories, but inevitably there will be some overlap.

Content

I Intro: Which V form groups do you have this year?

1. Do you find V form English teaching is very different from English teaching lower down the school?

   .... What ways (things) particularly?

2. Is there any real difference between the courses for GCE and CSE?

   .... What about literature?
   .... Could you go into some details?

3. What do you find you put most emphasis on in V year?

   .... Do you divide the work up into categories you want to cover?
   .... Do you find you have to vary your emphasis according to the class?
   .... Would you say the emphasis changes during the year?

Method

II 1. How would you advise a beginner about teaching *method* in V?

   .... Would you say there's a general pattern to your lessons?
   .... (if necessary relate a pattern to suggest)

.... Do you think most of your colleagues teach in a very similar way to you?

.... How do they differ?

2. Do you find the class work on their own, in groups, or do you teach them most of the time?

3. We're interested in how you apportion time for different activities...

    .... Can you say roughly what proportions of your time over the year is devoted to:
    - — work on literature (including writing)? (perhaps plays, stories, poems)
    - — essay writing (not based on literature)?
    - — discussion of general (including social) issues?
    - — comprehension?
    - — punctuation, spelling and other language exercises?
    - — acting without text?
    - — anything else?

4. How much homework can you expect from the class you're teaching?

Constraints

III 1. Is there anything particularly that you'd like to change or do differently?

.... Would you choose any different topics or books if there wasn't an examination? What books do you like to use?

.... Are you happy with the setting/streaming system you have?

2. Would you teach differently if there was money for more resources — books etc.?

.... What would you do with them?

3. Do you have enough time?

   (To H.o.D. How far are your time-table requests for the V able to be met in practice?)

4. What kind of reactions do you get to English from colleagues?

   .... Do they make comments or try to influence your teaching?

Exams and Standards

IV

1. Do you think standards have changed whilst you've been teaching/over X years? (as appropriate). (Find out how long)

   .... What do you put this down to?

2. How do you expect your present class to get on with the books they're studying?

   .... with the kind of examination questions they'll have to answer?

Pupils

V

1. Would you say the group you're teaching this year are a typical (X band) class?

   .... In what ways are they/aren't they typical?
   .... Are they good at written work?
   .... Are they good at oral work?

2. What do you think makes a pupil good at English in V?

   .... What qualities in their work will get a good grade?

3. Is there any particular boy or girl I ought to notice?

4. How many do you expect will stay on?

   .... Do their parents expect them to? Are they ambitious for them.

5. Do you have much contact with parents?

   .... Do you have the feeling they're interested in the kind of English you're doing?

Additional
(if time)

I 4. What do you enjoy teaching most in the V?

   Which parts raise most problems?

III 5. If you had extra five hours for work each week which of the following would you choose to spend it on — number the first three for importance:

   parents' meetings
   departmental meetings
   class teaching
   individual teaching
   private preparation
   marking and correction
   in-service courses

   — if none of these are there any others?

IV 3. What do you think has most effect on the standards reached by your pupils?

   4. If you were devising an ideal English examination for this stage what would you want to include?

Appendix I (b): Lecturer Interview Schedules

Introductory — Can you tell us something about what you've done since you left school? (Qualifications. Experience outside colleges. Length of lecturing experience. (Age))

I

1. What groups which are mainly 16–17 year olds do you teach E. and C. to?
2. Which group will we be seeing?
3. Do you think they tend to differ from other groups? Could you say in what way?
4. How much time do you have with them?

Method and Content

II

1. What do you find you put most emphasis on in this first year of the course?
   Do you divide the work up into categories you want to cover?
   Do you find you have to vary your emphasis according to the class?
   Would you say the emphasis changes during the year?
2. .... Would you say there's a general pattern to your lessons?
   (if necessary relate a pattern to suggest)

   .... Do you think most of your colleagues teach in a very similar way to you?
   .... How do they differ?

3. Do you find the class work on their own, in groups, or do you teach them most of the time?

4. We're interested in how people apportion time for different activities — (We asked this question of school teachers; it may not apply in your case.)

   .... Can you say roughly what proportions of your time over the year is devoted to:—

   — general essay writing or situated assignments?
   — discussion of general (including social) issues?
   — comprehension?
   — punctuation, spelling and other language exercises?
   — work on literature (including writing)?
   — acting without text?
   — anything else?

5. Do you expect the students to do work outside class time?

   — How much? What kinds?

Constraints

III 1. Would you teach differently if there was money for more resources — books, etc.? What would you do with them?

2. What kind of reactions do you get to English and Communications from colleagues?

   — Do they try to make you conform to their idea of English?
   — What picture do you think they have of you and the other Eng./Com. specialists?

3. Is there any contact between you and the employers? Is your course influenced by their needs? Directly or indirectly?

Exams and Standards

IV

1. Do you think standards have changed whilst you've been lecturing over X years? (as appropriate)

   .... What do you put this down to?

2. How do you expect your present class to cope with the course?

   .... with the kind of examination they'll have to face?

3. What do you aim to do in your teaching? How far does the examination enable or prevent?

4. How would you rate the Communications element in X compared with 'O' level Language?

Students

V

1. Would you say the group you're teaching this year are a typical BEC/TEC/X class?

   .... In what ways are they/aren't they typical?

2. Do you know much about their aspirations?

3. Do you have any information about their background?

4. Is there any contact between the college and the schools they attended?

5. In what ways do you think the courses here differ from the students' experience of English at school?

---

1. We've talked about the examination, resources, colleagues and employers. Are there any other constraints or pressures that influence the course and how you teach it?

2. What kinds of English/Communications work brings out the best response from students?
3. What part of the course do you enjoy teaching the most?
4. If you were devising an ideal course what would you want to include? What would you want the examination to be like?

Appendix II Questionnaire for Teachers and Lecturers

1. How long have you been teaching?

   Full-time
   Part-time

2. What kinds of school or college have you taught in?
3. What other working experience (not vacation jobs) have you had? Has this any relevance to your present views about your students and about teaching?
4. What proportion of time do you at present spend teaching English or Communications? What other subjects have you taught/do you teach (if any)?
5. Did you undertake any professional training? We would be glad to know whether you took a B.Ed., College of Education Certificate, P.G.C.E. or any other qualification.
6. What experiences, qualifications or characteristics seem to you to weigh most heavily in promotion or appointment to senior posts?
7. It is sometimes said that teachers are 'put on a pedestal'. Do you feel that the public — students, their parents and others — expect you to be a particular kind of person?
8. Who or what do you think has had most influence on your views (and practice) in English or Communications teaching? (And this is where we would be grateful for your opinions at some length, whether they relate to your own education, to your specialisation, to people you have known, or whatever?)

Appendix III(a) Pupil Interview Schedules

A. 1. Do you know what you're going to do at end of year?

2. Is job same as anyone in your family?

3. What made you think of it?

B. 1. What do you like doing in spare time? Much TV? Reading?

2. Do you get a lot of homework? Parents involved?

C. 1. What school subjects do you like most? (Follow up preference — try to get criteria elucidated.) How about English?

2. What grade do you think you'll get in English? Do you think you'll do better in other subjects?

3. Do you think English is different from other subjects?
How are CSE/GCE groups decided?
What are people who are good at English like? (Probe.)

4. Some people seem to think English in V is very different from what it was earlier; do you?

5. When I came in you were (describe teaching style), was that typical?

6. What do you think of books you've read?

D. 1. Lots of jobs want English. Do you think what you do will be useful?

2. How important is it in your Dad or Mum's job?

3. Is talking well more important than writing well?

4. Would you want a job with a lot of writing?

E. (Based on written work)
1. What kind of writing do you like most? (Mention actual examples.)

2. Do you like writing about yourself, about characters in books, . . .
3. What do you think of the comprehension work you have to do?

   Useful ploy 'Talk me through what teacher does when he sets a piece of writing' cf. method of commentator in action replay when someone scores a goal. Follow up with questions, e.g. What kinds of comments does T. make? What do you do with the work when he gives it back?

Appendix III(b) Student Interview Schedules

1.1 Which school were you at? Do you live near? (Also establish student's identity and if class and teacher one of ours.)

1.2 What did you do immediately after the exams?
Did you try to get a job?
When did you decide to stay on/come to college?
What are most of your friends doing?

1.3 What made you decide to stay on at school/come to college?
Did school want you to come/go back?
What made you decide to follow this course? What else could you have done?
Did you consider staying on/going to FE?

2.1 What qualifications are you aiming to get?
What did you get in the summer?

2.2 Do you know what you're going to do at the end of the year?
What do you intend to do eventually — say in five (ten) years?

3.1 Is this year (course) different from school generally (fifth year)?
How? (Probe.)

3.2 What was your English like last year?
What did you tend to do in lessons? What else?
What did you do that was worth doing? (Is there any difference between liking something and it being important?)
Was there anything you really disliked?

3.3 How is English/Communications different this year from last?

3.4 Is English/Communications different from other subjects?

3.5 Would you say you were good at it — writing/talking? Why do you think you're not good?
Or when did you start being good? If not, what are people like who are?
How could you/someone get better?
What did you expect English/Communications to be like this year?

3.6 Are you having to work harder than you did last year? Do you decide how much work you do? Much spare time? If pressure to work hard, where from?

3.7 Do you like reading? If so, what?

4.1 How important do you think English/Communications will be in your job?
How important is it in your parents' jobs?

4.2 Is it generally useful?
Does it have anything to do with what you do in your spare time?
Do you read books or watch TV in any different way from your parents?

('A') only

5.1 Why have you chosen to do Literature?
Is it different from literature in the fifth?

5.2 What kind of reading do you do yourself?

5.3 Is there anything important to you that is left out? Would you say that there is anything that really matters to you in the English you're doing?
What things do you find yourself arguing about?

6. Do you regret deciding to stay/come to college?

APPENDIX IV

Teachers and lecturers involved in *Versions of English*

Schools

	Teacher	Year & level	Senior post	Main qualification English
INNER CITY				
Downtown	Mrs Brennan	5 T	✓	✓
	Mr Baxter }	6		✓
	Mr Underwood }		✓	✓
	Mr Richardson	5 M		✓
	Mr Holmes	6	✓	✓
	Mrs Williams	5 B		
Urban	Mr Callaghan	5 M		✓
	Mrs Sackville	5 T		✓
	Mrs Sutton	5 B	✓	✓
SUBURBAN				
Catchwide	Mr Gilham	5 B		✓
	Mr Keegan	5 M		✓
	Mr O'Donnell	5 T	✓	✓
New Suburbia	Mrs Harrison	5 M		✓
	Mrs King	6	✓	✓
	Mr Porson	5 T		✓
	Mrs Waterhouse	5 B		✓
SMALL TOWN				
Greentown	Mr Saxon	5 B		✓
	Mr Tremaine	5 B	✓	✓
Smalltown	Mr Anderson }	6		✓
	Mr Austin }	5 T		✓
		5 B		
	Mr Squires	5 M	✓	✓
	Mrs Wood	5 T	✓	✓

Further Education

	Lecturer	English/ Communi- cations Course		Senior post	Main qualifi- cation English
SMALL TOWN					
	Mr Hemmings	C	BEC		
	Mr Pattison	E	'O'		✓
	Mrs Sands	E	RSA		
CITY					
City Road	Mrs Brown	C	G&G		✓
	Mrs Fraser } Mr Turner }	C	TEC		
	Mr Blackburn	C	Coll		
High Street	Mr Davidson	C	BEC		✓
	Mrs Lincoln	E	'A' Lit RSA		✓
	Mr Peel	E	'O' Lit	✓	
Square Hill	Mr Benson	C	TEC		
	Mrs Brindley	C	C&G		✓
	Mr Wilkinson	C	C&G		✓

Senior Post = Head of Department
(school) Head of Year
Deputy Head

Senior Post = Senior lecturer
(college)

Index